DERIVATIVES,
REGULATION
AND BANKING

ADVANCES IN FINANCE, INVESTMENT AND BANKING

SERIES EDITOR: ELROY DIMSON

VOLUME 1

Japanese Financial Institutions in Europe
D. Arora

VOLUME 2

Empirical Issues in Raising Equity Capital
M. Levis (Editor)

VOLUME 3

Derivatives, Regulation and Banking
B. Schachter (Editor)

DERIVATIVES, REGULATION AND BANKING

Edited by
Barry Schachter

1997
ELSEVIER
Amsterdam – Lausanne – New York – Oxford – Shannon – Tokyo

ELSEVIER SCIENCE B.V.
Sara Burgerhartstraat 25
P.O. Box 211, 1000 AE Amsterdam, The Netherlands

ISBN: 0 444 82073 6

Introduction to the Series

This series, presents a number of hitherto unpublished studies on a variety of financial themes.

The subjects covered by the *Advances in Finance Investment and Banking* (AFIB) book series include financial institutions and markets, corporate finance, portfolio investment, regulatory issues in banking and finance, comparative surveys, international taxation and accounting issues, and relevant macro-economics and asset pricing research studies. Books in this series include contributed volumes and edited conference proceedings, as well as single authored monographs. The attributes which bind these contributions together into a series are the focus on theoretical, empirical and applied issues within the field of finance.

Contributions stem from authors all over the world; their focus is consistently international. The editors of the AFIB series join me in hoping that the publication of these studies will help to stimulate international efforts in achieving advances within the fields covered by the series.

Elroy Dimson

CONTENTS

ACKNOWLEDGMENTS

I am very grateful to Elroy Dimson, series editor, for his extensive support and patience during the preparation of this manuscript.

INTRODUCTION

1. THE GOAL OF THIS VOLUME

Most would agree that the relaxation of exchange controls, deregulation of domestic financial markets and advances in computer technology have reshaped banking. The emergence of an international marketplace in a rapidly growing set of financial products, most notably derivatives, has brought unique opportunities to banks and new challenges to regulators of these financial institutions. Trading revenues remain a relatively small component of the total income of internationally active banks, but that income source continues to grow and the instruments traded continue to become more sophisticated. Innovations in asset securitization may, one day, enable banks to become pure service providers, holding relatively few assets. These examples illustrate both the fundamental changes taking place and the challenge these changes provide to old methods of supervision. It is the purpose of this volume to provide some perspective on these changes, from the points of view of the banks and their supervisors. The papers collected here, when viewed as a whole, may also help provide a framework for evaluating future developments in banking and the appropriate regulatory responses.

The fifteen papers in this volume are divided, informally at least, into two groups. The first eight papers examine changes in bank activities from the banks' point of view. They discuss, among other things, financial innovation, the risks associated with trading activities, and the particulars of certain trading and retail innovations. The remaining seven papers explore issues that have been raised by bank supervisors. Of central importance is the somewhat ill-defined notion of systemic risk to the banking system.. The papers included here that address systemic risk explore both the regulatory challenges provided by financial innovation and the proposed supervisory responses, and speculate on the formal modeling of systemic risk analysis.

2. THE EVOLVING ACTIVITIES OF BANKS

Jagtiani, Saunders and Udell examine the assertion that off-balance-sheet ("OBS") activities of banks have evolved as a response to regulation. They view OBS activities as financial innovations that can be modeled using the theory of the diffusion of innovation in the real sector. They find that, at both the industry level and the individual bank level, capital regulation cannot explain the speed at which financial innovations such as swaps have been adopted by banks. These results do not support the assertion that OBS activity has been driven by regulatory capital requirements.

Sinkey and Carter examine non-regulatory reasons for banks to use derivatives products, such as revenue enhancement and hedging. Their analysis provides a profile of banks that use derivatives. They find that these banks, when compared to banks not using derivatives have weaker capital positions and lower net interest margins. They also find derivatives using banks have smaller duration gaps and higher liquidity ratios.

Azarchs provides an overview of the risks associated with derivatives activities. Her analysis focuses primarily on credit risk and its relation to capital. She contracts regulatory capital requirements with capital criteria developed by Standard & Poor's ("S&P"). She finds that S&P capital is greater than BIS capital, which is not supportive of the claim that regulatory capital for credit risk is excessive. This finding parallels, and provides insight into, a similar finding by Azarchs that BIS market risk capital is less than S&P market risk capital.

Riffe examines the relation between OBS disclosures and bank equity values. Her analysis focusses on the question of the information content of notional values, widely felt to be difficult to interpret as indicators of risk of derivatives positions. She finds only mixed support for the assertion that equity valuation of market-related OBS instruments is related to the level of interest rate risk.

The papers by Ammer and Brunner and by Leahy examine the largest volume trading activity, FX trading. Ammer and Brunner try to distinguish whether banks FX revenues are primarily related to proprietary trading or the provision of intermediation services. Their results suggests, that the primary source of profits is indeed market making and not position taking, suggesting that the market risk of this activity is smaller than has been suggested by some. Leahy asks whether the positions taken by banks reveals any forecasting ability. His results show some persistent ability to forecast exchange rates suggesting that banks's profits from position taking are greater than chance would suggest.

Financial innovation has not been restricted to trading and wholesale banking activities. Cantor and Schachter and Ogden examine a derivatives innovation on the retail side of banking, the index-linked CD. Indexed deposits are marketed widely in the US and Europe, under a variety of names. For example, in the UK they are commonly referred to as Guaranteed Unit Trusts. These instruments represent attempts to expand the choices available to the retail bank client, by linking the return on a deposit to the performance of a market factor other than the interest rate. Typically this factor is an equity index. Cantor and Schachter highlight the legal basis for this activity in the US, and discuss risk management issues. Ogden analyzes pricing of stock index linked CDS and finds that they are generally priced above their theoretical value, providing rents to the issuing banks. He provides insight into how these instruments could also aid the bank in an overall portfolio risk management strategy.

3. THE CHALLENGES TO BANK SUPERVISORS

Arguments that derivatives destabilize markets in some fashion are not new. For example, exchange-traded options were banned in the US in 1933 following a period of high price volatility. A committee representing grain exchanges stated at the time, "the elimination by the exchanges of trading in indemnities [i.e., options] has removed one of the prime causes of excessive price movements."[1] Darby considers several definitions of systemic risk and evaluates various arguments that have been put forward regarding the effect of derivatives on the level of systemic risk. He concludes that, rather than increase systemic risk, derivatives have reduced it, by enabling improved risk management. He argues that the Basle amendment aimed at imposing regulatory capital for market risk may increase systemic risk by discouraging certain portfolio management activities.

Board, Goodhart, Power and Schoenmaker examine the role for regulation aimed specifically at derivatives activities. They frame their analysis in the manner of Coase, in which negative externalities resulting from a market failure are a necessary prerequisite to regulatory intervention. They examine the accumulated evidence and conclude that neither theory nor observation support the argument that over-the-counter derivatives are destabilizing. They argue further that capital and control issues that arise in the context of derivatives transactions are not peculiar to derivatives, but are best dealt with as general banking issues.

Mullineux takes a more general perspective by examining the relation between regulation and financial innovation on the retail side of banking. His research focusses on the UK experience and extends prior to the current surge in derivatives and trading to the beginning of the wave of technological advances in banking, including the introduction of automated teller machines. He documents the regulatory responses to these innovations and evaluates the impact on the UK financial sector. Mullineux finds that these innovations have reduced transactions costs, increased liquidity of financial assets, increased competition and reduced credit rationing, while exposing banks to increased interest rate risk.

It is the increased risk from fluctuations in interests rates and other market (i.e.,

---

[1]Grain Futures Administration. 1930. *Wheat Futures Volume of Trading, Open Commitments and Prices*. Washington, DC: United States Department of Agriculture, statistical bulletin No. 31.

price) risks that has spurred the amendment to the Basle accord. Jackson, Maude and Perraudin and Kupiec and O'Brien look at the implications of this regulatory response. Jackson, Maude and Perraudin examine the efficacy of the Basle amendment when banks use their own internal risk management models, commonly referred to as Value-at-Risk ("VaR"), for determining regulatory capital. In a VaR model the bank forecasts the return distribution of its trading portfolio, and estimates the return at some percentile, usually the second or third. This return is referred to as the VaR. Jackson, Maude and Perraudin find that it is difficult to consistently accurately estimate the tail probability. They find that the assumption of normally distributed portfolio returns common in some VaR models results in less accurate estimates of tail probabilities. Finally, they find that backtesting, i.e., comparison of forecast with ex post performance, a key component of the Basle amendment, does have some power to identify very inaccurate VaR models.

Kupiec and O'Brien compare three alternative schemes for determining regulatory capital for market risk, the internal models approach (i.e., VaR), the standard approach (similar in spirit to that used for calculating regulatory capital for credit risk) and the pre-commitment approach, in which banks specify their regulatory capital and pay penalties if losses exceed the regulatory capital. They argue that the standard approach is too inflexible, and that while the internal models approach is superior, it focuses exclusively on the trading portfolio at the end of the day and does not consider underlying determinants of bank risk-taking. They conclude that in general all approaches suffer from an artificial segregation of trading risk from whole-bank price risk.

In evaluating credit risks from OBS contracts, it is generally believed that bilateral netting provisions of financial contracts, such as can be found in the ISDA and BBA master agreements, are risk reducing, and hence lessen potential systemic risks. Hendricks examines the effects of bilateral netting agreements on credit exposures, measured as the sum of current exposure and "potential" exposure from future changes in market values. He shows that while current exposures fall with bilateral netting, the same is not necessarily the case with potential exposures. The key to understanding this result he shows is the observation that in-the-money contracts (those with a positive market value) are the primary drivers of potential credit exposure. To the extent that in-the-money contracts are similar (e.g., mostly pay-fixed swaps), potential exposure can be very sensitive to changes in rates.

Unlike the perceived benefits of bilateral netting, there is no consensus on the advantages of multilateral netting from a systemic perspective. On the one hand, multilateral netting reduces settlement flows, which is perceived as risk reducing. On the other hand, multilateral netting provides a mechanism for isolated financial events to spill over into other segments of the financial sector. Arguments on both sides abound, but systematic analysis is in short supply. Schneck suggests an approach for evaluating the kind of risks associated with interconnected obligations. Schneck evaluates a banking system with multiple dealers who have interconnected cash flow obligations. Hedging by end-users shifts risks to dealers, who then share the risks. Schneck then illustrates how this model can be used to evaluate the probability of a "domino" effect of defaults.

It is an impossible task to keep up-to-date on the changes being undertaken by banks and their supervisors. Even as this book is going to press, several regulatory initiatives have been undertaken which will have significant impacts on the way banks do business. For example, the Basle market risk capital rules were put into place in the US in September 1996. These require international banks to measure market risk exposure for computing capital. Many issues about these rules remain unresolved, includingwhat exactly is meant by "specific risk" of debt and equity instruments held in trading portfolios. In November 1996, the US Comptroller of the Currency proposed a major relaxation of the activities that national banks can undertake in their operating subsidiaries. In the context of these rapid, ongoing changes, the papers in this volume constitute an essential element for placing those changes in the proper prospective.

Derivatives, Regulation and Banking
Edited by B. Schachter

Chapter 1
FINANCIAL INNOVATIONS AND THE GROWTH OF BANK DERIVATIVE ACTIVITIES

Julapa Jagtiani[†]
Baruch College, City University of New York, New York, USA
Anthony Saunders and Gregory Udell
New York University, New York, NY, USA

1. INTRODUCTION

Bank off-balance-sheet (OBS) activities grew dramatically in the 1980s. By the end of 1989, aggregate outstanding OBS activities for all banks was $5,692 billion, nearly double the $3,234 billion of outstanding on-balance sheet activities. As of December 1992, the notional amount of off-balance sheet derivative products alone (swaps, options, futures and forward contracts) at most money center banks was substantially larger than the respective asset levels at these banks. For example, the ratio of the notional amount of OBS derivatives to total assets at Bankers Trust, J.P. Morgan, and Chemical Bank was 9.6, 8.6, and 7.6 times respectively. The estimated at-risk exposure of these derivatives activities represent 230, 126, and 83 percent of stockholder equity for these three banks respectively.[1]

While OBS activities generate fee income for banks, they also potentially increase bank risk (Koppenhaver and Stover (1991) and Avery and Berger (1991a)). One popular hypothesis for the dramatic growth of bank OBS activities has been that banks may have used them as a means of augmenting earnings to offset reduced spreads on traditional on-balance sheet corporate lending business. Furthermore, the incentives to increase OBS risk may have been exacerbated by a flat-rate deposit insurance premium and capital requirements that did

[†]This paper is a more extensive version of our earlier paper published in the *Journal of Banking and Finance* 19 (1995). The authors would like to thank participants of the European Finance and the FMA Conferences, Allen Berger, and Sally Davies for their comments and suggestions.

[1]Source: Sheshunoff Information Services Inc. It should be noted that while these figures correctly present an overall growth of bank off-balance sheet activities, one must be cautious when comparing the dollar volume of different off-balance sheet products (such as swaps vs standby letters of credit) since they can be much different in nature and risk exposure.

not take into account OBS activities and risks.

There have been a number of studies that have examined the key motivations behind bank OBS activities; however, the results have been mixed. One group of studies has investigated whether banks engage in OBS activities in order to reduce "regulatory taxes." Jagtiani (1995) and Pavel and Phillis (1987) find that banks with binding capital constraints are more likely to engage in swaps and loan securitization than banks with excess capital. Their results are also consistent with Baer and Pavel (1987), who find that banks engage in loan securitization and standby letters of credit (SLCs) to avoid reserve requirements and deposit insurance premiums. However, these empirical findings are not consistent with those of Benveniste and Berger (1987) and Koppenhaver (1989), who find that the bindingness of capital constraints is not a significant factor in a bank's decision to engage in SLCs and other OBS guarantees.

A second group of studies has examined the relationship between bank OBS activities and risk. Interestingly, Avery and Berger (1991b) find that better performing banks tend to issue more OBS commitments -- a finding that is inconsistent with the capital avoidance hypotheses which suggests that banks with low capital (i.e. binding minimum capital constraints) are more likely to engage in OBS activities.

One explanation for these ambiguous results may lie in the failure of this literature to recognize that OBS activities represent financial innovations. Consequently, testable models which do not reflect adoption patterns associated with the introduction of an innovation within an industry may be seriously misspecified. The purpose of this paper is to revisit the issue of the relationship between capital requirements and OBS activities by specifically modelling the introduction of each OBS activity as an innovation whose adoption by the banking industry follows a pattern specific to that activity.

Our approach borrows from the theory of the diffusion of innovations as it applied to the real (i.e. industrial) sector. It has been shown in the literature that the adoption pattern of real innovations usually follows a logistic time curve -- see, for example, Davies (1979), Griliches (1957), and Mansfield (1961). In a similar fashion, we model bank off-balance sheet activities -- interest rate swaps, SLCs, loan securitization, interest rate options, and interest rate futures and forward contracts -- as financial innovations whose adoption should reflect a diffusion pattern similar to that observed for real-sector product innovations.[2] These

---

[2]Logistic analysis of innovations has also been applied to studies of other financial innovations. For example, Keeley and Zimmerman (1985) studied the differences among banks in the time pattern of adoption of money market deposit accounts, Hannan and McDowell (1987) studied the adoption of automatic teller machines (ATM), Murphy and Rogers (1986) studied the life cycle and the adoption of ATM and IRA deposit accounts, and Mandell (1972) studied the adoption of credit cards.

off-balance sheet financial innovations (FIOBS) are expected to grow over time as OBS financial technology is diffused among banks; i.e. as more banks develop the expertise required to offer these new products. Moreover, we examine factors that are important in determining OBS growth including capital requirements.

During our data period (1984-1991), several important regulatory changes regarding bank capital requirements took place. This allows us to examine the effect of these changes on the diffusion of OBS activities. In particular, an increase in U.S. capital requirements in 1985 based only on bank on-balance sheet assets can be viewed as inducing banks to undertake greater OBS activities; i.e. an OBS growth rate exceeding that predicted by the "pure" diffusion model. Conversely, risk-based capital requirements, which were approved in July 1988 and based on bank OBS activities as well as on-balance sheet activities, can be viewed as imposing a regulatory tax on OBS activities that should have led to slower growth than predicted by the diffusion model.[3]

Our analysis starts by examining the effects of regulation on *aggregate* OBS activities for the whole industry. In this industry level analysis, we measure OBS activities both in terms of the number of banks that engage in OBS activities (as a proportion of the overall sample) and in terms of notional dollar volume of OBS activities. We then conduct an analysis of *individual banks*. This bank level analysis allows us to explore the effects of factors that are specific or idiosyncratic to individual banks such as their risk (creditworthiness) and size.

Our empirical evidence suggests that changes in capital regulations had little or no impact on the speed of adoption or diffusion of FIOBS activities. This is inconsistent with the popular explanation for the explosive growth of OBS activities, which is that banks engaged in these activities to avoid or minimize capital requirements. An analysis at the individual bank level also suggests that the diffusion pattern varies substantially across different OBS products and across banks. Interestingly, our bank level analysis does not reveal that creditworthiness is an important factor in determining differences in the speed of adoption of derivative products (including swaps, options, and futures and forwards) across banks. However, creditworthiness seems to play a role in the speed of adoption for SLCs and

---

[3]Under the risk-based capital requirements, banks are required to hold 4 percent core capital (tier I) and 8 percent total capital (tier I and tier II) as a proportion of their risk-adjusted assets -- banks are required to hold additional capital to support their OBS activities for the first time. The new requirements were approved in July 1988, and the transition period for its implementation ended on December 31, 1992. However, banks were required to meet the interim standard (3.25 percent core capital and 7.25 percent total capital to the risk-adjusted assets) by December 31, 1990. In addition to the risk-based requirements, banks are also required to meet a leverage ratio of 3 percent core capital to total assets under the new requirements. See Table 1 for summary of changes in capital regulations.

loan securitization.

The remainder of the paper is organized as follows: Section 2 describes the data. Section 3 presents the research methodology in three sub-sections: a) the basic properties of the logistic diffusion model, b) the model used for analyzing the diffusion pattern of FIOBS activities for the whole banking industry and c) the model used for analyzing the variation of diffusion patterns across FIOBS products and banks. Section 4 discusses the empirical results. Conclusions and policy implications are presented in Section 5.

2. THE DATA

This paper utilizes quarterly data from the Report of Income and Condition (Call Report) during the period January 1984 to September 1991 (31 quarters). Note that banks were required to report their FIOBS activities for the first time in September 1983, except for interest rate swaps (which were reported for the first time in June 1985). Consequently, our analysis is based on the period beginning June 1985 for swaps and January 1984 for all other activities. The sample includes 91 large commercial banks as listed in Appendix I.

The definitions of the dollar amount of swaps, options, futures and forwards, loan sales, and SLCs used in this paper are the notional dollar amounts reported in the Call Report. Specifically, they are the total principal notional amounts of interest rate swaps outstanding, outstanding obligations to purchase or sell under options contracts (excluding contracts involving foreign exchange)[4], obligations to purchase or sell under futures and forward contracts (excluding contracts involving foreign exchange), loans sold in each particular quarter, and SLCs outstanding.

It can be argued that some FIOBS activities are substitutable among themselves. For example, interest rate swaps, futures & forwards, and options may all be used as alternative hedging instruments against an underlying on-balance sheet position. Banks may shift from one activity to another due to changes in prices, costs, or regulations (such as capital requirements).[5] To account for this substitutability, we also examine these four FIOBS activities collectively – "market risk FIOBS" – which are defined as the combined value of all swaps, futures, forwards, and options of a bank.

---

[4]Theoretically, the delta or option values of these contingent assets and liabilities may be better measures of outstanding "values."

[5]See Jagtiani, Nathan, and Sick (1992) for discussion on economies of scale and cost complementarities among on- and off-balance sheet activities. To the extent that capital requirements differ across OBS activities, they may affect demand side decisions (see discussion on risk-based capital).

3. RESEARCH METHODOLOGY

The analysis of this paper is divided into three parts: (a) the basic properties of the logistic diffusion model, (b) the diffusion pattern of FIOBS activities for the whole banking industry and (c) the variation in the diffusion pattern across banks for different FIOBS products.

3.1 The Logistic Diffusion Model

The underlying hypothesis of the logistic innovation model takes the form of equation (1) below, where m_t is the number of firms that have already adopted the innovation at time t, and n is the total number of firms in the industry. The model assumes that the number of firms that adopt an innovation between time t and t+1 depends on the number of firms which had previously adopted the innovation. Specifically, it is proportionate to the product of the number of firms that have not adopted at time t and the proportion of the population that have already adopted the innovation at time t. The magnitude of the proportion (β) represents the speed of adoption, and depends on several factors such as the characteristics of the innovation and the characteristics of the firms in the industry.

$$m_{t+1} - m_t = \frac{\beta(n - m_t)m_t}{n}, \ \beta > 0. \tag{1}$$

If the period t to t+1 is very small, the solution of the differential equation of (1) can be written as shown in (2) below -- see Davies (1979) for detail. Equation (2) is a well known logistic time curve, which predicts that the proportion of the population having adopted the innovation will increase at an accelerating rate until 50 percent adoption (half of the population) is attained at time $t=-(\alpha/\beta)$. Thereafter, adoption increases at a decelerating rate, and 100 percent adoption is approached asymptotically. This logistic prediction of innovation adoption has been justified on imitative and bandwagon behavior (see Mansfield and Hensley (1960), Mansfield (1961), Romeo (1977), and Davies (1979)). A graphic presentation of the proportion of firms having adopted (m_t/n) over time is an S-shaped curve which has a point of inflexion, indicating a maximum rate of increase in the adoption, at the 50 percent adoption level (see Davies (1979), 10 and 115).

$$P_t = \frac{m_t}{n} = \frac{1}{1 + e^{(-\alpha - \beta t)}}. \tag{2}$$

$$Ln(\frac{P_t}{1 - P_t}) = \alpha + \beta t. \tag{3}$$

Using an appropriate transformation, the logistic time curve in equation (2) can be estimated using OLS as shown in equation (3) above. The model we use in this paper is an expansion of equation (3) to incorporate the effects of regulatory changes, as described in the next section. The parameter β is defined as measuring the speed of diffusion. Specifically, it can be shown that $t_2-t_1 = \beta^{-1} Ln[m_2(n-m_1)/m_1(n-m_2)]$ (see Davies (1979) for details). It is obvious that the adoption of the innovation is more rapid the larger β. In this paper, we also examine factors that are important in determining the variation in β across banks.

In order to test how robust our results are to model specification, we also perform our analysis using respectively a Linear Model, Normal Model, and Lognormal Model instead of a logistic time curve. In the Linear Model, we assume that $P_t = \alpha + \beta t$. In the Normal Model, it is assumed that Q_t, the probability that a firm chosen randomly at time t will have adopted the innovation, follows a normal distribution; i.e. $Q_t = N(t|\mu,\sigma^2)$. The graphic presentation of P_t, the proportion of population having adopted the innovation at time t, is presented by the cumulative normal curve in Appendix 2. The Lognormal Model assumes $Q_t = N(Ln\ t|\mu,\sigma^2)$.[6]

3.2 Methodology: Diffusion Pattern For the Banking Industry

The methodology we use to study the adoption pattern of various FIOBS activities incorporates the effects of regulatory changes on their speed of adoption. As discussed earlier, the explosive growth of bank FIOBS activities may, in part, reflect banks' attempts to avoid capital requirements. If this is the case, the announced changes in capital requirements during the period of study may have had a significant impact on the adoption of these activities beyond those predicted by the logistic model in equation (3).

Two capital requirement changes were announced during the period of our study. The first, in June 1985, involved moving from different capital adequacy requirements for the multinationals, regional banks, and small banks to a uniform minimum capital to on-balance sheet asset ratio requirement (see Table 1 for details).[7] As a result, capital adequacy

---

[6]These alternative specifications differ from the logistic model in that they are not based on any underlying assumption of imitative behavior.

[7]Banks are divided by the Federal Reserve into three different categories. The three categories are (1) "multinationals" which are the seventeen largest banks in the United States; (2) "regional banks" which are banks not included in category one but have total assets over $1 billion; (3) small banks with

Table 1
Summary of Changes in the U.S. Capital Adequacy Standards

Year	Dummy Variables For Regulatory Effects and Expected Signs	Multinationals[a]	Regional Banks[a]	Small Banks[a]
1981		No Capital	Primary 5%	Primary 6%
1983		Increased to Primary 5%	No Change	No Change
June 1985	- Subsidy for OBS Activities - <u>Regime 1</u> 1985:III-1988:II DUM1=1; Positive Coef	Increased to Primary 5.5%	Increased to Primary 5.5%	Decrease to Primary 5.5%
July 1988	- RBC - Tax on OBS Activities - Non-Risk-Based - Subsidy to OBS - <u>Regime 2</u> 1988:III-1990:III DUM2=1; Empirical Issue			
Dec 1990	- RBC - Tax on OBS Activities - Lower Leverage Ratio - Tax OBS - <u>Regime 3</u> 1990:IV-1991:III DUM3=1; Non-Positive Coef			

July 1988:
- Approval of the Risk-Based Capital (RBC) Requirements for All Banks in July 1988
- Partial Effect on December 31,1990 Full Effect on December 31, 1992
- Note: Leverage Ratios are In Place Until End 1990

Dec 1990:
- Partial Implementation of RBC Requirements (7.25% Total and 3.25% Tier I Capital to *Risk-Adjusted* Assets) on December 31, 1990
- OBS Activities were Subject to the Capital Requirements for the First Time
- Leverage Ratio was Reduced (from 5.5% Primary to 3% Tier I Capital to *Total Assets*)

[a] Multinationals are defined to be the seventeen largest banks in the United States; Regional banks are defined to be those non-multinationals with total assets over $1 billion; Small banks are defined to be banks with total assets under $1 billion

requirements were increased for large multinational banks and regional banks, but decreased for small banks. Since our sample does not include small banks, the 1985 change can be viewed as increasing capital requirements for all the banks in our sample. This change created incentives to move activities off balance sheet since no capital was required to be held against such activities.

The second announced change in capital requirements was from a non risk-based to a risk-based capital requirement in July 1988. This requirement had to be partially satisfied by the end of 1990 and fully satisfied by the end of 1992. Given advanced knowledge of the new risk-based capital requirements, banks may have started adjusting their position in FIOBS activities prior to its partial (1990) and final (1992) implementation. That is, the risk-

---

total assets under $1 billion.

based capital requirements may have started affecting the diffusion process of bank FIOBS activities as early as July 1988.[8] In contrast to the 1985 change in capital requirements, risk-based capital requirements can be viewed as discouraging the growth of OBS activities.[9]

We analyze the effects of changing capital requirements on the diffusion of FIOBS activities by dividing our sampling period using time dummy variables into four different regimes. The initial regime is the base period from 1984:I to 1985:II. The next regime is the period from 1985:III to 1988:II during which the dummy variable DUM1 equals one (and is otherwise equal to zero). DUM1 captures the effect of capital related incentives to increase FIOBS activities due to the implicit subsidy inherent in the 1985 change. We expect DUM1 to have a positive coefficient because the 1985 change represented higher regulatory taxes for the on-balance sheet activities of large banks while leaving their OBS activities untaxed.

The third regime covers the period 1988:III (the announcement of risk-based requirements) through 1990:III (the quarter prior to their binding implementation). DUM2 variable is equal to one from 1988:III to 1990:III, and equal to zero otherwise. DUM2 is used as a measure of banks' reactions to the planned imposition of risk-based capital requirements. Note that in this regime, there are two effects counteracting each other. On the one hand, the binding leverage ratio requirements (non risk-based) in place in this period may be viewed as encouraging OBS growth. On the other hand, the risk-based requirement being phased-in according to the July 1988 announcement can be viewed as discouraging OBS growth. Whether DUM2 has a positive or negative coefficient is an empirical question.

Finally, the last regime (from 1990:IV to the end of our sample 1991:III), is captured by the dummy variable, DUM3. DUM3 is equal to one beginning 1990:IV, and equal to zero from 1984:I to 1990:III. DUM3 is included in the analysis to reflect the impact of the risk-based capital regulations after their implementation. The risk-based capital requirements, which require banks to hold capital as a ratio of *risk-weighted* assets, should discourage OBS growth since OBS activities were subject to capital requirements for the first time.

---

[8]Eyssell and Arshadi (1990) found that equity values of large, publicly traded banks decreased at the time of announcement of the new risk-based capital plan on July 11, 1988.

[9]Risk-based capital requirements also affected the relative regulatory taxation of on-balance sheet activities, leading some to speculate that the imposition of these requirements precipitated a credit crunch in business lending (see Breedan and Isaac (1992)). This has spawned a growing empirical literature (see Berger and Udell (1994) for a review of this literature). Recent evidence predicted by Berger and Udell (1994), who compare pre and post risk-based-capital regimes, caste doubt on the proposition that Tier I and Tier II risk-based capital requirements affected bank business lending negatively. However, they did find some evidence suggesting that new (implicitly CAMEL-adjusted) leverage requirements may have had some albeit small effect.

Furthermore, the leverage ratio for on-balance sheet activities was reduced from 5.5 percent primary capital to 3 percent Tier I capital to *total* assets -- which by itself could be viewed as encouraging on-balance sheet (discouraging OBS) activities. However, the 3 percent leverage requirement is a minimum only applicable to the most highly rated banks. For other banks, the Tier I leverage ratio is 3 percent plus a cushion of at least 100 to 200 basis points based on bank examination and regulator discretion (see Berger and Udell (1994)). On balance, DUM3 is expected to have a non-positive coefficient in the OBS diffusion equation.

Equation (4) is an expansion of the traditional logistic adoption model in equation (3) which incorporates these capital requirement effects. While the dummy variables, DUM1, DUM2, and DUM3, are intended to capture regulatory effects on the intercept of the logistic time curve, the cross product terms, will capture regulatory effects on the slope.

$$Ln(\frac{P_{it}}{K_i - P_{it}}) = \alpha_i + \beta_i t + \mu_i DUM1 + \Theta_i DUM2 + \Phi_i DUM3$$
$$+ \rho(t \times DUM1) + \delta(t \times DUM2) + \epsilon(t \times DUM3) \tag{4}$$

t	=	Number of quarters from the beginning of the sample ($t=1,2,..31$)
β_i	=	Estimated speed of adoption based on the traditional diffusion model for FIOBS activity i (for the banking industry)
DUM1	=	Dummy variable which is equal to one from 1985:III to 1988:II (when $t=7,8,..18$), and equal to zero otherwise.
DUM2	=	Dummy variable which is equal to one from 1988:III to 1990:III (when $t=19,20,..27$), and equal to zero otherwise.
DUM3	=	Dummy variable which is equal to one from 1990:IV to 1991:III (when $t=28,..31$), and equal to zero otherwise.
K_i	=	Equilibrium level of P_{it} (when $t = \infty$), where P_{it} is defined below.

Following the theory of real innovations, the logistic diffusion function for FIOBS activities can be measured either by a) the percentage of firms adopting an innovation or b) the percentage of output reflecting the innovation. Specifically, Model (1) measures adoption as *the percentage of banks* engaging in FIOBS activities at time t. Model (2) measures adoption as the *dollar volume of the FIOBS* activities as a proportion of assets at time t. This may be seen as a measure of a bank's off-balance sheet innovation relative to its asset growth. Note that the definition of adoption used in Model 2 is particularly appropriate for our purpose since we focus on the effect of capital regulations on banks' incentive to move their activities off balance sheet.

We estimate only one equation for each FIOBS activity i. Each regression has 31 observations (31 quarters), and is estimated by weighted least squares to avoid heteroskedasticity problems.[10] Independent variables are the same for both Models (1) and (2), as shown in equation (4). The specific definitions of the dependent variables are as follows:

Model (1) - Percentage of Issuing Banks:

P_{it} = Number of banks in the sample that engage in FIOBS activity i at time t divided by number of all banks in the sample.

K_i = 1 (i.e., all banks will engage in FIOBS activity i at $t=\infty$)

Model (2) - Dollar Volume of FIOBS Activities:

P_{it} = Aggregate dollar amount of FIOBS activity i issued by all banks in the sample at time t divided by the aggregate dollar amount of total assets plus FIOBS activity i offered by all banks in the sample at time t.

K_i = Equilibrium level of P_{it} (when $t = \infty$), not equal to 1 by definition.

Unlike Model (1), the value of K in Model (2) -- i.e. the maximum potential dollar size of each market when $t=\infty$ -- is by definition not equal to one. Since we do not know, and cannot observe, the correct value of K in Model (2), we assume two different values of K_i for each FIOBS activity i: $K=Max(P_{it})+\sigma(P_{it})$ and $K=Max(P_{it})+2\sigma(P_{it})$, where $Max(P_{it})$ is the maximum value of P_{it} over the sampling period and $\sigma(P_{it})$ is the standard deviation of P_{it} . The results, presented in Tables 2A through 2F, show that the estimates are not sensitive to the assumed values for K.[11] We also assume in Model (2) that the value of K is constant over the period of study.[12]

3.3 Methodology: Diffusion Pattern Across FIOBS Products and Across Banks

The methodology used in examining the variation across banks in adoption patterns consists of two stages. Each bank's pattern of adoption is determined (for each FIOBS activity) in stage one, the individual bank's estimated adoption coefficient is then modeled

---

[10]Following Berger and Udell (1992), each observation is divided by the estimated standard deviation of its error term, $[(1/P_{it} + 1/(1 - P_{it}))/N]^{1/2}$, where N is the denominator in calculating P_{it} , depending on the definition of P_{it}.

[11]This is consistent with Globerman (1974) who also found the diffusion in the tool and die industry to be insensitive to the assumed values of K.

[12]This assumes regulatory changes do not affect K, while in reality regulatory changes could have a significant impact through the intercept, slope, and the K value. The assumption of constant K is made by all other diffusion studies (Globerman (1974), Keeley and Zimmerman (1985), and Hannan and McDowell (1987)). Given the data constraint, K is not endogenous.

as a function of various bank characteristics in stage two. Specifically:

Stage 1: The logistic curve is fitted to the data for each FIOBS activity i at each bank j, based on equation (5) below. In this stage, the diffusion factor for each FIOBS activity i for each bank j is estimated. Since we have 91 banks in our sample, we estimate 91 equations for each FIOBS product. The independent variables are the same as those in equation (1). The estimated coefficients measure the diffusion pattern over time and the effects of regulatory changes on that pattern of FIOBS activity i at bank j. The coefficient of time, b_{ij}, which represents the speed of adoption for FIOBS activity i at bank j, is then further examined in Stage 2.

$$Ln(\frac{P_{ijt}}{K_{ij} - P_{ijt}}) = a_{ij} + b_{ij}t + c_{ij}DUM1_j + d_{ij}DUM2_j + f_{ij}DUM3_j$$
$$+ g_{ij}(t \times DUM1_j) + h_{ij}(t \times DUM2_j) + k_{ij}(t \times DUM3_j). \tag{5}$$

P_{ijt} = Dollar amount of FIOBS activity i at bank j at time t divided by dollar amount of total assets plus FIOBS activity i offered by bank j at time t.

K_{ij} = $Max(P_{ijt}) + 2\sigma(P_{ijt})$ for each FIOBS activity i; where $Max(P_{ijt})$ is the maximum P_{ijt} for FIOBS activity i at bank j over the period of study.

Stage 2: In this stage, we examine the variation in the adoption pattern across FIOBS products and across banks. The estimated coefficient b_{ij} is used as a dependent variable to examine factors that are important in determining the variation of the adoption pattern of OBS activities across banks. The estimated b_{ij} is regressed on the characteristics of the bank concerned, as shown in equation (6). In this stage, we estimate one regression for each FIOBS activity. Each regression uses 91 observations (banks).

Table 2A
Diffusion Pattern for Banking Industry: Volume of Innovations: Effects of Regulatory Changes on the Logistic Adoption Curve

Variable	SLCs (K=.1091)		Loan Sales (K=.2451)		Swaps (K=.8024)		Options (K=.5747)		Futures & Fwd (K=.6508)		Market Risk FIOBS (K=1.0)	
Intercept	17681** (.0001)	18259** (.0001)	13834** (.0001)	14354** (.0001)	26815** (.0001)	26720** (.0001)	11997** (.0001)	17022** (.0001)	21135** (.0001)	23178** (.0001)	30914** (.0001)	-30360** (.0001)
Time	-0.041* (.0331)	-0.004 (.9445)	0.018 (.3799)	0.096 (.2845)	0.050** (.0001)	0.050** (.0001)	0.142** (.0001)	0.408† (.0932)	0.066** (.0001)	0.102† (.0596)	0.057** (.0001)	0.055** (.0001)
Time. DUM1	0.006 (.9066)		-0.034 (.6790)		N/A		-0.425† (.0690)		-0.077 (.1119)		N/A	
Time. DUM2	-0.007 (.9062)		-0.044 (.6034)		0.003 (.1559)		-0.392 (.1021)		-0.063 (.2174)		0.003 (.3477)	
Time. DUM3	-0.0005 (.9938)		-0.077 (.3646)		0.001 (.7564)		-0.373 (.1207)		-0.056 (.2750)		0.003 (.3484)	
DUM1	0.670** (.0047)		N/A		N/A		-2.984** (.0001)		-0.706** (.0005)		N/A	
DUM2	0.723† (.0730)		0.763 (.1102)		0.065 (.1642)		-3.429** (.0001)		-0.746** (.0095)		0.012 (.8378)	
DUM3	1.108* (.0378)		-0.036 (.9534)		0.016 (.8063)		-3.365** (.0002)		-0.674† (.0520)		0.027 (.7419)	
Quarters	31	31	31	31	26	26	31	31	31	31	26	26
R-Square	.386	.149	.789	.778	.993	.992	.876	.778	.955	.947	.991	.991
(Adjusted)	(.291)	(.018)	(.757)	(.744)	(.992)	(.992)	(.857)	(.744)	(.949)	(.939)	(.990)	(.990)

The estimation is based on Equation (4) Model (2), where the adoption growth is measured as a ratio of FIOBS activity issued by the industry to the industry's total assets plus the FIOBS activity. The equilibrium ratio K is assumed to be equal to the maximum adoption ratio during the sampling period plus 2 standard deviations (Max+2σ) but not greater than 1. Period of study is January 1984 to September 1991, total 31 quarters (except 26 quarters for swaps). P-values are reported in parentheses. Significance at the 1, 5, and 10 percent level is indicated by **, *, and † respectively.

Table 2B
Diffusion Pattern for Banking Industry: Volume of SLCs: Effects of Regulatory Changes on the Adoption; Comparing Various Models

Variable	Model (a) Logistic (K=Max+2σ) K=1091		Model (b) Logistic (K=Max+1σ) K=1046		Model (c) Linear		Model (d) Normal		Model (e) Log Normal	
Intercept	17681** (.0001)	18259** (.0001)	21279** (.0001)	22454** (.0001)	938.7** (.0001)	942.5** (.0001)	0.092** (.0001)	0.092** (.0001)	-2.390** (.0001)	-2.393** (.0001)
Time	-0.041† (.0331)	-0.004 (.9445)	-0.059* (.0235)	-0.021 (.8046)	-0.0003 (.3375)	0.001 (.6333)	-0.0006** (.0088)	0.000 (.8983)	-0.006* (.0137)	0.002 (.8354)
Time.DUM1		0.006 (.9066)		0.019 (.7859)		-0.000 (.9664)		-0.0001 (.7937)		-0.002 (.7424)
Time.DUM2		-0.007 (.9062)		0.004 (.9577)		-0.0004 (.7165)		-0.0003 (.5913)		-0.004 (.5445)
Time.DUM3		-0.001 (.9938)		0.012 (.8752)		-0.0003 (.7547)		-0.0002 (.7312)		-0.003 (.6795)
DUM1	0.670** (.0047)		0.932** (.0038)		0.013** (.0039)		0.007** (.0038)		0.078** (.0059)	
DUM2	0.723† (.0730)		1.048† (.0559)		0.012 (.1066)		0.007 (.1127)		0.074 (.1433)	
DUM3	1.108* (.0378)		1.576* (.0297)		0.017† (.0849)		0.013* (.0326)		0.135* (.0442)	
R-Square (Adjusted)	.386 (.291)	.149 (.018)	.394 (.301)	.151 (.021)	.387 (.293)	.144 (.012)				
Log Likelihood							133.2	129.4	58.8	55.2

The estimation assumes that the adoption growth of SLCs, which is measured as a ratio of SLCs issued by the industry to the industry's total assets plus SLCs, follows various patterns in Models (a) to (e). Period of study is January 1984 to September 1991, total 31 quarters. P-values are reported in parentheses. Significance at the 1, 5, and 10 percent level is indicated by **, *, and † respectively.

Table 2C
Diffusion Pattern for Banking Industry: Volume of Loan Sales: Effects of Regulatory Changes on the Adoption; Comparing Various Models

Variable	Model (a) Logistic (K=Max+2σ) K=.2451	Model (b) Logistic (K=Max+1σ) K=.1995		Model (c) Linear		Model (d) Normal		Model (e) Log Normal	
Intercept	-13834** (.0001)	-13370** (.0001)	-13964** (.0001)	-85.1 (.4538)	-106.1 (.4799)	0.008 (.4414)	0.005 (.7449)	-4.071** (.0001)	-4.141** (.0001)
Time	-0.018 (.3799)	0.022 (.4332)	0.131 (.2947)	0.003 (.1176)	0.010 (.1960)	0.004** (.0037)	0.005 (.2181)	0.076** (.0001)	0.114* (.0185)
Time.DUM1	-0.034 (.6790)		-0.044 (.7038)		-0.002 (.7443)		0.001 (.7139)		0.008 (.8306)
Time.DUM2	-0.044 (.6034)		-0.057 (.6312)		-0.004 (.5931)		0.0002 (.9575)		-0.025 (.5583)
Time.DUM3	-0.077 (.3646)		-0.104 (.3868)		-0.007 (.3365)		-0.003 (.4679)		-0.061 (.1608)
DUM1	0.547† (.0878)	0.842† (.0585)		0.066* (.0186)		0.018 (.3079)		0.497* (.0186)	
DUM2	0.763 (.1102)	1.195† (.0721)		0.077† (.0618)		0.022 (.4862)		0.263 (.4872)	
DUM3	-0.036 (.9534)	0.116 (.8915)		0.003 (.9578)		-0.061 (.1415)		-0.769 (.1234)	
R-Square (Adjusted)	.789 (.757)	.803 (.773)	.786 (.753)	.876 (.857)	.868 (.848)				
Log Likelihood						73.5	74.5	-3.4	-1.6

The estimation assumes that the adoption growth of loan sales, which is measured as a ratio of loan sales issued by the industry to the industry's total assets plus loan sales, follows various patterns in Models (a) to (e). Period of study is January 1984 to September 1991, total 31 quarters. P-values are reported in parentheses. Significance at the 1, 5, and 10 percent level is indicated by **, *, and † respectively.

Table 2D
Diffusion Pattern for Banking Industry: Volume of Interest Rate Swaps: Effects of Regulatory Changes on the Adoption; Comparing Various Models

Variable	Model (a) Logistic (K=Max+2σ) K=.8024		Model (b) Logistic (K=Max+1σ) K=.6590		Model (c) Linear		Model (d) Normal		Model (e) Log Normal	
Intercept	-26815** (.0001)	-26720** (.0001)	-26249** (.0001)	-25983** (.0001)	-295.7 (.1818)	-471.05* (.0383)	-0.042** (.0011)	-0.055** (.0001)	-2.848** (.0001)	-2.990** (.0001)
Time	0.050** (.0001)	0.050** (.0001)	0.070** (.0001)	0.069** (.0001)	0.020** (.0001)	0.021** (.0001)	0.021** (.0001)	0.022** (.0001)	0.100** (.0001)	0.113** (.0001)
Time.DUM1	N/A		N/A		N/A		N/A		N/A	
Time.DUM2	0.003 (.1559)		0.005 (.1556)		-0.001 (.1663)		-0.001* (.0286)		-0.020** (.0001)	
Time.DUM3	0.001 (.7564)		0.002 (.4765)		-0.003** (.0005)		-0.004** (.0001)		-0.035** (.0001)	
DUM1		N/A		N/A		N/A		N/A		N/A
DUM2		0.065 (.1642)		0.080 (.2378)		-0.005 (.7169)		-0.013 (.3151)		-0.294** (.0085)
DUM3		0.016 (.8063)		0.047 (.6190)		-0.063** (.0059)		-0.082** (.0001)		-0.791** (.0001)
R-Square (Adjusted)	.993 (.992)	.993 (.992)	.992 (.991)	.993 (.992)	.994 (.993)	.995 (.994)				
Log Likelihood							70.6	73.4	15.1	19.7

The estimation assumes that the adoption growth of swaps, which is measured as a ratio of swaps issued by the industry to the industry's total assets plus notional amount of swaps, follows various patterns in Models (a) to (e). Period of study is January 1984 to September 1991, total 26 quarters. P-values are reported in parentheses. Significance at the 1, 5, and 10 percent level is indicated by **, *, and † respectively.

Table 2E
Diffusion Pattern for Banking Industry: Volume of Options: Effects of Regulatory Changes on the Adoption; Comparing Various Models

Variable	Model (a) Logistic (K=Max+2σ) K=.5754		Model (b) Logistic (K=Max+1σ) K=.4575		Model (c) Linear		Model (d) Normal		Model (e) Log Normal	
Intercept	-11997** (.0001)	-17022** (.0001)	-11713** (.0001)	-17265** (.0001)	-175.9 (.3412)	-650.2* (.0105)	-0.036* (.0422)	-0.041 (.1245)	-6.152** (.0001)	-6.085** (.0001)
Time	0.142** (.0001)	0.408† (.0932)	0.176** (.0001)	0.474† (.0907)	0.023** (.0001)	0.052† (.0845)	0.0116** (.0001)	0.011 (.1481)	0.179** (.0001)	0.173** (.0001)
Time.DUM1		-0.425† (.0690)		-0.473† (.0790)		-0.044 (.1308)		-0.005 (.3984)		0.022 (.4086)
Time.DUM2		-0.392 (.1021)		-0.440 (.1107)		-0.042 (.1548)		-0.002 (.7309)		0.001 (.9621)
Time.DUM3		-0.373 (.1207)		-0.417 (.1319)		-0.040 (.1758)		0.002 (.7845)		-0.004 (.8860)
DUM1	-2.984** (.0001)		-3.273** (.0001)		-0.261** (.0009)		-0.078** (.0087)		0.284* (.0248)	
DUM2	-3.429** (.0001)		-3.875** (.0001)		-0.344** (.0012)		-0.084 (.1122)		-0.071 (.7537)	
DUM3	-3.365** (.0002)		-3.748** (.0004)		-0.337** (.0058)		0.021 (.7619)		-0.257 (.3899)	
R-Square (Adjusted)	.876 (.857)	.778 (.744)	.922 (.910)	.866 (.845)	.971 (.967)	.961 (.955)				
Log Likelihood							57.5	56.8	12.4	10.0

The estimation assumes that the adoption growth of options, which is measured as a ratio of options issued by the industry to the industry's total assets plus options, follows various patterns in Models (a) to (e). Period of study is January 1984 to September 1991, total 31 quarters. P-values are reported in parentheses. Significance at the 1, 5, and 10 percent level is indicated by **, *, and † respectively.

Table 2F
Diffusion Pattern for Banking Industry: Volume of Futures and Forward: Effects of Regulatory Changes on the Adoption; Comparing Various Models

Variable	Model (a) Logistic (K=Max+2σ) K=6508		Model (b) Logistic (K=Max+1σ) K=.5284		Model (c) Linear		Model (d) Normal		Model (e) Log Normal	
Intercept	-21135** (.0001)	-23178** (.0001)	-19939** (.0001)	-22562** (.0001)	8.073 (.9673)	-311.9 (.2770)	0.017 (.1586)	0.016 (.4011)	-3.064** (.0001)	-3.033** (.0001)
Time	0.066** (.0001)	0.102† (.0596)	0.094** (.0001)	0.140† (.0620)	0.018** (.0001)	0.023* (.0289)	0.013** (.0001)	0.011* (.0385)	0.087** (.0001)	0.058* (.0427)
Time.DUM1		-0.077 (.1119)		-0.099 (.1385)		-0.012 (.1973)		-0.003 (.5398)		0.010 (.6500)
Time.DUM2		-0.063 (.2174)		-0.082 (.2413)		-0.010 (.3168)		0.001 (.8794)		0.017 (.4929)
Time.DUM3		-0.056 (.2750)		-0.073 (.3056)		-0.009 (.3465)		0.002 (.6805)		0.013 (.6058)
DUM1	-0.706** (.0005)		-0.920** (.0008)		-0.112** (.0032)		-0.068** (.0008)		-0.236* (.0316)	
DUM2	-0.746** (.0095)		-1.027** (.0095)		-0.121* (.0277)		-0.048 (.1895)		-0.245 (.2149)	
DUM3	-0.674† (.0520)		-0.920† (.0540)		-0.127† (.0589)		-0.020 (.6838)		-0.430† (.0981)	
R-Square	.955	.947	.959	.951	.981	.978				
(Adjusted)	(.949)	(.939)	(.953)	(.944)	(.978)	(.975)				
Log Likelihood							69.2	67.5	16.8	14.9

The estimation assumes that the adoption growth of futures and forward contracts, which is measured as a ratio of futures and forward contracts issued by the industry to the industry's total assets plus futures and forward outstanding, follows various patterns in Models (a) to (e). Period of study is January 1984 to September 1991, total 31 quarters. P-values are reported in parentheses. Significance at the 1, 5, and 10 percent level is indicated by **, *, and † respectively.

Table 2G
Diffusion Pattern for Banking Industry: Volume of Market Risk FIOBS: Effects of Regulatory Changes on the Adoption; Comparing Various Models

Variable	Model (a) Logistic (K=Max+2σ) K=1.0		Model (b) Logistic (K=Max+1σ) K=.871		Model (c) Linear		Model (d) Normal		Model (e) Log Normal	
Intercept	-30914** (.0001)	-30360** (.0001)	-30837** (.0001)	-29925** (.0001)	-269.9 (.3148)	-392.5 (.1657)	-0.025† (.0507)	-0.032* (.0155)	-2.324** (.0001)	-2.422** (.0001)
Time	.057** (.0001)	.055** (.0001)	.074** (.0001)	.069** (.0001)	.026** (.0001)	.026** (.0001)	.027** (.0001)	.027** (.0001)	.086** (.0001)	.095** (.0001)
Time.DUM1	N/A	N/A	N/A	N/A	N/A	N/A	N/A	N/A	N/A	N/A
Time.DUM2		0.003 (.3477)		0.004 (.3574)		-0.001 (.1484)		-0.001* (.0370)		-0.015** (.0001)
Time.DUM3		0.003 (.3484)		0.006 (.2193)		-0.003** (.0022)		-0.003** (.0001)		-0.026** (.0001)
DUM1	N/A	N/A	N/A	N/A	N/A	N/A	N/A	N/A	N/A	N/A
DUM2	0.012 (.8378)		0.005 (.9493)		-0.017 (.2753)		-0.021 (.1017)		-0.228** (.0037)	
DUM3	0.027 (.7419)		0.065 (.5812)		-0.068** (.0048)		-0.076** (.0001)		-0.588** (.0001)	
R-Square	.991	.991	.989	.989	.996	.996				
(Adjusted)	.990	.990	.988	.988	.995	.996				
Log Likelihood							71.2	72.6	24.2	29.0

The estimation assumes that the adoption growth of market risk FIOBS (combined volume of swaps, options, and futures and forward contracts), which is measured as a ratio of market risk FIOBS issued by the industry to the industry's total assets plus market risk FIOBS volume, follows various patterns in Models (a) to (e). Period of study is January 1984 to September 1991, total 26 quarters. P-values are reported in parentheses. Significance at the 1, 5, and 10 percent level is indicated by **, *, and † respectively.

$$Y_{ij} = \Omega_i + \Gamma_i X_{ij}. \tag{6}$$

Y_{ij} = Estimated coefficients, b_{ij}, from stage one

Γ_i = Vector of sensitivities of the diffusion pattern of FIOBS activity i for various levels of the characteristics.

X_{ij} = Vector of characteristics of bank j (average across 31 quarters).

Specifically, these characteristics are:

1. Creditworthiness Factors:

     NPLOAN: Non-performing loans as a percentage of total assets

     PROFIT: Net income as a percentage of total assets

     CAPITAL: Equity capital as a percentage of total assets

     RISKWGT: Risk-adjusted assets (calculated from the new risk-based capital guidelines) as a percentage of total assets[13]

     ASSETS: Log of total assets (bank size)

2. Measure of Foreign Activities (or Degree of International Presence):

     FGNDEPO: Foreign deposits as a percentage of total deposits

4. EMPIRICAL RESULTS

The results are discussed in two parts: (a) diffusion of FIOBS activities for the banking industry and (b) diffusion of activities across banks.

4.1 Results: Diffusion Pattern for the Banking Industry

4.1.1 Model (1): Proportion of Banks Engaged in FIOBS Activities as Dependent Variable

     Speed of Adoption. The regression results for Model 1, equation (4), are shown in Table 3A. Figures 1 and 2 plot the proportion of banks engaged in FIOBS activities over time. From Table 3A, the speed of adoption (β) is positive and highly significant (as expected) for swaps, options, and market risk FIOBS, but significantly negative for SLCs, and insignificant for loan sales and futures and forward contracts. The unexpected results of SLCs could be because SLCs were around for a long period of time prior to our sampling period, thus they may not represent a "financial innovation." The insignificance of Loan Sales could be explained by two events which dampened loan sales during our sampling period -- the collapse in the LBO market in the late 1980s (most of the loans sold in the

---

[13]The RISKWGT variable is a measure of bank risk based on the new risk-based capital regulation, and was used earlier in Avery and Berger (1991b).

Table 3A
Diffusion Pattern for Banking Industry: Proportion of Banks Engaging Effects of Regulatory Changes on the Logistic Adoption Curve

Variable	SLC		Loan Sales		Swaps		Options		Futures & Fwd		Market Risk FIOBS	
Intercept	4.572** (.0001)	4.584** (.0001)	6.370** (.0001)	6.119** (.0001)	4.072** (.0001)	4.019** (.0001)	-5.829** (.0001)	-5.678** (.0001)	4.172** (.0001)	4.263** (.0001)	5.924** (.0001)	5.780** (.0001)
Time	-0.005** (.0005)	-0.010 (.2407)	0.001 (.9265)	0.040† (.0704)	0.039** (.0001)	0.041** (.0001)	0.064** (.0001)	0.047 (.2676)	-0.025 (.1796)	-0.035 (.4933)	0.016* (.0338)	0.021** (.0071)
Time.DUM1	0.007 (.2817)		-0.033† (.0573)		N/A		0.0001 (.9987)		0.029 (.4741)		N/A	
Time.DUM2	0.008 (.2769)		-0.039* (.0429)		0.0003 (.8824)		0.005 (.8868)		0.018 (.6895)		-0.010** (.0031)	
Time.DUM3	0.007 (.3902)		-0.038† (.0624)		-0.007* (.0220)		0.025 (.5163)		0.009 (.8479)		-0.018** (.0001)	
DUM1		0.036* (.0155)		-0.003 (.9789)		N/A		-0.172 (.3051)		0.221 (.3028)		N/A
DUM2		0.097** (.0014)		-0.118 (.5480)		0.028 (.5891)		-0.255 (.3840)		0.242 (.5347)		-0.177* (.0186)
DUM3		0.070* (.0401)		-0.045 (.8615)		-0.177* (.0345)		0.272 (.4809)		-0.011 (.9828)		-0.452** (.0005)
# Quarters	31	31	31	31	26	26	31	31	31	31	26	26
R-Square	.938	.878	.109	.203	.831	.830	.908	.906	.486	.513	.470	.545
(Adjusted)	(.918)	(.837)	(-.029)	(.081)	(.808)	(.807)	(.892)	(.894)	(.407)	(.438)	(.397)	(.483)

The estimation is based on Equation (4) Model (1), where the adoption growth is measured as the percentage of banks engaging in the innovations, and the equilibrium ratio K is equal to 1. Period of study is January 1984 to September 1991, total 31 quarters (except 26 quarters for swaps). P-values are reported in parentheses. Significance at the 1, 5, and 10 percent level is indicated by **, *, and † respectively.

Table 3B

Diffusion Pattern for Banking Industry: Proportion of Banks Engaging Effects of Regulatory Changes on the Linear Adoption Pattern

Variable	SLC	Loan Sales		Swaps		Options		Futures & Fwd		Market Risk FIOBS	
Intercept	0.985** (.0001)	2.193** (.0001)	1.929** (.0001)	3.234** (.0001)	3.137** (.0001)	0.770** (.0001)	0.826** (.0001)	3.294** (.0001)	3.327** (.0001)	3.007** (.0001)	2.948** (.0001)
Time	-0.0001** (.0006)	0.0005 (.9677)	0.044 (.1185)	-0.004 (.4868)	-0.002 (.7668)	0.016** (.0001)	0.012 (.1939)	-0.006* (.0429)	-0.008 (.3374)	-0.013 (.1343)	-0.011 (.2176)
Time.DUM1	0.0001 (.2878)		-0.035 (.1067)		N/A		0.002 (.7790)		0.006 (.3840)		N/A
Time.DUM2	0.0001 (.2827)		-0.043† (.0736)		-0.009** (.0006)		0.003 (.7579)		0.004 (.5788)		-0.007† (.0692)
Time.DUM3	0.0001 (.3986)		-0.039 (.1202)		-0.016** (.0001)		0.005 (.5397)		0.003 (.7187)		-0.009† (.0700)
DUM1	0.001* (.0180)	0.018 (.8789)		N/A		-0.013 (.7231)		0.054 (.1410)		N/A	
DUM2	0.001** (.0017)	-0.139 (.5660)		-0.184** (.0034)		-0.033 (.6091)		0.068 (.3010)		-0.146† (.0851)	
DUM3	0.001* (.0473)	0.010 (.9742)		-0.441** (.0001)		0.039 (.6472)		0.035 (.6828)		-0.230† (.0869)	
# Quarters	31	31	31	26	26	31	31	31	31	26	26
R-Square	.936	.148	.199	.733	.773	.926	.925	.592	.600	.633	.638
(Adjusted)	.915	.017	.076	.696	.742	.915	.914	.529	.539	.583	.589

The estimation assumes that the adoption growth, which is measured as a percentage of banks engaging in the innovations, follows a linear pattern (instead of the logistic pattern). Period of study is January 1984 to September 1991, total 31 quarters (except 26 quarters for swaps). P-values are reported in parentheses. Significance at the 1, 5, and 10 percent level is indicated by **, *, and † respectively.

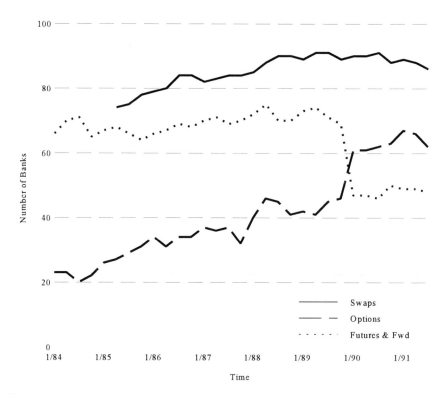

Figure 1
Number of banks engaging in swaps, options, and futures and forwards

1980s were loans made for LBO activity) and regulatory restriction on HLT purchases by banks (see Berger and Udell (1993).

The insignificance of futures and forwards may be explained using Figure 1, which shows that the number of banks adopting options dramatically increased, while those adopting futures & forwards dramatically decreased in 1990-1991. These results are consistent with a switch by banks from using (producing) futures & forward contracts to using (producing) options contracts during the 1990-1991 period. One important reason for this switch could be that exchange- traded derivatives are zero risk weighted for capital purposes under the 1988 risk-based capital plan, while OTC traded contracts have positive

Figure 2
Number of banks engaging in SLCs and loan sales

risk weights.[14] To the extent that options are more likely to be exchange-traded than forwards (which are virtually 100 percent OTC traded), banks had an incentive to switch out of forwards into exchange-traded instruments such as options.

Regulatory Effects. Table 3B suggests that for most FIOBS products, the coefficients

---

[14]Exchange traded contracts were given a zero risk-weight (conversion factor) on the basis that the exchange provides a guarantee against default on a contract. In the case of bi-lateral OTC contracts, no such guarantee is provided. Source: Federal Reserve Press Release (January 19, 1989) -- the final guidelines to implement risk-based capital requirements for state member banks and bank holding companies, based on the framework adopted on July 11, 1988 by the Basle Committee on Banking Regulations and Supervisory Practices, page 75. Reference #4480 Federal Reserve Bank of Philadelphia.

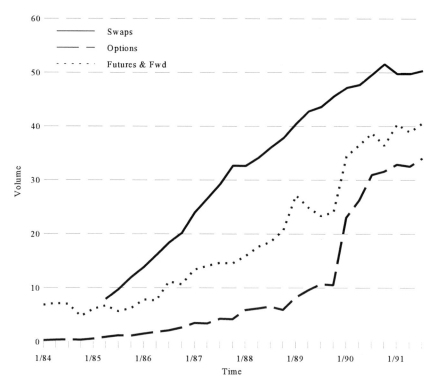

Figure 3
Aggregate dollar volume of swaps, options, and futures and forwards

of DUM1 and t.DUM1 are insignificant, with one exception for SLCs whose DUM1 coefficient is significantly positive. The results indicate that the OBS subsidies (due to the 1985 capital requirement increase) had little or no positive impact on the adoption of FIOBS products except for SLCs.

The SLC result could reflect the fact that SLCs may not be a financial innovation in the same sense as the other FIOBS products. SLCs may have been used by banks as an OBS substitute for traditional lending to avoid the increased on-balance sheet capital requirements. Unlike swaps, options, futures and forwards, and loan sales, issuing SLCs does not involve learning new technology, thus allowing more banks to issue SLCs as an alternative to expanding their on-balance sheet lending activity. Limited knowledge and expertise in offering derivative products and loan sales may have restricted less sophisticated banks from

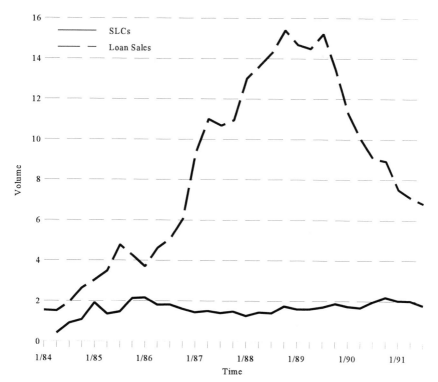

Figure 4
Aggregate dollar volume of SLCs and loan sales

participating in these markets in response to the regulatory subsidies in 1985, causing the coefficients of DUM1 and t.DUM1 to be insignificant for these products.

The coefficients of DUM2 and t.DUM2 are insignificant for swaps, options, and futures and forward contracts -- suggesting that the announcement of the risk-based capital requirements in 1988 had no significant impact on the adoption of these derivative FIOBS products. However, when all derivatives FIOBS are examined collectively, the coefficients of DUM2 and t.DUM2 are significantly negative for market risk FIOBS. The coefficient of t.DUM2 is significantly negative for loan sales, while the coefficient of DUM2 is positive for SLCs.

The coefficients of DUM3 and t.DUM3 are insignificant for loan sales, options, and futures and forward contracts, but are significantly negative for swaps and market risk FIOBS

-- implying that some banks may have withdrawn from the swap market due to the regulatory tax on off-balance sheet activities imposed by the risk-based capital requirements.

Our robustness test using the Linear Model is reported in Table 3A. The coefficients of time remain positive for options, but become insignificant for all other FIOBS activities. The results on regulatory effects, however, confirm those based on the logistic model. That is, with the exception of SLCs, the regulatory subsidies in 1985 had no effect on the adoption of other FIOBS products. In addition, the imposition of the risk-based capital regulation had a strong negative effect on the speed of adoption of swaps, but no significant impact on loan sales, options, and futures and forward contracts.

The results overall suggest that, with the exception of swaps, the risk-based capital requirements appear to have had little effect in discouraging banks from engaging in FIOBS activities both during the phase-in period and after the actual implementation. One possible explanation for this is that the leverage requirement, and not the risk-weighted Tier I and Tier II requirements, represented the binding constraint for most large banks. Therefore, our results for OBS activities can be viewed as consistent with recent empirical work which has found that the leverage ratio, and not the risk-based capital requirements, was most important in determining on-balance sheet activities during the recent bank credit slowdown (Berger and Udell (1994)).

4.1.2 Model (2): Volume of FIOBS Activities as Dependent Variable

Despite the "unobservable" value of K used in this model, Table 3 shows that with the exception for SLCs, the fit measured by R-Square using our assumed K values is very high (80 to 99 percent) for all other FIOBS products. The plots of FIOBS growth (measured in terms of dollar volume as a percent of total assets and the FIOBS activity) are presented in Figures 3 and 4.

Speed of Adoption. The coefficient of time is significantly positive (as expected) for swaps, options, futures & forward, and market risk FIOBS. Again, the coefficients are insignificant for SLCs and loan sales, probably because SLCs are not financial innovations and because of the events which affected loan sales during our sampling period -- as described earlier.

Regulatory Effects. Again, the coefficient of DUM1 is significantly positive for SLCs, implying that banks increased their SLCs activity probably as a substitute for on-balance sheet lending to take advantage of the regulatory subsidies in 1985. The coefficient of DUM1 is either insignificant or negative (unexpected) for other products. The coefficients of DUM2 and DUM3 are significantly negative for options and futures and forward contracts,

Table 4A

Diffusion Pattern Across Banks: Factors Determining Variation in Diffusion Pattern Across Banks

	SLCs	Loan Sales	Swaps	Options	Futures & Fwd	Market Risk FIOBS
Panel A: Summary of Cross-Sectional Speed of Adoption (Estimated Coefficients of Time) from $Ln[P_{it}/(K_i-P_{it})] = \alpha_i + \beta_i(Time) + \mu_i(DUM1) + \Theta_i(DUM2) + \Phi_i(DUM3)$						
Mean of β_i	0.0107	0.0182	0.1155	0.2592	0.0901	0.0794
Std. Dev.	0.0596	0.1369	0.1602	0.5900	0.4944	0.1115
Minimum	-0.0233	-0.3872	-0.7350	-0.4844	-1.3979	-0.2398
Maximum	0.1252	0.3680	0.6089	3.8351	3.4151	0.3504
Ave. Adj. R^2	.608	.377	.684	.404	.429	.645
Coef. of Var.	5.57	7.52	1.39	2.28	5.49	1.40
# Signif. at 5%	52/91	33/91	67/91	31/85	32/91	62/91
Panel B: Factors Determining Variation in Speed of Adoption Across Banks						
Intercept	-0.129	-1.602**	-0.337	-1.222	0.962	-0.551†
	(.3572)	(.0001)	(0.4922)	(.5851)	(.4961)	(.0824)
CAPITAL	0.022**	0.017	0.032	0.168	-0.080	0.019
	(.0023)	(.3520)	(.2031)	(.1242)	(.2728)	(.2366)
PROFIT	-0.014	-0.093	-0.084	-0.702†	0.355	-0.072
	(.6239)	(.2145)	(.4039)	(.0794)	(.2232)	(.2625)
NPLOAN	-0.022*	-0.051†	-0.012	-0.036	0.069	-0.014
	(.0382)	(.0632)	(.7443)	(.8123)	(.5178)	(.5573)
FGNDEPO	-0.0002	-0.004*	0.001	-0.008	-0.001	0.001
	(.6639)	(.0161)	(.4625)	(.3600)	(.8197)	(.6532)
RISKWGT	0.091	0.316†	0.253	-0.258	0.627	0.209
	(.2058)	(.0920)	(.3150)	(.8129)	(.3967)	(.1972)
ASSETS	-0.002	0.088**	0.004	0.060	-0.070	0.024
	(.8200)	(.0004)	(.8952)	(.6506)	(.4500)	(.2494)
R-Square	0.208	0.235	0.080	0.087	0.044	0.154
(Adjusted)	(.152)	(.181)	(.014)	(.012)	(-.028)	(.093)

The adoption growth is measured as the ratio of FIOBS activity issued by a bank to the bank's total assets plus the FIOBS activity. The equilibrium ratio K is assumed to be equal to the maximum adoption ratio during the sampling period plus 2 standard deviations (Max+2σ) but not greater than 1. Period of study is January 1984 to September 1991, total 31 quarters (except 26 quarters for swaps). P-values are reported in parentheses. Significance at the 1, 5, and 10 percent level is indicated by **, *, and † respectively.

positive for SLCs, and insignificant for all other FIOBS products -- suggesting that the risk-based capital requirements may have reduced the adoption of options and futures and forwards to a level below that predicted by the logistic time curve, while having no significant effect on other FIOBS products. Interestingly, the trade-off evident in the proportion tests (Figure 1 and Table 2) between options and futures and forward contracts is not evident in the volume tests (Figure 3 and Table 3). This casts some doubt on our original interpretation that banks may have shifted from non-traded futures and forward contracts to traded options because of the differential treatment under risk-based capital.

The coefficients of t.DUM1, t.DUM2, and t.DUM3 are not significant for all FIOBS products, suggesting that the regulatory changes had no effect on the slope of the logistic adoption curve.

As a robustness test, we perform the same analysis using the logistic model with different values of K, the Linear Model, the Normal Model, and the Lognormal Model (described in Section IIIa). The results presented in Tables 3A, 3B, 3C, 3D, 3E, and 3F confirm our main results that, for SLCs, loan sales, options, and futures and forwards, the coefficients of t.DUM1, t.DUM2, and t.DUM3 are insignificant -- indicating that the regulatory changes did not have any impact on the speed of adoption of these products through the slope of the diffusion curve.

The results also confirm that the imposition of the risk-based capital requirements did not discourage banks from engaging in SLCs and loan sales, since the coefficients of DUM2 and DUM3 are non-negative in all models. The results also suggest that the risk-based capital requirements may have reduced the adoption of options and futures and forwards. For swaps, the effect of regulatory changes is not sensitive to the assumed value of K, although it does seem to be sensitive to the model specification providing some evidence of a negative effect from risk-based capital.

In summary, the impact of capital adequacy changes had no consistent pattern on or across FIOBS products (when the adoption is measured either in terms of the proportion of banks adopting the innovation or the volume of the adopted FIOBS activities). The results also indicate that not all FIOBS activities behave in the same fashion in response to regulatory changes. The results overall seem to be relatively insensitive to the assumed value of K and the assumed diffusion model.

4.2 Results: Diffusion Pattern Across Banks

Panel A of Tables 4A and 4B summarize the speed of diffusion coefficients, b_{ij}, estimated from equation (5) using individual bank data. The mean and standard deviation results indicate considerable differences in the speed of adoption across FIOBS products and across banks. The degree of differences across banks in the speed of adoption, measured by the coefficients of variation (standard deviation divided by mean) suggests that the differences also vary widely across products. The proportion of the 5 percent significance of the coefficient b_{ij} is larger in Table 4A than in Table 4B for all FIOBS products, except for swaps which are about the same.

Panel B of Tables 4A and 4B present the results based on equation (6), which

Table 4B
Factors Determining Variation in Diffusion Pattern Across Banks

	SLCs	Loan Sales	Swaps	Options	Futures & Fwd	Market Risk FIOBS
Panel A:	**Summary of Cross-Sectional Speed of Adoption (Estimated Coefficients of Time) from**					
$Ln[P_{it}/(K_i-P_{it})] = \alpha_i + \beta_i(Time)+\mu_i(Time.DUM1)+\Theta_i(Time.DUM2)+\Phi_i(Time.DUM3)$						
Mean of β_i	0.0158	0.0337	0.1228	0.1185	0.0169	0.0707
Std. Dev.	0.0969	0.2991	0.1716	1.3688	0.6664	0.1450
Minimum	-0.2801	-0.8109	-0.7350	-9.1127	-2.4572	-0.7901
Maximum	0.4756	1.5614	0.6358	3.8351	3.4151	0.3404
Ave. Adj. R^2	.591	.365	.684	.392	.469	.649
Coef. of Var.	6.13	8.88	1.39	11.55	39.43	2.05
Signif. at 5%l	18/91	8/91	68/91	22/85	16/91	59/91
Panel B:	**Factors Determining Variation in Speed of Adoption Across Banks**					
Intercept	0.080	-1.020	-0.530	-6.376	-1.066	-0.690
	(.7775)	(.2759)	(0.3084)	(.2050)	(.5933)	(.1176)
CAPITAL	0.009	-0.023	0.037	0.556*	0.029	0.014
	(.5451)	(.6267)	(.1666)	(.0241)	(.7747)	(.5246)
PROFIT	0.014	0.016	-0.087	-2.673**	-0.028	0.004
	(.8063)	(.9328)	(.4132)	(.0034)	(.9457)	(.9679)
NPLOAN	-0.002	-0.030	-0.014	-0.252	-0.122	0.006
	(.9328)	(.6732)	(.7200)	(.4649)	(.4203)	(.8526)
FGNDEPO	0.0002	-0.005	0.001	-0.019	0.001	0.001
	(.8887)	(.1784)	(.4901)	(.3161)	(.8921)	(.5618)
RISKWGT	0.050	0.812†	0.215	-1.246	1.622	0.156
	(.7286)	(.0928)	(.4186)	(.6095)	(.1230)	(.4870)
ASSETS	-0.010	0.040	0.017	0.335	-0.016	0.033
	(.5915)	(.5142)	(.6220)	(.2627)	(.9014)	(.2577)
R-Square	0.016	0.088	0.087	0.190	0.037	0.123
(Adjusted)	(-.053)	(.024)	(.021)	(.123)	(-.036)	(.061)

The adoption growth is measured as the ratio of FIOBS activity issued by a bank to the bank's total assets plus the FIOBS activity. The equilibrium ratio K is assumed to be equal to the maximum adoption ratio during the sampling period plus 2 standard deviations ($Max+2\sigma$) but not greater than 1. Period of study is January 1984 to September 1991, total 31 quarters (except 26 quarters for swaps). P-values are reported in parentheses. Significance at the 1, 5, and 10 percent level is indicated by **, *, and † respectively.

attempts to explain the variation in the speed of adoption of FIOBS products across banks in terms of individual bank characteristics such as capital adequacy, size, creditworthiness (risk), and international presence. The results indicate that, for swaps, futures and forwards, and market risk FIOBS, none of these variables are significant in determining differences in the speed of adoption across banks. In the case of options, PROFIT is weakly significant with a negative sign, implying that more profitable banks seem to be slower in selling options. In the case of loan sales, the RISKWGT (risk-weighted assets as a percentage of total assets) and ASSETS (bank size) have a positive and significant effect in determining the speed of diffusion, while NPLOAN (non-performing loans) and FGNDEPO (international presence) have a negative effect. This implies that banks with proportionately larger loan portfolios (larger RISKWGT) were quicker to adopt loan sales activities -- probably because they tended to have an advantage in entering the loan sales market due to their portfolio allocation. Large banks also have an advantage because the loans sold tend to be relatively large because the borrowers are relatively large (see Berger and Udell (1992)). In addition, larger banks may have had an advantage in the loan securitization market because they were viewed as safer (less likely to fail), while banks with larger non-performing loans may have been disadvantaged in adopting loan sales due to a lack of credibility. The coefficient of non-performing loans in the case of SLCs is also negative possibly for the same credibility reason as in loan sales.

It is interesting to note that the simple capital to asset ratio (CAPITAL) is not significant in determining the speed of adoption for all FIOBS products, except for SLCs whose capital coefficient is positive, again possibly reflecting a credibility effect. This is consistent with the finding by Avery and Berger (1991b) that better performing banks issue more OBS commitments. Indeed, the results overall seem to suggest that banks' decisions to adopt various FIOBS products, with the exception for SLCs and loan sales (non-derivative products), are related to purely technological and learning factors as proxied by the time variable.

5. CONCLUSIONS AND POLICY IMPLICATIONS

This paper investigates the growth of FIOBS activities in the banking industry over the 1984-1991. The FIOBS activities examined are: swaps, SLCs, loan sales, options, and futures and forward contracts. In examining the dramatic growth of these activities, we employ for the first time the logistic diffusion model of product innovation. In using this approach, we test the hypothesis that this explosive growth has been driven by regulatory avoidance. That is, FIOBS activities may have been used to avoid increased on-balance-sheet capital requirements -- since capital was not required to support OBS activities until the end of 1990 (although the proposed changes were announced in 1988).

We examine the diffusion pattern of FIOBS products at two levels: (i) the banking industry level (aggregate) and (ii) individual bank level. At the industry level, we focus on whether changing capital regulations have had significant effects on the adoption pattern of FIOBS products in aggregate. The results suggest that changes in capital regulations have had no consistent effect on the adoption of FIOBS products. Not all FIOBS products behave in the same fashion in response to regulatory changes, suggesting that risk-based capital may have affected the composition of OBS activities after 1988. This is a surprising result given that the capital adequacy avoidance has been one of the most popular explanations for the dramatic growth of bank OBS activities in the past decade.

At the individual bank level, the results indicate a considerable variation in bank adoption patterns across different FIOBS products and across banks. In addition, we find that differences in the speed of FIOBS adoption across banks is not determined by a bank's size, capital ratio, and creditworthiness factors (international exposures, loan loss rates, and profitability) for most FIOBS (derivative) products. A bank's decision to adopt these products seems to generally be related to technological and learning factors as proxied by the time variable. Unlike derivative FIOBS products, creditworthiness factors seem to play a role in the speed of adoption for SLCs and loan securitization.

REFERENCES

Avery, R. and A. Berger, 1991a, Loan Commitments and Bank Risk Exposure, *Journal of Banking and Finance* 15, 173-192.

Avery, R. and A. Berger, 1991b, Risk-Based Capital and Deposit Insurance Reform, J*ournal of Banking and Finance* 15, 847-874.

Baer, H. and C. Pavel, 1987, Does Regulation Drive Innovation?, *Federal Reserve Bank of Chicago: Economic Perspectives*, 3-16.

Benveniste, L. and A. Berger, 1987, Securitization with Recourse: An Instrument that Offers Uninsured Depositors Sequential Claims, *Journal of Banking and Finance* 11, 403-424.

Berger, A. and G. Udell, 1994, Did Risk-Based Capital Allocate Bank Credit and Cause a 'Credit Crunch' in the U.S.?, *Journal of Money, Credit, and Banking*, forthcoming.

Berger, A. and G. Udell, 1993, Securitization, Risk, and the Liquidity Problem in Banking, in: M. Klausner and L.J. White, eds., *Structural Changes in Banking*, Homewood, IL: Irwin Publishing, 227-291.

Berger, A. and G. Udell, 1992, Some Evidence on the Empirical Significance of Credit Rationing, *Journal of Political Economy* 100 (October), 1047-1077.

Breeden, R.C. and W.M. Isaac, 1992, Thank Basel for the Credit Crunch, *Wall Street Journal*, December 4, A14.

Davies, S., 1979, *The Diffusion of Process Innovations*, Cambridge: Cambridge University Press.

Eyssell, T. and N. Arshadi, 1990, The Wealth Effects of the Risk-Based Capital Requirement in Banking: The Evidence From the Capital Market, *Journal of Banking and Finance* 14, 179-197.

Globerman, S., 1974, Technological Diffusion in the Canadian Tool and Die Industry, *The Review of Economics and Statistics*, 428-434.

Griliches, Z., 1957, Hybrid Corn: An Exploration in the Economics of Technical Changes, *Econometrica* 25, 501-522.

Hannan, T.H. and J.M. McDowell, 1987, Rival Precedence and the Dynamics of Technology Adoption: an Empirical Analysis, *Economica* 54, 155-171.

Jagtiani, J., 1995, Characteristics of Banks That Are More Active in the Swap Market, *Journal of Financial Services Research* 9 (4), forthcoming.

Jagtiani, J., A. Nathan, and G. Sick, 1995, Economies of Scale and Cost Complementarities in Commercial Banks: On- and Off- Balance Sheet Activities, *Journal of Banking and Finance* 19 (6) forthcoming.

Jagtiani, J., A. Saunders, and G. Udell, 1995, The Effect of Bank Capital Requirements on Bank Off-Balance Sheet Financial Innovations, *Journal of Banking and Finance* 19 (2) forthcoming.

Keeley, M.C. and G.C. Zimmerman, 1985, Competition for Money Market Deposit Accounts, *Economic Review: Federal Reserve Bank of Atlanta* (Spring), 5-27.

Koppenhaver, G.D., 1989, The Effects of Regulation on Bank Participation in the Guarantee Market, Chapter 7, in: G. Kaufman, ed., *Research in Financial Services: Private and Public Policy*, Vol. 1, JAI Press, 165-180.

Koppenhaver, G.D. and R.D. Stover, 1991, Standby letters of credit and Large Bank Capital: An Empirical Analysis, *Journal of Banking and Finance* 15, 315-327.

Mandell, L., 1972, Credit Card Use in the United States, Institute for Social Research, University of Michigan.

Mansfield, E., 1961, Technical Change and the Rate of Imitation, *Econometrica* 29, 741-766.

Mansfield, E. and C. Hensley, 1960, The Logistic Process: Epidemic Curve and Applications, *Journal of the Royal Statistical Society* B-22, 332-337.

Murphy, N.B. and R.C. Rogers, 1986, Life Cycle and the Adoption of Consumer Financial Innovation: An Empirical Study of the Adoption Process, *Journal of Bank Research*, 3-8.

Pavel, C. and D. Phillis, 1987, Why Commercial Banks Sell Loans: An Empirical Analysis, *Federal Reserve Bank of Chicago: Economic Perspectives* (May/June), 3-14.

Romeo, A., 1977, The Rate of Imitation of a Capital-Embodied Process Innovation, *Economica* 44, 63-69.

APPENDIX 1
LIST OF SAMPLED BANKS

American NB&TC	First Interstate Bk OR	Seattle First NB
American Security Bk NA	First Interstate Bk WA	Security Pacific NB
Ameritrust Co NA	First NB of Atlanta	Shawmut Bk NA
Amsouth Bk Birmingham NA	First NB of Boston	Signet Bk Virginia
Arizona Bk	First NB of Chicago	Sovran Bk NA
Bancohio NB	First NB of Louisville	State Street B&TC
Banco Popular De Puerto Rico	First NB of Maryland	Sumitomo Bk of California
Bank Leumi TC of NY	First Security Bk of Utah NA	Texas Commerce Bk NA
Bank of America	First Tennesee Bk NA	Trust Co Bk
Bank of Hawaii	First Union NB NC	United Jersey Bank
Bank of Tokyo	First Wisconsin NB	Valley NB of Arizona
Bank One	Fleet NB	United States NB
Bankers Trust	Hamilton Bank	Wachovia B&TC NA
Barnett Bk of South Florida	Harris T&SB	
California First Bk	Huntington NB	
Central Bank of the South	Idaho First NB	
Central Fidelity Bank	Indiana NB	
Chase Lincoln First Bank	Israel Discount Bk of NY	
Chase Manhattan Bank	Manufacturers Hanover TC	
Chemical Bank	Manufacturers NB	
Citibank NA	Marine Midland Bank	
Citibank New York State	Maryland NB	
Citibank South Dakota NA	Mellon Bank NA	
Citizens & Southern NB	Meridian Bank	
Citizens Fidelity B&TC	Midlantic NB	
Comerica Bank - Detroit	Morgan Guaranty	
Connecticut B&Tc NA	National Bk of Detroit	
Connecticut NB	National City Bank	
Continental Illinois NB&TC	National Westminster Bk USA	
Crestar Bank	NCNB NB of Florida	
Deposit Guaranty NB	NCNB NB of North Carolina	
Equibank	Northern TC	
First Bk NA	Northwest Bk Minneapolis NA	
First City NB of Houston	Philadelphia NB	
First Fidelity Bk NA NJ	Pittsburgh NB	
First Hawaiian Bank	Provident NB	
First Interstate Bk AZ	Rainier NB	
First Interstate Bk CA	Republic NB of New York	
First Interstate Bk NV	Riggs NB of Washington DC	

Derivatives, Regulation and Banking
Edited by B. Schachter
© 1997 Elsevier Science B.V. All rights reserved.

Chapter 2
DERIVATIVES IN U.S. BANKING:
THEORY, PRACTICE, AND EMPIRICAL EVIDENCE

Joseph F. Sinkey, Jr. and David Carter[†]
University of Georgia, Athens, Georgia USA

1. INTRODUCTION

"The six men who rule world derivatives" ply their trade for six major bank holding companies located in the United States.[1] BankAmercia, Bankers Trust, Chase Manhattan, Chemical Banking, Citicorp, and J.P. Morgan are the corporate entities where these "financial engineers" create derivatives products. The market dominance of these firms warrants an investigation of the role of derivatives in U.S. banking. This chapter investigates the theoretical, practical, and empirical aspects of this role.

The theoretical focus centers on contemporary theories of banking and hedging behavior as determinants of the use of derivatives activities. The practical side looks at derivatives as ways for banks to hedge their balance sheets, to generate revenues from engaging in proprietary trading, and to generate fee income and enhance customer relationships by selling risk-management services to clients. As the cases of Procter & Gamble and Gibson Greetings, Inc. have demonstrated, however, selling complex risk-management services to client firms may not always enhance bank-customer relationships, and it raises the specter of "derivatives liability." During 1994 and 1995, litigation based on

---

[†]Joseph F. Sinkey, Jr. is Edward W. Hiles Professor of Financial Institutions and David Carter is a Ph.D. candidate, both in the Department of Banking and Finance, Terry College of Business. EMAIL: jsinkey@cbacc.cba.uga.edu and dcarter@uga.cc.uga.edu. We thank Richard C. Aspinwall, Robert B. Avery, David W. Blackwell, M. Cary Collins, Edward J. Kane, William L. Megginson, Kevin Rogers, Sheridan D. Titman, James A. Verbrugge, and D. Lee Warren for their comments and suggestions at various stages in the development of this research. Earlier versions of the research were presented at finance workshops at The University of Tennessee, The University of Georgia, and Boston College; at the Conference on Bank Structure and Competition sponsored by the Federal Reserve Bank of Chicago; and at the 1995 Meetings of the American Finance Association, Washington, D.C.

[1]Bennett (1993) attributes the domination of world derivatives to the people at these six institutions. Since individuals come and go, we focus on the institutions behind these folks.

allegedly misleading selling practices threatened the financial capital, and the reputation capital, of the biggest derivatives players in the world.

The empirical evidence presented in this chapter relates to the use of derivatives (or lack of use thereof) by all U.S. commercial banks over the three-year period 1989 to 1991. Although the growth in the use of derivatives such as forwards, futures, options, and swaps by U.S. banks has been explosive, it has not been an industry-wide phenomenon. During the early 1990s, approximately 600 out of 11,000 or so U.S. commercial banks used derivatives, with the six large dealer banks (described above and hereafter referred to as the "Big Six") accounting for 70 percent of this usage. Further, at year-end 1991, 13 large banks (all members of the International Swaps and Derivatives Association, ISDA) accounted for 82 percent of the derivatives activities conducted by U.S. commercial banks. Using both descriptive tests and regression models, the empirical analysis focuses on differences in the financial characteristics between user and nonuser banks. Controlling for dealer activities, the investigation also attempts to analyze the use of derivatives for hedging.

The descriptive findings indicate that user banks, including large dealer banks, have weaker capital positions, smaller maturity gaps, lower net interest margins, and use more notes and debentures to fund assets; but, overwhelmingly, they are much larger than nonuser banks. Tobit regression results tend to confirm these findings consistent with those found by Nance, Smith, and Smithson (1993) for hedging by nonfinancial firms.

This chapter proceeds as follows: Section I presents a primer on derivatives and a summary of the derivatives debacles of 1994 and early 1995. Section II provides some background information on the what, why, how, and for whom of derivatives use by U.S. commercial banks. Section III presents a taxonomy of derivatives use by U.S. commercial banks for the years 1989 to 1991. Section IV establishes the empirical models, defines the variables, and identifies the data sources. Although our empirical models are ad hoc in nature, they derive from published research by Nance, Smith, and Smithson (1993) on the determinants of corporate hedging by nonfinancial firms with modifications for application to banks. Section V presents the descriptive findings while Section VI contains estimates of tobit regressions. Section VII summarizes and concludes the chapter, and draws policy and managerial implications.

2. A PRIMER AND SUMMARY OF THE DERIVATIVES DEBACLES OF 1994-95[2]

Derivatives are contracts whose values derive from an underlying bond, stock,

---

[2]This section draws on Sinkey (1995).

currency, or commodity. They are tools for managing risk. When used properly, derivatives essentially are benign as they allow organizations or individuals to modify or eliminate exposure to risks from <u>unexpected</u> changes in interest rates, exchange rates, or commodity prices. As with any tool, when derivatives are used improperly or without adequate controls and accountability or both, financial disasters such as the bankruptcies of Orange County, California and Barings PLC, a British investment bank, may occur.

A bank that finances long-term mortgages with short-term deposits can hedge its interest-rate risk using a variety of derivatives such as interest-rate swaps, futures, or options. A U.S. importer of foreign goods can protect against depreciation of the dollar by buying currency forward or futures contracts. A soybean farmer can hedge against lower crop prices at harvest by selling soybean futures or forwards at planting time.

Derivatives transactions are zero-sum games between buyers and sellers called counterparties. Although "hedgers" and "speculators" are the usual players, a hedger may contract with another hedger with the opposite risk exposure. Or, a speculator may strike a deal with another speculator with an opposite view on the future course of the price of the underlying asset, commodity, or currency. When one counterparty gains, the other loses.

Derivatives transactions span two markets: the cash market and the derivatives market. Soybean farmers bring their harvests to the cash market. To protect against declining (cash) prices for soybeans, they can sell soybean contracts in the futures market. Selling or "shorting" futures means that the investor gains when the price of the underlying asset/commodity declines; the zero-sum constraint means that the buyer of the futures contract loses. If the hedge is perfect (rare in the real world), the gain in one market exactly offsets the loss in the other market or vice versa.

All of this is benign and the basic transactions have been going on, not only for years, but for centuries with little attention or concern. During 1994 and the first part of 1995, however, derivatives have made headlines, most of them adversely associated with bankruptcy, earnings losses, or litigation. The bankruptcies of Orange County and Barings and the derivatives losses of Escambia County in Florida's panhandle have been the most recent fiascos. Prior to these messes, major corporations such as Metallgesellschaft AG, Procter & Gamble, Gibson Greetings, and Mead incurred financial losses associated with derivatives.

<u>Caveat emptor</u> means let the buyer beware. Because they deal in million-dollar transactions, the managers of banks, pension funds, mutual funds, government agencies, and the treasurers of major corporations should fully understand any contracts they enter. Moreover, as principals, stockholders, directors, and taxpayers should demand accountability and control mechanisms from these agent-managers. In the derivatives fiascos of 1994 and

early 1995, the traders/managers responsible for the losses did not necessarily act with criminal intent, instead they may be the modern equivalent of riverboat gamblers who simply bet and lost. Another explanation focuses on the complexity of derivatives contracts. Today's derivatives come in more flavors than those found at many popular ice-cream parlors. The menu ranges from plain vanilla (simple, traditional contract) to the exotic (complex, financially-engineered contract). Complexity, however, does not excuse neglect. While many managers who enter into complex contracts without complete understanding are undoubtedly guilty of neglect. some are simply responding to incentives without proper internal controls in place – neglect at a higher level.

Some buyers of derivatives have claimed fraudulent and deceptive practices by the sellers of derivatives products. For example, Bankers Trust of New York has recently settled out of court with Gibson Greetings, agreeing to accept only $6 million for a $20-million debt. Despite denying any guilt or wrong doing in this and other cases, Bankers Trust was fined $10 million by the Securities and Exchange Commission and signed an "unusual enforcement agreement" with the Federal Reserve Bank of New York to improve its supervision of the sale of risky derivatives to corporate clients. In addition, based on its own internal probe, Bankers Trust reassigned five executives involved in soured derivatives deals. These events notwithstanding, Bankers Trust has decided to do battle with Procter & Gamble in the courts over derivatives liability regarding their deals.

Both buyers and sellers of derivatives must have adequate internal controls and oversight. The Orange County and Barings cases appear to be the most blatant examples of these shortcomings. In the Barings fiasco, the fact that a 28-year old trader could bet $30 billion on the future course of interest rates and stock prices without top managers knowing strains credulity. The financial-engineering gap separating young traders from older managers is no excuse for an absence of managerial controls and oversight. Also, underestimating the cleverness of the criminal mind with access to computer stealth is understandable but not excusable.

Remembering that most derivatives deals are zero-sum games, the derivatives fiascos of 1994 and 1995 do not require any overreaction by government regulators or politicians. Except for mandating adequate disclosure and attempting to assure transparency, government should not interfere with private business decisions. Did the government prohibit Coca Cola from "gambling" when it changed its formula for Coke? Internal business controls and external market mechanisms to monitor and discipline corporate actions are preferred to government interference. Existing regulatory weapons of fines, consent decrees, and enforcement actions are adequate for policing derivatives abusers. Moreover, market forces, aided by ex-post settling up either in or out of the courts, will redistribute contested gains and losses. On balance, let both buyers and sellers beware, and let the government refrain from interfering with private business decisions.

3. BANK USE OF DERIVATIVES: WHAT, WHY, HOW, AND FOR WHOM

Derivatives contracts, defined to include interest-rate and foreign-exchange forwards, futures, options, and swaps, represent an area where banking has **not** been declining. Because they are classified as off-balance sheet activities (OBSAs), the explosive growth of derivatives activities has not been registered on banks' balance sheets.[3] The traditional OBSAs of commercial banks consist primarily of credit-related contracts such as lines of credit and loan commitments. In contrast, derivatives contracts represent the new and innovative tools of "financial engineering" (e.g., Smith and Smithson (1990) and Smith, Smithson, and Wilford (1990)) and can be viewed as potential means of increasing bank franchise value.

3.1. Why Do Banks Use Derivatives?

Banks engage in derivatives activities either as end-users to manage their own risks or as brokers/dealers in providing risk-management services to corporate customers.[4] In addition, commercial banks use derivatives contracts to speculate on the future course of interest rates, exchange rates, and commodity prices. Although bank regulators and their examiners frown on purely speculative transactions, the business of banking involves "bets" on the future course of interest rates, exchange rates, and commodity prices. Prudent bank managers restrict the sizes of their bets, whether made on or off the balance sheet, and market and regulatory discipline provide monitoring mechanisms.[5]

As end-users, banks attempt to hedge duration gaps on their balance sheets; as brokers/dealers, they provide risk-management or transactions services to customers in return

---

[3]Beginning with the first quarter of 1994, a new Financial Accounting Standards Board (FASB) rule requires that the unrealized gains on swaps, options, and other derivatives be recorded as assets; unrealized loses must be recorded as liabilities. Layne (1993, 1993a, 1993b) and Stern (1994) describe the growth and profitability of derivatives activities.

[4]Smith (1993) stresses that "hedging by the bank is not a substitute for hedging by the bank's customers" (p. 157).

[5]Regarding this, the Comptroller of the Currency (see OCC Guidelines (1993)), stated: "In derivatives, the slicing, dicing, and recombining of risk elements of products makes it harder to see the risk. Banks need to be prepared to expect the unexpected ..." Merton and Bodie (1992) discuss techniques for managing the guarantee business (e.g., deposit insurance).

for fees and commissions, and opportunities to strengthen customer relationships (Smith (1993) and King and Lipin (1994)).[6] Ironically, as the cases of Gibson Greetings, Inc., Procter & Gamble, Mead Corp., and Metallgesellschaft have demonstrated, placing clients in speculative contracts may harm customer relationships, and raises the specter of "derivatives liability" (see Overdahl and Schachter (1995)). To generate trading revenues and profits, banks engage in proprietary trading. Although this speculative activity worries some analysts, investors, lawmakers, and regulators (Bacon (1993, 1993a) or Layne (1993)), it does not seem to bother bank traders (e.g., Group of Thirty, (1993)).

3.1.1. Derivatives and Financial Management

By providing new tools for managing risk, derivatives contracts have "fundamentally changed financial management" (Group of Thirty, (1993)). Smith (1993) emphasizes that bankers must recognize the potential benefits of selling risk-management services. The obvious benefits come from the generation of fee income and opportunities for bankers to create value through cross-selling and enhanced customer relationships.[7] Less obviously, since derivatives reduce the probability of financial distress for client firms, banks also benefit by reducing their risk exposure to these customers.

3.2. Who Uses Derivatives?

While almost all banks have traditional OBSAs, only about five percent use derivatives. Why do so few commercial banks use derivatives? How do user banks differ from nonusers? How do end-users (hedgers) differ from dealers and how do ISDA-member banks differ from banks that are not members of ISDA? Finally, how do the six banks that rule world derivatives differ from other dealer banks? In analyzing these questions, this chapter presents evidence on the derivatives activities of U.S. commercial banks over the

---

[6]Knecht (1995) presents an opposing view regarding the development of bank customer relationships as practiced at Bankers Trust, one in which Charles Sanford, Bankers Trust chairman, presumably asked traders: "Have you made any money today?" not, "Have you built any relationships?" Since the derivatives debacles at Bankers Trust in 1994 and 1995, Knecht reports that "Mr. Sanford now talks about an effort to rebuild customer relationships, and a high-level committee has been formed to increase the emphasis on client relationships" (p. B12).

[7]Kane and Malkiel (1967) were one of the first to emphasize the importance of "other services" (beyond loans and deposits) to the bank-customer relationship. Wigler (1991) describes how to use derivatives to increase customer profitability.

years 1989 to 1991.[8]

This chapter analyzes derivatives data at the bank level. Within a holding company, some derivatives transactions are across subsidiaries and therefore netted out on a consolidated holding-company basis. For example, at year-end 1991, Citicorp reported derivatives contracts of $1.257 trillion while Citibank New York reported $1.293 trillion. Citibank South Dakota with $7.8 billion in assets (mainly credit-card receivables, see Sinkey and Nash (1993)) held $5.6 billion in interest-rate contracts. Another of Citicorp's credit-card banks, Citibank Maryland (Towson) with $3.9 billion in assets, held $2.1 billion in interest-rate contracts. In the case of a major BHC like Citicorp, almost all derivatives activities are conducted by its lead bank, Citibank New York.

3.3. Entry Restrictions, Informational Economies, and Correspondent Banking

Since the end-use of derivatives does not require a substantial financial commitment from a bank and since derivatives markets and over-the-counter (OTC) contracts are easily accessible to banks, wide-spread use of derivatives by banks should exist. Derivatives activities do, however, require an investment in "intellectual capital" in terms of understanding the transactions,[9] which may make some banks reluctant to participate. Instead, they may rely on securitization to remove on-balance sheet risk, utilize traditional risk-management techniques and tools, or perhaps do nothing. In contrast, to be a dealer and trader of derivatives products requires a substantial investment of financial, intellectual, reputational, and, to a lesser extent, physical capital – barriers to entry.[10] Since only the largest banks are able to muster such resources, dealing and trading activities are restricted to such entities in the United States. On a global basis, however, size may not be an appropriate proxy as reflected by the fact that of the six U.S. banks that rule the world of

---

[8]Banks outside the U.S. and nonbanking firms within the U.S. also engage in derivatives activities. Our analysis focuses only on the derivatives activities of U.S. commercial banks for the years 1989 to 1991. McDonough (1993) describes the global derivatives market.

[9]To illustrate, the Comptroller of the Currency, describes the kind of derivatives situation that concerns him: A bank with less than $200 million in assets has a structured note in its investment portfolio whose interest rate is tied to the performance of the deutschemark and the Spanish peseta vs. the dollar. He says: "We are not convinced that they have this instrument for legitimate hedging purposes or that they understand it." Fact: the initial rate on this note was 9%, but it is currently paying no interest – and it has lost 20% of its market value.

[10]Although Tufano (1989) does not deal with "derivatives" per se, his analysis of financial innovation and first-mover advantages in investment banking describes the high costs associated with the development of new products in general, inclusive of derivatives.

derivatives only one (Citicorp) ranks among the world's 25 largest banks. This suggests that intellectual and reputational capital are the barriers to entry on a global basis. When these two factors are combined with an accounting, legal, regulatory, and technical environment conducive to financial innovation, U.S. dominance of the worldwide market for derivatives results.

Once entry has been achieved, derivatives activities benefit from substantial informational and scale economies. Although ISDA membership is not a requirement to be a dealer/trader, the asset size of the smallest U.S. bank that is a primary member of ISDA could be treated as the threshold size for a dealer/trader. Based on 1991 data, the critical mass needed to be a dealer/trader bank would be $12 billion in assets or roughly $1 billion in equity capital.

On balance, entry restrictions and informational economies of scale or scope may be the underlying reasons why so few banks engage in derivatives activities. Based on survey data, Booth, Smith, and Stolz (1984) report that smaller banks have a problem hiring and retaining the skilled employees needed for an effective program of financial risk management. Nevertheless, bank holding companies and correspondent banking, traditional mainstays of U.S. banking, offer convenient and efficient ways for banks that do not use derivatives to obtain such services not only for themselves but also for their customers. Within large bank holding companies, the lead bank can provide risk-management services to subsidiaries and their clients. Small banks that are not members of a holding company or belong to a small BHC can obtain risk-management services for themselves or their clients from correspondent banks that deal in derivatives.

3.4. Derivatives Liability: *Caveat Emptor* and Accountability Versus "Aggressive" and "Deceptive" Sales Practices

At a derivatives conference held in Atlanta on September 13-14, 1994,[11] the corporate treasurers of several major corporations expressed dismay at the claims made in the press by major companies that they were effectively hood winked into buying derivatives contracts that they did not understand or need or both. These treasurers indicated they would have been embarrassed to make such claims. Caveat emptor (let the buyer beware) and accountability for one's actions represent the cornerstones of their arguments. Of course, they probably would have been less sanguine had the soured derivatives been in their portfolios.

---

[11]"Derivatives: Uses and Abuses, Managing Corporate Financial Exposure in Today's Markets," a conference and workshop presented by the Chicago Mercantile Exchange, KPMG Peat Marwick, and the Terry College of Business, The University of Georgia.

Nevertheless, their position was clear: Don't buy anything you don't understand or don't need.

The specter of derivatives liability became real on September 12, 1994 when Gibson Greetings filed a suit against Bankers Trust claiming the bank and its broker unit (BT Securities Corp.) failed to disclose fully the risks associated with the derivatives transactions Gibson had entered (see Thomas (1994)). On October 13, 1994, Bankers Trust asked the U.S. District Court in Cincinnati to throw out Gibson's suit and for Gibson to pay Bankers Trust's legal fees (Lipin (1994)). Bankers Trust claims that Gibson was fully aware of the risk of such investments and that senior officials approved the transactions.

Procter & Gamble (P&G) filed suit against Bankers Trust on October 28, 1994, claiming fraud and deception in its sales practices, and seeking $130 million plus punitive damages. Pre-dating these events, Fortune (March 7, 1994) warned: "Like alligators in a swamp, derivatives lurk in the global economy. Even the CEO of companies that use them don't understand them" (Loomis (1994), pp. 40-41). In a 1994 speech, Charles Sanford, the chairman of Bankers Trust, stated that corporate leaders must "... know enough about the business to be the risk manager of risk managers" (Sanford (1994), p. 27). On November 14, 1994, Bankers Trust announced that, as part of an internal probe into the bank's sales practices, it had reassigned five executives involved in soured derivatives deals (Lipin (1994a)).[12]

The threat and reality of derivatives liability should caution dealer banks to make sure that their clients understand the contracts they enter (see Schachter (1995)). On balance, both banking and nonbanking firms need policies, procedures, and controls regarding derivatives activities, especially speculative contracts.

3.4.1. Market Reactions to the Threat of Derivatives Liability

On April 13, 1994, Procter & Gamble announced a $102-million, after-tax loss to close out two interest-rate swaps arranged for it by Bankers Trust of New York. To shift some of the blame for the loss on Bankers Trust, P&G raised the threat of "derivatives liability" by indicating that it was "seriously considering our legal options relative to Bankers Trust" (Stern and Lipin (1994)). The stock-market reaction to P&G's threat was negative as a portfolio of the Big Six had a market-adjusted average return of -1.62 percent on April 13,

---

[12]Corrigan and Hargreaves (1994), Culp and Miller (1994), Lipin, Bleakley, and Granito (1994), Stern and Lipin (1994), and The Economist (April 16, September 21, and October 1, 1994,) report related stories.

Exhibit 1
A Chronology of Major Economic/financial, Legal, and Regulatory Announcements Related to the Derivatives Deals of Procter and Gamble and Gibson Greetings, Inc. With Bankers Trust, April 1994 Through May 1996.

Date	Event
April 13, 1994	Procter & Gamble to Take a Charge to Close out Two Interest-rate Swaps
April 14, 1994	Portfolio Poker: Just What Firms Do with "Derivatives" Is Suddenly a Hot Issue, P&g's Loss Shows Pitfalls in Getting into the Game of Options and Swaps, Some Hedge Some Speculate
April 21, 1994	Bankers Trust Gets a Big Boost from Sale of Derivatives; Another Client Has Loss
April 22, 1994	Fancy Footwork: Bankers Trust Thrives Pitching Derivatives, but Climate Is Shifting, Losses by Clients like P&g May Crimp Plan to Move to Relationship Banking, Some Intense Pressure to Sell
September 13, 1994	Gibson Sued its Longtime Bank, Bankers Trust, over the Greeting-card Firm's Disastrous Encounter with Derivatives Earlier this Year (In November, the Case Was Settled out of Court.)
October 28, 1994	Procter & Gamble Sues Bankers Trust Because of Huge Losses on Derivatives/derivatives Are Going Through Crucial Test: a Wave of Lawsuits
December 6, 1994	Bankers Trust Signs Accord with New York Fed on Derivatives
December 23, 1994	Bankers Trust Settles Charges with Sec/cftc on Derivatives
January 17, 1995	Sec Plans to Expand Disclosure Rules Covering Derivatives Used to Hedge Risk
January 20, 1995	Bankers Trust 4th-period Net Fell 64% as Many Derivatives Pacts May Default (Bt Also Announced That it Was Setting Aside $423 Million for Potential Losses on Derivatives-related Business, the Bulk of it to Cover Any Claims Arising from P&g's Suit)
February 7, 1995	P&G Amends Lawsuit Naming Bankers Trust
May 10, 1996	Bankers Trust Reaches Out of Court Settlement With P&G

Sources: the Wall Street Journal (Dates as Indicated).

1994.[13] Removing Bankers Trust from the portfolio resulted in an average return of -1.48 percent. The market-adjustment process netted out the return on the S&P 500, which on that day was -0.29 percent. On April 22, 1994, The Wall Street Journal carried a front-page story that raised some questions about banks' derivatives activities with emphasis on the losses experienced by P&G and other companies (e.g., Gibson Greetings Inc.). On this day, the market-adjusted average return for the Big Six was -1.71 percent; removing Bankers Trust, the return was -1.96 percent. The S&P return on April 22, 1994 was -0.25 percent.

Both of these negative market reactions suggest that bank dealers, who are under varying degrees of pressure to sell derivatives, make sure that clients understand the difference between hedging and speculating with derivatives. The events also suggest that

---

[13]Excess returns tests are based on market-adjusted returns; they are not risk-adjusted.

client firms have appropriate policies, procedures, and controls regarding their derivatives activities.

The market reaction to the filing of the suit against Bankers Trust by Gibson was negative for dealer banks but not very substantial, perhaps because the litigation was partially anticipated given P&G's threat. Specifically, a portfolio of the Big Six was down -0.60 percent (-0.49% less BT) while a portfolio of nine other dealer banks was down -0.68 percent. The market, as captured by the S&P 500, was up 0.28 percent on the day of the announcement. The market's reaction to P&G's suit also was muted as the stock prices of a portfolio of the Big Six was up 1.29 percent, which was 41 percentage points less than the increase in the S&P 500. A portfolio of seven other ISDA member banks was up 2.30 percent or 60 percentage points more than the S&P 500.

On October 13, 1994, Bankers Trust asked the U.S. District Court in Cincinnati to throw out Gibson's suit and for Gibson to pay Bankers Trust's legal fees (Lipin (1994)). Bankers Trust claims that Gibson was fully aware of the risk of such investments and that senior officials approved the transactions. Although stock prices for the Big Six were unchanged or up on this news, they were up less than the S&P 500 (+0.5%). On November 14, 1994, Bankers Trust announced, as part of an internal probe into the bank's sales practices, that it had reassigned five executives involved in soured derivatives deals (Lipin (1994a)). Bankers Trust's common stock was down 1.61 percent on the news as it recorded a two-year low of 60.625 before closing at 61. The S&P 500 was up 0.80 percent for the day. Shortly thereafter, Bankers Trust arranged an out-of-court settlement with Gibson, in which it agreed to accept $6 million out of about $20 million owed to it by the card company. The employee who sold the derivatives to Gibson is no longer with Bankers Trust.

On December 23, 1994, The Wall Street Journal reported that Bankers Trust had signed consent decrees with the SEC and the Commodity Futures Trading Commission (CFTC), and agreed to pay a $10 million fine over its derivatives sales. The settlement was not unexpected and Bankers Trust neither admitted nor denied guilt. In the consent decree, the CFTC said that Bankers Trust was a "commodity trading adviser" rather than simply a seller of certain products. In addition, on a broader scale, the SEC and CFTC ruled that the swaps sold to Gibson are being treated as securities for regulatory purposes because the agencies found securities embedded within the swaps. The result is that securities laws, which are tougher than common law, would apply to any derivatives with embedded securities. The business implication is that derivatives dealers will be required to provide more information in the future, and that they might be liable for past "omissions" (e.g., about what you failed to say). Prior to the SEC/CFTC decree, Bankers Trust signed what was described as an "unusual enforcement agreement" with the Federal Reserve Bank of New

Table 1
The Derivatives Activities of U.S. Commercial Banks Dollar Amounts Outstanding as of December 31, 1991

Instrument		$ billions	% of type	% of total
Total Interest-rate		3,836	100.00	52.42
	Swaps	1,757	45.79	24.00
	Futures & forwards	1,226	31.95	16.75
	Written options	427	11.14	5.84
	Purchased options	426	11.12	5.83
Currency contracts		3,344	100.00	45.70
	Swaps	306	9.16	4.19
	Futures & forwards	2,583	77.24	35.30
	Written options	232	6.95	3.18
	Purchased options	222	6.64	3.04
Other contracts		138	100.00	1.88
All contracts		7,318	100.00	100.00

Source: Figures calculated from Reports of Condition and Reports of Income and Dividends computer tapes, National Technical Information Service, Springfield, VA.

York to improve its supervision of the sale of risky derivatives to corporate clients.[14] See, also, the analysis in Overdahl and Schachter (1995).

An important financial/accounting development regarding derivatives occurred on January 20, 1995, when Bankers Trust announced that it was reclassifying $423 million payable to it under derivatives contracts as "receivables". The economic meaning of this accounting maneuver was to recognize the probability of default associated with the contracts. Interestingly, however, the probability of default cannot be traced so much to a lack of ability to pay – the focus of traditional credit risk, as to an unwillingness to pay because of obligors' concerns about the possibility that they were misled/misinformed about their risk exposures. Thus, this particular type of credit risk traces to derivatives liability, which should be linked to selling and disclosure practices rather than to credit analysis and assessing a counterparty's ability to pay. Traditional credit analysis views a borrower's unwillingness to repay as a character flaw; in the case of derivatives liability, however, the character flaw arises from the seller's behavior, resulting in the counterparty's refusal to pay.[15]

---

[14]For additional details on the two agreements reported in this paragraph, see Lipin and Taylor (1994) and (1994a).

[15]The five Cs of credit analysis are: character (willingness to pay), capacity (cash flow), collateral (liquid assets), capital (net worth and access to capital market), and conditions (economic and interest-rate cycles), see Sinkey (1992). The "credit risk" arising from derivatives contracts has not been traditional in the sense that the counterparties (e.g., P&G and Gibson) had the cash flow, collateral, or

Exhibit 1 presents a chronology of some of the major events of 1994 and 1995 in terms of their economic/financial, legal, and regulatory effects on derivatives activities.

4.   A TAXONOMY OF THE DERIVATIVES CONTRACTS HELD BY U.S. COMMERCIAL BANKS

The growth in the use of derivatives by U.S. commercial banks over the past decade has not been an industry-wide phenomenon. For example, at year-end 1991 roughly 600 commercial banks used derivatives either as end-users or for other reasons; in contrast, over 11,000 banks did not use derivatives. Within the user's group, derivatives activities are highly concentrated in the 13 "primary members" of the International Swaps and Derivatives Association (ISDA)[16], which accounted for 81.7 percent of U.S. derivatives activities undertaken by commercial banks in 1991. Of these 13 ISDA-member banks, Bennett (1993) describes six of them (BankAmerica, Bankers Trust, Chase, Chemical, Citicorp, and Morgan) as "ruling world derivatives."[17] These six banks accounted for 85.9 percent of the derivatives held by the 13 dealers and 70.3 percent of the derivatives held by all 612 user banks at year-end 1991.[18] The bulk of derivatives contracts used by U.S. commercial banks have either interest rates or foreign-exchange rates as the underlying factor. Both the interest-rate and foreign-exchange contracts include swaps, futures, forwards, and options. Any additional contracts on other commodities or precious metals are reported in the "other" category. This paper defines a "user bank" as one with derivatives contracts reported on lines 11, 12, or 13

---

capital to repay their obligations but they refused to do so for other reasons.

[16]Prior to August 13, 1993, ISDA was the International Swap Dealers Association.

[17]Evans (1994) provides a broader survey of "derivatives superstars" by focusing on 115 of the world's top players.

[18]Except where noted otherwise, the derivatives contracts reported in this paper represent notional principal amounts as reported by banks on Schedule RC-L of the Report of Condition, see Table 1 below. Notional values cannot be equated with actual risk exposures, estimated at two-to-three percent of nominal values. Our data, however, should accurately reflect relative exposures, e.g., roughly 11,000 banks have no exposure to derivatives. Section 3 provides some estimates of real exposures for the largest U.S. banks.

Table 2
The Derivatives Activities of U.S. Commercial Banks Stratified by Total Assets, December 31, 1991

Total Assets	Number of banks		Percent
($ millions)	with derivatives	without derivatives	with
< 100	69	8,938	0.77
100 - 300	127	1,836	6.47
300 - 500	60	293	17.00
500 - 1,000	87	156	35.80
1,000 - 5,000	164	84	66.13
5,000 - 10,000	57	1	98.28
> 10,000	48	0	100.00
< 1,000	343	11,223	2.97
> 1,000	269	85	75.99
All banks	612	11,308	5.13

Source: Figures calculated from Reports of Condition and Reports of Income and Dividends computer tapes, National Technical Information Service, Springfield, VA.

of Schedule RC-L of the Report of Condition.[19]

Table 1 reveals that three contracts dominated the derivatives activities of commercial banks in 1991: futures and forwards based on currency contracts totaled $2.6 trillion, accounting for 77 percent of currency contracts and 35 percent of all contracts; interest-rate swaps had a notional value of $1.7 trillion, accounting for 46 percent of interest-rate contracts and 24 percent of all contracts; and interest-rate futures and 24 percent of all contracts; and interest-rate futures and forwards totaled $1.2 trillion, accounting for 32 percent of interest-rate contracts and 17 percent of all contracts. Combined, these three contracts totaled almost $5.6 trillion or 76 percent of all the derivatives held by U.S. commercial banks on December 31, 1991.[20] These figures represent notional principal amounts or the gross value of all contracts written; they do not reflect net market position or actual risk exposure. Regarding real exposures, Mark Brickell of J.P. Morgan (see Euromoney (September 1992), p. 37) estimated the "gross credit risk exposure" at the top 30 U.S. banks at $150 billion. He estimated the three largest exposures as: Bankers Trust with $25.6 billion (40% of total assets), Chase with $25 billion (25%), and Morgan with $17.7

---

[19]On March 10, 1994, the Federal Financial Institutions Examination Council (FFIEC) announced proposed changes in Schedule RC-L.

[20]As of June 30, 1994, 668 commercial banks held $15.4 trillion in derivatives contracts; the 15 largest participants held 95% of the contracts or $14.6 trillion (FDIC Quarterly Banking Profile, Second Quarter, 1994).

Table 3
The Distribution of Derivatives Contracts Stratified by Total Assets for User Banks, December 31, 1991

Stratification		Interest-rate contracts		Currency contracts		Other contracts	
Size	number	number	percent	number	percent	number	percent
<100	69	62	89.9	3	4.3	4	5.8
100-300	127	120	94.5	9	7.1	0	0.0
300-500	60	55	91.7	7	11.7	0	0.0
500-1,000	87	74	85.1	30	34.5	1	1.1
1,000-5,000	164	139	84.8	84	51.2	3	1.8
5,000-10,000	57	55	96.5	45	78.9	2	3.5
>10,000	48	48	100.0	45	93.8	17	35.4
Total	612	553	90.4	223	36.4	27	4.4

Notes: Banks with derivatives are ones that held such contracts at year-end 1991; banks without did not hold any of these contracts at the end of 1991. Schedule RC-L indicates that some of the amounts reported are regarded as volume indicators and not necessarily measures of risk. In Panel B, the percent of banks with derivatives is calculated based on the total number of banks in the size class. Source: Figures calculated from Reports of Condition and Reports of Income and Dividends computer tapes, National Technical Information Service, Springfield, VA.

billion (17%). Chemical and Citicorp were reported with exposures to total assets of 16 percent and 14 percent, respectively.

Table 2 shows how derivatives were distributed by bank size at year-end 1991. As expected, as bank size increases, the percentage of banks using derivatives increases. Somewhat surprisingly, 343 banks with assets less than $1 billion had outstanding derivatives contracts at the end of 1991. Although 69 of these 343 banks had total assets less than $100 million, they represented less than one percent of the 9,007 banks in the size class. The typical user bank in this smallest size class had average assets of $57.5 million and average interest-rate contracts of $8.2 million (standard deviation = $20.4 million). At the other end of the size spectrum, all 48 banks with total assets greater than $10 billion (average assets = $27 billion) had derivatives contracts outstanding, on average, $75 billion of interest-rate contracts, $68 billion of currency contracts, and $2.8 billion of other contracts. Within this group, however, the 13 banks that are "primary members" of ISDA dominate with almost $6 trillion in derivatives (81.7% of all contracts); within the ISDA members, BankAmerica, Bankers Trust, Chase, Chemical, Citicorp, and J.P. Morgan dominate with 85.9 percent, and 70.3 percent of the derivatives held by all 612 user banks.

Table 3 shows the distribution of derivatives contracts stratified by total assets for the user banks. Banks with assets under $1 billion primarily have interest-rate contracts in their

Table 4
Total Derivatives, Total Assets, and Noninterest Income for U.S. Commercial Banks December 31, 1991

Bank	Total derivatives	Total assets	Derivatives to Assets	Noninterst income to total income
Panel A. Banks Listed as Primary Members of ISDA				
Chemical	$ 851,020	$ 47,654	17.2	0.1995
Bankers Trust	854,860	52,490	16.2	0.3259
FNB Chicago	381,511	34,928	11.8	0.1676
Morgan Guar.	902,080	70,778	11.4	0.2151
Chase Man.	776,181	78,774	10.3	0.1569
Continental	195,538	71,716	8.2	0.1558
Citibank	1,292,798	160,830	7.9	0.1534
Bank of Amer.	454,395	94,212	4.6	0.1795
Republic NY	107,182	22,997	4.3	0.1210
Bank of NY	85,951	41,739	2.3	0.1822
FNB Boston	49,224	27,021	1.8	0.1294
Mellon Bank	19,291	22,695	0.69	0.2229
Maryland NB	6,494	11,793	0.55	0.1395
Mean	459,730	53,272	7.5	0.1807
(st. dev.)	(428,847)	(11,794)	(5.6)	(0.0535)
Panel B. Group Data				
Mean ("Big 6")	855,216	41,287	11.28	0.2050
(st.dev.)	(268,561)	(47,654)	(4.83)	(0.0638)
Mean ("ISDA-7")	120,742	26,829	4.26	0.1598
(st.dev.)	(131,306)	(9,538)	(4.24)	(0.0351)
Mean (612)	11,957	2,639	0.32	0.1245
(st.dev.)	(NA)	(5,624)	(2.31)	(0.0894)
Mean (11,308)	0.0	91	0.0	0.0794
(st.dev.)	(0.0)	(200)	(0.0)	(0.0676)

Notes: Total derivatives and assets are in millions. The "Big Six" includes Bankers Trust, BOA, Chase, Chemical, Citibank, and Morgan. Panel A shows U.S. bank membership in the International Swaps and Derivatives Association (ISDA) as of December 1, 1991 as supplied by ISDA. As of January 4, 1994, First Union National Bank and NationsBank were listed as primary members of ISDA, expanding the number of U.S. bank primary members to 15.

Source: Figures calculated from Reports of Condition and Reports of Income and Dividends computer tapes, National Technical Information Service, Springfield, VA.

derivatives portfolios.   The number of banks using currency contracts increases monotonically with bank size and, except for the 48 largest, most banks do not hold other contracts. Table 4 compares the total derivatives for the 13 ISDA-banks to their total assets (Panel A) and for groups of user and nonuser banks. The typical ISDA-member U.S. bank held (at year-end 1991) a dollar (notional) volume of derivatives contracts that was 7.5 times

Table 5
Ranking of 27 Banks with Derivatives Contracts Exceeding Their Total On-Balance Sheet Assets,
December 31 ,1991

Bank	Derivatives contracts			Total	Ratio
	Interest	Currency	Other	assets	
Mitsui Trust, NY	0.5	29.2	0.0	0.6	47.94
First Inter., CA	14.3	0.0	0.0	0.5	27.74
Chemical Bank	458.9	392.1	0.1	49.4	17.21
Bankers Trust	413.8	380.8	60.1	52.7	16.22
FNB Chicago	151.6	229.7	0.02	32.4	11.78
Morgan Guaranty	524.6	359.3	18.2	79.0	11.42
Chase Manhattan	354.9	409.4	11.9	75.1	10.33
Continental Bank, IL	155.0	39.0	0.1	23.8	8.22
Citibank	536.4	716.2	40.2	162.7	7.93
Manufacturers Han.	270.3	172.8	0.3	59.6	7.44
Security Pac., CA	192.2	175.7	0.0	53.4	6.89
Bank America	214.4	239.9	0.0	99.6	4.56
Republic Nat., NY	37.1	67.1	3.0	24.7	4.34
Greene County, MO	0.1	0.0	0.0	0.02	3.98
First Inter. Bank, CA	54.4	6.2	0.0	19.7	3.07
Bank of New York	33.5	52.4	0.0	36.6	2.35
Seattle-First NB, WA	0.8	0.1	0.0	12.0	2.30
FNB Boston	35.7	13.4	0.1	26.2	1.88
IBJ Schroder, NY	79.5	0.6	0.0	4.6	1.84
Banc One, OH	10.1	0.03	0.0	5.9	1.72
Norwest Bank, MN	18.5	0.3	0.0	11.0	1.71
First Union, NC	24.5	2.6	0.0	15.9	1.71
First Sec., Boise, ID	4.4	0.0	0.0	2.6	1.68
J.P. Morgan, DE	8.4	0.0	0.0	5.1	1.66
First Dep., Tilton, NH	2.4	0.0	0.0	1.5	1.56
Harris Trust, IL	6.6	9.1	0.0	11.7	1.35
River Forest, IL	0.3	0.0	0.0	0.3	1.02

Notes: All figures in billions of dollars. Contracts are expressed as notional values and total assets are
expressed as book values.
Source: Figures calculated from Reports of Condition and Reports of Income and Dividends computer
tapes, National Technical Information Service, Springfield, VA.

its total on-balance sheet assets. Chemical Bank's ratio of 17.2 topped the list while
Maryland National Bank ranked 13th at 0.55. The dominance of the 13 ISDA-member banks
leaves about $1.3 trillion in notional derivatives spread across 585 banks, an average of $2.2
billion per bank.

Table 5 shows the 27 banks with derivatives contracts exceeding their total on-
balance sheet assets as of December 31, 1991. The two banks with the largest ratios of
derivatives to total assets, Mitusi Bank and Trust (47.9) and First Interstate Bank of Los

Angeles (27.7), are not ISDA members and not listed in Table 5. For the years 1989 to 1991, these two banks had average on-balance sheet assets of $433 million and $639 million, respectively; their fee incomes accounted for 30 percent and 48 percent of their total revenues.

Table 4 also shows an important symptom of banks' derivatives activities: the ratio of noninterest (or fee) income to total income or "sales". Panel A shows these data for each of the 13 ISDA-member banks while Panel B presents the information by groups for the "Big Six," the 13 ISDA banks less the Big Six, the user banks less the 13 ISDA banks, and the nonuser banks. Starting with the Big Six, the fees-to-sales ratio declines steadily across the four groups: 0.2050, 0.1598, 0.1245, and 0.0794.

To summarize, Tables 1 through 5 show the kinds of derivatives contracts commercial banks hold and the dominance of the 13 ISDA-member banks, especially the Big Six, in the uneven development of these contracts.

5. DERIVATIVES AND CONTEMPORARY THEORIES OF BANKING AND HEDGING BEHAVIOR

Finance theory suggests that hedging increases firm value by reducing expected costs associated with (1) taxes, (2) financial distress, or (3) other agency problems. Nance, Smith, and Smithson (1993, hereafter NSS) provide evidence that 104 nonfinancial firms, which used hedging instruments in 1986, faced more convex tax functions, had less coverage of fixed claims, were larger, had more growth options in their investment opportunity sets, and employed fewer hedging substitutes. Since the major theoretical arguments for hedging presented in this chapter follow NSS's presentation, we do not repeat their arguments here. We extend their analysis by applying it to hedging by the banking firm and by incorporating the determinants of bank dealer activities. Adjusted for regulatory and deposit-insurance constraints, their approach also should apply to commercial banks. Banking behavior is more complicated, however, because banks, in addition to acting as end-users or hedgers, also engage in dealing and trading activities using derivatives. Moreover, since current bank financial statements do not separate the activities of end-users from dealers or traders, it is difficult to empirically separate hedging motives from other reasons for engaging in derivatives transactions. Nevertheless, with dealer activities concentrated in the 13 ISDA-member banks and with activities in this group further concentrated in "Big Six," the major dealer banks can be isolated and controlled for in our experiments. This section reviews existing banking and hedging theory, identifies economic incentives for banks to hedge or to deal in derivatives, and presents testable hypotheses.

5.1. Contemporary Banking Theory

In their survey of the contemporary theories of financial intermediation, Bhattacharya and Thakor (1993) describe banks as providing "brokerage" and "qualitative asset transformation (QAT)" services. The traditional brokerage services provided by commercial banks include transactions accounts and origination and renewal of loan contracts; as QAT providers, banks transform or modify claims (mainly deposits) with respect to credit risk, liquidity, duration, and divisibility. Regulatory discipline encourages bankers to diversify and to hedge the risks created by these transformations, e.g., to hedge the interest-rate risk created by duration and liquidity transformations. Mispriced deposit insurance (Kane (1985, 1989)), however, encourages bankers to bet the bank using either on- or off-balance sheet activities or both.

5.1.1. Lessons from the S&L Crisis

The U.S. savings-and-loan (S&L) crisis of the 1980s provides a glaring example of how volatile risk mismanagement and mispriced deposit insurance can be. Mismanagment of interest-rate risk was the fundamental cause of the S&L mess. The extreme duration mismatches accepted by S&Ls document the need to manage interest-rate risk effectively, and to provide an incentive-compatible, deposit-insurance contract. With the collapse of the S&L industry, many commercial banks have taken up the slack in residential real-estate lending (Eisenbeis and Kwast (1991)). Moreover, in the absence of off-balance sheet hedges in most of these banks, the duration mismatches of borrowing short and lending long may portend an S&L-type crisis for real-estate-lending depositories during the next major upswing in interest rates.

5.1.2. Financial Innovation to the Rescue

Because on-balance sheet methods of managing interest-rate risk (e.g., duration matching) may conflict with customers' preferences for products and services, banks employ various financial innovations for managing interest-rate risk. Two key methods are: securitization, which through selling assets removes risk from the balance sheet, and derivatives contracts, which employ off-balance sheet techniques to manage portfolio risks. While Burger and Udell (1993), among others, analyze the importance of securitization to banks, this chapter focuses on the use of derivatives activities by U.S. commercial banks. Banks without the skilled personnel to have a derivatives-based, risk-management program can obtain such services from correspondent banks or subsidiaries within their holding company, or they can participate in governmental or privately sponsored securitization programs.

*5.1.3. The Roles of Regulation, Deposit Insurance, and the Federal Safety Net: Moral
          Hazard and Market and Regulatory Discipline*

Commercial banks operate in a highly regulated and protected environment. One
important form of bank protection is the deposit-insurance guarantee that historically has
provided a de facto 100-percent safeguard for all of an insured bank's liabilities. In addition,
although the FDIC Improvement Act of 1991 (FDICIA) calls for "prompt corrective action"
for banks whose capital ratios fall below two percent, large banks still may be perceived as
"too-big-to-fail" (TBTF) or "too-big-to-liquidate" (TBTL). Nevertheless, the OCC's
treatment of Citibank during the early 1990s suggests that large banks will **not** be treated as
"too-big-for-corrective-action."

The combination of the deposit/liability guarantee and access to the Federal Reserve's
discount window provides a federal safety net for all banks, but especially the largest
institutions. While the federal safety net helps ensure confidence in the banking system, it
encourages moral-hazard behavior because both deposit insurance and the discount window
are mispriced.[21]

Banks with greater propensity to exploit FDIC subsidies should make less use of
derivatives for hedging on-balance sheet risks. Nevertheless, since derivatives also can be
used for speculative purposes, moral hazard may encourage riskier banks to use derivatives
to increase off-balance sheet risk-taking. The moral-hazard problem, however, may be
mitigated by regulatory discipline or "regulatory interference" (Buser, Chen, and Kane
(1981)). For example, the CAMEL rating system for banks, where C = capital adequacy, A
= asset quality, M = management, E = earnings, and L = liquidity, implicitly prices bank risk-
taking, which may offset or at least reduce the explicit mispricing. In addition, risk-based
capital standards price bank OBSAs explicitly by requiring them to be supported by bank
capital. A market-discipline hypothesis also suggests that external monitoring encourages
riskier banks to hedge, although only banks with large CDs and actively traded debt and
equity shares are subject to market discipline. Together market and regulatory discipline
should encourage banks to hedge.

5.2. Hedging to Increase Firm Value

If hedging increases the value of the banking firm, it does so by reducing expected

---

[21]Beginning January 1, 1993, the FDIC set its deposit-insurance assessments on the basis of a
bank's riskiness as captured by its supervisory (CAMEL) rating and its capital adequacy.

costs associated with taxes, financial distress, or other agency problems.[22] Also, if banks can increase the net asset values of client firms by selling them risk-management services, client firms will be able to reduce their chances of encountering financial distress. However, if banks (e.g., Bankers Trust) place client firms in speculative contracts, the costs and probabilities of financial distress might increase (e.g., Metallgesellschaft) or customer relationships might be injured (e.g., Gibson Greetings and P&G) or both.

5.3. Bank Substitutes for Hedging

As suggested by contemporary banking theory, asset sales, securitization, or duration matching offer alternatives to off-balance sheet hedging. We refer to this behavior as the substitutes-for-hedging hypothesis. Testing for its existence is complicated because a bank's use of OBSAs is also influenced by its decisions with respect to other financial policies. A further complicating factor is bank regulatory restrictions that attempt to shape bank decision-making (e.g., risk-based capital requirements affect both asset allocations and capital structure). For example, by increasing their capital adequacy (reducing leverage), banks placate their regulators but at the same time they reduce debt-related tax shields and increase tax liabilities. Other techniques for controlling agency problems include the use of convertible debt or preferred stock rather than straight debt, reducing on-balance sheet risk by holding safer assets, and imposing restrictions on dividends. These alternatives are also influenced by bank regulation and deposit insurance. To the extent that the deposit-insurance contract is incentive-incompatible, it may discourage hedging and encourage risk-taking by riskier banks. This adverse effect, however, may be offset or at least reduced by regulatory discipline, the implicit-pricing component of fixed-rate deposit insurance.

5.4. Recapitulation of Banking and Hedging Theories

Derivatives offer three attractive alternatives to banks: (1) acting as end-users, banks attempt to hedge on-balance sheet risk, (2) acting as dealers, they increase noninterest revenue (e.g., fees) without a substantial increase in risk exposure,[23] and (3) acting as risk

---

[22]We refer the interested reader to Nance, Smith, and Smithson (1993) and the references therein for the details of these aspects of modern corporation finance.

[23]While the popular press and Congress have emphasized the riskiness of bank derivatives, more serious studies have not found compelling reasons for concern. For example, the Group of Thirty (1993) concluded: "... derivatives by their nature do not introduce risks of a fundamentally different kind or of a greater scale than those that already exist in the financial markets. Hence, systemic risks are not appreciably aggravated, and supervisory concerns can be addressed within present regulatory structures and approaches" (p. i).

managers for their clients, banks attempt to reduce clients' risk exposures and enhance customer relationships, the cases of Gibson Greetings and P&G notwithstanding. Contemporary banking and hedging theories suggest that derivatives activities can increase the value of the banking firm by increasing bank fees, by reducing the expected costs associated with financial distress (either for the bank or for client firms or both), by enhancing bank-customer relationships, by reducing expected taxes, or by reducing agency costs. The existence of barriers to entry and informational and transactional scale/scope economies imply that large banks are more likely to deal in derivatives. Arguments based on agency costs predict that banks with more leverage (lower capital adequacy) and more growth opportunities are more likely to engage in hedging. A regulatory hypothesis, however, suggests that banks must have less leverage to be permitted to enter new activities. Based on mispriced deposit insurance and TBTF, a moral-hazard hypothesis implies that riskier banks and TBTF banks might refrain from hedging to exploit government subsidies or engage in derivative activities for speculative reasons. Moral-hazard behavior, however, can be offset or at least reduced by market or regulatory discipline or both. A tax hypothesis suggests the benefits of hedging should increase with the probability that the bank's pretax income is in the progressive region of the tax schedule. The existence of substitutes for hedging implies that the chances of a bank using derivatives for hedging are lower the more convertible debt the bank issues, the more preferred stock the bank issues, the safer the bank's assets, and the smaller the bank's dividend payout. Since these substitutes for hedging all are reinforced by bank capital and liquidity requirements, effective regulatory discipline encourages such substitution.

6. EMPIRICAL MODELS AND DATA

This section presents the empirical methods, data sources, sample banks, and definitions of the variables.

6.1. Empirical Methodology

The empirical methods consist of descriptive statistics focused on differences in group means (users vs. nonusers) and multivariate analyses based on the tobit model. We define a "user bank" as one with derivatives contracts on lines 11, 12, or 13 of Schedule RC-L of the bank call report. The items include forwards, futures, options, and swaps written on interest rates, currencies, and commodities. Tables 1-3 summarize these data for U.S. commercial banks as of December 31, 1991. A "nonuser bank" is one without any derivatives contracts at year-end 1991.

6.1.1. Descriptive Statistics

To test whether the theoretical relationship between users and nonusers of derivatives is supported empirically, the sample banks are divided into users and nonusers of derivatives and group means for each of the explanatory variables (discussed in C below) are calculated. A t-test based on unequal group variances determines the statistical significance of the differences in the means. In addition, dealer banks, identified as "primary members" of ISDA, are compared with nondealer users.

6.1.2. Tobit Estimation

A tobit regression is employed to estimate the relationship between the extent of derivatives use by banks and the explanatory variables. In the tobit specification, first proposed by Tobin (1958), the dependent variable is defined as (see Maddala (1983) or Kmenta (1986)):

$$y_i^* = b'x_i + u_i, \tag{1}$$
$$y_i = y_i^*, \text{ if } y_i^* > 0, \text{ and}$$
$$y_i = 0, \text{ otherwise.}$$

In (1), y_i is a linear function of the explanatory variables, b is a vector of unknown parameters, x_i is the vector of m characteristics, and μ is the error term. The dependent variable or "index" can be thought of as a "predisposition for y," which in our case is a predisposition to use derivatives. Although the managers of nonuser banks may not have been able to overcome the barriers to enter derivatives activities, they may have **desired** to do so. In studying consumer expenditures on durable goods, based on survey data, Tobin faced a similar problem with his dependent variable, i.e., consumers revealing no expenditures on durable goods may have desired to make such purchases.

6.2. Data Sources

The data for the empirical analysis are from the Federal Reserve System's <u>Report of Condition and Income for Commercial Banks</u> ("Call Report"), provided on computer tapes by the National Technical Information Service (NTIS). The analysis focuses on the derivatives activities of U.S. commercial banks at year-end 1991 as measured by the notional value of outstanding derivative contracts divided by total assets. The explanatory variables (described in detail in part C below) are three-year averages (1989 to 1991). The use of three-year averages for the explanatory variables follows Nance, Smith, and Smithson (1993).

Descriptive statistics for the 13 banks which are members of the ISDA are reported separately. The largest six of these banks are designated "Big Six" while the remaining seven members are designated "ISDA-7." These 13 banks are analyzed separately because of their role as major dealers of derivatives, and to attempt to separate dealing and hedging from pure hedging.

6.3. Variables and Expected Relations

For the tobit estimates, the dependent variable is the December 31, 1991 notional value of outstanding derivatives divided by total assets. It is designed to measure a bank's derivatives activities. In their study of the determinants of hedging by nonfinancial corporations, Nance, Smith, and Smithson (1993) provide a vector of proxies for the independent variables in equation (1). This paper builds on their specification with modifications to capture bank behavior with respect to derivatives contracts. The explanatory variables, described in ratio form, are discussed below.

6.3.1. Bank Size (ASSETS) and Dealer Dummies

If a barriers-to-entry/economies-of-scale hypothesis is correct, a positive relationship should exist between the use of derivatives by commercial banks and their size as measured by total assets (ASSETS). Lack of a significant positive relationship implies a lack of barriers to entry or lack of scale economies or both in the use of derivatives by banks. A negative relationship suggests that large banks refrain from hedging or speculate with derivatives because of moral hazard or because they perceive themselves as too big to fail or both. To test for nonlinear effects associated with bank size, as suggested by a plot of total derivatives against total assets, quadratic and logarithmic forms of ASSETS are added separately to equation (1). Alternatively, since dealer activity in derivatives is strongly correlated with bank size, dummy variables based on ISDA membership and total assets greater than $1 billion also are employed to test for size/dealer effects. These dummies, tested as intercept and interaction terms with total assets, are defined as

ISDA DUMMY = 1, if bank is an ISDA member, 0 otherwise;
BIG 6 DUMMY = 1, if bank is one that "rules world derivatives," 0 otherwise;
ISDA-7 DUMMY =1, if bank is ISDA member but not one of Big 6, 0 otherwise; and
NON-ISDA DEALER DUMMY = 1, if bank is not member of ISDA and has total assets
    greater than $1 billion, 0 otherwise.

The non-ISDA dealer dummy is included to capture the willingness of billion-dollar or bigger banks, that do not actively trade derivatives, to supply risk-management services to their customers.

6.3.2. Leverage/Capital Adequacy (CAPRATIO and NOTES)

CAPRATIO is the ratio of equity capital to total assets. If banks hedge to reduce the likelihood of default when debt levels are high (i.e., low capital adequacy), the empirical relationship between CAPRATIO and a bank's derivatives activities will be negative. Conversely, a positive relationship indicates that banks only use derivatives when they have sufficient capital to meet regulatory requirements. The moral-hazard hypothesis implies that banks with low capital ratios will not hedge. NOTES is a bank's outstanding notes and debentures as a percentage of its total assets. A positive relation is expected between NOTES and a bank's use of derivatives.

6.3.3. Exposure to Interest-Rate Risk (GAP60)

A bank's use of certain derivative securities (e.g., interest-rate swaps, futures, etc.) is related to its exposure to interest-rate fluctuations. Exposure to interest-rate risk reflects a bank's mismatch in the repricing of its assets and liabilities. Following Kim and Koppenhaver (1993), GAP60 is the absolute value of the difference between assets repricing or maturing between 12 and 60 months and liabilities repricing or maturing between 12 and 60 months, divided by total assets. Banks with a greater exposure to interest-rate fluctuations (large values for GAP60) are expected to use derivatives to a greater extent. A negative relationship suggests moral-hazard behavior.

6.3.4. Intermediation Profitability (NIM)

Net interest margin (NIM) is a measure of intermediation profitability before credit losses. It is calculated as net interest income, the difference between total interest income and total interest expense, as a percentage of total assets. Banks with low NIMs should attempt to increase fee income by selling derivatives products while banks with high NIMs should attempt to lock-in their "spreads" by using derivatives to hedge. The moral-hazard hypothesis suggests that banks with low NIMs will speculate using derivatives while banks with high NIMs will not hedge.

6.3.5. Growth Opportunities (ASSETG or EQUITYG)

If firms with more growth options are more likely to hedge, a positive relationship should exist between a bank's use of derivatives and the present value of its growth opportunities (PVGO). Two accounting proxies for PVGO used here are: (1) the growth rate of total on-balance sheet assets (ASSETG) and the growth rate of total equity capital (EQUITYG).

6.3.6. Tax Effects (PROG and TAX)

Two variables, PROG and TAX, are used to examine the relationship of taxes to a bank's derivatives activities. PROG measures whether a bank's pretax income falls within the progressive region of the tax schedule. The standard deviation is calculated for pretax earnings for the period of 1987 to 1991. Using the standard deviation, a 95% confidence interval is constructed around the 1991 pretax income. If any part of the confidence interval falls within the progressive tax region ($0 - $100,000), the variable PROG is coded as a one; otherwise, PROG is coded as zero. If, as NSS (1993) argue, the convexity of the U.S. corporate tax schedule provides incentives for firms to hedge, then firms with a greater portion of their pretax earnings in the progressive region of the tax schedule should have a positive relationship between PROG and their use of derivatives.

The other tax-related variable is TAX, which measures the effective tax rate paid by each bank. As such, it is a proxy for tax-preference items (e.g., tax loss carry forwards, tax credits, etc.) that a bank can use to reduce its taxes. It is calculated by dividing taxes actually paid by taxable income, then deflating by total assets. The more tax-preference items a bank has, the lower its effective tax rate will be. When a firm has more tax-preference items, NSS (1993) argue that the tax benefit of hedging is greater. Therefore, a negative relationship should exist between the use of derivatives and the effective tax rate (TAX).

6.3.7. Alternatives to Hedging (LIQUID, PREF, and DIV)

To capture alternatives to hedging three variables are employed: liquidity (LIQUID), preferred stock (PREF), and dividends (DIV). LIQUID is calculated by dividing a bank's liquid assets by total assets. Liquid assets consist of cash and balances, federal funds sold, and securities purchased to resell. PREF is the percentage of total assets financed by preferred stock, and DIV is dividends paid divided by total assets. If these variables truly represent alternatives to hedging, banks will be less likely to use derivatives as they issue more preferred stock, hold more liquid assets, and have smaller dividend payouts. This implies an expected negative relationship between a bank's use of derivatives and LIQUID and PREF. The relationship between the use of derivatives and DIV, however, should be positive.

7. DESCRIPTIVE RESULTS

Tables 6 and 7 present differences between derivatives users and nonusers. These results must be interpreted with care because the tests ignore interaction among variables.

Table 6
Differences Between Users and Nonusers of Bank Derivatives All Insured Commercial Banks (average annual data of year-end figures for 1989-1991)

Variable	Group means		Difference in	"t"-stat
	Users	Nonusers	means	
Total assets	$3.7B	$.091B	$3.6B	40.1
Progress. tax	2.8%	19.0%	-16.20%	-21.3
Capital ratio	7.2%	9.25%	-2.03%	-12.7
GAP60	21.1%	27.0%	-5.90%	-10.9
NIM	3.74%	4.00%	-0.25%	-4.7
Notes & deb.	0.36%	0.03%	0.33%	4.6
Equity growth	19.8%	8.4%	10.40%	2.6
Div. payout	0.52%	0.45%	0.07%	2.2
Liquidity	14.9%	14.0%	0.90%	2.1
Preferred st.	0.06%	0.03%	0.03%	1.5
Asset growth	10.6%	7.8%	2.80%	1.5
Tax rate	27.1%	24.8%	2.30%	0.4

Notes: U = user bank (599 to 612 observations) and NU = nonuser bank (10,986 to 11,308 observations). The t-statistic is based on unequal group variances. Variables are defined in the text. Source: Figures calculated from Reports of Condition and Reports of Income and Dividends computer tapes, National Technical Information Service, Springfield, VA.

7.1. Users Versus Nonusers

In Table 6, nine of the 12 variables have differences in means that are statistically significant at the five-percent level or better employing a t-statistic based on unequal group variances. The profile of a user bank that emerges from these data reveals an average institution that is 40-times larger with a lower capital ratio, smaller maturity gap, lower NIM, more notes, and debentures, greater equity growth, higher dividend payout, greater liquidity, and less income in the progressive region of its tax schedule.

The results in Table 7 control for dealer activities by separating the ISDA primary members from non-ISDA users, and separating the Big Six from the ISDA-7. The average Big-Six bank is three-times as large as the average ISDA-7 bank, 32-times larger than the average nondealer user, and more than 900-times larger than the average nonuser. Even when the 13 ISDA members are excluded from the sample of users, a similar profile emerges; in this case, nondealer users of derivatives are almost 30-times larger than nonusers.

The substantial differences in bank size among the groups described above suggests that (1) barriers to entry and informational and scale economies play an important role in determining who deals in derivatives and (2) after excluding dealers, size still plays an important role in determining the use of derivatives for hedging.

Table 7
Financial Characteristics of Banks That Use and Do Not Use Derivatives (Average Data for
December 31, 1989-1991)

Financial characteristic	ISDA primary members "Big six"	seven others	Users (non ISDA-member)	All nonusers
Equity/assets	0.0462	0.0533	0.0726	0.0924
	(0.0047)	(0.0107)	(0.0374)	(0.0520)
GAP60/assets	0.0977	0.0617	0.2140	0.2696
	(0.0402)	(0.0389)	(0.1286)	(0.1110)
Total assets	$84.1B	$26.8B	$2.6B	$0.091B
	(41.3)	(9.5)	(5.3)	(200.1)
NIM	0.0251	0.0227	0.0377	0.0399
	(0.0105)	(0.0064)	(0.0124)	(0.0098)
N&D/assets	0.0202	0.0118	0.0033	0.0003
	(0.0061)	(0.0090)	(0.0174)	(0.0090)
Equity growth	0.0078	0.2344	0.1993	0.0839
	(0.0637)	(0.2956)	(1.0550)	(0.7839)
Div./Assets	0.0028	0.0047	0.0052	0.0045
	(0.0014)	(0.0075)	(0.0066)	(0.0115)
Liquid/assets	0.1438	0.2245	0.1481	0.1397
	(0.0293)	(0.1024)	(0.1068)	(0.0852)
Pref./assets	0.0005	0.0012	0.0005	0.0003
	(0.0013)	(0.0016)	(0.0032)	(0.0041)
Asset growth	0.0155	0.0570	0.1079	0.0783
	(0.0310)	(0.1134)	(0.4611)	(0.1947)
Prog. tax	0.00	0.00	0.0284	0.1898
	(0.00)	(0.00)	(0.1662)	(0.3921)
Tax rate	2.5895	0.3347	0.2463	0.2477
	(5.6289)	(0.2724)	(1.1778)	(0.8318)

Notes: The variables are defined in the text. The number of banks for the last two columns are 599
(or fewer) and 11,005 (or fewer). The "fewer" occurs because of missing observations on some
variables and "fewer" is never more than 33 banks.
Source: Figures calculated from Reports of Condition and Reports of Income and Dividends computer
tapes, National Technical Information Service, Springfield, VA.

7.1.1. Capital Adequacy, Debt Capital, and Equity Growth

User and nonuser banks (Table 6) show a statistically significant difference in their
mean capital ratios (t = -12.7), 7.22 percent (users) versus 9.25 percent (nonusers). The finer
breakdown of users in Table 7 reveals that the Big 6 (4.5%) and ISDA-7 banks (5.3%) have
even lower mean capital ratios. Since inadequate capital translates as greater leverage, these
results are consistent with hedging theory. An important component of bank capital is debt
capital. Users have a significantly higher amount of debt capital (i.e., notes and debentures
as a percent of total assets) than nonusers, and as shown in Table 7 this relative amount of

debt capital increases with bank size within the user group. This greater leverage is expected based on hedging theory. No significant differences were observed with respect to the use of preferred stock. The average growth rate of equity capital at user banks (19.8%) was over twice as large as the average growth rate at nonuser banks (8.4%), t = 2.6. This finding is consistent with two alternative expectations: (1) a growth-opportunities explanation or (2) simply a reflection of user banks maneuvering to meet the new risk-based capital requirements. The latter seems more plausible.

7.1.2. Net Interest Margin (NIM) and Fee Income

Table 6 shows a statistically significant difference (t = -4.7) between the mean NIM for user banks (3.75%) and the mean NIM for nonuser banks (4.00%). Table 8 reveals that the Big Six and ISDA-7 banks have even lower mean NIMs at 2.51 percent and 2.27 percent, respectively. If a bank loses franchise value in the traditional business of borrowing and lending, it can be expected to seek alternative sources of value (e.g., fee income from derivatives). The data shown in Table 4 reflect this tradeoff between traditional and nontraditional sources of revenue, and reveal a strong positive relation as dealer activity increases across the three categories of user banks.

7.1.3. Maturity Gap (GAP60)

Table 7 shows an inverse relation between the GAP60 ratio and bank size as captured by the three classes of users. The ratio differs significantly between all users (21.1%) and nonusers (27.0%) with a t-statistic of -10.9 (Table 6). If gap or duration management is a substitute for hedging, then banks not engaging in off-balance sheet hedging should have relatively smaller gaps, which is not observed. Lack of regulatory discipline might be the culprit as only recently have bank regulators attempted to incorporate interest-rate risk into risk-based capital requirements. Additional negative factors include the lack of market discipline on smaller (nonuser) banks and barriers to entry (e.g., intellectual capital) for smaller banks.

7.1.4. Liquidity, Taxes, and Other Considerations

From an economic standpoint, the difference in the liquidity ratios (0.9%) does not appear meaningful, although the t-statistic (2.1) is significant. Moreover, as Table 7 shows the difference is driven by the ISDA-7 banks which have an average liquidity ratio of 22.4 percent. Neither of the two tax variables is statistically significant and the difference in asset growth, while higher at user banks, also is not statistically significant.

Table 8
Tobit Estimates of the Determinants of Derivatives Contracts for All Insured Commercial Banks
Dependent variable (Y) = the ratio of the notional value of derivatives contracts to the book value of total
assets as of December 31, 1991, where Y = Y* for banks with derivatives and Y = 0 for banks without
derivatives and where Y* represents an index of the "desire" of banks to use derivatives contracts. *Table
entries include the estimated parameter, chi-square in ( ), and probability value in [ ].*

Independent variables	Specification		
(annual averages 89-91)	1	2	3
INTERCEPT	-1.35E+5	-1.04E+5	-1.00E+5
	(264.6)	(172.8)	(172.2)
	[0.0001]	[0.0001]	[0.0001]
ISDA DUMMY (1 = member)	–	-1.17E+8	–
		(6.8)	
		[0.0091]	
BIG-6 DUMMY (1 = Big 6)	–	–	14.0E+8
			(27.1)
			[0.0001]
ISDA-7 DUMMY (1 = ISDA, not Big 6)	–	–	-5.43E+7
			(1.07)
			[0.2950]
NON-ISDA DEALER DUMMY	–	-1.93E+6	-9.69E+5
(Non-ISDA bank with total assets > $1B = 1;		(9.7)	(2.30)
0 otherwise)		[0.0018]	[0.1290]
ISDA DUMMY * ASSETS	–	11.9885	–
		(29.2)	
		[0.0001]	
BIG 6 DUMMY * ASSETS	–	–	-13.4026
			(6.08)
			[0.0136]
ISDA-7 DUMMY * ASSETS	–	–	6.3570
			(5.89)
			[0.0152]
NON-ISDA DEALER DUMMY * ASSETS	–	3.4140	2.6438
		(90.2)	(47.0)
		[0.0001]	[0.0001]

8. REGRESSION FINDINGS

To provide evidence on conditional relations, we employ tobit regression analysis.
The dependent variable is the ratio of derivatives to total assets at year-end 1991; the
independent variables are averages of year-end data for three years: 1989, 1990, and 1991.
Banks with derivatives have noncensored dependent values while banks without derivatives
have left-censored dependent values equal to zero. In logistic or logit regression, as used by

Table 8 continued
Tobit Estimates of the Determinants of Derivatives Contracts for All Insured Commercial Banks

Independent variables	Specification		
(annual averages 89-91)	1	2	3
TOTAL ASSETS	-1.1628	-2.2327	-2.2796
	(10.4)	(35.9)	(39.9)
	[0.0012]	[0.0001]	[0.0001]
TOTAL ASSETS SQUARED	1.49E-7	2.43E-8	9.10E-8
	(222.6)	(1.60)	(13.3)
	[0.0001]	[0.2059]	[0.0003]
GAP60	-3.5504	-2.7882	-2.6111
	(34.4)	(20.7)	(19.4)
	[0.0001]	[0.0001]	[0.0001]
LIQUIDITY	2.3658	2.3456	2.3963
	(11.8)	(11.2)	(12.5)
	[0.0006]	[0.0008]	[0.0004]
NET INTEREST MARGIN	-17.2454	-13.1997	-11.7922
	(5.92)	(3.49)	(2.99)
	[0.0150]	[0.0619]	[0.0839]
DIVIDENDS	10.8112	7.7498	6.8855
	(5.64)	(2.72)	(2.24)
	[0.0174]	[0.0989]	[0.1346]
CAPITAL NOTES	7.5739	6.2535	5.5495
	(5.20)	(3.23)	(2.57)
	[0.0226]	[0.0725]	[0.1091]
EQUITY RATIO	-4.7489	-3.2438	-2.7569
	(4.60)	(2.23)	(1.74)
	[0.0320]	[0.1351]	[0.1865]
Log likelihood for NORMAL	-2,243.99	-2156.30	-2138.22

Noncensored values (banks with derivatives) = 592
Left-censored values (banks without derivatives) = 10,771
Observations with missing values = 557 consisting of 20 users and 537 nonusers
Notes: Four additional variables included in all the specifications but not found to be statistically significant are PROG, TAX, ASSETG, and PREF. The Big 6 banks are Bankers Trust, BOA, Chase, Chemical, Citicorp, and J.P. Morgan; the ISDA-7 are FNB Chicago, Continental Bank (acquired by BOA in 1994), Republic NY, Bank of New York, FNB Boston, Mellon Bank, and Maryland National Bank.

Nance, Smith, and Smithson (1993) to study the determinants of hedging for nonfinancial corporations, the dependent variable is binary with users coded as "1" and nonusers coded as "0." Although we estimated both tobit and logit models, we report only the tobit results. We do so for two reasons. First, we favor this technique because it does not "waste" information about the dependent variable. Second, the tobit and logit estimates obtained were similar, though not identical.

8.1. Tobit Estimates

Table 8 presents tobit estimates for all insured commercial banks consisting of 592 user banks and 10,771 nonuser banks. The specifications in Table 8 differ only in how they test for the effects of bank size and dealer activity on the use of derivatives. They also serve as sensitivity tests for the other variables in the model.

In column (1), the estimated coefficient for total assets squared is positive and highly significant (chi-square = 222). The estimated coefficient for total assets is negative but less significant (chi-square = 10). We interpret this result as consistent with barriers to entry or informational and scale economies as important factors separating users of derivatives from nonusers.

Given the controls for the effects of bank size, six of the ten other regressors in column (1) are statistically significant at the five-percent level or better. The signs for these estimated coefficients suggest that banks with greater liquidity, higher dividend payouts, and more capital notes are associated with the use of derivatives. In contrast, banks with larger maturity gaps, higher NIMs, and higher capital ratios are associated with nonuse of derivatives. Alternatively, banks that use derivatives have smaller maturity gaps, lower NIMs, and lower capital ratios. The GAP60 variable and the equity ratio support the moral-hazard hypothesis. The liquidity measure suggests either moral-hazard behavior or the need for liquidity to support derivatives activities. The NIM estimate is consistent with the notion that banks losing franchise value in the business of traditional intermediation seek alternative sources of value. The positive signs for notes and debentures and dividend payout suggest that debt capital does not represent an alternative to hedging while dividend payout does. Alternatively, since notes and debentures count, in part, for meeting bank capital requirements, their greater use may be for this reason.

Specification (2) in Table 8 adds four dummy variables: the ISDA dummy, the non-ISDA dealer dummy, and the separate interactions of these two dummies with total assets. Non-ISDA banks are those with total assets greater than $1 billion that are not members of ISDA (341 banks). Each of these four variables is highly significant, indicating substantial differences in derivatives activities across the three groups of banks. Because of the high positive correlation between total assets and the ISDA dummy ($p = 0.69$, significant at the 0.0001 level), the standard error on the square of total assets blows up and its coefficient is no longer significant. The inclusion of dummy variables to further delineate the effects of size and dealer activity also affects the stability of the other independent variables. For example, using a strict cutoff at a five-percent significance level only GAP60 and liquidity maintain their significance. The other four variables and their significance levels are: NIM (6.2%), capital notes (7.2%), dividends paid (9.9%), and the ratio of equity capital to total assets (13.5%).

Specification (3) in Table 8 splits the ISDA dummy into Big Six and ISDA-7 components. Since both intercept and interaction terms are employed, four variables are added to the model while the two ISDA-13 dummies are deleted. The significant correlations of the Big Six and ISDA-7 dummies with total assets (e.g., the correlation between the Big Six dummy and total assets is 0.74, significant at the 0.0001 level) make it difficult to identify the separate influences of these variables. Nevertheless, the stability and significance of the GAP60 and liquidity variables are essentially unchanged by these size sensitivity tests.

9. SUMMARY, CONCLUSIONS, AND POLICY IMPLICATIONS

This chapter has focused on derivatives in U.S. banking by examining both theory and practice, and by describing and investigating empirically the use and determinants of derivatives activities by U.S. banks over the years 1989 to 1991. Derivatives activities represent an area where banking has **not** been declining. The explosive growth of derivatives, however, has not been registered on banks' balance sheets since they are classified as off-balance sheet activities. In addition, the growth has not been an industry-wide phenomenon. At year-end 1991, 612 commercial banks used derivatives either as end-users or for other reasons; in contrast, over 11,000 banks did not use derivatives. Within the user's group, derivatives activities are highly concentrated in the 13 "primary members" of the International Swaps and Derivatives Association (ISDA) which held 81.7 percent of the contracts reported by U.S. commercial banks on December 31, 1991. Six of these 13 ISDA-member banks (BankAmerica, Bankers Trust, Chase, Chemical, Citicorp, and Morgan) accounted for 85.9 percent of the derivatives of the 13 dealers and 70.3 percent of the derivatives of 612 user banks.

The concentration of derivatives activities in the largest banks supports a joint hypothesis of barriers to entry and informational and scale/scope economies as the primary determinants of dealer activity in derivatives. On a global basis, however, size may not be an appropriate proxy for non-entry in the derivatives business. For example, the six U.S. banks that rule the world of derivatives have only one firm (Citicorp) that ranks among the world's 25 largest banks. This fact suggests that intellectual and reputational capital are the barriers to entry on a global basis. When these two factors are combined with an accounting, legal, regulatory, and technical environment conducive to financial innovation, the dominance of U.S banks in the worldwide market for derivatives is not surprising. On balance, the descriptive and regression findings are consistent with banking and hedging theories presented in the paper, and consistent with those of Nance, Smith, and Smithson (1993) for nonfinancial corporations.

Since the 11,000 banks that are not using derivatives are also unlikely to have duration-matched balance sheets, they and the FDIC (taxpayers) are exposed to interest-rate risk. Bank owners, regulators, and uninsured depositors should provide the proper incentives or disciplines to encourage managers to hedge this risk. Incorporating interest-rate risk into risk-based capital requirements represents a step in the right direction. Since the barriers to entry and informational and scale/scope economies in derivatives activities seem to be so great, correspondent banking, a traditional mainstay of U.S. banking, would seem to offer a convenient and efficient way for the numerous nonuser banks to obtain such services not only for themselves but also for their customers. The threat of derivatives liability should caution dealer banks to make sure that their clients understand the contracts they enter. On balance, both banking and nonbanking firms need policies, procedures, and controls regarding derivatives activities, especially speculative contracts. Proper internal controls (apparently absent in the Barings case) and existing banking rules and regulations, along with ex-post settling up through the courts, lead us to conclude that additional external controls over derivatives decisions are not needed.

REFERENCES

Bacon, Kenneth H., 1993, U.S. Issues Guidelines on 'Derivatives' Obliging Banks to Mull Customer Needs, *The Wall Street Journal* (October 28).

Bacon, Kenneth H, 1993a, Lawmakers Question Agencies' Ability To Regulate the Derivatives Market, *The Wall Street Journal* (October 29).

Bennett, Rosemary, 1993, The six men who rule world derivatives, *Euromoney* (August), 45-49.

Bhattacharya, Sudipto and Anjan Thakor, 1993, Contemporary Banking Theory, *Journal of Financial Intermediation* 3, 2-50.

Block, S.B. and T.J. Gallagher, 1986, The Use of Interest-Rate Futures and Options by Corporate Financial Managers, *Financial Management* 15, 73-78.

Booth, James R., Richard L. Smith, and Richard W. Stolz, 1984, Use of Interest-Rate Futures by Financial Institutions, *Journal of Bank Research* (Spring), 15-20.

Burger, Allen N. and Gregory F. Udell, 1993, Securitization, Risk, and the Liquidity Problem in Banking, in Structural Changes in: *Banking* Klausner and White, Eds., Homewood, IL, Irwin.

Buser, Stephen, Andrew Chen, and Edward Kane, 1981, Federal Deposit Insurance, Regulatory Policy, and Optimal Bank Capital, *Journal of Finance* (March), 51-60.

Corrigan, Tracy and Deborah Hargreaves, 1994, Eyeballing the Finance Director, *Financial Times* (January 26), 9.

Culp, Christopher L. and Merton H. Miller, 1994, Hedging a Flow of Commodity Deliveries with Futures: Lessons from Metallgesellschaft, *Derivatives Quarterly* (Fall), 7-15.

Economist, 1994, Corporate Hedging: Hard Soap, (April 16), 82 (and various other issues, see footnote 2).

Eisenbeis, Robert A. and Myron Kwast, 1991, Are Real Estate Depositories Viable? *Journal of Financial Services Research* (March), 5-24.

Euromoney, 1992, (September).

Evans, Richard, 1994, Derivatives Superstars: Anonymous No Longer, *Global Finance* (February), 39-74.

FDIC Quarterly Banking Profile (Second Quarter), 1994, Washington, D.C.: FDIC.

Group of Thirty, 1993) *Derivatives: Practices and Principles.* Global Derivatives Study Group, Washington, D.C. (July), 64

Group of Thirty, 1993a) Derivatives: *Practices and Principles, Appendix I: Working Papers.* (1993a, Global Derivatives Study Group, Washington, D.C. (July), 140

Group of Thirty, 1994, *Derivatives: Practices and Principles, Appendix III: Survey of*

Industry Practice. Global Derivatives Study Group, Washington, D.C. (March), 130

Hu, Henry T.C, 1993, Misunderstood Derivatives: The Causes of Informational Failure and the Promise of Regulatory Incrementalism, *The Yale Law Journal* (April), 1457-1513.

Hunter, William and Stephen Timme, 1986, Technical Change, Organization Form, and the Structure of Bank Production, *Journal of Money, Credit and Banking* (May), 152-166.

Kane, Edward J, 1989, *The S&L Insurance Mess: How Did It Happen?* Washington D.C.: The Urban Institute Press.

Kane, Edward J, 1985, *The Gathering Crisis in Deposit Insurance.* Cambridge, MA: MIT Press.

Kane, Edward J. and Burton G. Malkiel, 1967, Bank Portfolio Allocation, Deposit Variability, and the Availability Doctrine, *Quarterly Journal of Economics* (February), 113-134.

Kane, Edward J. and Haluk Unal, 1990, Modeling Structural and Temporal Variation in the Market's Valuation of the Banking Firm, *Journal of Finance* 45 (March), 113-136.

Kim, Sung-Hwa and G.D. Koppenhaver, 1993, An Empirical Analysis of Bank Interest-Rate Swaps, *Journal of Financial Services Research* (February), 57-72.

King, Ralph T. Jr. and Steven Lipin, 1994, New Profit Center: Corporate Banking, Given Up for Dead, Is Reinventing Itself, *The Wall Street Journal* (January 31), 1+.

Kmenta, Jan, 1986, *Elements of Econometrics.* New York: Macmillan Publishing Company.

Knecht, G. Bruce, 1995, Bankers Trust Risk Apostle Faces Tough Strategic Play, *The Wall Street Journal* (April 18), B1 and B12.

Kuprianov, Anatoli, 1993, Over-the-Counter Interest Rate Derivatives, Federal Reserve Bank of Richmond *Quarterly Review* (Summer), 65-94.

Layne, Richard, 1993, Banc One Discloses Details of Giant Swaps Portfolio, *American Banker* (December 2), 1, 22.

Layne, Richard, 1993a, BT's Bet on Derivatives Business Paying Off, *American Banker* (August 10), 20.

Layne, Richard, 1993b, Newcomers Pile Into Booming Swaps Field, *American Banker* (June 9), 1+.

Lipin, Steven, 1994, Bankers Trust Says Gibson Greetings Was Fully Aware of Derivatives Risk, *The Wall Street Journal* (October 13), A4.

Lipin, Steven, 1994a, Bankers Trust Reassigns Executives in Midst of Internal Sales-Practice Probe, *The Wall Street Journal* (November 14), A3.

Lipin, Steven, Fred R. Bleakley, and Barbara Donnelly Granito, 1994, Portfolio Poker: Just

What Firms Do With 'Derivatives' Is Suddenly a Hot Issue, *The Wall Street Journal* (April 14), 1+.

Lipin, Steven and Jeffrey Taylor, 1994, Bankers Trust Settles Charges on Derivatives, *The Wall Street Journal* (December 23), C1, C22.

Lipin, Steven and Jeffrey Taylor, 1994a, Bankers Trust Signs Accord on Derivatives, *The Wall Street Journal* (December 6), A3, A12.

Loomis, Carol J, 1994, The Risk That Won't Go Away, *Fortune* (March 7), 40-57.

Maddala, G.S, 1983, *Limited-Dependent and Qualitative Variables in Econometrics.* Cambridge: Cambridge University Press.

McDonough, William J. The Global Derivatives Market, Federal Reserve Bank of New York *Quarterly Review* (Autumn), 1-5.

Merton, Robert and Zvi Bodie, 1992, On the Management of Financial Guarantees, *Financial Management* (Winter), 87-109.

Nance, Deana R., Clifford W. Smith, Jr., and Charles W. Smithson, 1993, On the Determinants of Corporate Hedging, *Journal of Finance* (March), 267-284.

OCC Issues Guidelines on Bank Derivatives Activities, (1993, News Release, Comptroller of the Currency Administrator of National Banks (October 27), NR 93-116.

Overdahl, James and Barry Schachter, 1995, Derivatives Regulation and Financial Management: Lessons From Gibson Greetings, *Financial Management* 24 (Spring 1995), 68-78.

Report of Condition and Income for Commercial Banks and Selected Other Financial Institutions, Computer Tapes 1988-1991. National Technical Information Service, U.S. Department of Commerce, Springfield, VA.

Sanford, Charles S. Jr, 1994, Financial Markets in 2020, *Economic Review* (First Quarter), Federal Reserve Bank of Kansas City, 19-28.

Schachter, Barry, 1995, Suitability, Legal Risk, and Derivatives Regulation, *Journal of Financial Engineering* 4 (June 1995), 147-156.

Sinkey, Joseph F. Jr, 1995, Let derivatives buyers beware and government keep hands off, *The Atlanta Journal/Constitution* (April 2), R6.

Sinkey, Joseph F. Jr, 1992, *Commercial Bank Financial Management in the Financial-Services Industry* (fourth edition, New York: Macmillan Publishing Company.

Sinkey, Joseph F. Jr. and David A. Carter, 1995, The Determinants of Hedging and Derivatives Activities by U.S. Commercial Banks, Working Paper, The University of Georgia.

Sinkey, Joseph F. Jr. and David A. Carter, 1994, The Derivatives Activities of U.S. Commercial Banks,

Proceedings of the 30th Annual Conference on Bank Structure and Competition (May), Federal Reserve Bank of Chicago.

Sinkey, Joseph F. Jr. and Robert C. Nash, 1993, Assessing the Riskiness and Profitability of Credit-Card Banks, *Journal of Financial Services Research* (June), 127-150.

Smith, Clifford W. Jr, 1993, Risk Management in Banking, in Advanced Strategies in: *Financial Risk Management*, Robert J. Schwartz and Clifford W. Smith, Jr., eds. Englewood Cliffs, NJ: New York Institute of Finance, 147-162.

Smith, Clifford W. Jr. and Charles W. Smithson, eds, 1990, *The Handbook of Financial Engineering*. New York: Harper Business.

Smith, Clifford W. Jr., Charles W. Smithson, and Sykes D. Wilford, 1990, *Financial Risk Management*. New York: Ballinger/Institutional Investor.

Stern, Gabriella, 1994, Banc One's Sliding Stock Price Scuttles Accord to Acquire Nebraska's FirsTier, *The Wall Street Journal* (February 15), A5.

Stern, Gabriella and Steven Lipin, 1994, Procter & Gamble to Take a Charge To Close Out Two Interest-Rate Swaps *The Wall Street Journal* (April 13), A3

Tobin, James, 1958, Estimation of Relationships for Limited Dependent Variables, *Econometrica* 26 (January), 24-36.

Thomas, Paulette, 1994, Procter & Gamble Sues Bankers Trust Because of Huge Losses on Derivatives, *The Wall Street Journal* (October 28).

Tufano, Peter, 1989, Financial Innovation and First-Mover Advantages, *Journal of Financial Economics* 25, 213-240.

Wigler, Lester, 1991, Using Financial Derivatives: Customer Profitability Can Be Increased, *American Banker* (December 26), 4.

Derivatives, Regulation and Banking
Edited by B. Schachter
© 1997 Elsevier Science B.V. All rights reserved.

Chapter 3
DERIVATIVES DEALERS AND CREDIT RISK

Tanya Azarchs
Standard & Poor's, New York, New York USA

1. INTRODUCTION

The focus of intense public concern pertaining to derivatives has shifted away from derivatives dealers to end users of derivatives. Part of the reason is that dealers generally aquitted themselves well over the last couple of years since S&P first addressed the risks of their business (See Credit Week Nov. 9, 1992). Thus, developments so far support S&P'soriginal assessment that the derivatives business for experienced dealers, if prudently conducted, does not pose undue or unmanageable risk. The dealers' record is the more encouraging because this was a period which included a fair amount of turbulence in the bond and currency markets. In contrast, rising interest rates produced a spate of well publicised snafus for end users.

S&P continues to believe that the market making function of derivatives represents a valuable new franchise or intermediation service. It performs a useful economic function in producing more choises for managing or hedging risks. It also replaces the business lost when large banks' most creditworthy clients turned away from banks and securities markets for short-term funds. Earnings from derivatives have grown rapidly, paralleling the growth of the derivatives market, which has been nothing short of explosive. But given that derivative instruments are new, that they have not been tested through a wide variety of stress scenarios, careful vigilence is warranted. In addition, while the risks of the derivatives business are not new, and are ones that banks have long experience in manageing, the risks are more complex. S&P takes comfort that the risk management systems at major dealers worldwide (see Table 1) have improved dramatically in the last decade, in answer to that complexity. At this point, those management techniques are well understood and are well along in implementation. The risks appear to be both quantifiable and manageable.

The Group of Thirty (G-30) report, published in 1993, founded on a survey of major dealers and end users of derivatives, did a very credible job of describing the best practices of the industry. Some of the respondents appear to have been very optimistic or prospective in characterising the extent to which their policies and practices conformed to the receommendations. Nevertheless, the work has precipitated a lot of self-examination on the part of institutions, as intended. It should go a long way to self regulation, which was the motivation for the study. The report's recommendations are not really contraversial except possibly in the area of disclosure recommendations. It demonstrates the degree to which industry practices were generally understood amongst the largest players.

The principal risks of derivative dealings are:

- **Credit risk.** This is the risk that a counterparty will default on a contract with a positive market value. On the whole, S&P believes that credit risk is the largest but the most easily managed of the risks.

- **Market risk.** This is the risk that the net value of the entire derivatives portfolio will change based on interest rate fluctuations because the portfolio is not perfectly hedged, or matched.

- **Accounting risk.** This arises since significant discretion is permitted in the area of marking derivative contracts to market; computed prices can vary greatly depending on assumptions used and resulting in some contracts being mispriced and subject to revaluation, and

- **Legal and operating risks.** Legal risk can be triggered for example when a seller fails to adequately document and present the risks inherent in derivative instruments to a buyer or when a seller or buyer lacks corporate authority to enter into derivative transactions. Operating risk or documentation risk can arise for example when dealers do not ensure that the master swap agreements are in place for all contracts and for all subsidiaries of parents with agreements.

In addition, there are the broader systemic issues of liquidity risk and legal risk that impact the industry as a whole, not just parties to contracts. While the derivative business represents manageable levels of risk, it has become a substantial user of capital for major dealers and thereby presents liquidity issues.

2. ASSESSING CREDIT RISKS

Evaluating credit risk in a derivatives portfolio involves not only assessing the probability of a counterparty default; it presents the additional difficulty of quantifying a maximum potential exposure to loss. In the case of a loan, the maximum loss risked is the amount of the loan. In contrast, in the case of a derivative contract the maximum potential loss is not

Table 1
Derivatives Exposure as of December 31, 1993.

Intstitution	Swaps	Notional Amounts Forwards and Futures	Notional Amounts Options Purchased	Total	Replacement Value
BankAmerica	255,252	580,987	45,492	881,731	14,209
Bankers Trust NY	405,362	926,413	194,366	1,526,141	21,521
Chase Manhattan	233,678	555,927	96,957	886,562	13,650
Chemical Banking	686,795	1,462,547	138,220	2,287,562	24,167
Citicorp	278,057	1,402,817	154,025	1,834,899	22,151
Continental Bank	47,667	53,970	17,347	118,984	1,905
First Chicago	115,055	235,118	39,712	389,885	6,517
J.P. Morgan	689,337	558,299	222,241	1,469,877	30,740
Nationsbank	32,777	49,029	72,022	153,828	1,020
Republic New York	56,900	66,179	21,617	144,696	1,520
Australia (Mil. A$),					
Westpac (§)	232,082	392,329	34,571	658,981	20,364
England (Mil. £)					
Barclays Plc	248,729	N.A.	N.A.	608,487	7,741
Natwest Plc*	N.A.	N.A.	N.A.	531,022	6,774
France (Mil. Ffr)					
Banque Indosuez	1,141,159	2,393,364	418,321	3,952,844	N.A.
BNP*	969,503	1,303,185	190,720	2,463,408	N.A.
Paribas (§)	2,805,303	1,151,292	1,082,964	5,039,559	N.A.
Societe Generale	2,887,963	1,904,977	2,929,046	7,721,986	N.A.
Germany (Mil. DM)					
Deutsche Bank	468,000	N.A.	148,000	616,000	20,000
Switzerland (Francs)					
Credit Suisse	N.A.	1,680,785	N.A.	1,680,785	N.A.
Swiss Bank Corp.*	411,300	860,900	921,700	2,193,900	32,100
Union Bank Suisse	N.A.	1,877,838	437,973	2,315,811	N.A.
U.S. Brokers (Mil. $)					
Merrill Lynch ¶	560,000	259,000	N.A.	819,000	6,483
Morgan Stanley **	198,000	460,000	N.A.	658,000	6,500
Salomon **	265,000	632,000	N.A.	897,000	8,581

(§)Includes options written. ¶Options are contained within swaps. *Includes exchange traded instruments. **Options are contained within futures and forwards. N.A.—Not available.

the notional amount of the contract, but rather the cost of replacing the contract. This will be the contract's current market value (MV), but only if it is positive. The MV represents the present value of the stream of remaining net receipts (receipts minus payments) on the contract. On average, the positively valued MV of contracts in a diversified portfolio is a small fraction (under 2%) of the notional amount of the portfolio. Naturally, many individual contracts can have much higher proportional value to rational amount.

Credit risk exposure is affected by market fluctuations. Fluctuating market prices can alter the market value of a contract and hence alter the amount of credit risk exposure of a derivative contract as well. Contract market values are likely to fluctuate over time in response to the movement in various underlying rates. For example, in the case of an interest rate swap of fixed-rate payments for floating-rate payments, in a rising rate environment, the swap's value increases for the party paying fixed rates when rates rise. Conversely, the swap's value decreases for the counterparty paying floating rates. At origination, the swap contract's value would be zero, but over its life it could attain a significant positive or negative value.

As previously mentioned, credit risk exists only for the contracts with positive current market values. This positive market value (PMV) is also known as the replacement cost. In the event of a default by a counterparty, the contract would need to be replaced with a contract with a contract with similar cash flows, at a cost similar to the market value of the defaulted contract (assuming there is a liquid market for the instrument). Negatively valued contracts (NMV), on the other hand, represent a potential economic gain to the counterparty if they are abrogated. In a perfectly a matched book, the PMV's would equal the NMV's, and the net value is zero.

2.1 Volatility Affects Credit Exposure

Dealers typically model the potential increase in value of derivative contracts by employing statistical methods or simulation techniques to estimate the volatility of the underlying interest, currency, or commodity rates, and how that volatility will affect the price of the contracts. These techniques can generate estimates of maximum potential market values (MPMV) for replacement costs. Conservative risk management techniques set limits for exposure to each counterparty based on these estimated MPMVs.

In estimating credit risk a kind of model risk comes into play. Quality of risk models can vary greatly. In general, models and systems capabilities for tracking credit exposures are in a catch-up mode, and have experienced difficulty keeping up with the growth of the business. Additionally, for all of their sophistication, the risk models depend on historical records of volatility. A risk remains that a sudden sharp deviation from historical rates .could occur. Furthermore, the compounding of assumptions upon which the models are built can lull unwary model users into a specious sense of precision. S&P assesses the conservatism of the estimation assumptions built into the models.

S&P believes it is possible to quantify the amount of credit exposure banks assume in their derivative dealings within reasonable parameters of accuracy. While modeling

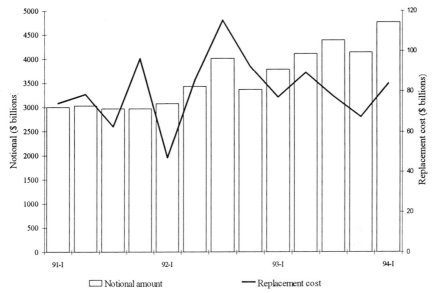

Figure 1
Aggregate exposures, currency and commodity contracts, for nine major U.S. commercial bank dealers.

techniques may tend to underestimate the MPMV of any one contract, S&P takes comfort that two countervailing tendencies exist that can combat an underestimating of MPMV: these are the portfolio effect and the effect of netting.

The portfolio effect reduces estimates of the change in market value associated with adverse changes in underlying rates because in very large portfolios, offsetting changes tend to occur in instruments that are not perfectly positively correlated. Dealers have varying abilities to estimate this portfolio effect. Netting effects can vary according to documentation on a case-by-case basis.

2.2 Netting Assumptions Influence MPMVS

Assumptions about exposure netting can influence the MPMV calculations substantially. In the event of a bankruptcy of a counterparty, the courts can allow netting, or the offsetting of positively valued contracts against negatively valued ones to the same counterparty when a "master netting" agreement exists. Without the documented ability to net, in the event of a counterparty's bankruptcy, a court may be likely to "cherry pick" the contracts, i.e., allow default on contracts with positive values and continue to collect on negatively valued ones. However, an operating risk or a documentation risk also exists in netting. In the past, not all dealers have been careful to ensure that the master swap agreements are in place for all contracts and for all subsidiaries of parents with agreements. Building legal and regulatory support for netting was one of the major recommendations of the G-30 report, since the ability to net reduces credit exposure, and limits systemic risk. In fact, statutory support for netting has been growing. For example U.S. bankruptcy code has accepted netting and made it satutory in the banking acts of 1989 and 1991 as long as the counterparties are covered by a master swap agreement. For accounting purposes, FASB Interpretation 39 to FASB 107 (which forces most U.S. banks to represent the entire credit exposure of derivatives on the asset side of the balance sheet, with negatively valued contracts on the liabilities side) also allows netting by counterparties covered by master swap agreements deemed legally enforceable.

     S&P is fairly comfortable that the U.S. and certain other advanced countries will recognize the agreements, but doubt remains on their enforceability in other countries. The calculations that follow do not incorporate the effect of netting, however, due to the lack of quality data.

2.3 Credit Risk Is Moderate

How grave is credit risk in the derivatives business? Certainly it is substantial. However, it must be emphasized that the credit risk of derivatives is proportionately less than the risk taken by a bank's on-balance sheet lending. With derivatives, the credit ratings of the counterparties tend to be solidly investment grade—-much higher than the average ratings of borrowing clients. For example, Citicorp, Bankers Trust, and Chemical revealed in their annual reports that over 95% of their counterparties are investment-grade-rated. S&P has found the average rating to be 'A'. In general, given the rating and maturity distribution of bank portfolios, the expected cumulative default rate would be about 0.8%. Over its short life span, the swaps businesses has suffered very few defaults. Other than the case of the British municipalities, most occured in the 1992-1993 period with the failure of some major insurance companies and Olympia & York. New disclosure requirements for U.S. banks to report exposures of 90-days past due assets shows that they were 0.03% or less of replacement cost at March 31, 1994-a negligible amount.

     When quantifying credit exposure or MPMV in a diversified derivatives portfolio that is part of a large, diversified operating company, S&P believes there is no need to calculate the potential maximum market values of each specific product for each tenor, as it would in a monoline-enhanced subsidiary to which a 'AAA' rating is assigned. S&P examines the general mix of counterparties, products, and tenors of contracts in portfolios

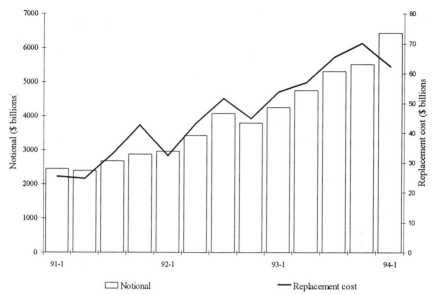

Figure 2
Aggregate Exposures, interest rate contracts, for nine major U.S. commercial bank dealers.

periodically and formulates an opinion of how risky the portfolio is based on that mix.

3. PRODUCT MIX DETERMINES VOLATILITY

S&P has an estimate of the volatility of market values for each broad product category in large diversified portfolios. This affords some idea of how high the credit exposure (PMV) can reach relative to notional amounts of those products. For example, the MVs for the whole range of currency or foreign-exchange (FX) contracts and equity and commodity contracts have been very volatile: they virtually doubled over the fourth quarter of 1991 in response to the drop in interest rates, then fell sharply in the following quarter, only to shoot up in the second quarter of 1992 *(see figures 1 and 2)*. Interest-rate contract portfolios are considerably less volatile, but nevertheless their MVs also jumped when rates eased. Relative to notional amounts, the PMV has fluctuated between 1.1% and 3.8% for FX contracts during the period shown, and 0.6% and 2.4% for interest-rate contracts.

Refining the general categories of currency and interest rate contracts, S&P ranks the various derivative product types by volatility. Commodity and equity contracts clearly are substantially more volatile than the average portfolio product. This means they can reach higher levels of market value relative to notional amounts than do other products. Within the currency category, currency swaps tend to be highly volatile. Currency options are less volatile, followed by currency futures and forwards. The risk factors appear to be highly influenced by the average tenors of the products in diversified bank portfolios, with longer-dated contracts being much more volatile than shorter-dated ones. Swaps tend to be of longer tenor than options or futures/forwards.

Interest-rate contracts are, in general, less risky than currency contracts. Within the interest-rate category, interest-rate swaps are the most risky, with options a little less so, and forwards representing very little credit exposure relative to notional amounts, again because they tend to be very short dated. Exchange traded instruments such as futures represent negligible credit risk because they are collateralized.

In analyzing the mix of the various bank portfolios, Bankers Trust New York Co.and J.P. Morgan & Co. have the highest risk profile because they are more involved with commodity and equity contract. In addition, J.P. Morgan, and to a lesser extent Bankers Trust, have the greatest proportion of contracts maturing in more than one year*(see table 2)*. This translates into generally higher market values relative to notional amounts, because contracts near expiration have few remaining cash flows.

4. MANAGEMENT POLICY IS KEY TO MARKET RISK

Changes in the net value of all contracts, positively (PMV) and negatively valued (NMV) are recognized as trading gains or losses in earnings and on the balance sheet for those using mark-to-market accounting. Market risk is at least as great a risk as credit risk but more difficult to measure. More than credit risk, much depends on the day to day decisions of management as to whether to neutralize risk or maintain an open position.

In theory it is possible for dealers to be completely neutral to changes in underlying rates. Each contract benefiting from an increase in a particular rate can be hedged, or matched, with a contract or security benefiting from a decrease in the same rate. The major dealers with large distribution networks and intimate knowledge of supply and demand in the marketplace often enter into contracts knowing they can offset the position with another client or dealer with a similar contract on the other side of the market. At times, however, this may not be the case, or there may be a time delay. The dealer can then offset the position with an on-balance-sheet transaction, in treasuries, for instance. Or the dealer can purchase a contract to hedge the position with another dealer. With the best of intentions, perfect hedges are elusive. Often there is basis risk or small mismatches in maturities that

Table 2
Derivatives Maturity Mix as of March 31, 1994

Institution	Currency and commodities		Interest rate	
	<1 Yr.	Others	<1 Yr.	Others
BankAmerica Corp.	55.2	2.8	19.0	23.0
Bankers Trust N.Y. Corp.	43.5	5.9	24.3	26.3
Chase Manhattan Corp.	48.1	2.9	22.9	26.1
Chemical Banking Corp.	33.0	1.5	41.5	24.0
Citicorp	56.9	2.9	26.3	13.9
Continental Bank Corp.	23.5	1.4	37.4	37.6
First Chicago Corporation	51.1	3.1	23.9	21.8
J.P. Morgan & Co. Inc.	24.8	8.4	26.0	40.7
Nationsbank Corp.	23.0	0.8	51.3	24.9
Republic New York Corp.	56.5	1.2	27.1	15.3

Source: FRY-9c Regulatory Reports

under some market conditions will prevent the two instruments from moving in two equal but opposite directions.

But the key to the degree of market risk is management policy. Given that the tools exist to hedge, management discretion as well as policies that identify and place limits on risk taking are the determinants of the degree of risk. Another important element is the management information systems that can present a comprehensive global picture of positions.

In managing market risk, dealers use many of the same techniques employed in managing any other type of trading risk. Common methods employ some notion of setting limits per trader based on statistical calculations of earnings at risk. Once again, model risk comes into play.

The potential impact of imperfectly hedged positions is very large. Market risk is the most difficult for outsiders to assess. No public disclosure currently addresses this risk. Nor is it easy to conceive of a useful measure of risk that could be comparable for all dealers. Given the complexity of the products and the element of "art" versus "science" involved in constructing simulation models that depict the risk profiles of portfolios such disclosure may be a long way off. However, the major dealers appear to practice good risk management with very little intentional position taking. One evidence of this is revenues from derivatives have been relatively stable—one of the more stable elements of the trading revenue line. If portfolios were grossly mismatched the revenue, which is the change in net market value (PMV-NMV) of the portfolio over the period, would be very volatile.

5. LEGAL AND OPERATING RISKS

Legal risk is looming ever larger. It was thrust into the forefront with Procter and Gamble's suit of Bankers Trust for selling its treasurer highly leveraged products he allegedly did not understand or have the authority to purchase (an out of court settlement was reached in May, 1996). Credit Suisse also agreed to cover a $40 million loss due to alleged unauthorized trading on the part of the client. Regulators in the U.S. have promulgated regulations requiring banks to ascertain the suitability or appropriateness of products to the purchaser (see Schachter (1995)). For example, in May 1996 the Office of the Comptroller of the Currency issued guidance for banks selling derivatives to counterparties acting as fiduciaries. Prudent dealers would do well to document the presentations of the risks inherent in instruments sold to clients.

A related legal risk, ascertaining the authority of officers of client organizations to enter into derivative transactions is also a serious matter. Unauthorized trading by certain British municipalities (the Hammersmith and Fulham case), and their consequent default on contracts has produced the largest credit losses in derivatives to date. Another related legal risk is that the documentation needs to be in order—confirm slips matched and swap agreements signed.

6. ACCOUNTING PRACTICES VARY

As one would expect with rapidly developing new products, accounting standards have been hard pressed to keep up, creating what could be called accounting risk. Most major dealers have at this time accepted the use of mark-to-market accounting rather than accrual accounting, as recommended by the Group of 30. But significant discretion is permitted in the area of marking derivative contracts to market. Public quotes do not exist for some types of contracts, particularly the most esoteric ones. In some cases, prices can be derived from publicly quoted swaps curves. In others, mathematical formulas may be used. In both cases computed prices can vary greatly depending on assumptions used, resulting in some contracts being mispriced and subject to revaluation.

Dealers generally use so-called mid-point pricing, the point between the bid and offer price. More conservative pricing policies withold some or all of the gain between the midpoint and the bid or offer. The Group of 30 recommends midpoint pricing but witholding for specific identified risks—credit, liquidity, legal, etc. While many claim to practice such witholding, the amount of such witholding "reserves" varies tremendously between firms. This results in more income being recognized up front by the less conservative dealers,

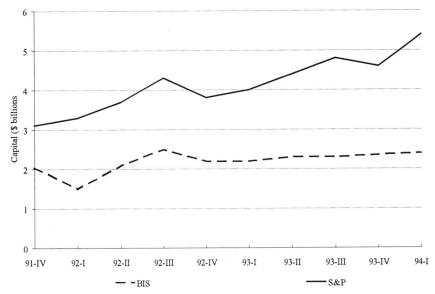

Figure 3
A comparison of BIS credit-risk required capital with S&P "all-in" required capital, aggregated, for ten U.S. commercial bank dealers.

rendering comparisons of income statements and balance sheets of these business lines among dealers very difficult. The risk is that standardization of methods of marking to market could result in significant revaluations for some dealers.

7. CAPTIAL NEEDED TO COVER ALL RISKS

The derivatives business has grown to be a substantial user of capital at the major dealers. It is a larger user of capital, in S&P's estimation, than it generally is in management's eyes. Most of the capital allocated by bank managements covers credit risks, with generally a small concession for market risk. Till recently, BIS regulations also only addressed credit risk and are lower than S&P assessments (*figure 3*). S&P believes that for derivatives, just as for lending, substantial additional capital is needed to cover risks other than the most probable credit loss level. For example, there is a risk that losses would approach a higher-than-expected, or worst-case level. Capital is also needed to cover market risk. Banks generally allocate modest levels of capital for market risk. It covers the

Table 3
Capital assessments in millions of U.S. dollars for derivatives for the year ended March 31, 1994

Institution	Actual Market Value	Maximum Potential Market Value	2% 'A' Level Capital Charge	BIS Capital
BankAmerica Corp.	14,510	27,033	541	220
Bankers Trust N.Y. Corp.	24,012	41,705	834	382
Chase Manhattan Corp.	14,731	27,557	551	241
Chemical Banking Corp.	26,175	51,811	1,036	386
Citicorp	26,116	51,845	1,037	449
Continental Bank Corp.	1,613	2,660	53	37
First Chicago Corp.	7,910	12,327	247	127
J.P. Morgan & Co. Inc.	29,807	53,451	1,069	506
Nationsbank Corp.	1,339	6,468	129	31
Republic New York Corp.	1,982	9,528	191	25

losses that could be incurred based on volatility levels incorporated in their models. However, S&P believes that market risk could be much higher, especially in periods of market disruption or sudden deviations from historic rate levels. Legal risks, such as the enforceability of contracts, are very unpredictable but may become an increasing factor. As a final catch-all category, capital is needed to general business risk. Taken together, these risks are substantial and require appropriate levels of capital. S&P assigns provisionally 2% capital against the credit exposure (MPMV) *(see table 3)*. This ranks the business risk of derivatives among the lowest of bank activities. Should evidence mount that the risks are higher, capital assessment could be revised.

S&P adjusts capital levels on a case-by-case basis depending on its assessment of the risks of individual bank portfolios. Capital requirements also vary depending on the rating level. The 2% capital assessment is commensurate with an 'A' rating. More capital is required for higher ratings.

The major dealers have the financial resources to cover the capital needs of the derivatives activities indicated by the S&P methodology, and S&P does not expect to make any rating changes as a result of these calculations. In fact, S&P does not view the existence of a large derivatives operation to be inconsistent with high ratings. For example, two of the largest derivatives dealers, J.P. Morgan and Bankers Trust, are also among the highest rated. 'AAA' and 'AA', respectively.

Table 4 1993 Derivatives Income in millions of U. S. dollars

Institution	Revenue	Percent of Total Bank Revenue
BankAmerica Corp.	80	0.7
Chase Manhattan Corp.	201	3.1
Chemical Banking Corp.	434	5.1
Citicorp	800	4.9
J.P. Morgan & Co. Inc.	797	12.4

Source: Annual reports

8. BANKS BENEFIT FROM DERIVATIVES PROFITS

Profits derived from derivatives activities have become very important to the major dealers. U.S. money center banks have begun disclosing income from derivatives *(see table 4)*. The derivative business can be seen as a replacement for the old interest income money-center banks enjoyed from their top-tier clients, who have since turned directly to the commercial paper and other securities markets to obtain funds. The cash flows from interest-rate swaps, for instance, resemble cash flows from lending activities: the bank collects monies based upon one rate schedule, while paying out monies on another schedule. For example on fixed/floating-interest swaps, the bank may receive from its counterparty a fixed rate on a given notional amount, which is analogous to a loan amount, while receiving a floating rate on a like notional amount from that same counterparty. Of course, income from derivatives is accounted for on a mark-to-market basis. Nevertheless, most income comes from a different kind of spread—the bid/offer spread on contracts. Prices of contracts conceptually represent the present value of expected net cash flows that are amortized over the life of the contract. This spread income has been fairly stable and dependent more on volume than on rate volatility. Some additional earnings on the float from payments received but not yet paid out is recognized in interest income. These stable sources of income should be viewed as good-quality earnings for banks.

The derivative business has become an important one to both the banks and to the economy. It carries certain risks but these risks are familiar to banks. Key among them—credit risk—is adequately quantifiable and less likely to cause as many difficulties for banks as have their lending operations, given the higher credit quality of the counterparties. Continued vigilance is needed to ensure that the risks remain adequately supported by capital. The industry needs to continue to improve monitoring systems and public disclosure to increase the transparency of the business.

REFERENCES

Schachter, Barry, 1995, Suitability, Legal Risk, and Derivatives Regulation, *Journal of Financial Engineering* 4 (June 1995), 147-156.

Derivatives, Regulation and Banking
Edited by B. Schachter
© 1997 Elsevier Science B.V. All rights reserved.

Chapter 4

THE VALUATION OF OFF-BALANCE-SHEET FINANCIAL INSTRUMENT DISCLOSURES IN THE BANKING INDUSTRY

Susan M. Riffe[†]

Southern Methodist University, Dallas, TX USA

1. INTRODUCTION

The objective of this paper is to determine if notional values of OBS financial instruments[1] are relevant in explaining the market value of bank equity. Notional values are the par value or face amount of the underlying positions in financial instruments. It is important to investigate notional values because they were the first OBS instrument disclosures required by bank regulators and the FASB. Since 1986, the Federal Reserve has required BHCs to disclose notional values in their Y-9 reports. In Statement of Financial

---

[†]Assistant Professor, Edwin L. Cox School of Business. I gratefully acknowledge the assistance of my dissertation chairman, Jim Manegold, and committee members, Walt Blacconiere, Kim Dietrich, and Andrew Weiss. Randy Beatty, Ravi Bhushan, Wayne Shaw, Ross Jennings, and especially Jody Magliolo also provided helpful comments. E. Ramesh provided SFAS 107 data used in a previous draft of this paper, and Anne Beatty provided related financial statement disclosures. The data used in this study were obtained from public sources. Y-9 data is available from the National Technical Information Service. A list of sample firms is available from the author upon request. I am appreciative of the financial support of the SMU Cox School of Business, USC School of Accounting, Deloitte & Touche Foundation, and the American Woman's Society of Certified Public Accountants/American Society of Women Accountants.

[1]The FASB defines a financial instrument as cash, evidence of an ownership interest in an entity, or a contract that both:

a. Imposes on one entity a contractual obligation (1) to deliver cash or another financial instrument to a second entity or (2) to exchange financial instruments on potentially unfavorable terms with the second entity

b. Conveys to that second entity a contractual right (1) to receive cash or another financial instrument from the first entity or (2) to exchange other financial instruments on potentially favorable terms with the first entity. (March 1990, par. 6)

Accounting Standard (SFAS) 105, the FASB required all firms to disclose notional values[2] for financial instruments with off-balance-sheet risk[3] for fiscal years ending after June 15, 1990 (FASB 1990). Subsequent FASB disclosure requirements have built on the base-line information provided by notional values. SFAS 107 requires disclosure of the fair value of all financial instruments for fiscal years ending after December 15, 1992 (FASB 1991a).[4] SFAS 119 requires more extensive fair value disclosures for derivative financial instruments such as swaps, options, and futures for fiscal years ending after December 15, 1994 (FASB 1994). Despite the plethora of disclosure requirements for OBS instruments, this is the first research to investigate the relevance of the initial, base-line notional value disclosures. This research provides a unique opportunity to examine the valuation of notional values during a period before other information was available about OBS instruments.

Notional values provide an objective measure of the extent of activity in these OBS instruments, but they have been criticized because they do not provide specific estimates of instrument values like the fair value disclosures in SFAS 107 and SFAS 119 (*Risk* 1994). However, these fair value disclosures have also been criticized because they are subjective. Further, these disclosures may be unreliable because fair values are difficult to estimate for the many instruments that are not traded on an open market. This paper provides an important first step in understanding the information provided by these alternative sets of disclosures by documenting that notional values are significant in explaining the market value of bank equity. It would be difficult for future research to determine the incremental information contributed by fair value disclosures until the information provided by notional values has been established.

This research is important for several reasons. First, developing appropriate OBS instrument disclosures is a priority to the FASB, and this research is among the first to investigate the relevance of these alternative disclosures. The FASB has been criticized because it does not currently have a comprehensive policy that addresses how to account for these evolving and increasingly complex financial instruments. Further, well-publicized

---

[2]SFAS 105 also required nonquantitative information about the extent, nature, and terms of the instruments. Because these descriptive disclosures tend to be very general in nature, they are not examined explicitly in the analysis.

[3]Financial instruments have OBS risk if they expose a firm to (1) incurring an instrument-related loss greater than the amount recognized as an asset on the balance sheet or (2) obtaining an instrument-related obligation greater than the amount recognized as a liability (FASB 1990, 4).

[4]Fair value was defined as the amount that the instruments could be exchanged for between willing parties. Firms only had to disclose fair values if it was practicable to do so.

losses related to these instruments have led to growing concern about the effect these instruments could have on the viability of firms (Andrews and Sender 1986; Smith and Lipin 1994). The FASB has responded to these criticisms and concerns by issuing three standards since 1990 dealing with financial instrument disclosures. At the same time, the FASB has called for research assessing the relevance of the disclosures they have required (FASB 1991b). This paper examines the relevance of OBS disclosures from the perspective of investors, who are identified by FASB Concepts Statement No. 1 (1978) as primary users of financial information. Relevance is defined as a significant association between disclosures and equity values.

Second, the paper extends the body of literature that has investigated the association between equity values and other accounting disclosures (Landsman 1986; Barth 1991; Harris and Ohlson 1987; Shevlin 1991; Sougiannis 1994; Amir 1993; Beaver et al. 1989; Barth et al. 1991; Barth 1994; Wahlen 1994). This paper is closely related to the work by Eccher et al. (1995), Barth et al. (1994), and Venkatachalam (1995) that has examined the relevance of on and off-balance-sheet financial instrument disclosures. The extension of the valuation literature to OBS instruments is crucial because these disclosures are extremely important to the FASB and the financial community. Furthermore, this paper makes a significant contribution because it is the only work to focus on notional value disclosures before other information was available about these instruments.

Third, the research helps to explain the difference between market and book value of equity. Previous research has suggested that the difference is partially explained by the lagged nature of historical cost accounting (Beaver and Ryan 1993). Underlying assets, liabilities, gains, and losses from OBS instruments are fully recognized in financial statements only on an ex post basis after uncertainty surrounding their effect on the financial condition of the firm has been sufficiently resolved. However, these OBS instruments are expected to significantly affect the market's perception of banks' values on an ex ante basis before the value is reflected on the balance sheet. Accordingly, this ex ante recognition of OBS values should help to explain some of the divergence between the market value and book value of equity. Accountants are criticized for neglecting to fully recognize the value of OBS items in financial statements (Kane and Unal 1990). Understanding the relationship between OBS instruments and bank equity values is a helpful starting point for resolving related recognition and measurement issues.

Fourth, the research provides additional understanding about the six instruments examined, loan commitments, standby letters of credit, commercial letters of credit, interest rate swaps, futures, and options. Banks are motivated to be involved in these OBS products because they may add value. However, much has been written about the riskiness of these instruments and the losses they can cause. Because of the challenging bank management issues that these instruments have introduced, it is important to use empirical analysis to evaluate these instruments. The analysis presented provides evidence concerning the economic characteristics of these instruments. In particular, the research will provide some insights into whether the instruments were positively or negatively associated with bank values in the late 1980s and how these values were affected by the risk characteristics of banks.

The chosen context for investigating the valuation of OBS items has several advantages. It is helpful to examine these disclosures for a relatively homogenous group of firms (Bernard 1989). Assessing the value of disclosures in a multi-industry context would be difficult because of different capital structures and production functions; thus, focusing on one industry may increase the signal-to-noise ratio (Beaver et al. 1989). Also, it is advantageous to examine OBS items within an industry where the positions are large and the instruments are an important part of operations. OBS positions were substantial and they experienced significant growth during the sample period. From June of 1986 to December of 1989, aggregate notional value positions for the 242 sample BHCs grew 155 percent. In addition, careful management of OBS positions are crucial to bank success (Sinkey 1989). Revenues from OBS instruments allow banks to offset lower earnings caused by increased competition in the direct lending markets and loan portfolio problems. The instruments also help banks and their customers manage the risk associated with increasingly volatile financial markets.

This paper is organized as follows. Section I introduces the research. Section II describes the OBS disclosures. Section III develops the valuation model and summarizes the research design. Section IV presents the sample selection procedures and the empirical analysis. Section V summarizes the research and discusses the conclusions.

2. OBS INSTRUMENT DISCLOSURES

The disclosures examined in this research are the notional values provided in Y-9 reports filed with the Federal Reserve. BHCs with assets greater than $150 million and all multibank holding companies must file quarterly Y-9 reports (Board of Governors 1986). Y-9s are publicly available information used by regulators during the bank examination process. These reports include a consolidated balance sheet and income statement prepared in conformance with generally accepted accounting principles. BHCs are also required to disclose the notional value (i.e., face amount or par value) of OBS instruments in their Schedule HC-F. These notional values disclosed in the Y-9s are the same as the notional values required under SFAS 105.

The instruments examined in this research are classified as either credit-related or market-related. Credit-related items are used to guarantee credit or facilitate credit availability and include standby letters of credit (i.e., standbys), commercial letters of credit (i.e., commercial letters), and loan commitments (i.e., commitments). Market-related instruments are used either to generate fees and trading gains or to manage interest rate risk and include options written (i.e., options), futures and forwards (i.e., futures), and interest rate swaps (i.e., swaps).[5] Dividing the instruments into these categories is appropriate given the similarities within categories and the significant differences between categories. For example, financial services firms are the primary issuers of credit-related instruments, while a wide variety of firms participate in market-related instruments. Credit-related instruments primarily expose a bank to risk from customer default, while market-related instruments primarily expose a bank to risk from fluctuations in market rates. Also, credit-related instruments are not usually actively traded and are more difficult to measure at fair value, while market-related instruments often trade on organized exchanges and have readily available fair value estimates.

The total value of these instruments includes both the on-balance-sheet amount already recognized on the financial statements and the OBS amount, defined as the present value of the expected future cash flows not yet reflected on the financial statements. The market value of equity will reflect both the on-balance-sheet and perceived OBS value. Accordingly, this research examines whether there is a significant correlation between the market value of equity and (1) the book value of equity (which captures the on-balance-sheet value of financial instruments and other assets and liabilities) and (2) notional values (which capture the OBS value of financial instruments). Although notional values do not provide a direct measure of the OBS value of the instruments, they do provide an objective measure of the extent of activity in these items that are disclosed by virtually all banks. Accordingly, the OBS value of credit-related and market-related instruments is expected to be a function of the notional values. If the OBS value of these instruments is positive (negative), then the relationship between the notional values and equity should be positive (negative).

---

[5]Several instruments included in the Y-9 reports are not examined. The excluded items are securities borrowed and lent, commitments to purchase and sell when-issued securities, participations acquired in bankers' acceptances, and loan sales with recourse. On average, these excluded instruments each represent less than 1 percent of assets. Although commitments to purchase foreign exchange are material to BHCs, they are not examined because the Y-9 disclosures for foreign exchange are not sufficiently detailed to test their relationship to market value.

2.1 Credit-Related Instruments

Banks collect fees on credit-related instruments for agreeing to guarantee their customers' credit or for facilitating their customers' access to credit. With commitments, banks agree to provide loans to customers under specified terms. With standbys and commercial letters, banks guarantee their customers' obligations to third-party beneficiaries. The notional values are essentially the par or face amount of the underlying contracts and represent either the amount the bank is agreeing to loan to the customer under the commitment or the amount of a customer's credit the bank is willing to guarantee to a third party under a standby or commercial letter. For example, if the bank has a commitment with a $100,000 notional value, then they have agreed to loan a customer $100,000 upon demand at either a fixed or floating interest rate. A standby with a $100,000 notional value obligates the bank to guarantee a $100,000 commitment that a bank customer has to a third party. If the bank pays out the $100,000 to the third party, the bank customer is then obligated to repay the bank.

When credit-related instruments are issued, banks usually receive up-front fees that are initially recognized as a deferred fees liability on the balance sheet and then gradually recognized as revenue over the life of the commitment (FASB 1986).[6] This deferred fees liability represents the on-balance-sheet value of the instruments at issuance and is determined by the risk of the underlying commitment and the competitiveness of the market for these instruments. Additional future cash inflows not reflected in this liability will be generated from subsequent fees or compensating balances required under the agreement. In addition, banks can anticipate future inflows from net interest revenue earned when customers take out loans under the instruments. The bank can also anticipate some future cash outflows if customers default on loans or if loans are issued at a substandard interest rate. Thus, the incremental OBS value of these instruments equals the present value of these expected future cash inflows and outflows that are not yet reflected on the balance sheet.

Notional values are expected to be related to the OBS value of these instruments because the future fees or compensating balances required will be a function notional values. Further, if the customers borrow under the standby, commercial letter, or commitment, the interest earned by the bank on the associated loan will be a function of the principal or notional value of the instruments. In addition, because the notional value represents the

---

[6]According to SFAS 91, if realization of the contingent obligation to loan out money is deemed likely, then the fees are deferred until the obligation is realized and the fees are amortized as an adjustment to the yield on the loan (FASB 1986).

maximum amount the bank may have to loan out under the instruments and accordingly the maximum amount the bank could lose if the customer defaults, the expected default losses will also be a function of the notional amounts. If the OBS value of the instruments is positive (negative), it suggests that the future expected cash inflows from fees and interest not yet reflected on the balance sheet are greater (less) than the future expected cash outflows from customer default, and there will be a positive (negative) relationship between the notional values and the market value of equity.

2.2 Market-Related Instruments

Market-related instruments fluctuate in value as interest rates change. Accordingly, banks use these instruments to manage interest rate risk, generate trading gains, or earn fees by serving as a market intermediary. For example, banks can use swaps to hedge their own interest rate risk by assuming one side of the swap, generate a gain by trading swaps in the open market, lock in a spread by arranging a swap between two parties, or, less commonly, earn a fee for initiating a swap transaction. The notional value of market-related instruments represents the par value or size of the underlying agreement and is used to calculate the interest cash flow streams. If the bank undertakes a $100 million swap transaction to pay fixed and receive floating interest rates, then the net amount of interest they will receive or pay is calculated as the spread between the two rates multiplied by $100 million. For futures and options, the $100 million notional value would represent the size of the basic trading unit underlying the contract.

With market-related instruments, fees or premiums collected for issuing these instruments, if any, are initially deferred and then generally recognized as revenue over the life of the agreement. The gains and losses on instruments used for trading purposes must be recognized immediately as incurred in the income statement. This is referred to as mark-to-market accounting. By contrast, gains and losses for instruments used for hedging may be initially deferred and gradually incorporated into the income statement as income and expense on the associated hedged items are recognized. This is called deferral or hedge accounting. Thus, the on-balance-sheet value of market-related instruments reflects the value of any deferred fees plus the recognized book value of the instruments given current market conditions and the accounting method used.

The OBS value is the difference between the recorded book value and the perceived value of these instruments reflected in stock prices. To the extent the mark-to-market amount does not fully reflect the market's expectations of changes in interest rates or market conditions, the OBS value will be different than zero. Also, if involvement in market-related instruments is perceived as providing opportunities for the bank to use its expertise in the area to enhance future value, then the OBS value would be positive.   In addition, using the instruments as a means of managing the risk of the firm may be perceived as a value-enhancing activity that is not reflected on the balance sheet.   Alternatively, as has become evident in recent years, large positions in these instruments may be indicative of impending losses not reflected in the on-balance-sheet amounts.   Because notional value is a measure of the extent of activity in these instruments, it should be significantly correlated with this OBS value.   Therefore, if the perceived OBS value is positive (negative) then a positive (negative) relationship should exist between notional values and the market value of equity.

3. RESEARCH DESIGN

3.1 Valuation Model

This study uses valuation models with data pooled across BHCs and time to examine the relationship between notional value disclosures of OBS instruments and the level of market values.[7]   A significant association between the disclosures and the market value of equity is interpreted as consistent with the information being relevant to investors in estimating the OBS value of these instruments.[8]   Because an observed relationship between the disclosures and the market value of equity could be driven by the omission of correlated variables in the analysis, it is important to include all obvious candidates as additional regressors in the model.   Although it is not possible to rule out the possibility of bias from correlated omitted variables, two alternative specifications of the market value of equity will be used to provide additional evidence that the relevance of the OBS disclosures can not be explained by other potentially relevant variables suggested by the accounting literature.

---

[7]Christie (1987) noted that these "levels" studies are economically equivalent with "returns" studies that use the percentage change in market value as a dependent variable and changes in accounting disclosures as independent variables. Landsman and Magliolo (1988) indicated the choice between levels and returns is a function of the assumed economic model and the econometric characteristics of the data. The levels approach is appropriate for this study because it investigates the relevance of the disclosed level of OBS items, and the analysis focuses on the cumulative effect of the OBS disclosures on market value. The returns approach would be appropriate if the research investigated how initially disclosing OBS information changed market values during a very short time period. However, this approach would be troublesome in this context because (1) many other pieces of information are released along with the OBS disclosures in the Y-9 reports, (2) the entire Y-9 report changed in June of 1986 when OBS disclosures were first required, and (3) subsidiary banks, but not BHCs, have been required to disclose some information about OBS instruments since 1983.

[8]It is not possible to determine if the OBS disclosures are actually used by investors to set prices or are correlated with other pieces of information that are used to set prices.

The first valuation model used is the accounting identity model, which assumes that the market value of equity equals the market value minus book value of assets and liabilities recognized on the balance sheet, plus the market value minus book value of unrecognized items. It has been used extensively in the accounting literature (Landsman 1986; Harris and Ohlson 1987; Beaver et al. 1989; Shevlin 1991; Barth 1991; Barth et al. 1991; Barth 1994). The model can be specified as follows:

$$MV = BV + (MA - BA) - (ML - BL) + (MOBS - BOBS) \qquad (1)$$

where BV is the book value of equity; MA is the market value of on-balance-sheet assets; BA is the book value of on-balance-sheet assets; ML is the market value of on-balance-sheet liabilities; BL is the book value of on-balance-sheet liabilities; MOBS is the market value of OBS items; and BOBS is the book value of OBS items.

The previous literature has incorporated several proxies for the difference between the market value and book value of on-balance-sheet assets (i.e., MA-BA) for banks. Beaver et al. (1989) used nonperforming loans and allowance for loan losses as proxies for the difference between the market value and book value of equity. They suggested that nonperforming loans provide additional information about the default risk associated with loans beyond what is reflected in the allowance for loan losses recorded on the balance sheet. In addition, Barth (1994) suggested that unrealized trading gains and losses on marketable securities impact the market value of equity. Following previous research such as Barth (1994), the difference between the market value and book value of liabilities (i.e., ML-BL) is assumed to be zero. This approach is appropriate either if liabilities are measured on the balance sheet at an amount that approaches their associated market value or if it can be assumed that a systematic component of this difference is captured in the intercept (Beaver et al. 1989).

Given the previous discussion in section II, this research extends the literature by including the notional value as a proxy for the OBS value of these instruments (i.e., MOBS-BOBS). Accordingly, the theoretical model of the market value of equity in equation (1) is operationalized as follows:

$$MV_{j,t} = \beta_0 + \beta_1 BV_{j,t} + \beta_2 DIFSEC_{j,t} + \beta_3 DIFLOAN_{j,t} + \beta_{OBS} OBS_{j,t} + \epsilon_{j,t} \qquad (2)$$

where $MV_{j,t}$ is the number of shares outstanding times the price per share for BHC j at the end of the quarter t; $BV_{j,t}$ is stockholders' equity minus preferred stock for BHC j at time t; $DIFSEC_{j,t}$ is the difference between the market value and book value of marketable securities for BHC j at time t; $DIFLOAN_{j,t}$ is the difference between the nonperforming loans and the allowance for loan losses for BHC j at time t; and $OBS_{j,t}$ is the notional value of OBS instruments for BHC j at time t.

Brennan (1991) criticized the accounting identity model, in general, because it does not properly consider both the income statement and the balance sheet. By incorporating balance sheet and income statement information, the model articulated in Ohlson (1993) and Feltham and Ohlson (1993) overcomes this potential shortcoming and has been used by Amir (1993) and Sougiannis (1994). The Ohlson model is derived from the clean surplus relationship that changes in book value equal earnings minus dividends. Accordingly, market value of equity (MV) at time t is defined as:

$$MV_t = BV_t + \sum_{\tau=1}^{\infty} \rho^{-\tau} \, E_t[E\tilde{A}RN_{t+\tau} - (\rho - 1)B\tilde{V}_{t+\tau-1} | OTH_t] \tag{3}$$

ρ is the discount rate plus one; $EARN_t$ is earnings at time t; and OTH_t is other information available at time t. The bracketed term is abnormal earnings, defined as earnings that exceed the required rate of return on the previous period's book value, given the firm's discount rate. Expected abnormal earnings is a function of other information available. Ohlson (1993) noted that although other information is not currently recognized in the financial statements, it will be reflected in earnings and book value in the future. Including other information in the model recognizes that some value-relevant items are incorporated into accounting numbers with a lag.

This model is operationalized by including book value (BV), earnings (EARN), and proxies for other information (OTH) as independent variables. Three variables are used as empirical proxies for OTH. The first two variables are growth in book value and systematic risk as suggested by Litzenberger and Rao (1971) and as included in Beaver at al. (1989). Risk is also implicitly a part of the Ohlson model because abnormal earnings in equation (3) depends on a risk-adjusted discount rate. The third element is the OBS value of the financial instruments examined in this research. These instruments are appropriately considered "other information" because they represent potential economic benefits or additional obligations not fully reflected on the balance sheet. These items provide an opportunity for banks to generate future cash inflows or outflows beyond what is reflected by the assets, liabilities, and equity recognized on the balance sheet.

Therefore, the empirical model based on Ohlson's formulation of the value of equity for BHC j at time t can be expressed as:

$$\begin{aligned} MV_{j,t} = \; &\beta_0 + \beta_1 \, BV_{j,t} + \beta_4 \, EARN_{j,t} + \beta_5 \, GROWTH_{j,t} + \beta_6 \, MKTBETA_{j,t} \\ &+ \beta_{OBS} \, OBS_{j,t} + \epsilon_{j,t} \end{aligned} \tag{4}$$

where $EARN_{j,t}$ is earnings before trading gains and losses for BHC j at time t;[9] $GROWTH_{j,t}$

---

[9]Beaver et al. (1989) and Barth (1994) used a similar variable because it is considered an appropriate proxy for operating earnings.

is the percentage change in assets over the previous four quarters for BHC j at time t;[10] $MKTBETA_{j,t}$ is the sensitivity of returns to a value-weighted market index estimated concurrently with the sensitivity of returns to 30-year Treasury bond index;[11] and $OBS_{j,t}$ is the notional value of the OBS financial instruments for BHC j at time t.

3.2 Deflation

Equations (2) and (4) are deflated by book value (BV) to help reduce problems with heteroscedasticity (Beaver et al. 1989). This approach is consistent with Christie's (1987) suggestion that levels models use deflators that are a function of the independent variables because this method reduces spurious correlation induced by inappropriate deflators. Ou and Penman (1993) noted that a book value deflator also controls for cross-sectional differences in accounting methods. Deflating equation (2) and (4) by $BV_{j,t}$ yields the following models:

$$\frac{MV_{j,t}}{BV_{j,t}} = \beta_0 \frac{1}{BV_{j,t}} + \beta_1 + \beta_2 \frac{DIFSEC_{j,t}}{BV_{j,t}} + \beta_3 \frac{DIFLOAN_{j,t}}{BV_{j,t}} + \beta_{OBS} \frac{OBS_{j,t}}{BV_{j,t}} + \epsilon_{j,t} \qquad (5)$$

$$\frac{MV_{j,t}}{BV_{j,t}} = \beta_0 \frac{1}{BV_{j,t}} + \beta_1 + \beta_4 \frac{EARN_{j,t}}{BV_{j,t}} + \beta_5 \, GROWTH_{j,t} + \beta_6 \, MKTBETA_{j,t}$$
$$+ \beta_{OBS} \frac{OBS_{j,t}}{BV_{j,t}} + \epsilon_{j,t} \qquad (6)$$

In equations (5) and (6), the intercept from equations (2) and (4) are reflected in the β_0 coefficient. Brennan (1991) noted that the intercept should be divided by the deflator when controlling for heteroscedasticity. When the BV term from equations (2) and (4) is deflated by BV, it yields the β_1 intercept.

3.3 Credit-Related versus Market-Related Categories

As explained in section II, the OBS instruments examined in the analysis are

---

[10]Kallapur and Trombley (1994) found that past growth in assets has a higher association with future realized growth in book value than past growth in book value.

[11]The following version of the two-index market model is used to estimate the sensitivity of returns to market and interest rate movements:

$$R_{j,d,t} = \alpha_0 + \beta_{M,j,t} R_{M,d,t} + \beta_{I,j,t} R_{I,d,t} + \epsilon_{j,d,t}$$

where $R_{j,d,t}$ is stock returns for BHC j on day d of period t after adjusting for infrequent trading; $R_{M,d,t}$ is return on value-weighted market portfolio of stocks on day d of period t; $R_{I,d,t}$ is holding period returns on 30-year Treasury bonds on day d of period t; $\beta_{M,j,t}$ is MKTBETA defined as market risk sensitivity for BHC j for period t after the Scholes and Williams (1977) adjustment; and $\beta_{I,j,t}$ is interest rate risk sensitivity for BHC j for period t and is used in defining IRDUM.

divided into credit-related and market-related categories:[12]

$$\frac{MV_{j,t}}{BV_{j,t}} = \beta_0 \frac{1}{BV_{j,t}} + \beta_1 + \beta_4 \frac{EARN_{j,t}}{BV_{j,t}} + \beta_5 \, GROWTH_{j,t} + \beta_6 \, MKTBETA_{j,t}$$
$$+ \beta_{CR} \frac{CROBS_{j,t}}{BV_{j,t}} + \beta_{MKT} \frac{MKTOBS_{j,t}}{BV_{j,t}} + \epsilon_{j,t} \qquad (7)$$

where $CROBS_{j,t}$ is the notional value of credit-related instruments defined as the sum of standbys, commercial letters, and commitments for BHC j at time t; and $MKTOBS_{j,t}$ is the notional value of market-related instruments defined as the sum of net options, net futures, and swaps for BHC j at time t. These two categories of instruments are considered value-relevant when the β_{CR} and β_{MKT} coefficients are significantly different from zero. Positive (negative) coefficients suggest that the OBS value is positive (negative) and that the future expected cash inflows not yet reflected on the balance sheet are greater (less) than the future expected cash outflows. The β_{CR} and β_{MKT} coefficients are expected to be less than one because as explained in section II the OBS value of the instruments should be much less than the notional or principal amount disclosed in the Y-9s.

According to SFAS 105, credit-related instruments primarily expose banks to risk of loss from customer default, or credit risk; thus, the valuation coefficients of these instruments should be inversely related to their credit risk exposure. For example, as the risk of customers defaulting on loans issued under commitments increases, the expected future cash flows from the commitments should decrease. The amount of nonperforming loans and past due loans relative to book value is used as a proxy for credit risk. This proxy represents cross-sectional differences in exposure to credit losses given the BHC's existing loan portfolio and is an appropriate proxy for the empirical analysis if the credit quality of the OBS portfolio and loan portfolio are similar. There are several factors that suggest this is an appropriate assumption. First, credit-related items are often extended to the same customers who are also involved with the BHC's traditional lending products. For example, over 70 percent of commercial loans are made through commitment contracts (Melnik and Plaut 1986). Second, discussions with an accounting officer at a money-center bank suggested that banks evaluate the risk of their credit-related instruments portfolio in the same manner that they evaluate their loan portfolios. Third, the footnotes for some banks also describe the similarity in credit risk between credit-related OBS items and loans. For example, Citizens Banking Corp. (1993, 42) stated that credit-related instruments "have essentially the same level of credit risk as that associated with extending loans to customers and are subject to the

---

[12]Although Ohlson's model is used to explain the research design, both the accounting identity model and Ohlson's model will be used to test these relationships.

Corporation's normal credit policies."

According to SFAS 105, market-related instruments expose banks to market fluctuations in interest rates or interest rate risk; thus, the valuation coefficients on these instruments should be related to this risk exposure. Previous research has documented that bank stock returns are significantly related to interest rates, and that the relationship varies cross-sectionally according to the composition of bank asset and liability portfolios (Flannery and James 1984a, 1984b). In this research, the sensitivity of market returns to interest rate movements is used as a cross-sectional measure of exposure to interest rate risk. Using an approach similar to Barth (1994), interest rate risk is assumed to be directly related to the extent of hedging activity in banks. Banks with high interest rate risk (nonhedgers) are expected to use OBS instruments more extensively for generating future fees or trading gains; banks with low interest rate risk (hedgers) are expected to use the instruments more extensively for hedging activity. Nonhedging banks that use these instruments more extensively for trading should have greater expected future cash flows from fees and trading gains not yet reflected on the balance sheet. For hedging banks, any future expected gains (losses) realized are expected to be offset against future losses (gains) for the on-balance-sheet instruments being hedged to yield lower incremental future expected cash flows. Thus, OBS instruments used by nonhedgers will have higher valuation coefficients compared to hedgers.

To test the relationship between credit risk, interest rate risk, and OBS instruments the following regression equation is estimated:

$$
\begin{aligned}
\frac{MV_{j,t}}{BV_{j,t}} = {} & \beta_0 \frac{1}{BV_{j,t}} + \beta_1 + \beta_4 \frac{EARN_{j,t}}{BV_{j,t}} + \beta_5\, GROWTH_{j,t} + \beta_6\, MKTBETA_{j,t} \\
& + \beta_{CR} \frac{CROBS_{j,t}}{BV_{j,t}} + \beta_{MKT} \frac{MKTOBS_{j,t}}{BV_{j,t}} \\
& + \beta_{CRDUM} \frac{CROBS_{j,t}*CRDUM_{j,t}}{BV_{j,t}} + \beta_{IRDUM} \frac{MKTOBS_{j,t}*IRDUM_{j,t}}{BV_{j,t}} + \epsilon_{j,t}
\end{aligned} \tag{8}
$$

where $CRDUM_{j,t}$ equals one if the firm is in the half of the sample with the most credit risk (defined as average nonaccruing and past due loans divided by book value for BHC j in period t) and zero otherwise; $IRDUM_{j,t}$ equals one if the firm is in the half of the sample with the most interest rate risk (defined as the sensitivity of returns to interest rate movements for BHC j during period t)[13] and zero otherwise. A negative β_{CRDUM} coefficient is consistent with a lower value for credit-related instruments for banks with higher credit risk. A positive

---

[13]$\beta_{1,j,t}$ described in footnote 11 estimates the sensitivity of returns to interest rate movements and is used to define IRDUM. The interest rate sensitivity ($\beta_{1,j,t}$) varies from -2.8 to +2.9 with a mean of .04.

Table 1
Mean and Median OBS Instrument Positions Among 242 Sample BHCs that Hold Specific Instruments During Fourteen Quarters from September 1986 to December 1989 (n=3,388)

OBS Instruments and Categories	Number of BHC/Qtrs with Instruments	% of BHC/Qtrs with OBS Instruments	Mean (Median) in $000s[a]
Standbys	3,314	97.8	$546,411 ($30,281)
Commercial Letters	2,758	81.4	125,861 (6,605)
Commitments	3,264	96.3	2,244,239 (218,203)
Total Credit-Related Instruments	3,386	99.9	2,800,688 (231,197)
Put Options	613	18.1	1,513,121 (51,000)
Call Options	616	18.2	721,809 (42,455)
Net (Puts - Calls)	757	22.3	637,924 (300)
Long Futures	1,001	29.5	2,283,214 (77,214)
Short Futures	1,091	32.2	2,513,326 (79,250)
Net (Long - Short)	1,234	36.4	-369,969 (-2,350)
Swaps	1,442	42.6	7,305,330 (157,682)
Total Market- Related Instruments[b]	1,742	51.4	6,062,373 (85,826)
Total OBS Instruments	3,386	99.9	5,919,605 (230,959)
Total Assets	3,388	100.0	8,512,391 (2,316,762)
Total Stockholders' Equity	3,388	100.0	440,643 (151,784)

[a]Means and medians are based on the number of BHC/quarters with nonzero positions in a particular instrument.
[b]Means and medians for market-related and total OBS instruments are calculated with net options and net futures.

β_{IRDUM} coefficient indicates the value of market-related instruments is higher for nonhedgers with greater interest rate risk exposure that are using these instruments more extensively for generating future fees and trading gains than for hedging on-balance-sheet exposure.

Table 2
Descriptive Statistics for Variables Used in the Empirical Models (n=3,388)

Variables[a]	Mean	25% Quartile	Median	75% Quartile	Standard Deviation
MV/BV	1.31	1.01	1.26	1.53	.50
(1/BV)*10^{-6}	14.	2.4	6.6	16.	51.
EARN/BV	.33	.18	.31	.43	.50
GROWTH	.03	.01	.02	.04	.05
MKTBETA	.47	.05	.37	.74	.45
DIFSEC/BV	.00	-.04	.00	.04	.49
DIFLOAN/BV	.07	-.03	.01	.09	.53
CROBS/BV	2.83	.85	1.73	3.42	3.62
MKTOBS/BV	1.19	.00	.00	.32	5.45

[a]Definitions follow:

MV	number of shares outstanding times the price per share at the end of the quarter;
BV	stockholders' equity minus preferred stock;
EARN	earnings before trading gains and losses;
GROWTH	percentage change in total assets over the previous four quarters;
MKTBETA	sensitivity of returns to value-weighted market index estimated concurrently with the sensitivity of returns to 30-year Treasury bond index (see footnote 12);
DIFSEC	market value of investment securities minus book value of investment securities;
DIFLOAN	nonaccruing loans plus loans 90 days or more past due but still accruing minus the allowance for loan losses;
CROBS	standbys + commercial letters + commitments; and
MKTOBS	net options + net futures + swaps.

4. ANALYSIS

4.1 Sample Selection

Quarterly BHC Y-9 information from September 1986 through December 1989 is used in the analysis because OBS instruments have been disclosed throughout this period. BHC data rather than subsidiary bank data are preferable because stock usually trades at the BHC level. Further, BHC Y-9 reports reflect information after eliminating intercompany transactions among subsidiaries. Because only BHCs with assets of $150 million or more must report Y-9 information on a quarterly basis, the sample is restricted to these larger firms. The number of BHCs with information available in any one quarter ranges from 891 in September of 1986 to 1,071 in December of 1989. Because all firms in the final sample must be publicly traded, 464 BHCs with data on both the Y-9 tapes and the Center for Research in Security Prices (CRSP) files are identified. Nine firms with negative book values are removed from the sample because a different valuation model may apply to these troubled institutions. Further, sample BHCs are required to have the following data for all

14 quarters: (1) Y-9 information, (2) quarter-end market values, and (3) at least 60 daily return observations per quarter. 149 firms did not meet the first requirement, 57 more did not meet the second, and 7 more did not meet the third. 242 BHCs met all three restrictions.

4.2 Descriptive Statistics

Table 1 includes descriptive information about OBS instruments for those nonzero positions in individual instruments during the sample period. The notional value of OBS items are material to BHCs. The mean (median) notional value of OBS instruments is $5.9 billion ($.23 billion). By comparison, the mean (median) total assets is $8.5 billion ($2.3 billion), and the mean (median) total stockholders' equity is $.44 billion ($.15 billion). It is interesting to note that market-related instruments are held in only 51 percent of BHC/quarters, while credit-related instruments are held in almost all BHC/quarters.

Table 2 presents the descriptive statistics for the variables in the empirical models developed in section 3. Similar to Barth (1994), the market value of equity tended to exceed the book value for these BHCs during the sample period. The relatively low values for MKTBETA are similar to those reported by Brewer and Lee (1986). Panels A and B of table 3 show the correlation between the variables in the accounting identity and Ohlson models, respectively. The deflated CROBS and MKTOBS are correlated. A potential consequence of this multicollinearity is that the variance of the OLS estimates may increase and make it difficult to determine the effect of these regressors on the dependent variable (Johnston 1984).

4.3 Fixed and Random Effects Models

The data is pooled across BHCs and time to investigate the relationship between OBS instruments and market value throughout the sample period. A pooled approach has the advantage of requiring interpretation of only a single regression rather than a series of regressions. However, nonspherical residuals that arise in either cross-sectional or time-series regressions can be a problem in a pooled model. Using ordinary least squares (OLS) may lead to inefficient estimates and biased standard errors. Judge et al. (1985) explained that fixed and random effects models can control for nonspherical residuals in pooled models. These models include intercepts for the j cross-sectional units and t time-series units to allow for differences between these additional intercepts and the overall intercept. They capture the impact of unobservable or unmeasurable effects that vary across firms or over time and reduce the potential for bias from correlated omitted variables (Dielman 1989). Fixed effects models assume that the additional intercepts are fixed parameters. By contrast, random effects models assume that the intercepts are random variables with a zero mean and

Table 3
Pearson Correlation Coefficients (n=3,388)[a]

Panel A: Accounting Identity Model

	1/BV	DIFSEC/BV	DIFLOAN/BV	CROBS/BV
1/BV				
DIFSEC/BV	-.27			
	(.00)			
DIFLOAN/BV	.77	-.26		
	(.00)	(.00)		
CROBS/BV	.22	-.12	.30	
	(.00)	(.00)	(.00)	
MKTOBS/BV	-.06	-.01	.04	.49
	(.00)	(.77)	(.01)	(.00)

Panel B: Ohlson Model

	1/BV	EARN/BV	GROWTH	MKTBETA	CROBS/BV
EARN/BV	.86				
	(.00)				
GROWTH	-.06	-.01			
	(.00)	(.47)			
MKTBETA	-.04	.01	-.01		
	(.02)	(.59)	(.62)		
CROBS/BV	.22	.26	-.10	.31	
	(.00)	(.00)	(.00)	(.00)	
MKTOBS/BV	-.06	-.05	-.07	.24	.49
	(.00)	(.00)	(.00)	(.00)	(.00)

[a]The numbers in parentheses are the p-values for the significance of the correlation between the variables.

an estimated variance.

The Breusch and Pagan Lagrange multiplier test and Hausman chi-squared test are used to compare the appropriateness of OLS, fixed effects, and random effects models given the econometric characteristics of the data (Greene (1992)). The estimated Breusch and Pagan Lagrange multiplier was significantly different from zero for these models at the p<.01 level. This result suggests that firm and/or period effects are not zero, and a random or fixed effects model is preferred to an OLS model. The Hausman chi-squared test was also significant at the p<.01 level. This finding suggests that the fixed effects model is preferred because the correlation between the random effects and the independent variables could bias the coefficient estimates. Thus, fixed effects estimation is used, requiring the inclusion of a separate dummy variable for each quarter and BHC.

4.4 Analysis of Credit-Related and Market-Related Instruments

The first columns in tables 4 and 5 report coefficient estimates for the accounting

Table 4
Accounting Identity Model: Results from Estimating Pooled Cross-Sectional Time-Series Model Using Two-Way Fixed Effects Estimation for the Full Sample, After Removing Outliers, and After Correcting for Autocorrelation (n=3,388)[a]

Variables[b]	Full Sample[c]	Outliers Removed[d]	Outliers Removed Auto. Cor.[e]
Degrees of Freedom	3,128	3,100	3,099
R^2 [f]	.75	.82	.88
β_0 1/BV	1642.33	6998.95	8052.76
	(1.85)*	(3.16)**	(8.66)**
β_1	1.24	1.26	1.24
	(11.55)**	(10.01)**	(13.30)**
β_2 DIFSEC/BV	.01	.03	.02
	(1.23)	(1.01)	(.70)
β_3 DIFLOAN/BV	-.07	-.59	-.55
	(-1.30)	(-10.59)**	(-16.22)**
β_{CR} CROBS/BV[g]	.05	.01	.02
	(1.82)*	(2.26)**	(4.00)**
β_{MKT} MKTOBS/BV	.01	.01	.01
	(3.49)**	(5.02)**	(5.29)**

$$\frac{MV_{j,t}}{BV_{j,t}} = \beta_0 \frac{1}{BV_{j,t}} + \beta_1 + \beta_2 \frac{DIFSEC_{j,t}}{BV_{j,t}} + \beta_3 \frac{DIFLOAN_{j,t}}{BV_{j,t}} + \beta_{CR} \frac{CROBS_{j,t}}{BV_{j,t}} + \beta_{MKT} \frac{MKTOBS_{j,t}}{BV_{j,t}} + \epsilon_{j,t}$$

[a] The coefficients are estimated using a two-way fixed model with data pooled across BHCs and time. The coefficients on the fixed effects variables are not presented.

[b] $MV_{j,t}$ number of shares outstanding times the price per share for BHC j at end of quarter t;

$BV_{j,t}$ stockholders' equity minus preferred stock for BHC j at time t;

$DIFSEC_{j,t}$ market value of securities minus book value of securities for BHC j at time t;

$DIFLOAN_{j,t}$ nonperforming loans plus loans 90 days or more past due but still accruing minus the allowance for loan losses for BHC j at time t;

$CROBS_{j,t}$ credit-related instruments (standbys+commercial letters+commitments) for BHC j at t;

$MKTOBS_{j,t}$ market-related instruments (net options+net futures+swaps) for BHC j at time t.

[c] t-statistics in parentheses. The t-statistics in the first and second columns are adjusted for heteroscedasticity using White's adjustment. ** indicates significantly different from zero at the p < .05 level (wo-tailed). * indicates significance at the p < .10 level (two-tailed).

[d] 28 observations with extreme values for studentized residuals, Cook's distance, or leverage are removed for the second and third columns.

[e] The third column adjusts for autocorrelation using the Yule-Walker method.

[f] Adjusted R-squared, first and second columns; total R-squared for the third column.

[g] The disclosures for the two categories of instruments are value-relevant if the β_{CR} and β_{MKT} coefficients are significantly different from zero.

identity and Ohlson model, respectively. Because the Breusch and Pagan test described in Johnston (1984) shows that heteroscedasticity of the residuals is a problem, the t-statistics are calculated using the White adjustment for heteroscedasticity.[14] Inspection of residual plots suggests that outliers may be a problem. Outliers are defined as observations with extreme values for studentized residuals, Cook's distance, or leverage. To ensure that the results are not driven by extreme values, the second column of these tables show the coefficient estimates after deleting the BHC/quarters defined as outliers according to any one of the three residual tests. Autocorrelation of residuals may lead to biased estimates of the standard errors as well as inefficient coefficient estimates. A Durbin-Watson test suggests that a fixed effects estimation of equations (5) and (6) reduces, but does not eliminate, the problem of autocorrelation. Consequently, the third column of these tables shows the coefficient estimates after using the Yule-Walker method to correct for this problem.[15]

CROBS and MKTOBS are significantly positively related to market values in the accounting identity model presented in table 4.[16] β_1 reflects the effect of book value and is also significant across estimation methods.[17] The coefficient on DIFLOAN is significantly negative as predicted after removing outliers and correcting for autocorrelation. However, the coefficient on DIFSEC is not significantly positive as predicted. This finding for DIFSEC is contrary to Barth (1994). Barth used data from annual reports, whereas this data was from Y-9s. The insignificance of the coefficients could be explained by the small difference between the market value and book value of securities for this sample; both the mean and median DIFSEC are zero.

---

[14]All of the t-statistics that are significant with the White's adjustment are also significant without the adjustment.

[15]The Yule-Walker method assumes that errors are generated by an autoregressive process. It is also known as a two-step full transform method where the OLS coefficients and autoregressive parameters are first determined and then generalized least squares is used to estimate the model by incorporating these parameters (SAS 1988). The autocorrelation correction increased the Durbin Watson statistic from .96 to 1.83 in table 4 and from 1 to 1.83 in table 5. Values close to 2 indicate that autocorrelation is not a significant problem.

[16]Because the value of put and call options as well as long and short futures are expected to offset one another, net options and net futures are used in the regressions. The results do not change significantly when put options, call options, long futures, and short futures are included as the gross rather than net amount in the MKTOBS variable.

[17]Barth (1994) did not include an overall intercept in her fixed effects model. The nature of the results for the CROBS and MKTOBS variables were not significantly affected by excluding the intercept.

Table 5
Ohlson Model: Results from Estimating Pooled Cross-Sectional Time-Series Model Using Two-Way Fixed Effects Estimation for the Full Sample, After Removing Outliers, and After Correcting for Autocorrelation (n=3,388)[a]

Variables[b]	Full Sample[c]	Outliers Removed[d]	Outliers Removed Auto. Cor.[e]
Degrees of Freedom	3,127	3,103	3,102
R^2 [f]	.75	.81	.87
β_0 1/BV	290.89	-559.56	1939.81
	(.30)	(-.96)	(4.96)**
β_1	1.21	1.14	1.20
	(11.27)**	(11.32)**	(14.01)**
β_4 EARN/BV	.08	.40	.14
	(1.41)	(6.31)**	(3.63)**
β_5 GROWTH	.32	.23	.03
	(3.28)**	(2.51)**	(.34)
β_6 MKTBETA	.03	.03	.01
	(2.30)**	(2.31)**	(.97)
β_{CR} CROBS/BV[g]	.06	.03	.03
	(1.87)*	(5.35)**	(6.35)**
β_{MKT} MKTOBS/BV	.01	.02	.01
	(3.69)**	(5.66)**	(7.28)**

$$\frac{MV_{j,t}}{BV_{j,t}} = \beta_0 \frac{1}{BV_{j,t}} + \beta_1 + \beta_4 \frac{EARN_{j,t}}{BV_{j,t}} + \beta_5 GROWTH_{j,t} + \beta_6 MKTBETA_{j,t} + \beta_{CR} \frac{CROBS_{j,t}}{BV_{j,t}} + \beta_{MKT} \frac{MKTOBS_{j,t}}{BV_{j,t}} + \epsilon_{j,t}$$

[a] The coefficients are estimated using a two-way fixed model with data pooled across BHCs and time. The coefficients on the fixed effects variables are not presented.

[b] $EARN_{j,t}$ = earnings before trading gains and losses for BHC j at time t; $GROWTH_{j,t}$ = percentage change in total assets over the previous four quarters for BHC j at time t; $MKTBETA_{j,t}$ = sensitivity of returns to value-weighted market index estimated concurrently with the sensitivity of returns to 30-year Treasury bond index (see footnote 11).

[c] t-statistics are reported in parentheses. The t-statistics in the first and second columns are adjusted for heteroscedasticity using White's adjustment. ** indicates the coefficients are significantly different from zero at the p < .05 level using two-tailed tests. * indicates significance at the p < .10 level using two-tailed tests.

[d] 24 observations with extreme values for studentized residuals, Cook's distance, or leverage are removed for the second and third columns.

[e] The third column adjusts for autocorrelation using the Yule-Walker method.

[f] The adjusted R-squared, first and second columns, total R-squared third column.

[g] The disclosures for the two categories of instruments are value-relevant if the β_{CR} and β_{MKT} coefficients are significantly different from zero.

The coefficients on CROBS and MKTOBS are also positive and significant when incorporated into the Ohlson model in table 5. EARN is significantly positively related to market value as predicted.[18] The coefficient on GROWTH is significantly positive as expected, except after correcting for autocorrelation. Apparently, the autocorrelation correction captures some of the explanatory power of the GROWTH measure.[19] Althoughtheory suggests that the sign on MKTBETA should be negative, it is positive. Beaver et al. (1989) also found a positive sign on a systematic risk variable and noted that this anomaly has been observed in previous research. The anomaly could be driven by measurement error in the risk variable from estimating a separate beta for every BHC and every quarter. Accordingly, one beta was estimated for each BHC using the entire sample period. The coefficient on MKTBETA was significantly negative as predicted, and the coefficients on CROBS and MKTOBS remained positive and significant. However, this alternative specification of the risk variable was not used in the final model because it violates an implicit assumption of two-way fixed effects regressions that there is a unique observation for every firm and quarter. However, this specification demonstrated that the significance of CROBS and MKTOBS does not appear to be driven by misspecification of the risk variable.[20]

In the regressions reported in tables 4 and 5, market value is measured at the end of the quarter. This approach assumes that analysts are closely monitoring financial institutions and are able to impound the Y-9 information at the report date. This is a reasonable approach widely used in the previous literature (Landsman 1986; Shevlin 1991; Kane and Unal 1990). However, it could be argued that investors have no way of impounding the information until it is formally released. Therefore, two additional dates are used to measure market values. The first alternative is 45 days after the report date, the due date for filing Y-9s with the Federal Reserve (Board of Governors 1986). The second alternative is three months after the

---

[18]Given Ohlson's model, abnormal earnings was also used as a proxy for EARN. Abnormal earnings was defined as earnings minus lagged book value times the firm's discount rate defined according to the Capital Asset Pricing Model. The abnormal earnings proxy was not generally significant and did not change the nature of the OBS results.

[19]For the third and fourth quarter of 1986 and the first quarter of 1987 GROWTH is measured as the percentage change from the second quarter in 1986. GROWTH was also measured as the percentage change for the previous eight quarters where possible. This specification did not change the nature of the OBS results.

[20]The coefficients on CROBS and MKTOBS are also significantly positive either when estimating a combined model that includes all of the control variables from both models or when none of the control variables are included.

report date, the standard period of time allowed in market-based research to ensure that information is publicly available. The regression equations were estimated for these two alternative dates after removing outliers and correcting for heteroscedasticity or autocorrelation. Credit-related and market-related instruments are significantly positively related to market values for these alternative valuation dates using both valuation models. The R^2s for these alternative regressions, which range from .75 to .82 do not differ significantly from those reported in tables 4 and 5. Therefore, the results do not appear to be especially sensitive to alternative valuation dates.

The reported regressions constrain the coefficients to be the same across instruments within the credit-related and market-related categories. This constraint was relaxed, and the models were estimated by including the six individual instruments as variables. The disclosures for commitments and swaps were positive and significantly related to the market value of equity, while the four other instrument disclosures were not generally significant. This finding is not surprising given that commitments and swaps are the largest OBS instrument variables with the most variability. In other words, the signal-to-noise ratio is larger with these two instruments. A t-test showed that the coefficients are not the same on the individual instruments within the credit-related or market-related categories. Thus, the models were also estimated when including only commitments and swaps. These regressions showed that the coefficients on commitments were very similar to the coefficients on credit-related instruments in tables 4 and 5, and the coefficients on swaps were very similar to those on market-related instruments. These findings suggest that the primary explanatory power for credit-related instruments comes from commitments, while the primary explanatory power for market-related instruments comes from swaps. The paper focuses on the results when the six instruments are combined into categories because it prevents excluding information captured by the four variables with less explanatory power (i.e., standbys, commercial letters, futures, and options). Combining the instruments into categories does not bias the conclusions that can be drawn from the analysis because the paper is designed to test whether the notional value disclosures are helpful in explaining the market value of equity, rather than to test for differences in the explanatory power across instruments.[21]

---

[21]There are several other advantages to combining the instruments into categories. First, the categorization of credit-related and market-related instruments makes sense economically because of the similarities of the instruments within categories and the differences in instruments across categories. Second, when estimating the models with individual instruments, eigenanalysis suggested by Belsley, Kuh, and Welsch (Johnston 1984) shows that the standby and commitment coefficients may be adversely affected by multicollinearity. Multicollinearity is of concern because it can make the coefficient estimates unstable (Johnston 1984). Combining the instruments into credit-related versus market-related categories helps to correct for this problem. Most of the high correlations between instruments are for

It appears that the notional value of credit-related and market-related instruments provide relevant information about the market value of equity. The coefficients on the OBS instruments are, as expected, much less than one, indicating that instrument values are less than the principal or par value amounts disclosed in the Y-9s. The disclosures are positively associated with the market value of equity. This suggests that the extent of involvement in these instruments as captured in the notional values is relevant in explaining market values. In particular, the positive coefficients on CROBS suggest that the OBS value or the present value of future fees and interest generated from these instruments and not yet reflected in the financial statements is greater than the estimated future losses from the contingent obligations that will be assumed. The positive coefficient on MKTOBS suggests that involvement in these instruments are perceived to enhance the value of the firm in ways not already reflected on the financial statements.

The regression coefficients provide an approximation of the value associated with these instruments.[22] The .03 coefficient on CROBS suggests that, on average, the incremental OBS value associated with these instruments is $37.44 million. The .01 coefficient on MKTOBS suggests that the incremental value associated with these instruments is $5.25 million. Thus, on average, these instruments together contribute approximately 8 percent of a BHC's total market value.

4.5 Analysis of Credit Risk and Interest Rate Risk

This section examines the effect of credit risk and interest rate risk on the value of the instruments. Table 6 shows the results from estimating equation (8). The negative β_{CRDUM} coefficients in panels A and B are consistent with the hypothesis that the valuation of credit-related instruments is negatively related to credit risk exposure. Thus, investors perceive that credit-related instruments decrease in value as credit risk increases because of

---

instruments within these two categories; thus, this approach effectively reduces the number of correlated variables in the model. Third, the analysis of the effect of credit risk and interest rate risk on the coefficients would be difficult to interpret when looking at the interaction of risk variables with six different instruments.

[22]The contribution of each instrument to market value was estimated as the coefficient times the mean value of the deflated variable times the mean value of the book value deflator for the sample after removing outliers. Thus, the commitment amount was estimated as .03 (CROBS coefficient from table 5) times 2.83 (mean CROBS/BV) times $441 million (mean BV). This MKTOBS amount was calculated as .01 (MKTOBS coefficient from table 5) times 1.19 (mean MKTOBS/BV) times $441 million (mean BV). The total value added of $42.69 million is 8 percent of the mean equity market value of $546 million. These approximations could be biased by the effect of correlated omitted variables on the coefficients.

Table 6
Effect of Credit Risk and Interest Rate Risk on Valuation of OBS Disclosures: Results from Estimating
Pooled Cross-Sectional Time-Series Model Using Two-Way Fixed Effects Estimation After Removing
Outliers (n=3,362)[a]

Panel A: Accounting Identity Model

$$\frac{MV_{j,t}}{BV_{j,t}} = \beta_0 \frac{1}{BV_{j,t}} + \beta_1 + \beta_2 \frac{DIFSEC_{j,t}}{BV_{j,t}} + \beta_3 \frac{DIFLOAN_{j,t}}{BV_{j,t}}$$

$$+\beta_{CR} \frac{CROBS_{j,t}}{BV_{j,t}} + \beta_{MKT} \frac{MKTOBS_{j,t}}{BV_{j,t}} + \beta_{CRDUM} \frac{CROBS_{j,t}*CRDUM_{j,t}}{BV_{j,t}}$$

$$+ \beta_{IRDUM} \frac{MKTOBS_{j,t}*IRDUM_{j,t}}{BV_{j,t}} + \epsilon_{j,t}$$

Degrees of Freedom = 3,098 $R^2 = .82$

β_0	β_1	β_2	β_3	β_{CR}	β_{MKT}	β_{CRDUM}[b]	β_{IRDUM}
7065.16	1.27	.02	-.59	.06	.01	-.06	.00
(3.18)**	(10.00)**	(1.00)	(-10.60)**	(4.26)**	(2.25)**	(-3.71)**	(.85)

Panel B: Ohlson Model

$$\frac{MV_{j,t}}{BV_{j,t}} = \beta_0 \frac{1}{BV_{j,t}} + \beta_1 + \beta_4 \frac{EARN_{j,t}}{BV_{j,t}} + \beta_5 \ GROWTH_{j,t} + \beta_6 \ MKTBETA_{j,t}$$

$$+\beta_{CR} \frac{CROBS_{j,t}}{BV_{j,t}} + \beta_{MKT} \frac{MKTOBS_{j,t}}{BV_{j,t}} + \beta_{CRDUM} \frac{CROBS_{j,t}*CRDUM_{j,t}}{BV_{j,t}}$$

$$+ \beta_{IRDUM} \frac{MKTOBS_{j,t}*IRDUM_{j,t}}{BV_{j,t}} + \epsilon_{j,t}$$

Degrees of Freedom = 3,101 $R^2 = .81$

β_0	β_1	β_4	β_5	β_6	β_{CR}	β_{MKT}	β_{CRDUM}	β_{IRDUM}
-497.84	1.14	.40	.22	.02	.06	.01	-.04	.01
(-.86)	(11.35)**	(6.39)**	(2.50)**	(2.15)**	(4.26)**	(2.46)**	(-2.55)**	(3.29)**

[a]The coefficients are estimated using a two-way fixed model with data pooled across BHCs and time.
The coefficients on the fixed effects variables are not presented. 28 (24) observations with extreme
values for studentized residuals, Cook's distance, or leverage are removed in panel A (B). Adjusted R-
squared is reported. t-statistics reported in parentheses. t-statistics are adjusted for heteroscedasticity
using White's adjustment. ** indicates that the coefficients are significantly different from zero at the
$p < .05$ level using two-tailed tests. * indicates significance at the $p < .10$ level using two-tailed tests.

$CRDUM_{j,t}$ 1 if BHC is in the upper half of credit risk in the sample, defined as average
                nonaccruing and past due loans divided by book value, zero otherwise.

$IRDUM_{j,t}$ 1 if BHC is in the upper half of interest rate risk in the sample defined as sensitivity
                of returns to interest rate movements using the two-index market model (see
                footnote 11), zero otherwise.

[b]Negative coefficient on β_{CRDUM} suggests that as credit risk increases, the OBS value of the credit-
related instruments decrease. Positive coefficient on β_{IRDUM} suggests the OBS value of market-related
instruments is higher for nonhedging banks with higher interest rate risk.

the increased potential for realizing losses from the instruments. In other words, investors appear to incorporate the credit risk associated with credit-related instruments into estimates of equity values.[23]

The β_{IRDUM} coefficient is not significant in the accounting identity model reported in panel A, but it is significant in the Ohlson model reported in panel B. This provides some mixed evidence that a relationship does exist between the valuation of market-related instruments and risk exposure. The positive β_{IRDUM} coefficient in panel B suggests that nonhedgers realize more incremental value from market-related instruments than hedgers. This result is anticipated because the future expected gains (losses) from market-related instruments used primarily for hedging activity will offset the expected losses (gains) from on-balance-sheet items; thus, the associated coefficient on the variables will be smaller for hedgers with low interest rate risk. By contrast, market-related instruments for banks that are nonhedgers with high interest rate risk will tend to use the instruments more extensively to generate fees and trading gains that will lead to more future expected incremental cash flows; thus, the valuation coefficient will also be larger for nonhedgers. The mixed results could also be driven by the fact that nonhedgers may have lower value because the risk of their earnings is higher. Thus, if the higher value nonhedgers realize from using these instruments to generate future expected gains is offset by the lower value nonhedgers experience because of riskier earnings, then there may not be a discernable relationship between the valuation of these instruments and hedging strategies. Further, since the results are not significant for the accounting identity model that directly controls for credit risk, it may suggest that interest rate risk does not add incremental information about the value of market-related instruments after controlling for credit risk.

5. CONCLUSIONS

The research uses notional values as a proxy for the OBS value of the financial instruments. The evidence demonstrates that the notional value disclosures for credit-related and market-related instruments are value-relevant. The positive relationship between the market value of equity and the disclosures indicates that the OBS value or expected future cash flows associated with these instruments not yet reflected in the financial statements are positive. This inference remains relatively consistent using two valuation models, after dealing with the econometric problems, and using alternative valuation dates. Also, the value

---

[23]The results are similar when CRDUM is defined using nonaccruing and past due loans divided by total assets.

of credit-related instruments falls for those BHCs with higher levels of credit risk exposure. As credit risk increases, the expected losses associated with instruments increase; therefore, the net value of the instruments declines. Although some evidence is presented that the value of market-related instruments are more positive for nonhedgers with higher interest rate risk, the empirical results are mixed.

The evidence presented suggests that notional values are informative in explaining equity market values during a period before other disclosures were available for these instruments. Finding that the OBS value of these instruments is helpful in explaining the divergence between the market value and book value of equity motivates a closer examination of the recognition issues for these items. This research suggests that more complete recognition of the value of these instruments in the financial statements would tie market value of equity more closely to book value.[24] Finally, the research suggests that these instruments are positively associated with the value of BHCs. A great deal of concern has been expressed about the risk of loss associated with these instruments. While investors appear to take risk exposure into account when estimating the OBS values of these instruments, on average, investors believe that BHCs will be adequately compensated for any risk they assume. A possible extension of this research could determine if investors' perceptions of the value of these instruments have changed over time as they have learned more about the potential risk of loss.

---

[24]This research does not normatively suggest, however, that regulators should pursue the goal of matching market value with book value.

REFERENCES

Amir, E., 1993, The Market Valuation of Accounting Information: The Case of Postretirement Benefits Other than Pensions. *The Accounting Review* 68 (October), 703-724.

Andrews, S., and H. Sender, 1986, Off Balance Sheet Risk: Where is it Leading the Banks? *Institutional Investor* (January), 75-84.

Barth, M. E., 1991. Relative Measurement Errors Among Alternative Pension Asset and Liability Measures, *The Accounting Review* 66 (July), 433-463.

Barth, M. E., 1994, Fair Value Accounting: Evidence from Investment Securities and the Market Valuation of Banks, *The Accounting Review* 69 (January), 1-25.

Barth, M. E., W. H. Beaver, and C. H. Stinson, 1991, Supplemental Data and the Structure of Thrift Share Prices, *The Accounting Review* 66 (January), 56-66.

Barth, M. E., W. H. Beaver, and W. R. Landsman, 1994, Value-Relevance of Banks' Fair Value Disclosures under SFAS 107, Working paper, Harvard Business School, Boston, MA.

Beaver, W. H., C. Eger, S. Ryan, and M. Wolfson, 1989, Financial Reporting, Supplemental Disclosures, and Bank Share Prices, *Journal of Accounting Research* 27 (Autumn), 157-178.

Beaver, W. H. and S. Ryan, 1993, The Accounting Fundamentals of the Book-to Market Ratio, *Financial Analysts Journal* 49 (November/December), 50-56.

Bernard, V. L., 1989, Capital Markets Research in Accounting During the 1980's: A Critical Review, In *The State of Accounting Research as We Enter the 1990's*, ed. T. Frecka, 72-120, Champaign, IL, University of Illinois.

Board of Governors of the Federal Reserve System, 1986, *Instructions for Preparation of Consolidated Financial Statements for Bank Holding Companies with Total Consolidated Assets of $150 Million or More or with More than One Subsidiary Bank Reporting Form FR Y-9 C*, Washington, D. C., GPO.

Brennan, M. J., 1991, A Perspective on Accounting and Stock Prices, *The Accounting Review* 66 (January), 67-79.

Brewer, E., and C. F. Lee, 1986, The Impact of Market, Industry, and Interest Rate Risks on Bank Stock Returns, Staff Memoranda 86-4, Federal Reserve Bank of Chicago.

Christie, A., 1987, On Cross-Sectional Analysis in Accounting Research, *Journal of Accounting and Economics* 9 (3), 231-258.

Citizens Banking Corp. 1993, Annual Report.

Dielman, T. E., 1989, *Pooled Cross-Sectional and Time Series Data Analysis*. New York, Marcel Dekker.

Eccher, E. A., K. Ramesh., and S. Ramu Thiagarajan, 1995. Fair Value Disclosures by Bank Holding Companies, Working paper, Northwestern University, Evanston, IL.

Feltham, G. A., and J. A. Ohlson. 1993, Valuation and Clean Surplus Accounting for Operational and Financial Activities, Working paper, University of British Columbia, Vancouver, BC.

Financial Accounting Standards Board, 1978, *Statement of Financial Accounting Concepts No. 1: Objectives of Financial Reporting by Business Enterprises*, Stamford, CT, FASB.

Financial Accounting Standards Board, 1986, *Statement of Financial Accounting Standards No. 91: Accounting for Nonrefundable Fees and Costs Associated with Originating or Acquiring Loans and Initial Direct Costs of Leases*, Stamford, CT, FASB.

Financial Accounting Standards Board, 1990, *Statement of Financial Accounting Standards No. 105: Disclosure of Information about Financial Instruments with Off-Balance Sheet Risk and Financial Instruments with Concentrations of Credit Risk*, Stamford, CT, FASB.

Financial Accounting Standards Board, 1991a, *Statement of Financial Accounting Standards No. 107: Disclosures about Fair Values of Financial Instruments*, Stamford, CT, FASB.

Financial Accounting Standards Board, 1991b, *Prospectus: Research on Disclosure*, Stamford, CT, FASB.

Financial Accounting Standards Board, 1994, *Statement of Financial Accounting Standards No. 119: Disclosure about Derivative Financial Instruments and Fair Value of Financial Instruments*, Stamford, CT, FASB.

Flannery, M. J., and C. M. James, 1984a, The Effects of Interest Rate Changes on Common Stock Returns of Financial Institutions, *The Journal of Finance* (September), 1141-1153.

Flannery, M. J., and C. M. James, 1984b, Market Evidence on the Effective Maturity of Bank Assets and Liabilities, *Journal of Money, Credit, and Banking* (November), 435-445.

Greene, W. H., 1992, *Limdep User's Manual and Reference Guide*, Bellport, NY, Econometric Software, Inc.

Harris, T. S., and J. A. Ohlson, 1987, Accounting Disclosures and the Market's Valuation of Oil and Gas Properties, *The Accounting Review* 62 (October), 651-670.

Judge, G. G., W. E. Griffiths, R. C. Hill, H. Lutkepohl, and T. Lee, 1985, *The Theory and Practice of Econometrics*, 2d ed. New York, Wiley.

Johnston, J., 1984, *Econometric Methods*, 3d ed. New York, McGraw-Hill.

Kallapur, S., and M. A. Trombley, 1994, The Association Between Realized Growth and Investment Opportunity Set Proxies, Working paper, University of Arizona, Tucson, AZ.

Kane, E. J., and H. Unal, 1990, Modeling Structural and Temporal Variation in the Market's Valuation of Banking Firms, *The Journal of Finance* (March), 113-136.

Landsman, W. R., 1986, An Empirical Investigation of Pension Fund Property Rights, *The Accounting Review* 61 (October), 662-691.

Landsman, W. R., and J. Magliolo, 1988, Cross-Sectional Capital Market Research and Model Specification, *The Accounting Review* 63 (October), 586-604.

Litzenberger R., and C. Rao, 1971, Estimates of the Marginal Rate of Time Preferences and Average Risk Aversion of Investors in Electric Utility Shares, 1960-66, *Bell Journal of Economics and Management Science* (Autumn), 503-514.

Melnik, A., and S. Plaut, 1986, Loan Commitment Contracts, Terms of Lending, and Credit Allocation, *The Journal of Finance* (June), 425-435.

Ohlson, J. A., 1993, Earnings, Book Values, and Dividends in Security Valuation, Working paper, Columbia University, New York.

Ou, J. A., and S. H. Penman, 1993, Financial Statement Analysis and the Evaluation of Market-to-Book Ratios, Working paper, University of California at Berkeley, Berkeley, CA.

Risk., 1994, Notions about Notionals, 7 (March).

SAS/ETS User's Guide. 1988, 6th ed, Cary, NC, SAS Institute, Inc.

Scholes, M., and J. Williams, 1977, Estimating Betas from Nonsynchronous Data, *Journal of Financial Economics*, 309-327.

Shevlin, T., 1991, The Valuation of R&D Firms with R&D Limited Partnerships, *The Accounting Review* 66 (January), 1-21.

Sinkey, J. F., Jr. 1989, *Commercial Bank Financial Management in the Financial Industry*, 3d ed, New York, Macmillan.

Smith, R., and S. Lipin, 1994, Beleaguered Giant: As Derivatives Losses Rise, Industry Fights to Avert Regulation, *Wall Street Journal* (August 25), A1.

Sougiannis, T., 1994, The Accounting Based Valuation of Corporate R&D, *The Accounting Review* 69 (January), 44-68.

Venkatachalam, M. 1995. Value Relevance of Banks' Derivative Disclosures, Working paper, University of Iowa, Iowa City, Iowa (January), 44-68.

Wahlen, J., 1994, The Nature of Information in Commercial Bank Loan Loss Disclosures, *The Accounting Review* 69 (July), 455-478.

Derivatives, Regulation and Banking
Edited by B. Schachter
1997 Elsevier Science B.V.

Chapter 5
SOURCES OF BANK FOREIGN EXCHANGE TRADING PROFITS:
TAKING POSITIONS OR MAKING MARKETS?

John Ammer and Allan D. Brunner[†]

Board of Governors of the Federal Reserve System, Washington, DC USA

1. INTRODUCTION

Over the past several years, foreign exchange trading profits of U.S. commercial banks have increased sharply. In this paper, we examine the sources of these profits for seven of the largest foreign exchange players among U.S. commercial banks. As shown in Figure 1, foreign trading profits for these institutions grew at a 17 percent annual rate between 1984 and 1993. These profits accounted for about 60 percent of all trading profits for those years and about 20 percent of total bank earnings. These trends have led many observers to question the sources of these profits: Were these revenues the result of banks taking profitable positions in currency markets? Or, were they derived from an increasing demand for banks' intermediation services?

The answer to this question has several important implications for economic theory and for investors in bank equities. First, if positions were a major source of profits, it would imply a failure of several forms of the efficient market hypothesis (EMH). As stated by Malkiel (1987), the semi-strong form of the EMH asserts that all publicly available information relevant to a particular exchange rate must be fully incorporated in the market rate, while the strong form further requires that the market rate include all information known

[†]Both authors are staff economists in the International Finance Division. Opinions expressed herein do not necessarily coincide with those held by Board of Governors or any other employees of the Federal Reserve System. We thank David Bowman, Hali Edison, Allen Frankel, Kausar Hamdani, Michael Leahy, Michael Martinson, Michael O'Connor, Larry Promisel, and Ted Truman for helpful comments. We also thank Don Adams, Mike Cicerone, Lauren Hargraves, Michael O'Connor, Mike Perozek, Doug Thomas, and Leeto Tlou for assistance with the data. The authors are solely responsible for any errors.

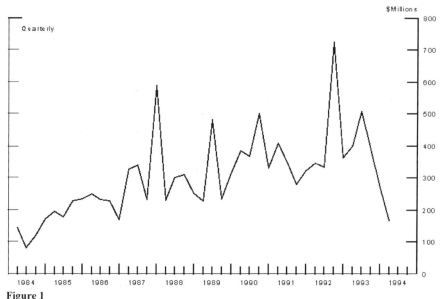

Figure 1
Foreign Exchange Trading Revenues of Seven U. S. Commercial Banks

to any market participant. Therefore, these versions of the EMH rule out the possibility that banks may have earned abnormal economic profits from taking positions in foreign exchange. Although the general tenets of the EMH are widely accepted on theoretical grounds, a few recent empirical studies have found evidence that some professional portfolio managers may be able to persistently outperform market benchmarks.[1]

Second, the source of foreign exchange trading profits also has implications for the sustainability of earnings. Although the persistence of intermediation earnings depends on aggregate volume, market share, and either bid-ask spreads (for generic instruments) or mark-ups (for customized products), they likely have longer-lasting effects on the bottom line than do profits from positions that may have been merely a temporary windfall. Equity securities of large U.S. commercial banks tended to trade in the early 1990s at significantly lower multiples of current earnings than the U.S. stock market as a whole, suggesting that

---

[1]For example, see Grinblatt and Titman (1992).

investors were relatively pessimistic about the likely stream of future bank earnings.[2] Moreover, articles in the popular financial press reported some misgivings on the part of investors concerning bank trading activities, indicating that at least part of the weakness in bank stock prices in the early 1990s can be attributed to investors' concerns regarding the sustainability of trading profits.[3]

Finally, the source of trading profits has implications for the variability of earnings and, consequently, for the riskiness of bank capital. It is possible that banks are devoting significant resources to proprietary trading activities without appropriate increases in economic profits. Such circumstances would tend to increase the volatility of earnings and possibly reduce the value of the banking firm.[4]

In this paper, we examine four possible sources of foreign exchange trading profits -- outright positions in spot and forward exchange contracts, outright positions in derivative securities, market-making services in spot and forward exchange contracts, and market-making services in derivative securities. The first two sources are associated with position-taking activity, and the last two sources are related to intermediation. We take several approaches to identify which sources can account for foreign exchange trading profits. We first test whether banks' foreign exchange positions predict future changes in exchange rates, which is a necessary condition for banks to generate position-taking profits (section 4). We then undertake some direct calculations of intermediation profits using available spread and volume data on spot and forward contracts (section 5). Finally, we indirectly examine whether these sources can actually account for observed bank earnings by regressing bank profits on data proxies for each of the four possible sources of foreign exchange profits (section 6).

On balance, our results are consistent with the efficient markets hypothesis. That is, our evidence does not support the notion that position-taking was, on average, a major source of foreign exchange trading earnings for the banks in our sample. To the extent that these

---

[2] Based on information extracted from the Value Line Investment Survey, we found that for the period 1990-1994, the average P/E ratio for the ten largest U.S. commercial bank players in foreign exchange markets was about 60 percent of the average P/E ratio for the U.S. stock market as a whole.

[3] See, for example, The Economist, April 10, 1993.

[4] Azarchs (1994) found that the trading income of a few large U.S. institutions accounted for less of the variance of total earnings than their did traditional lines of business. However, without accounting for the relative magnitude of the two activities, one cannot determine from these which activity tends to produce more volatile earnings.

earnings are derived from *conventional* market-making, they ought to be fairly stable and persistent over time. However, if *volatility-related* intermediation services are an important component of profits, the outlook is somewhat less clear. Foreign exchange option products are still relatively new, and the competitive structure of these markets may still be rapidly evolving.

2. SOURCES OF FOREIGN EXCHANGE REVENUES

For the purposes of this paper, we assume that banks' foreign exchange trading profits are derived from four identifiable sources. Banks could profit from outright positions (long or short) either in exchange rates themselves via spot and forward foreign exchange contracts or in the *second* moments of exchange rates (volatility) through derivative securities. For example, if a bank has a short yen position over a period during which the yen depreciates against the dollar, then the bank profits from its yen position.[5]

Note that it is also possible for a bank to take a position in the volatility of a currency while maintaining a zero position in the level of the currency. Suppose a bank writes (sells) both put and call options on the Swiss franc. The sold puts constitute a long position in the franc, and the sold calls are a short position. It is possible for the bank to arrange for these two holdings to balance to a net zero exposure to the level of the $/SFr exchange rate (although maintaining the neutral position over time would require dynamic hedging). Nevertheless, the bank is taking a short position in the volatility of the dollar-franc exchange rate, because the value of both the put and the call options are increasing in the volatility of the underlying assets. Ceteris paribus, this bank would profit from a decrease in volatility.

In addition, banks can profit from providing market-making services to their customers by intermediating in either spot and forward foreign exchange markets or in volatility-related markets, including the sale of customized derivative products. For example, if a bank stands ready to buy British pounds at $1.6415 and sell them at $1.6425, it will earn $1,000 from each "round trip" transaction (given a contract size of one million pounds). Similarly, a bank may profit from selling an option to a customer, if it can hedge its

---

[5]This conclusion ignores the complication that the bank is a net payer of yen interest and a net receiver of dollar interest over the period in question. If Japanese interest rates sufficiently exceeded U.S. interest rates over the period in question, a short yen position could be a losing position even if the yen depreciates. Because of data constraints that are mentioned below, we will not consider the effects of differentials between domestic and foreign interest rates.

consequent exposure at a lower cost than the option premium.

Let $\pi_{b,t+1}$ denote the trading profits earned by bank "b" between time t and t+1. The four components can be written as:

$$\pi_{b,t+1} = \sum_{c=1}^{C} \Delta e_{c,t+1} \cdot N_{bc,t} + \sum_{c=1}^{C} \frac{1}{2} \cdot S_{c,t+1} \cdot Q_{bc,t+1}$$
$$+ \sum_{c=1}^{C} \Delta \rho_{c,t+1} \cdot NV_{bc,t} + \sum_{c=1}^{C} \frac{1}{2} \cdot SV_{c,t+1} \cdot QV_{bc,t+1} \tag{1}$$

where $\Delta e_{c,t+1}$ denotes the change in the exchange rate of the US\$ relative to currency "c" between time t and t+1; $N_{bc,t}$ is the net position taken by bank b at time t in currency c; $S_{c,t+1}$ represents the average bid-ask spread for currency c between t and t+1; $Q_{bc,t+1}$ denotes the volume of spot and forward foreign exchange trades in currency c by bank b with customer counterparties; $\Delta \rho_{c,t+1}$ denotes the change in value of a unit position in volatility for currency "c" between time t and t+1; $NV_{bc,t}$ is the net position in volatility by bank b in currency c; $SV_{c,t+1}$ represents the average rate of profit for volatility-related intermediation in currency c between t and t+1; and $QV_{bc,t+1}$ denotes the volume of volatility-related activity by bank b for currency c.

If sufficiently high frequency data (i.e., transactions level) were available for all components in equation (1), it would be a straightforward accounting exercise to determine the proportion of bank trading profits that fell into each of our four categories. We will have to make do with lower frequency data and proxies for some of the variables. The next section of the paper describes survey data that regulatory institutions have collected on banks' trading positions.

3. SURVEY DATA ON BANK PORTFOLIO POSITIONS

Our empirical analysis uses survey data that has been collected by federal agencies.[6] Since 1990, federal financial regulators have required banks that undertake a significant volume of trading in foreign exchange and related instruments to file FFIEC form number 035, a fairly comprehensive monthly report on foreign currency portfolio positions.[7]

---

[6] These data are also examined in the next chapter by Michael Leahy, "Bank Positions and Forecasts of Exchange Rate Movements".

[7] Generally banks that have had gross foreign exchange trading volume of at least \$1 billion in the most recent third quarter are required to file the 035 report. Other banks with "significant

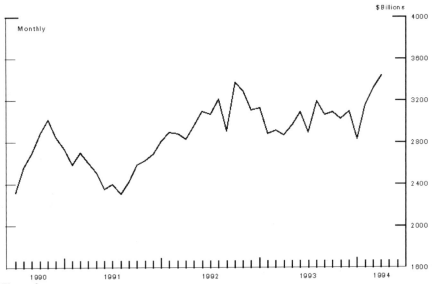

Figure 2
Gross Foreign Currency Dealing Activity
(spot, forward, and futures contracts in six currencies)

Respondents to this survey report details of their foreign exchange trading positions, including their gross open (i.e., unsettled) foreign exchange contracts (spot, forward, and futures) and their "net dealing position" in each of six major foreign currencies -- Deutsche marks, yen, sterling, Swiss francs, Canadian dollars, and Australian dollars.[8] The gross futures positions are reported separately, but forward and spot positions are lumped together as a single category. This last feature of the data is unfortunate, because it makes it

foreign exchange activities" may be specifically requested to file the 035 report by their primary federal regulator.

[8]Through 1992, the survey applied to close of business on the second Wednesday of the month. Since the beginning of 1993, it has been on a month-end basis. The net dealing position is the "actively managed" position in the currency that is used for internal risk monitoring of the bank's traders. This figure would generally account for Euro-deposits and derivatives positions as well as unsettled spot and forward currency commitments. The implicit underlying concept of this measure is the exposure of the bank to exchange rate fluctuations as a consequence of positions taken by its traders.

impossible to determine the contribution of interest rate differentials to profits. For example, suppose a bank has a net short position in yen of $10 million. This position might be comprised, in part, of a $20 million short position in forward yen. In this case, the bank would likely be earning (positive) net income on yen-denominated assets. Alternatively, the forward yen position might be neutral, in which case the bank would probably be a net payer of yen interest.

There are also some data on options positions. For each currency, the banks report the number of call options purchased, the number of calls written, the number of put options purchased, and the number of puts written. In addition, banks are asked to provide the consequent ("delta equivalent") position in each currency as a result of options contracts. However, no information is requested in the survey about the strike prices or the maturities of the options in the respondent bank's portfolio.

From among the respondents to the 035 survey, data limitations led us to focus on seven banks (henceforth, Banks A through G). Each of these banks was among the ten U.S. banks with the highest level of foreign exchange trading activity in April 1992, according to a joint central bank survey. Figure 2 depicts the gross positions (both long and short) for our sample of seven banks in unsettled spot, forward, and futures transactions in the aggregate of the six major currencies mentioned above. This rough measure of market activity (which may include long-term forward contracts entered into in previous years) has risen by about half since the summer of 1991 to approximately $3-1/2 trillion. The path of this variable over the past three years suggests that it is positively correlated with both domestic and foreign business cycles.

Figure 3 shows the aggregate of the net foreign currency dealing positions of these banks in the above-mentioned currencies expressed as a percentage of the aggregate gross position. The fact that the magnitude of this ratio has never exceeded 0.2 percent — so that open long positions are almost exactly balanced by open short positions — suggests that the scope of the banks' intermediation operations vastly exceeds that of their position-taking activities, at least to the extent that positions are held overnight.[9] It is also worth pointing out that the net foreign currency position of these banks has sometimes been short in the aggregate. As shown in Figure 4, these banks often had short positions in the Deutsche mark and Swiss franc which were offset by long positions in the yen and Australian dollar.

---

[9]This inference is further supported by the fact that the magnitude of this net-gross ratio is also consistently very small for individual bank positions in each currency. However, the need to respect the confidentiality of the individual banks' 035 responses precludes us from showing this ratio on a disaggregated basis.

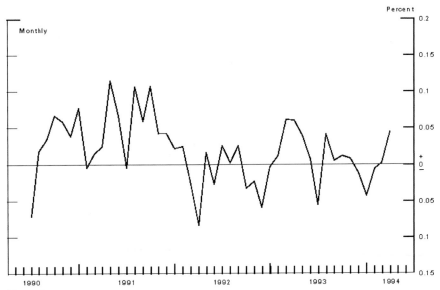

Figure 3
Net Foreign Currency Dealing Position
(as a percentage of dealing activity in six currencies)

To our surprise, the net dealing positions of the seven banks in our sample seem to be somewhat persistent over time, although they do appear to be mean-reverting. Table 1 shows that the first-order autocorrelations of the reported bank positions are nearly always positive, are positive with 95 percent confidence in 24 out of 42 cases, and run as high as 0.89.[10] For six of the seven banks, the total bank position exhibits a positive first-order autocorrelation significant at the 95 percent level. The results in Table 1 suggest that at least some of the positions are being taken with a view as to how markets will move over several weeks or more. This implication is puzzling, given that one would expect any advantage that traders might have in forecasting to be for shorter horizons associated with private information about order flow and market liquidity.[11] Similar time series properties are evident in a short span of daily net position data available for one of the banks.

---

[10]Again, autocorrelations for bank positions in individual currencies have been suppressed because the position data are confidential.

[11]Of course, it may be the case that most of the positions taken by these banks are unwound within the trading day. The 035 data give no hint of the typical magnitudes of intraday positions.

Table 1
First-order Autocorrelations of Foreign Exchange Positions, June 1990 - March 1994 summary of results by bank for 6 currencies

	Bank A	Bank B	Bank C	Bank D	Bank E	Bank F	Bank G
number positive	6	4	6	5	6	6	6
with 95% confidence	3	2	4	3	2	6	4
number negative	0	2	0	1	0	0	0
with 95% confidence	0	0	0	0	0	0	0
maximum estimate[a]	0.89	0.45	0.51	0.49	0.41	0.88	0.64
total position[a]	0.68	0.36	0.30	0.33	0.23	0.68	0.36

[a]Underlined coefficients are significant at the 95 percent confidence level.

4. FOREIGN CURRENCY POSITIONS AND ASSOCIATED PROFITS

If banks have some ability to forecast future changes in exchange rates, then they ought to be able to earn significant profits by actively seeking long and short positions in foreign currencies. That is, any predictive powers would be reflected in their foreign exchange positions. For example, one would expect a bank to be long in yen if it was forecasting a yen appreciation in the near future. Conversely, without any forecasting ability, they should reap zero profits, on average, from taking positions. In this case, banks' foreign exchange positions should have no predictive power for future exchange rate movements.

In this section, we explore this possibility using net dealing position data from the 035 survey. Figure 5 shows the total net position of the banks along with a trade-weighted index of the exchange value of the U.S. dollar. If the banks are typically taking what turn out to be profitable positions in foreign currencies, one would expect short positions to be followed by dollar appreciation and long positions to presage depreciation. It is difficult to discern such a pattern from the figure.

We pursue the question of whether positions predict exchange rates somewhat more systematically by estimating the following regression equation:

$$\Delta e_{c,t+1} = \mu_{bc} + \psi_{bc} N_{bc,t} + \epsilon_{bc,t+1} \tag{2}$$

for each bank (b) and currency (c). Here, Δe_c denotes the percent change in the (spot) exchange value of foreign currency c (e.g., dollar per yen), N_{bc} is the net dealing position of bank b in currency c, and the μ and ψ are parameters to be estimated. Positive estimates for

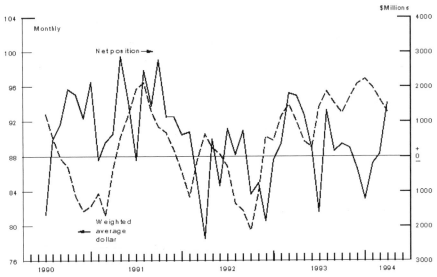

Figure 4
Net Foreign Dealing Position of Banks (includes positions in six currencies)

the ψ would imply that the banks are profitably predicting exchange rate movements.[12]

Note that equation (2) provides a direct test of the strong form of the efficient market hypothesis, which states that exchange rates should reflect all fundamental information known by any market participant. This test is somewhat stronger than the usual tests of whether publicly-available information can be used to forecast future exchange rate changes. These weaker tests have provided somewhat mixed results. Meese and Rogoff (1983a, 1983b) and others have found that random-walk models out-perform other models of exchange rates, indicating that all publicly-available information is incorporated in market rates. On the other hand, studies that have examined survey measures of exchange rate expectations reject that those data follow a random walk; see, for example, Frankel and Froot (1987).

---

[12] Note that we use only the spot exchange rate to judge profits, although the net positions (N) include open forward contracts and futures positions. If, for example, the interest rate differential changed during our measurement period, the forward exchange rate would not move one-for-one with the spot rate. However, in practice, changes in spot and forward exchange rates among major currencies have been highly correlated.

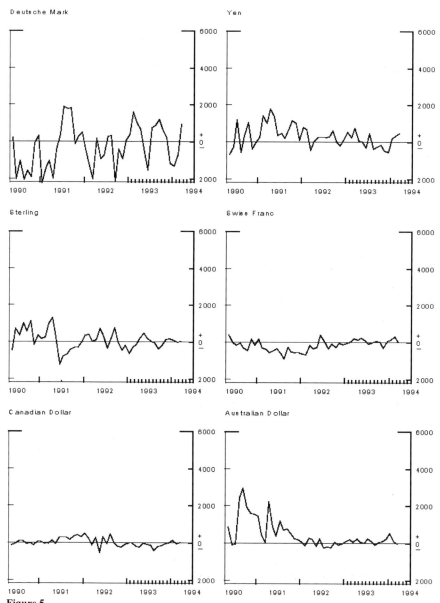

Figure 5
Net Dealing Positions of Banks By Currency (end of day positions in millions of US$)

Table 2
Do 035 FX Positions (5/90-3/94) Predict Exchange Rate Changes? (Overnight Horizon) Summary of
regression coefficients by bank for net dealing positions (in $US billions) in 6 currencies; dependent
variable is % change in exchange rate

	Bank A	Bank B	Bank C	Bank D	Bank E	Bank F	Bank G
number positive	4	3	2	0	3	3	5
95% confidence	0	0	0	0	1	0	0
number negative	2	3	4	6	3	3	1
95% confidence	0	0	0	1	0	0	0
total position[a]	-0.60	0.09	0.33	-2.95	-0.12	0.19	-0.07
	(-0.23)	(0.10)	(0.35)	(-0.28)	(-0.20)	(0.34)	(-0.11)

[a]The numbers in parentheses are t-statistics for the estimates for a null hypothesis of $\psi = 0$.

One remaining procedural issue is the length of the time period over which to measure
the change in the exchange rate; we report estimates for several time horizons. Results for
each bank are summarized in Table 2 for an overnight horizon — from 4 pm (the New York
close) on the day of the 035 survey until 9 am on the next business day.[13] Because it uses the
shortest possible horizon, this specification has the advantage that the banks' positions are
measured relatively accurately over the evaluation period. Because the New York market is
closed, many of the traders will not be changing their positions until the next morning.[14] The
drawback is that we are only assessing the performance of the banks' foreign exchange
positions for seventeen hours per month over our four-year sample. Note that roughly half
(22 out of 42) of the estimates of ψ are negative and that only about 5 percent of the
estimates (two out of 42) are significant at the 5 percent level. This evidence is consistent
with the notion that the banks are not able to predict overnight changes in exchange rates.

The first four rows of Table 2 suggest that overall, the banks were as likely to lose as
to profit from their positions in individual currencies. A natural question to ask is whether
the banks made or lost money on their overall foreign exchange positions. To address this
issue, we define a bank's overall net foreign exchange position as the sum of its positions in
each currency:

$$N_{b,t} = \sum_{c=1}^{C} N_{bc,t}. \qquad (3)$$

_____

[13]Note that this period runs over the weekend in a few cases. The confidential nature of the
035 data precluded reporting the regression coefficients.

[14] However, because these banks can also trade in the European and Asian markets, their net
dealing positions do not stay fixed even overnight.

Table 3

Do 035 FX Positions (5/90-3/94) Predict Exchange Rate Changes? (Horizon of 20 Business Days) Summary of regression coefficients by bank for net dealing positions (in $US billions) in 6 currencies; dependent variable is % change in exchange rate

	Bank A	Bank B	Bank C	Bank D	Bank E	Bank F	Bank G
number positive	5	1	1	4	2	2	2
95% confidence	0	0	0	0	0	0	1
number negative	1	5	5	2	4	4	4
95% confidence	0	0	0	0	0	0	0
total position[a]	8.17	-7.14	0.56	0.24	-2.40	-3.39	-1.22
	(0.71)	(-0.86)	(0.20)	(0.01)	(-0.60)	(-0.94)	(-0.16)

[a]The numbers in parentheses are t-statistics for the estimates for a null hypothesis of $\psi = 0$.

We also define an exchange rate index for each bank for each time period. The percent change in the exchange rate index for a bank is computed using the bank's foreign exchange positions as weights:

$$\Delta e_{b,t+1} = \frac{\sum_{c=1}^{C} N_{bc,t} \Delta e_{c,t+1}}{N_{b,t}}. \tag{4}$$

A bank's profit from its overall foreign exchange position in a period is given by the product:

$$\pi_{b,t+1} = \Delta e_{b,t+1} N_{b,t}. \tag{5}$$

Thus we can investigate whether banks' overall positions predict changes in the relevant exchange rate index by estimating:

$$\Delta e_{b,t+1} = \mu_b + \psi_b N_{b,t} + \epsilon_{b,t+1}. \tag{6}$$

The last row of Table 2 reports that there were positive estimates of ψ for three of the seven banks and negative estimates for four, although none of the banks exhibited a statistically significant correlation between its overall position and the subsequent change in the relevant exchange rate index. The overall position of the aggregate of the banks seems to have been only minimally profitable on average; the coefficient estimate — which is the estimate of ψ when equation (6) is estimated for the aggregate of the banks — is .02 (not shown) and insignificant from zero.

Table 3 summarizes estimates of equations (2) and (6) for exchange rate changes over the twenty business days following each 035 survey date. This specification has the advantage of assessing the positions relative to most of the exchange rate movements during the three-year sample period. The disadvantage is that the banks' positions are not measured accurately, as they evolve over the twenty days. However, the persistence in positions implied by Tables 1 suggests that foreign exchange positions often bear some resemblance

Table 4
Do 035 FX Positions (5/90-3/94) Predict Exchange Rate Changes? (Horizon of 5 Business Days)
Summary of regression coefficients by bank for net dealing positions (in $US billions) in 6 currencies;
dependent variable is % change in exchange rate

	Bank A	Bank B	Bank C	Bank D	Bank E	Bank F	Bank G
number positive	1	1	1	3	3	2	2
95% confidence	0	1	0	1	0	0	1
number negative	5	5	5	3	3	4	4
95% confidence	0	0	0	0	2	0	0
total position[a]	5.71	-1.54	-0.76	1.10	-0.74	-4.62	-0.64
	(1.29)	(-0.42)	(-0.75)	(0.21)	(-0.38)	(-1.11)	(-0.11)

[a]The numbers in parentheses are t-statistics for the estimates for a null hypothesis of $\psi = 0$.

to where they stood a month earlier. The 20-day results are similar to those of the overnight exercise in that roughly half of the ψ estimates are negative and that only one is statistically significant. The table implies that if positions were maintained for this horizon, four of the banks lost money on their foreign exchange positions as did the banks as a group.

Table 4 reports estimates for an intermediate horizon of five business days. These results are similar to those of Tables 2 and 3 — again, roughly half of the ψ estimates are negative and few are statistically significant. As at the overnight horizon, the seven banks as a whole appear to have made a small profit on their total position in foreign currencies, although the positive parameter estimate (not shown) is still not statistically significant from zero.

An issue that naturally arises is how much profit and loss is associated with the coefficients in the bottom row of Tables 2, 3, and 4. It is useful to decompose these position-taking profits into three pieces. First, a bank could have made money on its foreign exchange positions, if it had been long, on average, over the sample period in a currency that, on balance, rose over the period. Analogously, a short position, on average, in a currency that experienced a net depreciation over the sample period would also have been profitable. We can write profits from average positions of each bank (b) as

$$\sum_{t=1}^{T} \sum_{c=1}^{C} \Delta e_{c,t+1} \, \overline{N_{bc}}, \tag{7}$$

where $\overline{N_{bc}}$ denotes the average position over time of bank b in currency c.

Assuming that each bank's average currency positions over the four-year period are accurately reflected by the average of its positions reported on form 035, the above expression can be readily computed. The contribution of the average position component to average total foreign exchange earnings of the seven banks ranged from -1 percent to +7 percent. For the aggregate of the banks, this component seems to have contributed about $7 million per quarter, or less than 2 percent of foreign exchange earnings of these banks. The banks were fortunate that, on average, they were long in yen over the sample period. The yen was the only currency to appreciate significantly on balance over the sample period; it rose more than 50 percent, more than enough to produce quarterly earnings of $7 million on the average long yen position of the banks.

We next consider two separate types of *variation* in the banks' foreign exchange positions: i) changes in the bank's overall long or short position (total exposure) in foreign currency, and ii) variation in the mix of currencies. We can write profits from the long/short variation component as

$$\sum_{t=1}^{T} \frac{N_{b,t} - \overline{N_b}}{\overline{N_b}} \sum_{c=1}^{C} \Delta e_{c,t+1} \overline{N_{bc}}, \tag{8}$$

where $N_{b,t}$ is defined in (3) and $\overline{N_b}$ is its sample-period average. A trader that was able to predict the general direction of the U.S. dollar would have contributed to this component of trading profits. Measured at the overnight horizon (i.e., assuming that positions were held for precisely this period), this second component had a negligible effect, ranging from -2 to +1 percent of average foreign exchange earnings for the 7 banks. (Note that these numbers necessarily exclude any profits or losses from long/short variation that were not earned within 17 hours of an 035 reporting time.) At the 20-day horizon, this component contributed between -24 percent and +4 percent, and at the 5-day horizon it contributed between -17 and +6 percent. For the banks as a whole, the long/short component accounted for -4 to -1 percent of average foreign exchange profits at the three horizons.

The third profit component, due to variation in the currency mix, is

$$\sum_{t=1}^{T} \sum_{c=1}^{C} \left(N_{bc,t} - \frac{N_{b,t}}{\overline{N_b}} \overline{N_{bc}} \right) \Delta e_{c,t+1}. \tag{9}$$

This "mix" component would reflect profits from successful prediction of foreign currency cross rates. At the overnight horizon, this component had a negligible effect — between -3 and +1 percent of average foreign exchange earnings for each bank. At the 20-day horizon it contributed between -19 percent and +11 percent, and at the 5-day horizon it contributed between -3 and +7 percent. As a whole, the "mix" component accounted for between 0 and +1 percent of average foreign exchange profits at all three horizons.

The sum of the three components — (7), (8) and (9) — is a measure of the total profits derived from the 035 positions (conditional on our holding period assumptions):

$$\sum_{t=1}^{T} \sum_{c=1}^{C} \Delta e_{c,t+1} N_{bc}. \tag{10}$$

This sum accounted for -2 to +7 percent of bank foreign exchange earnings at the overnight horizon, -15 to +19 percent at the 5-day horizon, and -36 to +21 percent at the 20-day horizon. However, we measure the total contribution to average foreign exchange earnings at the aggregate of the banks at only about +2 percent at the overnight horizon, about +1 percent at the 5-day horizon, and about -1 percent at the 20-day horizon. Overall, the results suggest that foreign currency position-taking has little effect on industry-level bank profits but may help explain cross-sectional variation in earnings. This possibility will be further explored in section 6.[15]

Our analysis suggests that the banks' end-of-day positions accounted for less than 10 percent of their foreign exchange income during 1990-1994, and may have made a negative contribution. Nevertheless, it is possible that these banks are systematically earning profits on intraday positions that we cannot observe. However, the taking of positions in currency is essentially a zero-sum game, at least in money terms (but not necessarily utility). If the banks are making money, someone must be losing.[16] Because random trading would tend to lead to zero profits (net of transactions costs, including the bid-ask spread), the notion of a systematic loser is somewhat paradoxical. Perhaps the most plausible candidate is central banks, the only market participants not pursuing a goal of profit maximization. Occasionally circumstances have arisen, such as the faltering of the Exchange Rate Mechanism (ERM) in Europe in August and September 1992, that appear to offer an ex-ante profit opportunity to anyone in a position to trade foreign exchange.

5. DIRECT CALCULATIONS OF FOREIGN EXCHANGE INTERMEDIATION RETURNS

In this section, we attempt to measure intermediation earnings directly. If complete data were available on every foreign exchange trade that a bank made — including the transaction price, the quantity traded, and the prevailing bid and ask prices in the market at the time of the trade — it would be possible to construct a fairly precise measure of the returns to market-making. For example, for each trade, one might multiply the quantity traded by the difference between the transaction price and the prevailing mid-market price (i.e., the midpoint between the bid and ask prices).

---

[15] We also conducted a similar analysis using the short span of daily data that was available for one bank. Our results were similar to those reported in Tables 2, 3, and 4.

[16] However, to the extent that, with a single transaction, banks may be both taking a position and providing intermediation services to a customer, such a transaction would not be purely of a zero-sum nature.

It is also possible to estimate intermediation earnings with less comprehensive price and volume data. Turnover data for the seven most important foreign exchange markets (ranked by the trading volume involving U.S. counterparties) in April 1992 were collected from the seven banks in our sample, among other financial institutions, in a survey compiled by the Bank for International Settlements (BIS).[17] The survey distinguished between trades among foreign exchange dealers and trades between a dealer and a non-dealer. The latter transactions are those in which we expect our banks to be compensated for providing liquidity services.

A rough estimate of the portion of the foreign exchange earnings of our seven banks that can be attributed to intermediation in these currency markets can be obtained by multiplying their volume of trade in these markets with non-dealer counterparties by half of the average market bid-ask spread during April 1992.[18] (These seven markets, defined to include both spot and forward transactions, account for about 85 percent of the foreign exchange trading of the seven banks.) This measure amounted to $115 million (at a quarterly rate) for the aggregate of the seven banks, about 30 percent of both 1992 Q2 foreign exchange earnings and of the average for these banks between 1990 Q3 and 1994 Q1.

For several reasons, the above measure likely understates banks' earnings from providing liquidity services in foreign exchange markets. Perhaps the most obvious is that the estimate does not take account of all of the currencies in which the banks trade. Furthermore, minor currency markets are less liquid, and the spreads are wider in those markets, so that a given volume of trading will be more profitable to a market-making bank.

Second, the measure does not include any measure of the banks' trading in foreign exchange derivatives markets, including customized over-the-counter products. These activities have grown rapidly in magnitude and may contribute significantly to profits. Anecdotal evidence suggests that banks may earn more from providing liquidity to a customer who wishes to take or hedge a position in the second moment of a price (e.g., exchange rate risk) than from servicing a customer concerned with the first moment (e.g., taking a position in the level of an exchange rate).

Third, spreads in forward currency markets are almost invariably wider than in the

---

[17] The seven markets are the U.S. dollar markets for yen, DM, sterling, Swiss francs, Canadian dollars, Australian dollars, and French francs.

[18] Only about a quarter of the trading volume was with non-dealer counterparties.

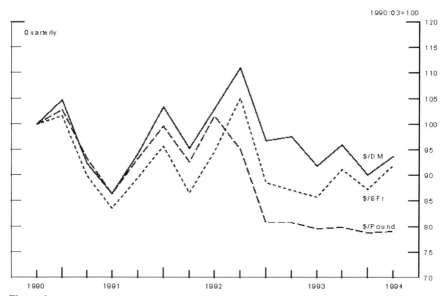

Figure 6
Exchange Rates

spot market.[19] About half of the trading volume of the six banks was in forward contracts. A casual inspection of wire service quotes undertaken recently suggested that 12-month forward spreads could be up to twice as much as spot spreads, even in heavily-traded currencies. In addition, Bessembinder (1994) reports average spreads for 6-month forwards that are 1-1/2 to 2 times as large as spot spreads. Lacking proper data on forward spreads, we used the spot spread on forward contracts in the above calculation.[20]

Fourth, our calculation was based on market spreads — the difference between the highest bid and the lowest ask. This is merely a lower bound on an individual bank's bid-ask spread. Some non-dealer customers may face a spread that is wider than the market spread.

Fifth, April 1992 was almost certainly a below-average month for intermediation profits. The mean spread was about 20 percent below its 1985-1993 average in all of the currencies except the Canadian dollar. Second, a proxy for exchange market activity drawn from the 035 data (the same that was shown in figure 2) was 3 percent below trend in the

---

[19] The manner in which forwards are quoted — as add-ons to the spot rate — practically ensures that forward spreads will be wider than spot spreads.

[20] Nor did we have a comprehensive breakdown of forward contracts by maturity.

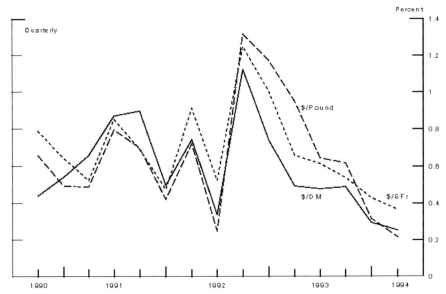

Figure 7
Standard Deviation of Exchange Rates

April 8 survey.

Finally, intermediation earnings may be further understated because of a positive correlation between volume and spreads that is masked by time aggregation of the data. Both trading volume and bid-ask spreads are thought to increase during episodes of market volatility, spreads because market makers are believed to require compensation for increased risk.[21] If trading tends to be concentrated when the spread is highest, the product of total monthly volume by an unweighted average of the spread will fall short of a (more accurate) higher frequency calculation.

Given that all the sources of error discussed above bias these calculations in the same direction, it seems plausible to speculate that earnings from intermediation could be understated by as much as a factor of three or four, that is, enough so that if earnings were

---

[21]Bessembinder (1994) found that spreads in four major currency markets were increasing in both conditional exchange rate volatility and innovations to trading volume. In the model of Tauchen and Pitts (1983), asset market trading volume is associated with the rate of information arrival.

correctly measured, they could completely account for the observed mean foreign exchange earnings.

6. A REGRESSION APPROACH TO EXPLAINING OBSERVED PROFITS

In the two previous sections, we examined two possible sources of foreign exchange trading profits -- position-taking and intermediation activity in spot and forward foreign exchange rate markets. This section uses an indirect method to determine the importance of these and other sources of profits for which data are not available, by regressing quarterly bank profits on proxies for the unobserved data.

Although the 035 data provide banks' net positions in several currencies, these data provide only proxies for intermediation volumes, net positions in volatility, and volatility-related activity for those currencies. In addition, although we were able to obtain bid and ask exchange rates for several currencies, we were not able to obtain either the changes in value of net positions in volatility or bid and ask rates for volatility-related activity, both of which are required to decompose profits as described in equation (1).

As a consequence, we made several assumptions about those missing variables. First, we assume that the volume of customer-related activity of a bank is proportional to the gross sum of all purchased and sold foreign exchange spot and forward contracts. Second, we assume that a bank's net position in volatility is proportional to the number of put and calls purchased less those sold; and we assume that the change in the value of these positions for a particular currency is a linear function of the change in the volatility of that currency. Also, we assumed that a bank's volume of volatility-related intermediation activity is proportional to the number of put and calls written and that the bid-ask spreads on these activities are linear functions of the currency volatility. Finally, we assumed that, for each variable reported by a bank on the 035, a simple average of the three numbers in any given quarter equalled the appropriately weighted mean value of the variable in that quarter.

Using these assumptions, the profits decomposition in equation (1) can be rewritten as a panel regression equation:

$$
\pi_{b,t+1} = \mu_b + \sum_{c=1}^{C} \alpha_c \cdot \Delta e_{c,t+1} \cdot N_{bc,t} + \sum_{c=1}^{C} \beta_c \cdot S_{c,t+1} \cdot Q_{bc,t+1}
$$

$$
+ \sum_{c=1}^{C} \gamma_c \cdot \Delta \sigma^2_{c,t+1} \cdot NV_{bc,t} + \sum_{c=1}^{C} \delta_c \cdot \sigma^2_{c,t+1} \cdot QV_{bc,t+1} + \epsilon
$$

(11)

where μ_b represents a bank-specific constant; where α_c, β_c, γ_c and $\hat{Q}$ are expected to be

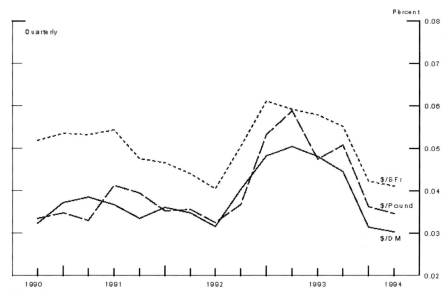

Figure 8
10am Bid-Ask Spreads in NY Foreign Exchange Market
(as a percentage of mid-point price; monthly average)

positive; and where the remaining components have been described above. The change in each exchange rate is measured over the whole quarter, and volatility is computed as the variance of daily log changes. The change in volatility in the third summation term is the difference between this measure and the value for the previous quarter. Also note that, except for bank-specific intercepts, we restrict the coefficients to be the same across banks. These restrictions are motivated by a desire to conserve degrees of freedom.

Figures 6, 7, and 8 present some of our exchange rate variables. Figure 6 demonstrates significant comovement among the European currencies. Not surprisingly, all of the exchange rate volatility measures in Figure 7 are also positively correlated. Figure 8 shows monthly averages of 10 am bid-ask spreads for U.S. dollars in terms of seven foreign currencies.[22] Note that these are highly liquid markets — the spreads seldom exceed 0.1 percent of the midpoint price.[23]

---

[22] The Australian dollar spread is measured at 9 am.

[23] Interestingly, although the quoted spreads are constrained by a discrete tick size (one 'pip'), the relative spreads (measured as a percent of the midpoint exchange rates) appear to be uncorrelated

Table 5
Explaining 1990-1994 Quarterly Foreign Exchange Trading Profits at 7 U.S. Commercial Banks

Parameter	Estimate	t-Statistic	Parameter	Estimate	t-Statistic
α_{DM}	-.08	-0.54	γ_{DM}	.002	0.20
α_{SFr}	.23	0.74	γ_{SFr}	.040	3.92
$\alpha_{£}$	-.12	-1.08	$\gamma_{£}$	.007	0.43
$\alpha_{¥}$	-.10	-0.33	$\gamma_{¥}$	.122	2.18
$\alpha_{A\$}$	.05	0.18	$\gamma_{A\$}$	.141	1.67
$\alpha_{C\$}$	1.02	0.84	$\gamma_{C\$}$	-.209	-2.97
β_{DM}	.000	0.17	δ_{DM}	.000	0.24
β_{SFr}	-.012	-2.14	δ_{SFr}	.003	2.53
$\beta_{£}$	.001	0.12	$\delta_{£}$	-.001	-0.49
$\beta_{¥}$	.003	2.18	$\delta_{¥}$	.005	2.43
$\beta_{A\$}$	.031	0.76	$\delta_{A\$}$	-.009	-1.29
$\beta_{C\$}$	.005	0.18	$\delta_{C\$}$	-.029	-1.25
R^2		0.60	Number of Observations		15
Number of Banks		7	Degrees of Freedom		74

The panel regression in equation (11) was estimated using quarterly data from 1990:Q3 through 1994:Q1. Estimated coefficients are presented in Table 5. The adjusted R^2 indicates that about 60 percent of the variance in profits can be explained by the model variables, but about a third of the coefficients have the "wrong" sign.

It is conceivable that a component of profits, such as position-taking, could account for a significant amount of the time series variation in profits but, on average, add nothing to the *level* of profits. Table 6 provides some information about the extent to which different types of regressors account for average foreign exchange earnings at each bank. The contribution of a right-hand-side variable to the mean is computed as the product of the estimated coefficient and the sample mean of the regressor. We report these contributions as a proportion of average foreign exchange earnings for the bank. The table indicates that about 50 percent of average profits can be accounted for by the variables that represent our four sources of foreign exchange earnings.

Note that the parameter estimates and the profits decomposition for position-taking and intermediation activity in currencies are roughly consistent with the results obtained in the previous two sections. All of the parameter estimates for position-taking variables (the

---

with the exchange rates (the denominator in the definition of the relative spread).

Table 6
Explaining 1990-1994 Average Quarterly Foreign Exchange Trading Profits

| | | Percent of Average Profits Attributable to: | | | |
	Constant	Positions in Currencies	Intermediation in Currencies	Positions in Volatility	Intermediation in Volatility
Bank A	87	-2	5	0	10
Bank B	69	0	0	8	23
Bank C	14	4	27	11	46
Bank D	88	0	-15	1	27
Bank E	71	0	4	-1	26
Bank F	82	0	9	9	0
Bank G	-21	0	77	3	42
Total	51	0	17	2	29

αs in Table 5) are insignificant from zero, and the contribution of these variables to average profits is negligible. Intermediation activity in currencies appear to account for only 17 percent of average profits, largely associated with two banks and activity in the Japanese yen.

Although parameter estimates for positions in volatility variables (the γs) are often significant, these variables account for about 2 percent of average profits. This is likely because the banks in our sample write nearly as many options as they buy. In contrast, two of the parameters for intermediation in volatility variables (the δs) are significant from zero, and these variables account for nearly 30 percent of average explained profits.

In summary, our cross-sectional regression suggests that about 50 percent of banks' foreign exchange earnings are associated with some type of financial intermediation, and the profit contribution of their position-taking activities is close to zero, on average. As before, there are numerous caveats to these results. First, there are very few degrees of freedom in the regression. In addition, these estimates could be contaminated for several reasons, including problems with the proxies for unobservables, omitted currencies, time aggregation, and correlation among the regressors.

References

Azarchs, Tanya, 1994, Market Volatility Impacts Bank Trading Operations, *Standard and Poor's Financial Institutions Rating Service* CC-65, June 30.

Bessembinder, Hendrik, 1994, Bid-Ask Spreads in the Interbank Foreign Exchange Markets, *Journal of Financial Economics* 35, 317-348.

Economist, The, 1993, Survey: International Banking (April 10), 3-38.

Frankel, Jeffrey A., and Kenneth A. Froot, 1987, Using Survey Data to Test Standard Propositions Regarding Exchange Rate Expectations, *American Economic Review* 77, 133-153.

Grinblatt, Mark and Sheridan Titman, 1992, The Persistence of Mutual Fund Performance, *Journal of Finance* 47, 1977-1984.

Leahy, Michael, 1994, Bank Positions and Forecasts of Exchange Rate Movements, in: *Derivatives, Regulation and Banking*, ed. Barry Schachter (North-Holland, Amsterdam).

Malkiel, Burton G., 1987, Efficient Market Hypothesis, in: *The New Palgrave: A Dictionary of Economics* (Macmillan Press, London).

Meese, Richard A. and Kenneth Rogoff, 1983a, The Out-of-Sample Failure of Empirical Exchange Rate Models: Sampling Error or Misspecification? in: *Exchange Rates and International Macroeconomics*, ed. Jacob A. Frankel (University of Chicago Press, Chicago).

Meese, Richard A. and Kenneth Rogoff, 1983b, Empirical Exchange Rate Models of the 1970s: Do They Fit Out of Sample? *Journal of International Economics* 14, 3-24.

Tauchen, George and Michael Pitts, 1983, The Price Variability-Volume Relationship on Speculative Markets, *Econometrica* 51, 485-505.

Value Line Investment Survey, The, 1994, Bank Industry (September 9), 2001-2035.

Derivatives, Regulation and Banking
Edited by B. Schachter
1997 Elsevier Science B.V.

Chapter 6
BANK POSITIONS AND FORECASTS OF EXCHANGE RATE MOVEMENTS

Michael P. Leahy[†]
Board of Governors of the Federal Reserve System, Washington, DC USA

1. INTRODUCTION

The profitability of banks' foreign exchange trading has been trending upward in recent years, prompting questions about the source of those profits. In particular, do the profits arise from providing market-making services in an environment where the demand for those services is growing? Or do the profits arise from savvy position-taking and superior abilities to forecast exchange rate movements?

This paper investigates the second question. Its specific objective is to study whether the position data reported on the form FFIEC 035, our best source of information on the positions banks take, indicate any special abilities on the part of the reporting financial institutions in predicting exchange rate changes. A bank will be successful in its position-taking to the extent that it takes long positions in currencies that eventually appreciate and short positions in currencies that eventually depreciate (more than the interest rate differential). If the reporting financial institutions have a better-than-average ability to forecast changes in exchange rates, their positions, and ultimately trading profits, would presumably reflect that ability.

Overall, the position data appear to provide some evidence that the performances of some financial institutions are 1) better than one might expect if their forecasts were purely random and 2) consistent with the possibility that they may possess information that would

---

[†]The author is a staff economist in the Division of International Finance, Board of Governors of the Federal Reserve System. This paper has benefited from many helpful discussions with Jon Faust and Matt Pritsker. I would also like to thank John Ammer, David Bowman, Allan Brunner, Hali Edison, Allen Rrankel, Dale Henderson, Deborah Lindner, Michael Martinson, Michael O'Connor, Larry Promisel, Ralph Smith, Charlie Thomas, Leeto Tlou, and participants in the IF Monday Workshop. Nathan Corson provided valuable research assistance. This paper represents the views of the author and should not be interpreted as reflecting those of the Board of governors of the Federal Reserve System or other members of its staff.

be valuable in forecasting changes in exchange rates. These results are suggested in the analysis of individual currency performances by the fact that some institutions appear more often in the top tenth of the performance distributions than one might expect if the top performances were merely the outcome of good luck. Furthermore, when the performances are evaluated for a group of currencies rather than for individual currencies, the number of institutions that appears in the top tenth of the performance distributions seems to be relatively high, with the same institutions again appearing relatively frequently.

These results are consistent with other findings of persistently good performances in financial markets[1] and are intriguing because they seem to indicate that some institutions may have either monopolistic access to information, such as private information about order flows, or superior insight into the implications of publicly available information. On the other hand, if the institutions' positions are correlated with a time-varying risk premium, the superior performances can be interpreted as compensation for bearing risk rather than as an indication of any special abilities to forecast movements in exchange rates.

There are at least two problems one must recognize in linking the results of this study with the profitability of banks' foreign exchange trading. First, the position data may not be representative of the positions that the financial institutions actually take when they make their profits. The FFIEC 035 position data are measures as of the close of business on one day per month. Even if position-taking has made a significant contribution to the profits of these institutions, one might not detect it with this sample. Banks whose profits are made largely on intra- day positions or on positions taken on other days of the month will not show strong performances here. Second, the usefulness of these data in determining the profitability of position-taking in general by these institutions is severely hampered by our ignorance of the horizons over which the positions are held. The reported positions might well be profitable over a horizon not considered in this analysis.

Two types of statistical approaches are used in this paper. One is a nonparametric approach that focuses on the frequency with which the signs of the positions match the signs of changes in exchange rates. The other is a parametric approach that uses logit models to incorporate information on the magnitude of positions as well as their signs and to determine how well the position data predict the direction of currency movements. A third approach, not presented here, involves fitting a linear regression model that includes information on the magnitudes and signs of not only the position but also the change in the exchange rate. The results of this third approach are described in a companion paper in this volume by Ammer and Brunner (1996).

---

[1]See, for example, Grinblatt and Titman (1992).

The data used in this analysis come from several sources. The position data are drawn from the monthly FFIEC 035 reports of five leading financial institutions over a period from June 1990 to March 1994. Because these reports are confidential, the institution names are suppressed in this paper; the five banks are referred to only by letters of the alphabet chosen at random (G, P, R, W, and Y). Data are available for other institutions, but it was determined that due to various reporting problems the data for those institutions would not be appropriate for this study. Line 11 in the FFIEC 035 report, the net reported dealing position, is used for the position data. According to the report instructions, the net reported dealing position is "the actively managed net dealing position for currencies . . . as reported to senior management for internal risk management purposes." The 035 report provides positions for six major currencies—the Australian dollar, Canadian dollar, mark, yen, Swiss franc, and U.K. pound. The exchange rate changes are derived from 4 p.m. exchange rates in New York, as reported by the Federal Reserve Bank of New York, and they are adjusted for interest rate differentials using Eurocurrency deposit rates maintained by the BIS for all currencies except the Australian dollar. For the Australian dollar, we used the domestic cash rate. The changes in the six exchange rates, adjusted for interest rate differentials, are calculated over eight horizons extending from 1 to 20 business days.[2]

2. NONPARAMETRIC ANALYSIS

One of the simplest ways to measure the performance of the position data in forecasting exchange rate changes is to calculate the proportion of times the signs of the position data match the signs of the change in the exchange rates. If the positions were taken randomly, with an equal probability of being long or short, one would expect that roughly half the time the signs would match. If, however, the positions taken reflect some ability to predict exchange rate changes, the proportion of correct sign matches would be greater than half. Under the assumption that the sign of position is independent of the sign of the change in the exchange rate, the number of correct guesses has a binomial distribution. Using this distribution, we can test whether the number of correct forecasts is significantly better than what we might expect if the positions were taken at random. Outcomes that appear in the higher end of the distribution, which would be represented by a percentile ranking, say, between 90 and 100, are more likely to be indicative of better-than-random performance. In those cases, the position data might have some positive value as a forecasting tool. On the contrary, outcomes that appear in the middle of the distribution

---

[2]The horizons considered are 1,2, 3,4, 5, 10, 15, and 20 business days.

Table 1
Simple Matching of Signs of Positions and Exchange Rate Changes: Frequency of Appearance of Individual Institutions in the Top Decile of the binomial Distribution (48 appearances per institution are possible)

Institution	Appearances
G	0
P	3
R	0
W	5
Y	5
TOTAL	13

would show little support for the hypothesis that the position data indicate any significant information value.[3]

Table 1 shows the number of individual performances that score a percentile ranking of 90 or better.[4] The maximum number of performances that could appear for any one institution is 48, which would occur if the institution earned percentiles of 90 or above in all six currencies at each of the eight horizons. If the performances were purely random draws from the interval between 0 and 100, we might expect that 10 percent or about 4 or 5 of the outcomes to be at 90 or better for each institution. Table 1 shows an average of less than 3 outcomes in the top tenth for each institution. In addition, the frequency with which the various institutions appear in the top decile is not uniform. Institutions W and Y appear relatively more frequently than the others, although not more than one might reasonably expect if their performances were random.

Merton (1981) has criticized the use of this test, arguing that the proportion of correct forecasts may not be useful in determining whether the forecasts reflect any special abilities or information not already available to the market. For example, suppose that a particular currency is expected to appreciate more often than it depreciates during some period but that the timing of the ups and downs is not known. An investor with no special information about the timing could take a long position in the currency throughout the period. This position will correctly forecast the changes in the exchange rate more than half the time if the

---

[3]Ironically, outcomes in the lower tail of the distribution are also indicative of information value, i.e., consistently wrong forecasts also contain useful information.

[4]With about 45 observations at each horizon, the sign of the position would have to match the sign of the change in the exchange rate at least 60 percent of the time to be in the top decile. Also, because the outcomes and associated probabilities in this analysis are discrete, there will always be some spanning of percentiles. In an attempt to avoid biasing the results one way or the other, I report the mid-point of the probability interval as the percentile.

Table 2
Conditional Matching of Signs of Positions and Exchange Rate Changes: Frequency of Appearance of Individual Institutions in the Top Decile of the Hypergeometric Distribution (48 appearances per institution are possible)

Institution	Appearances
G	4
P	1
R	0
W	5
Y	4
TOTAL	14

currency does indeed appreciate more often than it depreciates. However, those position data would not provide any information to market participants that they do not already have.

In an efficient-market equilibrium, the high score associated with this forecasting strategy can be thought of as an indicator of the return to bearing risk in the presence of a risk premium. Under the assumption that the risk premium is known to investors, the fact that one investor takes a risky position and is compensated for bearing that risk is not a sign of any special forecasting ability. To determine whether the FFIEC 035 position data offer information useful in forecasting exchange rate changes, we would like to exclude from our tests, to the extent possible, successful forecasts associated merely with compensation for bearing risk.

Merton (1981) offers an alternative measure that can, in principle, detect special forecasting ability in the presence of a risk premium. In the context of exchange rate forecasting, this measure is the sum of the probability of a correct forecast when the currency is appreciating and the probability of a correct forecast when the currency is depreciating. The sum of these conditional probabilities indicates the value of the position data as a forecasting tool. A position that is always positive would always correctly forecast the upward movements of the currency and never correctly forecast the downward movements. In this case, the sum of the probabilities would equal one, identical to the sum had random positions been chosen that would correctly forecast only half the upward movements and half the downward movements. Merton demonstrates that the sum of these conditional probabilities must be greater than one for the forecasts to have any positive value to agents interested in timing the movements of market prices.[5]

---

[5] In the special case in which the probability of a correct forecast in an up-market is equal to the probability of a correct forecast in a down-market, Merton's model is equivalent to the simple binomial model presented here. However, Merton's more general model allows these conditional probabilities to be equal without imposing that equality by assumption.

Michael P. Leahy

Table 3
Logit Estimation of Extent To Which Sign and Magnitude of Position Predict Direction of Exchange
Rate Change: Frequency With Which an Institution's Performance Appears in the Top Decile of the t-
Distribution (48 appearances per institutions are possible)

Institution	Appearances
G	6
P	7
R	4
W	1
Y	9
TOTAL	27

Henriksson and Merton (1981) provide a nonparametric test of the hypothesis that these conditional probabilities sum to one. If the forecasts are purely random, the number of times the position data correctly forecast an upward movement follows a hypergeometric distribution. Cumby and Modest (1987) note that this test is an application of Fisher's (1935) exact test of the independence of row and column classifications in a two-by-two contingency table. Cumby and Modest also demonstrate that the Henriksson-Merton test is biased when there is a time-varying risk premium that is correlated with the forecasts. A constant risk premium, however, which could create problems for the simpler binomial test, would not bias the Henriksson-Merton test of market timing abilities.

Table 2 shows the number of performances that score a percentile of 90 or better under the assumption that forecasts are purely random. The results are similar to Table 1, though institution G looks a bit better, while institution P looks a bit worse. Still, there is little evidence of any better-than-random forecasting ability across all the banks—with an average of less than 3 performances appearing for each institution. As before, the frequency with which the various institutions appear in the top decile is not uniform.

3. LOGIT ANALYSIS

One might think that the confidence an institution attaches to its belief about exchange rate movements is related to the size of the position it takes. An institution might take a large position when it is more confident about its forecast of an exchange rate and a small position when it is less confident. To incorporate information about the confidence with which a bank might forecast an exchange rate change, one can consider a logit model of the probability that a currency will appreciate. In this framework, if the position data do contain information useful in predicting exchange rates, a larger (more positive or less negative) position would imply a larger probability that a currency would appreciate. The

Table 4
Distribution of Performance In Individual Currencies by Horizon Based On Results of Nonparametric Estimation (Henriksson-Merton Test)

Horizon (days)	Number of Cases In			Q	K-S
	Bottom 3rd	Middle 3rd	Top 3rd		
1	10	10	10	0.0	0.62
2	10	6	14	3.2	0.98
3	7	16	7	5.4*	0.80
4	8	9	13	1.4	0.63
5	13	7	10	1.8	0.81
10	9	9	12	0.6	0.89
15	12	9	9	0.6	0.77
20	10	12	8	0.8	0.67
Average	9.9	9.7	10.4		
Average share	0.33	0.32	0.35		

Q is Pearson's Q-statistic; under the null hypothesis that the distribution of outcomes is uniform, a Q-statistic for three-celled decomposition is distributed chi-squared with 2 degrees of freedom. Column headed K-S contains the Kolmogorov-Smirnov statistic. An * indicates that the test rejects the hypothesis of uniform distribution at the 10 percent level.

estimated distribution of the coefficient on the position variable is used to determine how well the position data perform. A coefficient that is positive and significantly different from zero at a 90 percent confidence level is interpreted as signaling a better-than-random performance by the bank. As with the nonparametric test of Henriksson and Merton, a good performance in the logit estimation may be indicative of an ability to forecast exchange rates not generally available to the market. Such a conclusion is warranted, however, only if one is willing to assume that any risk premium that might exist is either constant or uncorrelated with the positions taken.

As shown in Table 3, 27 individual performances earned a percentile ranking of 90 or better. While this is a considerable increase from the number of performances that appeared in Tables 1 and 2, it is still only a bit more than the 5 per institution one might expect with purely random forecasting. The frequency with which individual institutions appear in the top decile remains uneven. This is so even though three institutions — Y, P, and G — appear somewhat more frequently than one might expect with just random forecasting.

4. ADDITIONAL ANALYSIS

Additional analysis of the distribution of performance percentiles over the bottom, middle, and top thirds of the interval between 0 and 100 is shown in Tables 4 and 5. Table

Table 5
Distribution of Performance In Individual Currencies by Horizon Based On Results of logit estimation

Horizon (days)	Number of Cases In			Q	K-S
	Bottom 3rd	Middle 3rd	Top 3rd		
1	7	12	11	1.4	0.72
2	8	6	16	5.6*	1.25*
3	11	6	13	2.6	0.78
4	11	9	10	0.2	0.46
5	12	11	7	1.4	0.77
10	12	6	12	2.4	0.67
15	15	7	8	3.8	1.12
20	12	8	10	0.8	0.62
Average	11.0	8.1	10.9		
Average share	0.37	0.27	0.36		

Q is Pearson's Q-statistic; under the null hypothesis that the distribution of outcomes is uniform, a Q-statistic for three-celled decomposition is distributed chi-squared with 2 degrees of freedom. Column headed K-S contains the Kolmogorov-Smirnov statistic. An * indicates that the test rejects the hypothesis of uniform distribution at the 10 percent level.

4 reports on results from the nonparametric estimation suggested by Henriksson and Merton; Table 5 reports on the results of the logit estimation. If the positions taken by the institutions were random, the distribution of the percentiles would be roughly even across the thirds, as appears to be the case on average in Table 4. The last two columns on the tables display information on more formal statistical tests of the uniformity of the distribution of results. Pearson's Q statistic, which is distributed as a chi-squared random variable with 2 degrees of freedom under the null hypothesis that the distribution of the percentiles is uniform, supports a rejection of the null hypothesis only at a horizon of three days in Table 4. However, this rejection occurs because of the large number of performances in the middle third of the distribution, not because of an inordinately large number of good performances. In addition, the Kolmogorov-Smirnov statistic fails to come in large enough to reject the null hypothesis at any horizon. The logit estimation analyzed in Table 5 shows a bit more promising results at the horizon of two days, with both the Q-statistic and the Kolmogorov-Smirnov test detecting a statistically significant (at the 10 percent level, at least) deviation from uniformity that corresponds to a large number of performances in the top third of the distribution. While Table 4 provides little support for the hypothesis that the top performances in Table 2 are indicative of anything more than good luck, Tables 3 and 5 support the better-than-random hypothesis at one horizon at least.

Furthermore, a look at the whole distribution of outcomes reveals a slight tendency for there to be more outcomes in the top and bottom thirds of the distribution than in the

Table 6
Multinomial Logit Estimation of Extent to Which Signs and Magnitudes of Positions in Marks, Yen and UK Pounds Predict Directions of Corresponding Dollar Exchange Rate Changes: Frequency With Which Individual Institutions Exhibit Successful Prediction Histories and Performances That Appear in the Top Decile of Chi-Squared Distribution (8 appearances per institution are possible)

Institution	Appearances
G	3
P	4
R	0
W	1
Y	2
TOTAL	10

Position data for institution R delivered performances that ranked in the top decile at four horizons, but these performances were not reported in the table because the data show an unsuccessful prediction history. A prediction history is defined as the sum over the sample period of the product of the sign of the exchange rate change at a given horizon (adjusted for interest rate differentials) and the position taken. A successful prediction history is defined as a positive sum. All the performances reported in the table had successful prediction histories.

middle third. This kind of result might occur when banks take positions in all currencies against the dollar, essentially betting that the dollar will move one way or the other against them all. When the bet turns out to be correct, the bank could get credit for up to six correct forecasts instead of one; when the bet turns out to be incorrect, the bank could show as many as six incorrect forecasts rather than one. In this case, even random forecasting would tend to generate more outcomes at the extremes of the distribution than one might otherwise expect.

5. MULTINOMIAL LOGIT ESTIMATION

To attempt to deal with this problem, a multinomial logit model was estimated for trios of currencies and corresponding positions. In the simple logit estimation conducted above, there were only two categories of outcomes—the currency either rose against the dollar or fell. In the multinomial logit model, the number of categories of outcomes can be larger than two. With three exchange rates, the number of categories can be as large as eight—all three currencies can appreciate, all three can depreciate, two can appreciate and one depreciate (in 3 different ways), and one can appreciate and two depreciate (in 3 different ways). In both the simple and multinomial logit estimation, the purpose of the estimation is see whether the position data have any power to predict the probability of being in a category.

With the multinomial categorization of the outcomes, correctly guessing a decline of the dollar against three currencies counts as one correct forecast, not three.

More currencies were not used in the multinomial logit analysis because of data limitations. With as many as six currencies, up to 64 categories can be generated. There are, however, only about 45 monthly observations in sample currently available. Even with only three currencies, it is often difficult to estimate the coefficients on the position data with any precision. Nonetheless, it is possible to test hypotheses about groups of coefficients with some precision even when individual coefficient estimates are imprecise. In particular, the hypothesis considered here is whether the position data as a group contribute to the explanatory power of the model over and above the constant terms. More formally, the null hypothesis is that the vector of coefficients on the positions are all zero. Under the null, the position data have no explanatory power. In this case, the likelihood ratio has a chi-squared distribution.

Table 6 shows individual institution performances that fall into the top decile of the chi-squared distribution for the mark-yen-U.K. pound trio. An additional complication arises because of the multivariate nature of this analysis. The percentile test cannot distinguish performances that are very good from those that are very bad, because a consistently bad performance is just as useful a predictor as a consistently good one. Consequently, the table reports only those performances that fall into the top decile and show a successful prediction history. A prediction history is defined as the sum over the sample period of the product of the position and the sign of the exchange rate change at a given horizon (adjusted for interest rate differentials). A successful prediction history is a positive sum. As noted in the table, Institution R is not listed as a top performer in the table, even though its performance shows up in the top decile as many as four times on the basis of the likelihood ratio test, because its position data generate unsuccessful prediction histories.

If all five banks had successful prediction histories and delivered performances that were in the top decile, the table would list a total of 40 appearances. Under the assumption that the forecasts are random, however, one would expect to see only about ten percent or about four listed in the table. Thus, the fact that 25 percent of the total are in the top decile and have successful prediction histories appears to be a rejection of randomness, particularly for some institutions. Institutions P and G appear much more frequently than one might expect, and Institution Y appears somewhat more frequently. While one should keep in mind that the sample size in this exercise is not large for this type of estimation procedure, the multinomial logit estimation appears to reveal that the position data for these banks show better-than-random performances and therefore these results may be indicative of some predictive power.

6. CONCLUSIONS

In general, these results are consistent with the hypothesis that the FFIEC 035 position data contain some information that would be helpful in forecasting movements of exchange rates, but it is difficult to provide outright support. The nonparametric analyses, which consider how well the signs of the positions predict the signs of changes in the exchange rate, seem to provide little or no support for the hypothesis. However, the logit analyses, which incorporate the magnitudes of positions as well as their signs into models that predict the signs of changes in the exchange rate, appear to provide more support. In particular, the relatively frequent appearance of two or three institutions in the top tenth of the performance distributions under the logit estimations is indicative of some better-than- random forecasting ability by those institutions and possibly some special forecasting ability. However, these conclusions are limited by the possibility that there exits a time-varying risk premium which is correlated with the positions taken by the top performers. In that case, what appears to be special forecasting ability may be only normal compensation for bearing risk.

REFERENCES

Ammer, John and Allan D. Brunner, 1996, Are Banks Speculators or Market Makers? Explaining Foreign Exchange Trading Profits, in: *Derivatives, Regulation and Banking*, Barry Schachter, ed., Amsterdam, North-Holland, 123-146.

Cumby, Robert E. and David M. Modest, 1987, Testing for Market Timing Ability: A Framework for Forecast Evaluation, *Journal of Financial Economics* 19, 169-189.

Fisher, Ronald A., 1935, The Logic of Inductive Inference, *Journal of the Royal Statistical Society* 98, part I, 39-54.

Grinblatt, Mark and Sheridan Titman, 1992, The Persistence of Mutual Fund Performance, *Journal of Finance* 47, 1977-1984.

Henriksson, Roy D. and Robert C. Merton, 1981, On Market Timing and Investment Performance. II. Statistical Procedures for Evaluating Forecasting Skills, *Journal of Business* 54, 513-533.

Merton, Robert C., 1981, On Market Timing and Investment Performance. I. An Equilibrium Theory of Value for Market Forecasts, *Journal of Business* 54, 361-406.

Derivatives, Regulation and Banking
Edited by B. Schachter
© 1997 Elsevier Science B.V. All rights reserved.

159

Chapter 7
INDEXED CERTIFICATES OF DEPOSIT

Eugene H. Cantor and Barry Schachter[†]
Comptroller of the Currency, Washington, DC 20219

1. INTRODUCTION

Indexed deposits have become popular bank products in the US and Europe. This chapter provides background and discusses risk management and supervisory issues related to the issuance by US national banks of indexed certificates of deposit ("Indexed CDs"). The term "Indexed CD" refers to a bank deposit product that uses some outside interest rate or composite index to determine its own interest rate. Typical examples include "stock indexed CDs," whose interest rates are tied to increases in the S&P 500 or some other equity index (see, e.g., Ogden (1996)); "commodity linked CDs," whose interest rates are keyed to increases in the price of gold or other commodities, or commodities indices; and "bonus CDs," whose interest rates increase when particular events occur, such as the victory of a particular football team in the Superbowl or the occurrence of a prescribed minimum amount of rainfall or snowfall in the issuing bank's local area.

2. SUMMARY OF REGULATION OF INDEXED CD PRODUCTS

National banks may offer Indexed CDs pursuant to their express power to receive deposits under 12 U.S.C. § 24(Seventh).[1] While unconventional, Indexed CDs are fundamentally deposit products updated to meet the contemporary needs of customers. These deposit products are (1) functionally equivalent to and a logical outgrowth of a traditional

---

[†]Eugene H. Cantor, Securities & Corporate Practices Division, Barry Schachter, Risk Analysis Division. The views expressed by the authors are their personal views, and do not necessarily reflect the views of the Office of the Comptroller of the Currency.

[1]The powers granted to state banks are generally found in the applicable state banking statute. Federally insured state banks may not engage as principal in any activity not permissible for a national bank, unless specifically approved by the FDIC. Federal Deposit Insurance Act ("FDIA") § 24, 12 U.S.C. § 1831a.

banking activity; (2) respond to customer needs or otherwise benefit the bank or its customers; and (3) involve risks similar to those already assumed by banks. The FDIC takes the position that Indexed CDs are federally insured as to principal. However, the computation of interest on Indexed CDs raises significant, unresolved federal insurance issues. This is because FDIC regulations provide that interest is federally insured only to the extent it is accrued and owed. Interest on Indexed CDs is generally computed and treated as accrued between computation dates. As a result, inceases, if any, in the computation index that occur between the last computation date and the date the institution fails (but before the next computation date) may not be insured because the interest is not considered accrued and owed as of the failure date (i.e., not determined between computation dates).

A CD generally is not a security under the Securities Act of 1933 (the "1933 Act") and the Securities Exchange Act of 1934 (the "Exchange Act"). The courts, however, have not provided a blanket exclusion for CDs from the federal securities laws, noting instead that their status depends on the facts and circumstances applicable to each instrument. Nevertheless, while there is no case law directly addressing whether an Indexed CD is a federal security, cases on bank deposit products indicate an Indexed CD probably would not be classified as a security because the principal amount of the deposit is not placed at risk.

Indexed CDs generally fall outside the scope of the Commodity Exchange Act ("CEA") and Commodities Futures Trading Commission ("CFTC") regulations for reasons that vary, depending on the structure of the deposit instrument. Indexed CDs (1) linked to securities indices, generally should fall outside the scope of the CEA because the CEA directs that they be evaluated under the federal securities laws; (2) tied to commodities such as oil or gold, are exempt by the "hybrid exemption" or the CFTC's "statutory interpretation;" and (3) related to foreign exchange and government securities, may be exempted by the "Treasury Amendment" to the CEA (the scope of which has been the subject of much litigation) or may be structured to fall under the hybrid exemption or the CFTC's statutory interpretation. Indexed CDs tied to unconventional commodities-like items, such as the amount of rainfall in the issuing bank's local area or the record of a local sports team, might be considered options on or contracts for the future delivery of commodities (i.e., a payment stream based on the applicable item), in view of the expansive definition of "commodities" used in the CEA. However, the CFTC likely would only pursue instruments with the types of commodities that are or are likely to be the subject of exchange trading. As a practical matter, weather and sports Indexed CDs may be structured to fall within the hybrid exemption or statutory interpretation, thereby avoiding the CEA problem.

Since Indexed CDs are deposit products, they are subject to the Truth in Savings Act. They are not subject to any other specific OCC or FDIC disclosure requirements, including the Joint Banking Agency Statement on Nondeposit Investment Products (February 16, 1994). For federal income tax purposes, interest income earned on an Indexed CD with a term of one year or less, is reported by the taxpayer when payment is received. Interest income on a CD with a term in excess of one year is generally estimated and reported for income tax purposes on a yearly basis. When the taxpayer receives actual payments, the tax return filed for the payments is adjusted to reflect the estimates used on previous tax returns.

The commodity component of an Indexed CD is similar to a sold option (or possibly a sold forward). The associated risk should be managed as part of the overall portfolio exposure of the bank. However, certain aspects of risk management may be unique to these instruments. It may not be possible to identify traded instruments with which to hedge the exposure. The exposure may be new to the bank and management may be unfamiliar with potentially useful hedging instruments. Responsibility for hedging may rest with the funds sourcing area which may be unfamiliar with the embedded risks. The administrative costs of maintaining a hedge may be high because of low volume and small transaction size. Taken together, these issues may represent a risk management challenge.

3. INDEXED CD PRODUCT DESCRIPTIONS

In general, an Indexed CD is a bank certificate of deposit that uses some index or event, not within the control of the bank, to determine all or a portion of the interest payable on the deposit. The CD's interest rate may be keyed to yields on specific financial instruments, such as a percentage of the yield on six-month Treasury bills; pegged to various financial indices, such as the S&P 500 stock index or gold or oil indices; or linked to nonfinancial indices, such as the amount of seasonal rainfall or snowfall experienced in a particular area or the won/loss record of a sports team.

In addition, the Indexed CD may be structured to provide a minimum annual yield regardless of the performance of the applicable index, with the index or bonus feature providing a sweetener. The index's performance affects only the interest paid on the CD; the bank must always return the customer's deposit irrespective of the performance of the index in order to obtain deposit insurance and to avoid commodities law related problems.

3.1 CDs Indexed to Specific Assets or Financial Instruments

An Indexed CD may reference the interest rate paid on another financial instrument for its own rate. Typical references include Treasury bill interest rates and the London Interbank Offer Rate ("LIBOR"). The amount payable on the Indexed CD may be less than the yield on the referenced instrument, based on a preexisting formula intended to take into account the value of FDIC insurance accorded the CD, or a multiple of the index if the reference element warrants.

Several depository institutions have issued so-called "indexed asset" CDs, which provide for a minimum fixed rate of interest, supplemented by contingent interest that is based on a percentage of the earnings, cash flow, and appreciation derived from selected bank assets.[2] The fixed rate component of the instrument may also be indexed. In one case, the fixed rate is indexed to two-thirds of the average yield for AAA-rated corporate bonds (Moody's Seasoned) most recently preceding the date of issuance of the CDs.[3]

Another group of Indexed CDs offers depositors a hedge against inflation by providing a variable feature keyed to an "inflation index." Columbia First Bank FSB in Arlington, Virginia, for example, offers the "Triple Bump-up" certificate. Depositors in the Triple Bump-up program are allowed three rate increases over the two-year life of the deposit. Columbia First publishes a weekly update of the rate index offered under the program. In exchange for the option to bump-up rates in the future, the customer initially receives a slightly lower rate than that paid by the bank on its regular two-year CDs. This arrangement allows the depositor to achieve a higher potential return by assuming some additional interest rate risk through acceptance of a lower initial return.

3.2 CDs linked to financial indices

The concept of offering a CD linked to a stock market index appears to have originated with the Chase Manhattan Bank ("Chase") and its Market Index Investment ("MII").[4] The MII is a non-transferable time deposit account that pays interest at a rate based in part on changes in the Standard & Poors' 500 Composite Stock Index ("S&P Index")[5].

---

[2]See, FDIC Interp. Ltr. 86-26 (September 9, 1986); and FDIC Interp. Ltr. 86-7 (April 9, 1986).

[3]FDIC Interp. Ltr. 86-26 (September 9, 1986).

[4]On August 8, 1988, the OCC issued a letter to Chase finding that the MII is a permissible banking product under applicable banking statutes. Decision of the Comptroller of the Currency on the Request by Chase Manhattan Bank, N.A., to Offer the Chase Market Index Investment Deposit Account (August 8, 1988) (the "Chase Decision"). The Investment Company Institute ("ICI") brought suit against Chase and the OCC, claiming the MII violated Glass-Steagall. In Civil Action No. 87-1093 (TPG), USDC, D.C. (1995) (unpublished) (the "Chase Court Opinion"), the court affirmed the OCC's decision, stating the Agency properly allowed Chase to sell the MII under 12 U.S.C. § 24(Seventh). ICI's time for appealing the decision has expired.

[5]The S&P Index is a market value-weighted arithmetic index of 500 stocks (generally the largest firms) quoted on the New York Stock Exchange. The calculation of the value of the S&P Index is based on the relationship between the current aggregate market value of the common stocks of those 500

Interest on the MII is equal to the percentage increase, if any, in the S&P Index from the date the MII is opened to the date it matures. The maturity date of the MII is selected by the depositor from among a range of maturities offered by Chase (generally three, six, nine, or twelve months). Each maturity also offers the depositor guaranteed interest rate alternatives of 4%, 2% or 0% (the "Guaranteed Return"). A minimum deposit of $5,000 is required.

The maturity and the interest rate alternative the depositor selects determine that fractional portion of the percentage increase in the S&P Index (referred to as the "Index Multiplier") that is used to calculate interest on the MII. Generally, the higher the Guaranteed Return selected by a depositor and the shorter the maturity, the lower the Index Multiplier for that depositor's MII.

The rate of interest based on the Index Multiplier is referred to as the "Index Rate," and is determined by multiplying the percentage increase in the S&P Index from the opening of the MII to its maturity. At maturity the depositor's account is credited with interest at the greater of the Index Rate or the Guaranteed Return. If there has been no increase in the S&P Index during the term of the deposit, then no interest is paid on the Index Rate and the depositor receives the Guaranteed Return. In every case, the depositor receives a full return of principal at maturity, subject to the application of an early withdrawal penalty, if any.

Since Chase began offering its MII, other banks have followed suit with similar products. In 1993, Cleveland's Charter One Bank offered three-year and five-year CDs that return 100 percent of the gain in the S&P 500 plus a minimum interest rate of 4 percent and 5 percent respectively. In effect, the depositor receives either the guaranteed yield or the appreciation in the S&P 500 index, whichever is higher. Shawmut Bank in Hartford, Connecticut, offers a one-year CD whose return is one-half the increase in the S&P 500. The First National Bank of Maryland offered the "Mint CD" whose interest rate was several percentage points less than the gain of the S&P 500.

The number of different formulas that may be used for Indexed CDs is unlimited. Some banks take the average of the monthly S&P index for a one-year period to decide the annual interest rate. A drop in the index in some months brings the entire average down for the year, lowering the yield to the consumer. Other banks calculate the interest rate by comparing where the index stands on the date the account is opened with the position of the index on the date the certificate matures. In this case, interim (weekly, monthly or even yearly) fluctuations in the index do not matter, since the interest is computed solely on the basis of the difference in the index based on two points in time, ignoring interim fluctuations.

---

companies and the aggregate average market value of the common stocks of 500 similar companies during a certain base period in the 1940s.

NationsBank's Private Bank offers a "Stock Market CD" that sets interest annually by determining the difference between the index level on the first day of the period and the average of the S&P levels on the last day of each month in that year. The percentage increase, if any, is used to compute the annual interest rate. If the S&P has decreased or stayed the same, on average for the year, no interest is paid. Republic National Bank, New York, offers three- and five-year CDs that pay 150 percent and 200 percent of the S&P increase, respectively. Each carries a minimum 1 percent interest rate guarantee.

Financial indices besides the S&P 500 are used. For example, College Savings Bank, Princeton, N.J. offers the "College CD" whose interest rate is based on the average tuition increases at 500 colleges. A formula is used to compute the average tuition increases at the 500 colleges and universities, and the annual interest is computed based on the overall increase.[6] The copyrighted formula is a tuition index for the nation's 500 largest private colleges. To cover tuition and other costs, the savings bank invests in adjustable-rate mortgage-backed securities with returns expected to track tuition inflation.

3.3 Commodity Linked CDs

Indexed CDs may be linked to commodities indices. In 1986, Wells Fargo Bank, N.A. offered the Wells Fargo Gold Market Certificates.[7] Purchasers of these certificates deposited a sum of money (ranging from $2,500 to $1 million) with the bank and paid a non-refundable premium or fee for the right to earn a return based on the increase, if any, in gold prices at the conclusion of a 26 week deposit period. The investor in this program could select a "Full Option" or "Half Option." Under the former, the investor's earnings were calculated by multiplying the deposit amount by 100% of any increase in the price of gold at the conclusion of the 26 week period.

Half options were multiplied by 50% of the increase in gold prices and could be purchased for a lower premium than a Full Option. In addition to paying a premium, investors had to forego interest on the deposit of their funds. Indexed CDs have also been offered based on an index of spot gold prices. Other commodities related indices might include oil and gas indices, foreign exchange rates, and other mineral indices. Note also that

---

[6]College Savings Bank owns a patent on the investment method for the product and has brought suit in federal district court against the State of Florida, claiming its college tuition program is a infringement on the bank's patent.

[7]The CFTC took enforcement action against Wells Fargo and obtained a permanent injunction that enjoined the bank from selling the instruments. The CFTC's position on similar instruments has since changed, and is more fully discussed in the section of this chapter on Commodities Regulation Issues — Historical Perspective.

stock indices may be considered commodity related, an issue more fully discussed later in this chapter under the section dealing with "Commodities Regulation Issues".

3.4 Bonus CDs

Depository institutions also offer Indexed CDs that pay bonus interest keyed to certain nonfinancial events or indices. Examples include the "Wildcat CD," offered by Kentucky's Salyersville National Bank, which is linked to the performance of the University of Kentucky's basketball team; the "World Cup CD," offered by Peterson Bank in Chicago, with a base rate of 4.40%, which would have doubled in the event the U.S. soccer team had won the world championship; and the "Superbowl XX CD" offered by Skokie Federal Bank in Chicago which was tied to the outcome of Superbowl XX in 1986, when the Chicago Bears played the New England Patriots. Other CD rates have been keyed in part to the average temperature for a particular year or season, and the amount of seasonal snowfall or rainfall in a particular area.

3.5 Periodic Withdrawal ("Retirement") CDs

The most recent entry into the Indexed CD market is the so-called Periodic Withdrawal "Retirement" CD (the "Periodic Withdrawal CD") which pays interest based in part upon the customer's life expectancy.[8] The product, initially offered by the Blackfeet National Bank, Browning, Montana, has been offered by an estimated dozen banks. The Periodic Withdrawal CD is in effect a combination Indexed/bonus CD. While variations may exist, Periodic Withdrawal CDs are generally structured in two phases: an "accumulation phase" and a "withdrawal phase." During the accumulation phase, deposits are made and interest is credited to the account. During the withdrawal phase, the depositor receives periodic amounts from the account for the depositor's life.

During the accumulation phase, interest accrues on the account, and depositors are permitted to make additional deposits to the account, but may not withdraw any funds without incurring a substantial penalty for early withdrawal. The interest rate in effect during the accumulation phase is generally fixed for a period of time, and then fluctuates based on

---

[8]Letter to Jack Kelly, President & Chief Executive Officer, Blackfeet National Bank from William P. Bowden, Chief Counsel, (May 12, 1994) (the "Blackfeet Letter"). On April 7, 1995, the Department of the Treasury, Internal Revenue Service, published a notice of proposed rulemaking which would, if finalized, eliminate the tax-deferred status of the Retirement CD, effectively destroying the product's marketability to depositors. The founder of the product, American Deposit Corp., is contesting the I.R.S. action in federal district court. In the meantime, banks offering the product have suspended their marketing efforts pending resolution of the tax issue.

an interest rate index. Past versions of the product have included an index based on the "bank's cost of funds," later revised to the U.S. Government Treasury Bill effective yield less one and one-half percent (Blackfeet N.B.); "current market conditions" (FNB Santa Fe, New Mexico); and the bank's "current 2-year CD rate" (MetroBank, N.A., Houston, Texas).

On or before the maturity date, the customer determines how the balance of funds in the account (principal plus accrued interest) (the "Maturity Balance") will be repaid by the institution. The customer is permitted at maturity to withdraw a certain percentage of the account (the "Maturity Withdrawal") without incurring any penalty. The rest of the Maturity Balance must remain in the account, and is distributed to the customer during the withdrawal phase in fixed, equal periodic (*e.g.*, monthly) amounts which include interest, for the customer's life.

The periodic distributions are based on three factors: (1) the balance of funds left in the account after the customer makes the Maturity Withdrawal; (2) an imputed interest rate; and (3) the remaining life expectancy of the depositor based on mortality tables. The depository institution guarantees the periodic amounts will continue for the remainder of the depositor's life, even if the balance in the account is exhausted. The Periodic Withdrawal CD generally contains a refund feature which provides that, during the withdrawal phase, the customer (or his estate or beneficiary) will receive aggregate payments at least equal to the Maturity Balance net of the Maturity Withdrawal.

The Periodic Withdrawal CD is a hybrid Index/bonus CD because the ultimate return to the depositor is based on a combination of an index and sweetener or bonus. The index is the interest rate index used during the Accumulation Phase. The bonus or sweetener is based on the period of time the depositor lives during the Withdrawal Phase, throughout which the bank guarantees payments will continue, no matter how much the depositor previously has received in payments. The longer the depositor lives during the Withdrawal Phase, the greater the depositor's overall return.

4. LEGAL AUTHORITY TO OFFER INDEXED CDS

The authority of national banks to offer Indexed CDs and related deposit products fits squarely within the specific authorization contained in 12 U.S.C. § 24(Seventh) that national banks may receive deposits.[9] The Supreme Court recently rejected a narrow view of the bank

---

[9]Under 12 U.S.C. § 24(Seventh) national banks have the power to exercise —
all such incidental powers as shall be necessary to carry on the
business of banking; by discounting and negotiating promissory notes,
drafts, bills of exchange, and other evidences of debt; by receiving

powers clause that would interpret the National Bank Act as granting to national banks only the five specified powers and such ancillary powers needed to perform those five. See, NationsBank v. Variable Life Annuity Co., __ U.S. __, 115 S.Ct. 810 (1995).[10] The bank powers clause is a broad grant of the power to engage in the business of banking, including, but not limited to, the five specifically recited powers and such other powers that are reasonably necessary to perform not just the enumerated powers, but the business of banking as a whole. Id. Many activities that are not included in the enumerated powers, including brokerage of a wide variety of financial investment instruments as a financial intermediary, are also inherent parts of the business of banking. Judicial cases affirming OCC interpretations establish that an activity is within the scope of this authority if the activity: (1) is functionally equivalent to or a logical outgrowth of a traditional banking activity; (2) responds to customer needs or otherwise benefits the bank or its customers; and (3) involves risks similar to those already assumed by banks.

4.1 Functionally Equivalent to or Logical Outgrowth of a Traditional Banking Activity.

An Indexed CD clearly meets the test of being an outgrowth of a traditional banking activity. The OCC has opined that the Chase MII is "clearly a deposit," Chase Decision at 22, a position that has been affirmed in federal district court, Civil Action No. 87-1093 (TPG), USED, D.C. (1995).

The term "deposit" is not specifically defined in 12 U.S.C. § 24(Seventh). While unconventional, Indexed CDs represent a manifestation of banks taking action to meet the changing investment requirements of their customers through the exercise of an express power. The legal authority of a national bank to alter and upgrade its deposit products to keep pace with the financial requirements of its customers has been affirmed by the OCC and the courts. In the Blackfeet Letter, OCC noted that a national bank has the authority "to offer its customers competitive and innovative financial products." Blackfeet Letter at 7.[11]

---

deposits; by buying and selling exchange, coin, and bullion; by loaning money on personal security; and by obtaining, issuing, and circulating notes. (Emphasis added.)

[10]See also, M & M Leasing Corp. v. Seattle National Bank, 563 F.2d 1377, 1382 (9th Cir. 1977), Cert. denied, 436 U.S. 956 (1978); American Ins. Ass'n v. Clarke, 865 F.2d 278, 282 (2d Cir. 1988); New York State Ass'n of Life Underwriters v. New York State Banking Department, 83 N.Y.2d 353, 632 N.E.2d 876, 880-81 (1994).

[11]See also, Chase Decision, noting that Chase has the express power to offer the MII, and "to pay interest on time deposits according to market conditions, in order to remain competitive with savings

The OCC has opined that basing an Indexed CD's interest on an outside index does not otherwise alter the instrument's status as a deposit. See, Chase Decision at 26. Referring to the definition of "deposit" under the FDIA, the Chase Decision notes that the amount or type of interest payable on deposits is limited only by Federal Reserve Act § 19, 12 U.S.C. § 371(a), which prohibits the payment of interest on demand deposits. Since CDs are time deposits, that prohibition is not applicable to them. There is no legal restriction on the type or amount of interest a bank may pay on time deposits, nor is there any restriction against a time deposit accruing interest at a variable rate based on an index or standard ostensibly unrelated to interest rates or compiled by an entity other than the bank.

While Indexed CDs are clearly grounded in a national bank's authorizations to accept "deposits," the OCC has recognized that other bank authorizations may also be used as a basis for offering bank deposit products. In the Blackfeet Letter, the OCC concluded that the sale of so-called "Retirement CDs" is part of or incidental to the business of banking based on a bank's express authorizations to receive deposits under 12 U.S.C. § 24(Seventh) and to enter into contracts under 12 U.S.C. § 24(Third); and their implied powers to incur liabilities and fund their operations.

4.2 Responding to Customer Needs or Otherwise Benefiting the Bank or its Customers.

In offering Indexed CDs, national banks are responding to the ever changing and expanding needs of their customers. These instruments, through their indexing features, meet specific customer investment needs by offering hedges against such economic occurrences as inflation, stock market fluctuations, and commodity price changes. In addition to investment activities, customers may use Indexed CDs for hedging their business activities.

4.3 Involving Risks Similar to Those Already Assumed by Banks.

Indexed CDs generally involve the same or similar risks banks undertake in their other banking activities. Banks routinely engage in matched and unmatched commodity and index swap transactions, including related swap derivative products and over-the-counter

---

alternatives such as money market mutual funds . . . based on any index or standard selected by the bank, Chase Decision at 4; Securities Industry Association v. Clarke, 885 F.2d 1034 (2d Cir. 1989), cert denied, 110 S.Ct. 1113 (1990) (a national bank's express powers allow it to design products which augment its traditional bank activities).

options.[12] These transactions often involve securities and other financial indices and entail the same or similar risks as those found with Indexed CDs. Risk management primarily involves pricing and hedging exposures. Generally speaking, risks associated with the pricing of Indexed CDs and related hedging activities are not unique to the industry because the risks are similar to those associated with options. These instruments may, however, raise novel pricing and hedging issues where the bank itself has not dealt with Indexed CDs, or where the instruments contain particularly novel features (e.g., sports or weather related CDs). For a more detailed discussion of the risks attendant with Indexed CDs, see the section of this chapter on — Risk Management of Indexed CDs.

5. FDIC INSURANCE ISSUES

Indexed CDs raise unique federal deposit insurance issues. Generally speaking, an Indexed CD is an insured deposit product because it meets the requirements for FDIC insurance. Calculation of the amount of insurance, however, is more problematic due to uncertainties relating to accrued interest.

Bank deposits may be federally insured only if: (1) there is an unpaid balance of money or its equivalent received and held by the bank in the usual course of business; (2) the bank utilizes the funds received in the normal course of its banking business (e.g., to make loans or investments); (3) the bank gives credit for the funds received to an account evidenced by a certificate of deposit; and (4) the parties intend to create a deposit liability. FDIA § 3(l), 12 U.S.C. § 1813(l).

The term "deposit" is defined in § 3(l) of the FDIA, 12 U.S.C. § 1813(l). That section, which provides an extensive definition of the term, describes a "deposit" in part as:

> the unpaid balance of money or its equivalent received or held
> by a bank or savings association in the usual course of
> business and for which it has given or is obligated to give
> credit, either conditionally or unconditionally, to a
> commercial, checking, savings, time, or thrift account, or

---

[12]OCC Interpretive Letter (September 13, 1994), from Douglas E. Harris, Senior Deputy Comptroller for Capital Markets, to Carl Howard, Esq. Citibank, N.A.; OCC Interpretive Letter No. 632 (June 30, 1993); OCC Interpretive Letter (May 13, 1992), from Jimmy F. Barton, Deputy Comptroller of the Currency, to Carl Howard, Esq., Citibank, N.A.; OCC Interpretive Letter (March 2, 1992), from Horace G. Sneed, Senior Attorney, to Jeffrey S. Lillien, Esq., The First National Bank of Chicago; No-Objection Letter No. 90-1 (February 16, 1990), reprinted in [1989 - 1990 Transfer Binder] Fed. Banking L. Rep. (CCH) ¶ 83,095; OCC No-Objection Letter No. 87-5 (July 20, 1987), reprinted in [1987 - 1988 Transfer Binder] Fed. Banking L. Rep. (CCH) ¶ 84,034.

which is evidenced by its certificate of deposit.

An "insured deposit" is defined under the FDIA to mean the "net amount due to any depositor for deposits in an insured depository institution (after deducting offsets) less any part thereof which is in excess of $100,000." 12 U.S.C. § 1813(l)(1).

In FDIC Interpretive Letter 87-15 (September 18, 1987), the FDIC confirms the insurability of Indexed CDs. There, the FDIC examines the insurability of CDs that offer a fully or partially indexed interest return at maturity, with the index linked to either a stock index, the spot price of gold, or the spot prices of selected foreign currencies. Depositors are given a choice between "bull" direction CDs or "bear" direction CDs, and may elect to exercise a "lock-in" feature to fix the return until maturity. The principal due at maturity, however, is not indexed or put at risk. The FDIC concludes the CDs are insurable deposits, subject to normal limits.

It is the manner in which Indexed CD interest is calculated that raises the more difficult federal deposit insurance issues. FDIC regulations provide that the amount of a deposit is the balance of principal and accrued interest, and the amount of "ascertainable" interest "unconditionally credited" to the customer's deposit account as of the date the insured depository institution defaulted.[13] The ascertainable amount of interest accrued to the date of the default is computed at the CD contract rate (or the anticipated or announced interest or dividend rate), which the institution would have paid had the deposit matured on the date of the institution's failure.

To determine the interest rate on a CD lacking an announced or anticipated interest or dividend rate, the FDIC, as a general rule, uses the rate paid in the immediately preceding payment period.[14] With respect to Indexed CDs however, the interest not accrued as of the date of a bank's failure may not be federally insured. For example, the interest payable on a CD whose interest rate is based on the increase, if any, in the S&P 500 index calculated between two dates, becomes accrued and payable only when the calculation is made. Interim fluctuations in the index that occur before a computation date are not considered in the calculation of interest owed. In this case, the FDIC might insure only the actual interest accrued on the CD up to the last time the increase in the index was actually calculated. For example, if the depositor purchases an S&P 500 Indexed CD on January 1, 1994, with interest calculated yearly, and the bank fails on June 1, 1995, interest will have been calculated only for the period January 1, 1994 - January 1, 1995. When the bank fails on June 1, 1995, no interest is calculated for federal deposit insurance purposes, for the interim

---

[13] 12 C.F.R. § 330.3(h)(I)(1).

[14] Id.

period January 1, 1995 to the bank's June 1, 1995, failure date. Since the FDIC has not articulated a position on interest accruals and insurance for Indexed CDs, it is unclear whether the agency would adopt the above analysis.

The FDIC also appears to take the position that if the terms of the Indexed CD allow the customer's deposit balance to be placed at risk, (i.e., "invaded" if the applicable index goes down between the time of the initial deposit and maturity) the CD is not a deposit for FDIA purposes. Several FDIC approvals of Indexed CDs have been expressly conditioned on the fact that "the depositors' funds [are not] placed at risk by providing for negative interest or by limiting the obligation to repay principal on the basis of asset performance."[15]

It is noteworthy that the FDIA's definition of a deposit specifically includes money for which the bank has given credit "either conditionally or unconditionally."[16] The regulation does not indicate what types of "conditional" obligations to repay may be imposed on a deposit product, but it is apparent the Agency would not accept a condition placed in an Indexed CD where return of the principal amount in whole or in part is conditioned on the performance of an index.

6. SECURITIES ISSUES

A CD generally is not a security under the 1933 Act and the Exchange Act. In Marine Bank v. Weaver, 455 U.S. 552 (1982) ("Weaver"), the Supreme Court held that a certificate of deposit issued by a federally regulated national bank is not a security under the Exchange Act. Comparing bank CDs to long-term debt obligations, the latter of which generally are Exchange Act securities, the Court noted it is unnecessary to subject CDs to the antifraud provisions of the Exchange Act because of the comprehensive set of regulations governing the banking industry, including the reserve, reporting, and inspection requirements of the federal banking laws, restrictions on advertising interest rates, and the existence of federal deposit insurance for CDs.

Although Weaver was an Exchange Act case, it has been cited by the courts as a basis for excluding bank CDs from the definition of security under the 1933 Act because the two Acts define "security" so similarly. See, Wolf v. Banco Nacional de Mexico, S.A., 739 F.2d 1458 (9th Cir. 1984) ("Banco Nacional"). In Banco Nacional, the court concluded it was "compelled by the reasoning of Weaver that when a bank is sufficiently well regulated that

---

[15]See, e.g., FDIC Interp. Ltr. 86-35 (November 26, 1986); FDIC Interp. Ltr. 86-26 (September 9,1986).

[16]12 U.S.C. § 1813(l).

there is virtually no risk that insolvency will prevent it from repaying the holder of one of its certificates of deposit in full, the certificate is not a security for purposes of the federal securities laws." Id. at 1463.

Nonetheless, in Weaver the Supreme Court did not completely rule out the possibility that a CD could be a security under the federal securities laws. In a footnote of much notoriety, the Court said —

> It does not follow that a certificate of deposit or business agreement between transacting parties invariably falls outside the definition of a "security" as defined by the federal statutes. Each transaction must be analyzed and evaluated on the basis of the content of the instruments in question, the purposes intended to be served, and the factual setting as a whole.

455 U.S. 551 at 560 fn 11 (the "Weaver footnote").

In Brockton Savings Bank v. Peat, Marwick, Mitchell & Co., 577 F.Supp. 1281 (D. Mass. 1983), the district court examined the Weaver footnote in the context of a claim by the plaintiff that a bank's use of proceeds from CD deposits to fund oil and gas loans, constituted a "common enterprise" in which the CD holders could obtain a return of their deposits only if the oil and gas loans were successful. The court dismissed this argument, stating the depositors had no risk of loss as a result of the bank's oil and gas loans, short of total bank insolvency.

> A bank depositor such as Brockton, unlike holders of stocks and bonds, does not face the risk that the principal value of its investment will decline. Rather, a bank depositor's only risk is that the accepting bank will become insolvent. Such a risk does not transform a bank deposit, such as Brockton's CD, into a security especially in view of the virtually complete assurance of repayment depositors enjoy.

Based upon Weaver and Brockton, it is clear that only where the Indexed CD carries with it characteristics applicable to securities and not deposits will the instrument be characterized as a security. This might occur, for example, where principal is placed at risk or where the return is dependent on the profits of a business venture. In Gary Plastic Packaging Corp. v. Merrill Lynch, Pierce, Fenner & Smith, Inc., 756 F.2d 230 (2d Cir. 1985), the court ruled that a certificate of deposit was a security under circumstances generally distinguishable from typical CD programs, including Indexed CDs. In Gary Plastic Merrill Lynch published a list of available CDs, brokered the CDs to interested parties, and maintained a secondary market for the certificates. In holding that the CDs were federal securities, the court took note of

Merrill Lynch's significant marketing efforts on behalf of the program and the fact that investors expected not only a return of their cash investment, but the potential for price appreciation due to interest rate fluctuations. It was also significant that investors who purchased CD's directly from banks participating in the program obtained higher interest rates than those offered by the same banks through Merrill Lynch, a fact the court noted derisively was not disclosed to program participants.

Based upon the criteria cited in the Weaver footnote, and the discussion in Brockton, most Indexed CDs should continue to be viewed as bank deposits and not securities. The fact that a CD may be indexed or contain a bonus feature generally will not act to convert the deposit product into a security. It should also be noted that Indexed CDs are not securities under Glass-Steagall. See, OCC Chase Decision and Court Chase Opinion. Glass-Steagall is not intended to affect the authority of commercial banks to conduct activities which are part of the business of banking. Because Indexed CDs fall within the express power of national banks to take deposits, the activity is not one that falls under Glass-Steagall.

7. COMMODITIES REGULATION ISSUES[17]

Indexed CDs are a form of derivative instrument since a portion of the value of the CD (i.e. computation of the interest rate) is determined or "derived" from the value of another underlying instrument or asset. Derivatives instruments may take the form of swaps, forwards, futures, and options (including combinations thereof). The various elements embedded in the structure of a deposit based instrument such as an Indexed CD might take one or more of these various forms, raising the issue of how the instrument itself should be classified for regulatory purposes.

Classification of an Indexed CD is critical for determining whether the instrument falls outside the scope of the CEA and CFTC regulation, or whether the instrument is subject to an applicable exclusion or exemption from commodities regulation. If the instrument is deemed to be a future under the CEA, it may not be traded on an exchange that is not regulated by the CFTC.[18] If the instrument is deemed to be a commodities option, it falls under the jurisdiction of the CFTC and may only be conducted pursuant to authorization by

---

[17]The authors wish to thank Joanne T. Medero, Partner, Orrick, Herrington & Sutcliffe for her assistance on the implications of the commodities laws on Indexed CDs. Portions of this section are based on her article Jurisdictional Issues in U.S. Regulation of Derivative Products, Butterworths Journal of International Banking and Financial Law, 117 (March 1994).

[18]CEA § 4(a).

the CFTC.[19] As a result of the complications raised by CFTC regulation, banks should structure their Indexed CDs to fall outside the scope of the CEA. As discussed below, this generally can be accomplished through compliance with CEA exemptions and CFTC interpretations and regulations.

7.1 Indexed CDs Subject to Securities Indices

The regulatory framework applicable to derivatives instruments splits jurisdiction between the CFTC and the SEC along functional lines. The CFTC supervises the trading of futures contracts and commodity options, while the SEC regulates the offer and sale of securities and securities options.[20] This principal is enunciated in the CEA which excludes from CFTC jurisdiction —

> any transaction whereby any party to such transaction acquires any put, call, or other option on one or more securities [as defined in the 1933 Act and Exchange Act] . . . including any group or index of such securities, or any interest therein or based on the value thereof.

CDs with interest rates dependent on one or more securities or securities indices will generally fall outside the scope of CFTC jurisdiction under the § 2(a)(1)(B) delineation of authority between the SEC and CFTC. This is true provided that only the interest rate on the Indexed CD is dependent on the applicable index. If the return of the depositor's principal balance is also keyed to a securities index, it likely will be subject to CFTC regulation as a future. It is critical that the Indexed CD not be characterized as a future since the sale of a future not traded on an exchange regulated by the CFTC is illegal (unless the CFTC states that it is exempt from the exchange-trading requirement).

The CEA does not contain a definition of the term future. However, in general, it appears that the primary distinction between a securities option and a future, in the bank deposit context, is found in the nature of the deposit balance. If repayment of the deposit balance is not contingent on the applicable securities index achieving a certain level, the instrument is probably not a future. The Chase MII is an example of an Indexed CD structured as an option on securities and not a future, because the level of the S&P 500 at maturity is relevant only to the amount of interest paid on the instrument, and is irrelevant to the bank's obligation to return the depositor's principal. Accordingly, the Chase MII is not subject to the CFTC's jurisdiction under the CEA § 2(a)(1)(B) delineation of authority.

---

[19]CEA § 4(c)(b).

[20]CEA § 2(a)(1)(B).

7.2 Hybrid Instrument Exemption and Statutory Interpretation

Securities or bank deposit instruments that include features similar to those found in futures or commodity options are hybrid instruments. Indexed CDs that return the deposit balance at maturity with interest payments dependent on the increase in the price of a particular commodity, such as oil or gold, are examples of hybrid instruments. Indexed CDs with securities indices are generally hybrid instruments, but fall outside the scope of the CEA under § 2(a)(1)(B).

The CFTC has issued both an exemptive rule (the "exemption") and a statutory interpretation (the "statutory interpretation") that apply to hybrid instruments. A bank may use either of the two regulatory provisions depending on the structure it selects for its Indexed CD. Both the exemption and the statutory interpretation are intended to exempt instruments where the commodity price exposure does not predominate and where an alternative regulatory regime applies. In general, the Exemption allows more flexibility in structuring Indexed CDs than does the Statutory Interpretation.

The Exemption[21] is promulgated under the CFTC's general exemptive authority which allows the agency to exempt "classes of hybrid instruments that are predominantly securities or depository instruments, to the extent such instruments may be regarded as subject to the provision of this Act."[22] It applies to "depository instruments" with one or more commodity-dependent components that have payment features similar to commodity futures or commodity option contracts.[23] Under the exemption, a demand or time deposit, as defined in 12 C.F.R. § 204.2 (which includes a certificate of deposit) offered by a federally insured depository institution, is exempt from all provisions of the CEA provided certain requirements are met. Under the requirements applicable to the exemption, (1) the sum of the "commodity-dependent values" of the "commodity-dependent components" must be less than the "commodity-independent value" of the "commodity-independent components" (in general, the commodity dependent values of the commodity-dependent components for an Indexed CD will exceed the commodity-independent values of the commodity-independent components only if either a portion of the deposit's principal may be lost or the account is for a very long term, making the value of the commodity linked interest rate more significant); (2) the bank must receive full payment for the deposit and no additional out-of-pocket payments, including payments from accruing interest, are required during the life of the

---

[21]Regulation of Hybrid Instruments, 17 C.F.R. Part 34.

[22]CEA § 4(c)(5)(A).

[23]17 C.F.R. § 34.3.

instrument or at maturity; (3) the instrument may not be marketed as a futures contract or a commodity option; (4) the deposit must not provide for settlement in the form of a delivery instrument that is specified as such in the rules of a CFTC designated contract market; and (5) the instrument is initially issued or sold subject to applicable federal or state securities or banking laws to persons permitted thereunder to purchase or enter into the hybrid instrument.

The statutory interpretation[24] offers another means of exempting an Indexed CD from CFTC regulation. Only "bona fide debt or depository instruments" are eligible for the exemption. To qualify, the instrument must meet the following criteria: (1) the commodity index borne by the instrument must be no greater than on a one-to-one basis (i.e., the instrument's index must not be a multiple of the interest rate or index to which it is keyed); (2) the instrument must provide for a maximum loss which, generally speaking, for Indexed CDs is the amount of interest payable on the instrument (i.e., only the interest and not the principal amount may not be placed at risk); (3) the instrument must have a significant commodity-independent yield; (4) there must be no commodity component that is severable from the debt or depository instrument; (5) the instrument must not call for delivery of a commodity; and (6) the issuer must not market the instrument as having the characteristics of a futures contract or commodity option.

7.3 The Treasury Amendment

The Department of the Treasury was instrumental in causing passage of the so-called "Treasury Amendment" to the CEA in 1974. The Amendment was enacted in response to concerns of the Department of the Treasury that the definition of "commodity" under the CEA was too broad, and might act to extend the CEA and the CFTC's applicable regulatory jurisdiction into the foreign currency and other trading activities of banks and other institutions that do not take place on the foreign exchange markets.

The Treasury Amendment provides that —

> Nothing in this [CEA] shall be deemed to govern or in any way
> be applicable to transactions in foreign currency, security
> warrants, security rights, resales of installment loan contracts,
> repurchase options, government securities, or mortgages or
> mortgage purchase commitments, unless such transactions
> involve the sale thereof for future delivery conducted on a

---

[24]Statutory Interpretation Concerning Hybrid Instruments, 55 F.R. 13582 (April 11, 1990) (Reissued).

board of trade.[25]

Since its enactment, the Treasury Amendment has been the subject of numerous court cases that have raised significant interpretive issues. In general, the Amendment might offer some exemptive relief from the CEA and CFTC regulations for banks that issue Indexed CDs tied to government securities or foreign exchanges. An Indexed CD, for example, that offers depositors a return based on appreciation in a particular foreign currency might be exempt under the exemption for transactions in foreign exchange. The same result could occur for Indexed CDs with rates keyed to government securities. However, there is a split in the circuits on whether the Treasury Amendment excludes "options" from coverage by the CEA. In CFTC v. William C. Dunn and Delta Consultants, Inc., 58 F.3d 50 (2d Cir. 1995), the court held that the term "transactions in foreign currency," as used in the Treasury Amendment, does not include, and therefore does not exempt, options, even those options traded off-exchange.

> Our reasoning was that an option was simply the right to engage in a transaction in the future, and, until this right matured, there was no exempt "transaction." The exercise of an option would constitute a "transaction in a foreign currency," but the purchase or sale of the option itself would not be such a "transaction" under the Treasury Amendment.

Id. at 55. Under this approach, Indexed CD's with interest rates linked to foreign currencies or government securities, could be viewed as options on foreign currencies or government securities which are not exercised until the CD matures. In Salomon Forex v. Tauber, 8 F.3d 966 (4th Cir. 1993), cert. den. _ U.S. _ (1994), 114 S.Ct. 2156 (1994), on the other hand, the Fourth Circuit, using a plain meaning analysis, held that "negotiated, customized, large-scale" foreign currency transactions (including options) between "professionals" are excluded by the Treasury Amendment from CFTC jurisdiction. How the Supreme Court might resolve this issue between the circuits is unclear. This ambiguity may be avoided by a bank's structuring its Indexed CDs in accordance with the hybrid exemption or statutory interpretation, and not relying on the Treasury Amendment.

7.4 Sports and Weather Related Indices

Indexed CDs with indices or reference elements keyed to items not normally thought

---

[25]CEA § 2(a)(1)(A)(ii), 7 U.S.C. § 2(a)(1)(A)(ii).

of as "commodities" raise interesting issues under the CEA. First, there is some question as to whether these instruments involve "commodities" as defined by the Act. CEA § 1(a)(3), 7 U.S.C. § 2 in defining "commodity," lists various goods such as wheat, cotton, rice and barley, and contains the catch-all phrase — "and all services, rights, and interests in which contracts for future delivery are presently or in the future dealt in. . ." CEA § 2(a)(1)(A)(I), 7 U.S.C. § 2(a)(ii) states, subject to the carve out for SEC jurisdiction described above, that the CFTC shall have exclusive jurisdiction over "options," "puts," "calls," and "transactions involving sales of a commodity for future delivery."

A reasonable argument can be made that Indexed CDs with indices keyed to such esoteric items as snowfall and sports records are not intended to fall within the ambit of the CEA's commodity definition as it applies to options and contracts for future delivery.[26] Given the breadth of the CEA definition of commodity, however, a payment stream based on snowfall or sports results may be considered an option on a commodity, despite the fact that the subject of the instrument might not be commonly recognized as such. Even so, the CFTC likely will not attempt to bring within its jurisdiction commodities that are not and are unlikely to become the subject of exchange trading. Accordingly, these unusual indices are unlikely to be covered by the CEA. While this issue has not been litigated in the context of Indexed CDs, its resolution as a practical matter is not critical given the existence of the hybrid exemption and statutory interpretation under which Indexed CD's may be structured. Also noteworthy is the fact that State gambling laws might apply to these instruments, depending on the particular state law provisions and their application to and impact on bank deposit instruments.

7.5 Historical Perspective

The CFTC's current position has evolved from one that treated Indexed CDs as commodities subject to the CEA. In CFTC v. Wells Fargo Bank, N.A., Civ. No. 87-07992 Wdk. (BX) (Nov. 18, 1987), (described more fully in this chapter under the heading Product Descriptions — Bonus CDs) the CFTC charged that Wells Fargo was illegally offering and selling options contracts to the general public in the form of "Wells Fargo Gold Market Certificates." Wells Fargo consented to a permanent injunction that enjoined it from selling

---

[26]Determining whether a transaction constitutes a futures or options contract requires a review of the transaction as a whole with a critical eye toward its underlying purpose. The principal investment is generally not placed at risk with an option, whereas it is at risk with a future. See, 54 Fed. Reg. 1139 (January 11, 1989); CFTC v. Co. Petro Marketing Group, Inc., 680 F.2d 573, 581 (9th Cir. 1982) (transactions held to be futures contracts). In the Indexed CD context, to meet criteria applicable to bank deposits, the principal will generally not be placed at risk, making the instrument an option for any analysis under the CEA.

these instruments, and it agreed to refund the customer funds, premiums and to pay interest on the use of the customer funds.

The CFTC later allowed a depository institution to issue to their retail customers CDs with interest payable at maturity based on an index of spot gold prices. These Indexed CDs could be bears or bulls, i.e., the Indexed CDs could either increase as the value of the index increased or vice versa. The CDs also provided a guaranteed rate of interest that would equal or exceed 35% of the estimated annual yield of a Non-Indexed CD of like maturity and denomination. No up-front fees were charged and the CDs were subject to a substantial penalty for early withdrawal. CFTC Interpretive Letter No. 88-18, 2 Comm. Fut. L. Rep. (CCH) ¶24,321.

8. MARKETING AND ADVERTISING ISSUES IN GENERAL

As discussed above, Indexed CDs generally are bank deposit products. The OCC has no specific rules that address solicitations for deposit products. The primary standard for these types of solicitations is safety and soundness. Misleading or fraudulent solicitations may be inconsistent with safe and sound banking practices. Because they are deposit products, solicitations for Indexed CDs are not subject to the Interagency Statement on Non-Deposit Investment Products.

Section 709 of the United States Criminal Code, 18 U.S.C. § 709, makes it unlawful for anyone to "falsely [advertise] or otherwise [represent] by any device whatsoever the extent to which or the manner in which the deposit liabilities of an insured bank or banks are insured by the Federal Deposit Insurance Corporation . . ." As a result, banks that issue CDs whose index component does not allow interest to be determined if the bank fails before the index computation date (e.g., S&P 500 Indexed CDs or college tuition CDs) generally refer to the CDs as being "principal insured," omitting any reference that could be construed as indicating interest is insured.

Many states have unfair and deceptive practices laws that prohibit certain sales practices. These laws may be applicable to Indexed CDs, depending on the particular law and its application to bank deposit products.

8.1 Truth in Savings

Indexed CDs are subject to Federal Reserve Board ("FRB") Regulation DD, Truth in Savings, 12 C.F.R. Part 230. The Truth in Savings provisions require disclosures so that consumers can make "meaningful comparisons" between accounts offered by depository institutions. 12 C.F.R. § 230.1.

Under Regulation DD, required disclosures applicable to an Indexed CD's interest rate include informing customers (1) of the method used to determine the interest rate; (2) that the product's interest rate and annual percentage yield may change, including any limitations on the amount the interest rate may change; (3) when interest begins to accrue; (4) about the frequency with which the interest rate may change; (5) whether or not interest is compounded and credited, (including the frequency if it is); (6) of the method used to compute the account balance; (7) of fees; (8) of the applicable maturity date and the circumstances under which the bank may redeem the account (i.e., callable time accounts); and (9) about renewal policies. 12 U.S.C. § 230.4. The commentary to Regulation DD states that if the interest rate is tied to an index, institutions must identify the index and specific margin. Regulation DD, Comment 6-2077.

Disclosures are also required concerning penalties for early withdrawal, including the fact that a penalty will or may be imposed for early withdrawal, how it is calculated, and the conditions for its assessment. Id. Specific proscriptions against false and misleading advertising are also contained in Regulation DD. "An advertisement shall not be misleading or inaccurate and shall not misrepresent a depository institution's deposit contract." 12 C.F.R. § 230.8.

The key component for allowing customers to compare various bank products is the annual percentage yield ("APY"), which is required to be disclosed in the solicitation materials if a rate of return or bonus is stated. The APY for Indexed CDs will depend on the type of index referenced. In general, for variable rate accounts, such as Indexed CDs, the bank is required to base the APY, and assume the rate does not change during the year, on the variable interest rate that is in effect when the account is opened or advertised. 12 C.F.R. Part 230, Appendix A, Part IC ("Appendix A"). For example, a variable rate CD that pays interest in accordance with the six-month Treasury Bill rate ("T-Bill Rate"), will quote an APY based on the T-Bill Rate when the account is opened or advertised.

Applying the criteria of Appendix A to calculating the APY for Indexed CDs that are keyed to stock market and other indices is more problematic. These CDs may not quote a current APY since the yield will not be known until enough time has elapsed to allow for the comparison of the applicable index at two points in time. For example, the MII interest rate on a CD purchased in 1995 is determined by comparing the S&P 500 at the beginning and end of 1995, and paying interest based on the increase, if any, in the index. Therefore, at the time the CD is opened, there is no way to determine the yield on the instrument. The same problem is inherent in the College CD, the return on which is computed based on the increase in college tuition costs on a year to year basis.

These types of Indexed CDs are not specifically addressed in Regulation DD. The

FRB however, has informally indicated its position to the OCC. In situations where the index used necessitates computing the return subsequent to the customer's purchase of the CD, the FRB takes the position that the bank must quote the APY as 0%, subject to change. The bank also discloses the circumstances under which the CD rate and yield will change, e.g., if the applicable index is higher at the end of the year than it was at the beginning of the year, the APY will exceed 0%. The method used to calculate the APY must also be fully disclosed.

9. U.S. FEDERAL INCOME TAX ISSUES

Indexed CDs raise federal income tax timing issues. The fact that the exact amount of interest accrued on an Indexed CD may not be known at the end of the tax year, or, in some cases, until the CD matures, makes it difficult to know the amount of interest income that should be reported on the taxpayer's federal income tax return. This problem is similar to the problem faced by the FDIC when a bank fails on a date before the index is scheduled to be calculated. For this reason, many of the Indexed CD accounts are offered only for tax deferred accounts, such as IRA, SEP and Keogh plans where timing issues are not a problem since taxation of the income is deferred.

A comprehensive analysis of the federal income tax principles applicable to Indexed CDs is beyond the scope of this chapter. Certain basic principles, however, can be noted. The Internal Revenue Service ("IRS") has been reviewing the taxation of indexed instruments, and has issued proposed regulations for so-called "contingent debt instruments" which might be applicable to bank CDs.[27] In addition, the original issue discount rules[28] are applicable in computing the amount of interest income reportable for Indexed CDs. As noted above, interim computations for Indexed CDs to accommodate the calendar reporting period for most individual taxpayers, is problematic.

---

[27]Prop. Reg. § 1.175-4. See generally, Report and Recommendation for the Treatment of Contingent Debt Instruments Under Proposed Regulation Section 1.1275-4, 61 Tax Notes 1241 (December 6, 1993). The IRS takes the position the Contingent Debt Instrument regulations are applicable to indexed CDs, but there is some disagreement in the industry as to whether indexed CDs fit the definitions of the proposed regulations. The IRS often uses proposed regulations to articulate its current position on a tax matter, and encourages taxpayers to comply with the proposed regulations even though they have not been finalized.

[28]Internal Revenue Code § 1275. See, Comment by Peter A. Roberts, College Savings Bank, Princeton, N.J., 67 Tax Notes 473 (April 25, 1995) ("Proper application of the OID rules to state prepaid tuition programs is necessary for private sector college savings products to fairly compete with governmental programs.")

In general, the IRS takes the position that the income from Indexed CDs with terms of one year or less should be reported when the income is paid. These instruments are called "variable rate debt instruments" (VRDIs). The IRS does not require taxpayers to estimate the income on VRDIs since the income will be received no later than one year after the deposit is made.

Interest income accrued on CDs with terms in excess of one year must generally be estimated and reported on a yearly basis. The IRS calls these instruments "contingent payment debt instruments" ("CPDIs"). When payments are actually made on the CDs, taxpayers take an adjusting deduction or addition to their gross income based on the previous years' estimates. The IRS' primary tax concern with VRDIs and CPDIs is that the declaration of the interest income by the taxpayer not be postponed in excess of a year.

10. RISK MANAGEMENT OF INDEXED CDS

Sales of Indexed CDs expose the bank to market risk (e.g., equity price risk). The source of market risk may be new to the bank, or may be the same as or correlated with an existing source of market risk. In either case, unless the exposure is negligible, the bank must be able to manage it in order to match that exposure to the bank's appetite for risk. The purpose of this section is to discuss the nature of the exposures embedded in Indexed CDs and to identify risk management problems, if they exist.

10.1 The nature of the risk exposure

All Indexed CDs can be likened to derivatives in which the bank is the seller (or the "short"). They may be designed with many different final payment patterns, such as a European call or put option or a forward contract. In some structures, e.g., the forward, the total return at maturity to the purchaser may be negative.

To date, Indexed CDs have not provided for negative interest, i.e., principal cannot be invaded. For these instruments the indexed portion of the CD has the form of a (European exercise style) commodity option. For example, the MII (described above) offers a payment to the purchaser at maturity that can be compactly described as follows:

$$\text{Payment at} \atop \text{maturity} = {\text{Initial} \atop \text{deposit}} \left(1 + {\text{Guaranteed} \atop \text{Return}} \times {\text{CD term} \atop \text{in years}} + \right.$$

$$\left. {\text{Index Multiplier} \over \text{S\&P at purchase}} \times \max \left\{ {\text{S\&P at} \atop \text{maturity}} - {\text{S\&P at} \atop \text{purchase}}, 0 \right\} \right).$$

The first two terms on the right hand side of the equation represent the return of principal and the fixed interest promised on the CD. The last term represents the uncertain payment from the commodity component. The max function selects the larger of the two items inside the curly brackets, and it exactly describes the payoff on a European call option on the S&P with a strike price equal to the level of the S&P on the purchase date.

10.2 The risk management problem

The risk management problem can be divided into two parts. First, the instrument must be priced in such a way as to offer a return commensurate with the instrument's risk. Second the bank must have some mechanism to hedge any exposure above a level of exposure consistent with the bank's tolerance for risk. The pricing problem exists regardless of the extent to which the bank will hedge the exposure, but will depend on the hedging policy, because different approaches to hedging the exposure may entail different administrative and transactions costs.

10.2.1 Pricing an Indexed CD

Generally speaking, issues associated with the pricing of Indexed CDs are not unique to the industry because the issues are similar to pricing issues associated with options. On the other hand, these instruments may raise novel pricing issues in situations where the bank itself has not dealt with Indexed CDs, or where the instruments contain particularly novel features (e.g., sports or weather related CDs). The generic pricing problem is composed of two parts. First the fair or theoretical value of the instrument must be determined. This includes a normal return for the risk in the instrument. Second, the adjustments to the fair value that are necessary to cover administrative, hedging, and related costs must be determined. This pricing strategy is not unique to these instruments. To price an Indexed CD such as the MII CD requires an option pricing model and estimates of the model's parameters. For example, in the case of the MII CD, it may be appropriate to use the Black-Scholes model, in which case estimates of the volatility and dividend yield of the S&P must be obtained. The appendix details how the MII CD fair value would be determined.

In the case of the MII CD, the bank has an exposure to increases in the index. Significantly for hedging, this exposure entails negative convexity (an increase in the index induces a greater incremental loss than the incremental gain from a similar decrease in the index). The MII CD also causes the bank to have an exposure to increases in index volatility and declines in interest rates. CDs with option-like characteristics will leave the bank with an exposure with negative convexity if the embedded option is a call and positive convexity if the embedded option is a put.

10.2.2 Hedging the exposure arising from an Indexed CD

Indexed CDs will not raise unique or novel hedging issues for national banks unless either the bank itself has not previously transacted in options products or the structure of the CD is new. The hedging strategy employed by the bank should reflect its risk appetite, the incremental effect of the CD sales on the overall risk exposure of the bank, and the relative costs of alternative hedging mechanisms. To the extent possible, the hedging strategy should be part of the bank's overall portfolio hedging strategy. These elements of hedging policy hold for all products of the bank. The mechanics of hedge construction are discussed in the appendix for the case of the MII CD. Situations where Indexed CDs are new to the bank, or where novel structures raise special issues are discussed next.

First, the bank's standard hedging strategy may not be feasible, because the CD may entail an exposure that cannot be effectively hedged with available financial instruments (e.g. swaps, options, futures or cash market instruments). For example, the most direct means of offsetting the commodity-related exposure in the CD is to enter into "matched" transactions. A matched transaction exactly mirrors the exposure being hedged. Exact matching can probably only be obtained through trades with an over-the-counter ("OTC") derivatives dealer, because exchange-traded derivatives will not have tenors and notional amounts that exactly fit the hedging need. Even more sophisticated hedging techniques, for example, those based on the "delta" of the embedded option, may not be feasible for the types of risks sometimes found in "bonus" CDs, e.g., non market risks related to the outcomes of sporting events. For such instruments the bank may need to develop special hedging strategies.[29]

Second, the exposure may be new to the bank. For a new exposure, the bank may have no "natural" hedges in its portfolio. Further, the managers may be unfamiliar with the potential hedging instruments and market practices that would affect the cost of hedging and, therefore, the choice of the best hedging instrument.

Third, the managers may not have the technical expertise necessary to implement a hedge of the exposure. This problem could arise not only if central risk managers do not understand options risks, but also if the responsibility for risk management of the exposure remains with the funds sourcing managers where they may be unfamiliar with option type risks.

Fourth, the administrative costs of hedging the commodity related CD exposure could be large. For example, it is unlikely that the bank would want to attempt to match each CD

---

[29]According to Kevin Tynan, president of Tynan Marketing, banks take out insurance policies to hedge against the rate risk in a bonus CD (William Plasencia, "Many Banks Dusting Off The Bonus CD," American Banker January 9, 1995). Pricing details and covenant restrictions were not discussed in the article.

purchase, because the administrative costs would be high and the bid-ask spread paid on matching transactions with principal amounts below $1 million would likely be significantly higher. Thus the bank would probably choose to enter into matching transactions periodically, say daily or weekly, which would result in the bank having some exposure.

APPENDIX

The value at the purchase date of the maturity payment on the MII CD can be written as follows:

$$V_0 = D_0 \left(\frac{1 + GR \times T}{e^{rT}} + \frac{IM}{S\&P_0} C_0 \right).$$

D_0 is the amount of the initial deposit, GR is the annualized guaranteed return, T is the term of the CD in years, r is interest rate e^{rT} is the present value factor, IM is the index multiplier, $S\&P_0$ is the level of the S&P at the purchase date, and C_0 is the value of a call on the S&P 500. The present value of the guaranteed amount plus the dollar value of the call option on the purchase date. If the CD is fairly priced then V_0 should equal the price paid (i.e., the amount deposited). The depositor chooses all the features of the CD except the IM, which the bank sets. Whether the CD is fairly priced then depends on the IM. The fair value IM can be determined by first setting the payment value equal to the amount deposited, and then solving the resulting equation for the IM. Doing this gives the following expression for the IM that makes the deposit fairly priced:

$$IM = (1 - (1 + GR \times T)e^{-rT}) \frac{S\&P_0}{C_0}.$$

Because the strike of the call is equal to the level of the S&P at the purchase date, it is possible to show that the IM does not vary with the level of the S&P 500 index.[30] As would be expected the IM declines as the GR increases, and increases as the term of the CD increases.

Table 1 provides some illustrative values for the IM. For the parameter values specified in the table, any value of the IM greater than presented in the table would imply the bank has set the price of the instrument too low. Thus this represents an upper bound on the IM in order for the instrument to offer an appropriate return to the bank. Costs related to hedging would reduce the upper bound on IM further.[31]

---

[30]To show this it is necessary to use the result first established by Robert Merton (1973), that ordinary European call prices are "homogeneous of degree one" in the underlying and the strike. This means that a call with the strike equal to the index has the same value as a call with a strike of one on an underlying asset with a value of one, multiplied by the index level on the purchase date. When this result is substituted into the IM formula, the index level in the numerator cancels.

[31]This analysis focusses on the bank's pricing strategy independently of the purchaser. Several analyses of pricing and hedging commodity-linked deposits have been conducted by others. See, for

Table 1
Levels of the Index Multiplier in the Market Index Investment CD that result in an (actuarially) fair price for the instrument for various Guaranteed Rates ("GR") and terms (both chosen by purchaser) and various market interest rates and volatilities

Index volatility	Market interest rate	Term = 0.25 year		Term = 1 year	
		GR = 0%	GR = 4%	GR = 0%	GR = 4%
9%	7%	0.70	0.30	1.06	0.47
	14%	0.95	0.68	1.14	0.83
18%	7%	0.41	0.17	0.71	0.31
	14%	0.66	0.47	0.96	0.70

All values are rounded down. If the bank were to set an Index Multiplier value greater than that indicated in any given cell, the result would be under-pricing of the CD by the bank.

The exposure in the MII CD can be hedged in different ways. In order to keep the discussion below uncomplicated it is assumed that the exposure is to be hedged apart from the remainder of the bank's portfolio.

While the initial pricing of the CD should reflect hedging costs, initial pricing should not affect the hedging of post-purchase exposures. This is because the bank's exposure to a change in the index is the same whether the initial pricing of the CD embedded a large potential profit to the bank or was fair. When matching trades, for example, the bank will buy from a third party above fair value and sell (when the CDs mature) below fair value. This cost, i.e., the bid-ask spread paid to the third party, should be incorporated into the initial pricing of the CD. The bid-ask spread paid will vary with the type of commodity exposure, and will be greater for those risks that do not have active OTC markets.

Hedging the risk within the bank may be accomplished through "static" or "dynamic" techniques (or more likely a combination of the two). Either method requires that the bank be able enter into transactions in instruments whose returns are correlated with the exposure.[32] This may not always be possible, either because correlated instruments are not available (as may be the case with some bonus CDs), or because regulatory constraints

---

working paper, 1994), Chen and Kensinger ("An Analysis of Market-Index Certificates of Deposit," Journal of Financial Services Research, 1994) and King and Remolona ("The Pricing and Hedging of Market Index Deposits," FRBNY Quarterly Review, 1987). In a perfect world the bank would make no sales of the CD if it were priced above the fair value. However, because of market imperfections (for example, transactions costs incurred by investors), a positive demand can exist for the instrument even when priced above fair value.

[32] In order to hedge all the exposure, at least one of the instruments used must be instantaneously perfectly correlated with the exposure.

Table 2
Derivation of the position in the S&P 500 that provides a static hedge for the option embedded in the MII CD

Bank positions	Cash flows at purchase date	Cash flows at CD maturity	
		$S\&P_T > S\&P_0$	$S\&P_T \leq S\&P_0$
Sell calls (embedded in CD)	$\dfrac{IM}{S\&P_0}C_0D_0$	$-\dfrac{IM}{S\&P_0}(S\&P_T - S\&P_0)D_0$	0
Invest in S&P	$-X$	$X\dfrac{S\&P_T}{S\&P_0}$	$X\dfrac{S\&P_T}{S\&P_0}$
Net Position		≥ 0 *if* $X \geq$ $\dfrac{IM}{S\&P_T}(S\&P_T - S\&P_0)D_0$	$\geq 0,$ $\forall X \geq 0$

For the hedge to be successful the cash flows from the net position at maturity must always be non-negative. This can be assured by careful selection of the size of the initial hedge position in the S&P 500, X. When the option in the CD expires in the money, *as* $S\&P_T \to \infty$, $X \to IM \times D_0$. Therefore, the value of X that is large enough to ensure the net cash flow is positive in each state, irrespective of the level of the index is IMD. If it is *assumed* the S&P will not increase by more than "w" times its purchase date value over the term of the CD, then X may be set to $(IM)D_0(1 - 1/w)$.

prohibit the bank from transacting in the instruments correlated with the exposure.

A static hedge is one in which the bank, after entering into the hedge transaction, does not alter the hedge prior to the maturity of the hedged transaction. Consider the following illustration. Because the value of an option can never exceed that of the underlying, it is possible to enter into a static hedge of the commodity exposure embedded in the MII CD by purchasing a position in the S&P 500 equities equal to (D_0)IM (see Table 2 for the derivation). Table 3 provides an illustration that this static hedge will yield sufficient cash from the investment in the S&P to ensure the option obligation embedded in the CD can be met irrespective of the level of the S&P at the maturity of the CD. Note that the cost of the hedge is greater than the initial value of the commodity component of the CD. This is the price that is paid in order for the hedge to be static when the underlying exposure is option-like. Too much protection must be purchased for some eventualities if enough protection is to be available in all other eventualities.[33] If the index at the maturity of the CD is below the

---

[33]From Table 2 it can be seen that the difference between the value of the option paid for at the purchase date and the cost of the hedging position in the S&P is given by the following expression:

$$IM \times D_0 \left[\frac{C_0}{S\&P_0} - 1 \right] \leq 0.$$

Table 3
Illustration that a static hedge of the MII CD can provide cash flows on the maturity date sufficient to finance the commodity-related component of the payment due to the purchaser

S&P$_T$	Option value	S&P investment value
25	0	15.60
100	0	62.41
150	31.20	93.61
300	124.81	187.22
50,000	31,141.15	31,203.56

It is assumed that the CD was purchased with an original maturity of 0.25 years and with a guaranteed return of 0, the purchaser deposits $100, the S&P is at a level of 100 on the purchase date, the index volatility is 9% annualized, the rate of interest is 7% annualized, the dividend yield on the index is 0%, and the index multiplier is 0.624 (which would yield a fair price for the CD at purchase). In this scenario, the purchase date value of the option component of the CD is $1.73, and the purchase date investment in the S&P is $62.41.

level at the purchase date, then some portion of the initial excess investment in the hedge will be lost to the bank.

Of course, the bank could use different instruments in its static hedge, each with different initial costs. While the properties of these hedges may differ from the illustration, the hedging principles are the same. The bank can reduce the cost of the static hedge by not insuring against unlikely outcomes. The static hedge described above provides sufficient cash for any level of the underlying index. If the bank assumes, say, that the index will not increase by more than 5 times over the term of the CD, then the initial position in the index could be reduced (while accepting the small risk of a very large rise in the index).

As an alternative to the static hedge, the bank may choose a dynamic hedging strategy. In a dynamic hedging strategy, the hedge is adjusted throughout the life of the CD in response to changes in the market factors affecting the exposure. The advantage of a dynamic strategy is that the bank can mold the hedge more closely to the exposure, thereby reducing over-hedging. The disadvantages of a dynamic strategy are increased transactions costs, exposure to price "gapping" in the underlying, and a need for greater and more technically competent resources to maintain the hedge.

There are many possible approaches to dynamic hedging. A simple strategy would have the bank take an initial position in the hedging instrument based upon the "delta" of the option embedded in the CD, i.e., the change in the value of the option position corresponding to a one basis point change in the underlying. If, for example, the initial option position delta were -$250 (a negative delta position for the bank such as this would arise from a sold call option embedded in the CD), then the bank would hedge by purchasing a position in an instrument with a delta of +$250. Subsequent changes in the option position delta (as the index level or index volatility changes, or as time passes) would be mirrored by changes in the hedge position.

In a perfect environment with continuously open markets, no price gapping, and no hedging-related costs, it is possible to ensure that the dynamic hedge will provide for sufficient cash at the maturity of the CD to meet the commodity related obligation, while at the same time completely avoiding over-hedging. This ideal environment does not exist, however, and, to be practical, dynamic hedges can only be adjusted periodically. The frequency of hedge revisions could depend upon changes in the net value of the hedged position. The less frequent the adjustment, the less effective the dynamic hedge will be in terms of providing sufficient cash flows at the maturity of the CD.

Pricing of the CD in the dynamic hedge case is more complex. Because the level of costs incurred in hedging over the life of the CD is not known in advance, the adjustment to the fair price to reflect these costs will be imperfect.

When it is not possible to identify hedging instruments based on the same underlying risk as is in the CD, it may still be possible to design a hedge based upon the volatility of the risk being hedged, the volatility of the risk underlying the hedging instrument, and the correlation between the two sources of risk. However, when using imperfectly correlated instruments in a hedge, it is impossible to eliminate all the exposure. In this case the bank will have "correlation" risk or "basis" risk, and monitoring this risk may be difficult when the risk being hedged is not traded actively in a market.

REFERENCES

Merton, Robert, 1973, The Theory of Rational Option Pricing, *Bell Journal of Economics and Management Science* 4 (Spring), 141-183.

Ogden, Joseph, 1996, A Strategic Analysis of Stock Index-Linked CDs, in: Derivatives, Regulation and Banking, Barry Schachter, Ed., Amsterdam: North-Holland, 193-214.

Derivatives, Regulation and Banking
Edited by B. Schachter
© 1997 Elsevier Science B.V. All rights reserved.

Chapter 8
A STRATEGIC ANALYSIS OF STOCK INDEX-LINKED CDS

Joseph P. Ogden[†]
State University of New York at Buffalo, Buffalo, NY USA

1. INTRODUCTION

Among the most interesting of the myriad of recent developments in the financial markets is the stock index-linked certificate of deposit, or SIL CD. Offered in various forms, the SIL CD offers interest that is linked to the performance of a stock index such as the Standard and Poor's 500 index. The specification of the linkage varies according to the issuer. The first such CD, Chase Manhattan's market-index CD, was offered to the public in 1987. Other examples include Bankers Trust's "100-Plus Market Linked Deposit," which we will refer to as the generic SIL CD and provides a guaranteed return of principal plus interest equal to the percentage increase in the S&P 500 index (excluding dividends) over the life of the CD, applied to the principal. Citibank offers a "Stock Index Insured Account," in which the return is equal to two times the percentage difference between the average and beginning values of the index over the life of the CD, and also provides a guarantee of principal. (Republic New York offers a similar product.) We will refer to this type of CD as an average-value SIL CD. Both of these accounts are also covered by FDIC deposit insurance.[1] The original maturity of SIL CDs is generally five years.

This paper provides a detailed analysis of SIL CDs. The analysis consists of two

---

[†]Chairman, Department of Finance and Managerial Economics, Jacobs Center for Management Studies. Earlier drafts of this paper were presented at the 1993 Conference of the International Association of Financial Engineers in New York and at the 1994 Annual Meeting of the Decision Sciences Institute in Honolulu. I wish to thank conference participants for valuable comments and suggestions.

[1]Similar securities are offered by other firms in the form of a portfolio of stripped treasuries and a call option. They include **MITTS** from Merrill Lynch, **SIRS** from Paine Webber, **Stock Market Certificates** from IDS, **SPINS** from Salomon Brothers, and **SUPER CDs** from Warburg and Co.

major parts. The first part is a pricing analysis of SIL CDs. Initially, the put-call parity equation and option pricing models are used to calculate fair values for each of two types of SIL CDs in a perfect market. The two SIL CDs examined are the generic and average-value versions depicted above. Then the prices of actual SIL CD contracts are compared to their corresponding fair values in order to assess the competitiveness of the actual contract. The conditional risk and expected return of the fair and actual contracts are also computed and compared.

The second part of the analysis focuses on possible motivations for banks to issue SIL CDs. Banks continue to face swiftly changing economic conditions, changing regulations, and tremendous competition from various sectors in the financial marketplace. Banks have responded by expanding their product lines and adopting risk management strategies. The SIL CD may offer another means by which banks can compete.

In both parts of the analysis, this paper is distinguished from earlier analyses of SIL CDs, including Cantor and Schachter (1996) Chance and Broughton (1988), Chen and Kensinger (1990) and Chen and Sears (1990), all of whom focus on different, though related, issues pertaining to the pricing and use of SIL CDs or their equivalents.

2. BASIC PRICING ANALYSES

2.1 The Generic Stock Index-Linked CD

The value of the generic SIL CD can be analyzed by reference to the well-known put-call parity equation:

$$Se^{-\delta T} + P = Xe^{-rT} + C, \tag{1}$$

where S is the current spot price of an asset and P and C are the values of European put and call options, respectively, written on the asset, both with an exercise price of X and time to maturity of T years. δ and r are the continuous cash 'leakage' rate of the asset (which, in the context of stock indexes, is the dividend yield) and the riskfree rate, respectively, both at (assumed constant) annual rates. In a perfectly competitive market (i.e., a market with no transaction costs, taxes, or other imperfections or frictions), equation (1) is a no-arbitrage relation--that is, the equation must hold or arbitrage profits are possible.

Both the left-hand side and the right-hand side of equation (1) are the values of portfolios that are equivalent to the generic SIL CD. That is, the generic SIL CD can be seen as a portfolio, represented by the left-hand side of equation (1), that includes an underlying asset, but without the right to the asset's cash flow, plus a put option on the asset (where the put option serves to guarantee loss of principal below X), or, as represented by the right-hand side of equation (1), a portfolio consisting of a pure discount bond that pays X at maturity plus a call option on the underlying asset. The actual portfolio representing the generic SIL CD can be constructed by choosing a value of X equal to S; that is, using at-the-money options in the portfolio. So for this case equation (1) becomes:

$$Se^{-\delta T} + P = Se^{-rT} + C. \tag{2}$$

To see why this specification is equivalent to the generic SIL CD, focus on the right-hand side of equation (2). Note that the minimum payoff on the portfolio at maturity is S, the initial value of the spot asset. The payoff will exceed S if the value of the spot asset at maturity exceeds its initial value--that is, if the call option is in the money at expiration. Denoting as S_T the value of the asset at maturity, the payoff of the portfolio at maturity is S + max(S_T-S, 0). Thus if S_T>S, the payoff is S+(S_T-S)=S_T, while if S_T<S, the payoff is S.

In a perfect market, an investor would pay Se^{-rT}+C for the portfolio represented in equation (2). However, the generic SIL CD provides this portfolio at a price of S. Therefore, if Se^{-rT}+C=S, the SIL CD is fairly priced. Otherwise, if Se^{-rT}+C>S, the SIL CD is underpriced relative to its fair value (i.e., it is a bargain), while if Se^{-rT}+C<S, the generic SIL CD is overpriced. Thus the put-call parity analysis provides an arbitrage test to determine whether the generic SIL CD is overpriced or underpriced. This test can be implemented if the values of $Se^{-\delta T}$ and P, or Se^{-rT} and C, can be determined. If these values can be observed empirically in the market, the task is simplified. Otherwise, assuming that the values of the pertinent variables can be observed, the test can be carried out using a model for the value of either the call or the put option.

We examine the generic SIL CD in simulation using the Black-Scholes (1973) European call option pricing model. We use the version of the Black-Scholes model that adjusts for continuous leakage. According to this model, the value of a call option is

$$C = Se^{-\delta T}N(d_1) - Xe^{-rT}N(d_2),$$
$$d_1 = \frac{\ln(\frac{Se^{-\delta T}}{X}) + (r + 0.5\sigma^2)T}{\sigma\sqrt{T}}, \tag{3}$$
$$d_2 = d_1 - \sigma\sqrt{T},$$

where $N(\cdot)$ is the cumulative standard normal density function and σ is the per annum standard deviation of returns on the underlying asset.

The initial parameter values we use in the simulation analysis are selected to reflect values associated with the S&P 500 index, recent market conditions, and the specifications of the generic SIL CD. Specifically, we chose as base values for the simulation: S=X=500,

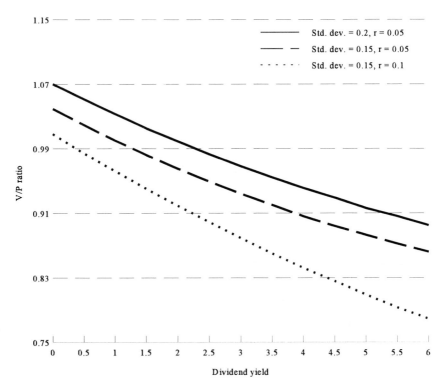

Figure 1
Value-Price ratios for generic SIL CDs by dividend yield

δ=0.03, σ=0.166, r=0.05, and T=5 years. Given these values, the sum of the values on the right-hand side of equation (2) (or equivalently, the left-hand side), and thus the estimated fair value of the generic SIL CD, is 472.38, composed of 82.98 in option value and 389.40 in bond value. However, since an investor would pay 500 for the contract, the contract is overpriced. Specifically, the investor would receive a portfolio that is worth 472.38/500=0.945, or 94.5 percent of the price paid. This ratio will henceforth be referred to as the value-price ratio, or V/P ratio.

Next, we assess the sensitivity of the V/P ratio to changes in the values of the estimated parameters, specifically δ, σ and r. The results are displayed graphically in Figure 1. Shown are V/P ratios for various values of δ ranging from 0.00 to 0.06 for each of three combinations of σ and r. The upper-most curve in the graph corresponds to σ=0.20 and r=0.05. The V/P ratio is inversely related to δ, ranging from 1.070 for δ=0.00 to 0.895 for δ=.060. The next curve corresponds to a smaller value of the standard deviation, σ=0.15 and r=0.05. Again, the V/P ratio is inversely related to δ, ranging from 1.039 for δ=0.000 to 0.862 for δ=0.060. Note that for each value of δ the V/P ratio is lower for σ=0.15 than for σ=0.20. Finally, the bottom curve corresponds to σ=0.15 and r=0.10. Again, the V/P ratio is inversely related to δ, ranging from 1.008 for δ=0.000 to 0.779 for δ=0.060.

The results in Figure 1 indicate that the V/P ratio for a generic SIL CD is quite sensitive to all of the estimated parameters; it is inversely related to δ and r and is directly related to σ. The results also indicate that, for all but the most extreme parameter values, the V/P ratio is likely to fall between 0.80 and 1.00. That is, *the price of a generic SIL CD generally exceeds its fair value.* Furthermore, the range of V/P ratios is sufficiently wide to be of concern to both issuers and investors as market conditions change over time.

2.2 The average-value Stock Index-Linked CD

The average-value SIL CD, such as that offered by Citibank, is a portfolio consisting of a pure-discount bond with a face value equal to S, the current value of the underlying asset (i.e., the index), and two at-the-money "average" options, each of which has a payoff at maturity of $\max(S^{av} - S, 0)$, where S^{av} is the average value of the underlying index over the life of the option, which extends from time 0 to time T. To see this, note that the payoff on this portfolio at maturity is

$$2[S^{av} - S] + S = 2S^{av} - S, \quad S^{av} > S,$$
$$S, \quad S^{av} \le S,$$

which is, of course, the payoff on the average-value SIL CD.[2]

The value of the average-value SIL CD also can be analyzed by reference to put-call parity, though in a more indirect fashion. Initially consider the basic put-call parity relation

$$S_0^{av} + P = Se^{-rT} + C, \tag{4}$$

where P and C are the values of European put and call average options maturing at T, both with an exercise price of X=S, and S^{av}_0 is the current value of an asset that pays S^{av} at time T. Solving (4) for C yields

---

[2] If $S^{av} > S$, the total return per dollar on the average-value SIL CD is $[1 + 2(S^{av} - S)/S]$, and thus given an initial investment of S the total return is $S[1 + 2(S^{av} - S)/S] = 2S^{av} - S$. If $S^{av} < S$, the payoff is S.

$$C = S_0^{av} + P - Se^{-rT}. \tag{5}$$

Now, if we multiply both sides of (5) by 2, add Se^{-rT}, and simplify, we obtain a put-call parity relation in terms of the portfolio that constitutes an average-value SIL CD:

$$2C + Se^{-rT} = 2(S_0^{av} + P) - Se^{rT}. \tag{6}$$

Thus, as with the generic SIL CD, we have an arbitrage test to determine whether the average-value SIL CD, whose price is S, is overvalued or undervalued. The test can be implemented if thevalues of C and Se^{-rT}, or S^{av}_0, P and Se^{-rT}, can be determined. If these values can be observed empirically, the task is simplified. Otherwise, assuming that the relevant parameter values can be observed, the test can be carried out using a model for the value of the call option.

We examine the average-value SIL CD in simulation using Turnbull and Wakeman's (1991) approximating pricing model for European average-value options. Modified for continuous leakage of the underlying asset, their equation for the value of a call average option is

$$C = e^{-rT}[Se^{-\delta T + \mu + \frac{1}{2}\sigma_a^2}N(d_3) - XN(d_3 - \sigma_a\sqrt{T})], \tag{7}$$

where $d_3 = \dfrac{[\ln(\dfrac{Se^{-\delta T}}{X}) + \mu + \frac{1}{2}\sigma_a^2 T]}{\sigma_a\sqrt{T}}$. In (7), μ and σ_a are the mean and standard deviation of

an approximating distribution for S^{av}. As Turnbull and Wakeman explain, μ is defined in terms of the riskfree rate r (given risk-neutral pricing of the option), and σ_a is defined in terms of σ, the standard deviation of the underlying asset.

Using parameter values equivalent to those used in the initial analysis of the generic SIL CD (i.e., S=X=500, r=0.05, δ=0.03, σ=0.166, and T= 5 years) the estimated fair value of the call option is 45.00, and thus the estimated fair value of the average-value SIL CD is $2(45.00) + 500e^{.05(5)} = 479.40$. The corresponding V/P ratio for the average-value SIL CD is 0.959 (=479.40/500). Thus, under current market conditions it appears that the average-value SIL CD is overpriced. However, the V/P ratio is slightly higher for the average-value SIL CD than the generic SIL CD (0.959 versus 0.945). Thus it appears that the average-value

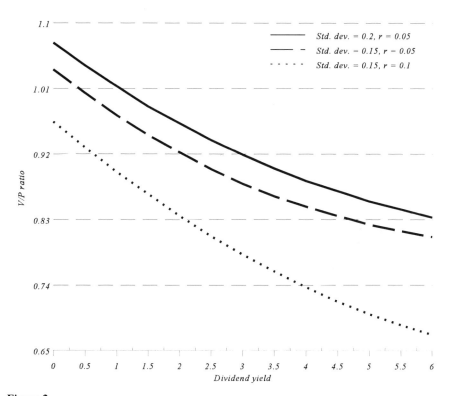

Figure 2
Value-Price ratios for average-value SIL CDs by dividend yield

SIL CD is slightly more favorably priced than the generic SIL CD.[3] Finally, we examine the sensitivity of the V/P ratio for the average-value SIL CD to changes in the values of the estimated parameters, calculating V/P ratios for the same combinations of parameters used in analyzing the generic SIL CD. The results are displayed graphically in Figure 2. We find that the results are qualitatively similar to those for the generic SIL CD. Specifically, the V/P

---

[3]This conclusion is consistent with statements in the financial press: "Take the case of Citibank's five-year index CD. A variety of different derivatives experts conclude that it's actually not a bad deal. In technical option-pricing terms, it gives somewhat better value to investors than Banker's Trust's CD ...." (Granito (1993)).

ratio is inversely related to δ and r and directly related to σ, and for the most empirically common sets of parameter values, the V/P ratio is between 0.80 and 1.00. As we will demonstrate later, neither of the contracts dominates (in terms of value) under all sets of parameter values.

3. CONDITIONAL EXPECTED RETURN, RISK AND EX ANTE PERFORMANCE OF STOCK INDEX-LINKED CDS

The value of a SIL CD also can be assessed in terms of its ex ante relative performance; that is, the expected return and risk of the SIL CD in comparison to its perfect market counterpart. Focusing initially on the generic SIL CD, recall that the perfect market counterpart of the generic SIL CD is a portfolio consisting of a riskless bond and a call option, both purchased at their fair values. The instantaneous expected return, $E(R_{pgen})$, and standard deviation, σ_{pgen}, of this portfolio are:

$$E(R_{pgen}) = W_b r + W_c E(R_c),$$
(8)

and

$$\sigma_{pgen} = W_c \sigma_c,$$
(9)

where W_b and W_c are the fractions of the value of the portfolio represented by the bond and the call option, respectively (i.e., they are portfolio weights), and $E(R_c)$ and q_c are the instantaneous expected return and standard deviation of the call option. Of course, both $E(R_c)$ and q_c are conditional upon the expected return and standard deviation of the underlying asset, the former denoted as $E(R_s)$. Under the assumptions of the Black-Scholes model, it can be shown that the instantaneous conditional expected return and standard deviation of the call option are:

$$E(R_c) = r + N(d_1)\frac{Se^{-\delta T}}{C}[E(R_s) - r],$$
(10)

$$\sigma_c = N(d_1)\frac{Se^{\delta T}}{C}\sigma.$$
(11)

The instantaneous expected return and standard deviation of the generic SIL CD, which we will denote as $E(R_{gen})$ and q_{gen}, respectively, will generally differ from their counterpart values $E(R_{pgen})$ and q_{gen} because the generic SIL CD is generally either overpriced or underpriced. The challenge here is to determine formulas for $E(R_{gen})$ and σ_{gen}

that correspond to those for $E(R_{pgen})$ and σ_{pgen}.

For simplicity, and without loss of generality, we assume that the investor always pays a fair value for the call option component of the SIL CD, so the difference between the fair value of the SIL CD and the actual price paid is represented as a payment of greater than or less than fair value for the riskless bond component, which in turn implies that the rate of return on the riskless bond will be either less than or greater than the actual riskless rate. Specifically, the price of the bond is:

$$Se^{-rt} + [S - (Se^{-rt} + C)] = S - C, \tag{12}$$

and thus the annual rate of return on the bond, denoted as r', is

$$r' = \frac{\ln[\dfrac{S}{S-C})]}{T}. \tag{13}$$

Therefore, the instantaneous expected return and risk of the generic SIL CD are

$$E(R_{gen}) = \frac{S-C}{S}r' + \frac{C}{S}E(R_c) \tag{14}$$

and

$$\sigma_{gen} = \frac{C}{S}\sigma_c. \tag{15}$$

The conditional expected returns and risk of the average-value SIL CD and its perfect market counterpart can be developed in an analogous fashion. The resulting conditional expected return and risk of the perfect market counterpart to the average-value SIL CD, denoted as $E(R_{pav})$ and σ_{pav}, respectively, are

$$E(R_{pav}) = [\frac{Se^{-rT}}{Se^{-rT} + 2C}]r + [\frac{2C}{Se^{-rT} + 2C}]E(R_c), \tag{16}$$

and

$$\sigma_{pav} = [\frac{2C}{Se^{-rT} + 2C}]\sigma_c, \tag{17}$$

where

$$E(R_c) = r + N(d_3)\frac{S^{av}}{C}[E(R_S) - r], \tag{18}$$

$$\sigma_c = N(d_3)\frac{S^{av}}{C}\sigma. \tag{19}$$

The corresponding conditional expected return and risk of the average-value SIL CD, denoted as $E(R_{av})$ and σ_{av}, respectively, are

$$E(R_{av}) = [\frac{S-2C}{S}]r' + [\frac{2C}{S}]E(R_c). \tag{20}$$

and

$$\sigma_{av} = \frac{2C}{S}\sigma_c, \tag{21}$$

where

$$r' = \frac{\ln[\frac{S}{S-2C}]}{T}. \tag{22}$$

Our initial assessment of the relative performance of the SIL CDs is obtained using the base values of the parameters established earlier. The results are displayed in Figure 3. The line depicts the linear relationship that must hold by arbitrage among (a) the riskfree asset, which is the point on the vertical intercept at 0.05, (b) the underlying index, which has expected return and risk of 0.10 and 0.166, respectively, (c) the (standard) call option, which has expected return and risk of 0.2251 and 0.5814, respectively, (d) the average-value call option, which has expected return and risk of 0.3343 and 0.9439, respectively, (e) the perfect market counterpart of the generic SIL CD, which has expected return and risk of 0.0808 and 0.1021, respectively, and (f) the perfect market counterpart of the average-value SIL CD, which has expected return and risk of 0.1034 and 0.1772, respectively.

The final two points on the graph in Figure 3 correspond to the generic and average-value SIL CDs. The expected return and risk of the generic SIL CD are 0.0676 and 0.0965, respectively, while the corresponding values for the average-value SIL CD are 0.0927 and 0.1699, respectively. Note that both of the SIL CDs plot below the fair-value line, indicating that both underperform their perfect market counterparts.

A more precise assessment of the ex ante performance of an SIL CD can be obtained by comparing its expected return to that of a portfolio that has the same risk. Using the base values of the parameters, a portfolio constructed using the riskfree asset and the underlying index with weights of 0.4187 and 0.5813, respectively, has the same risk as the generic SIL

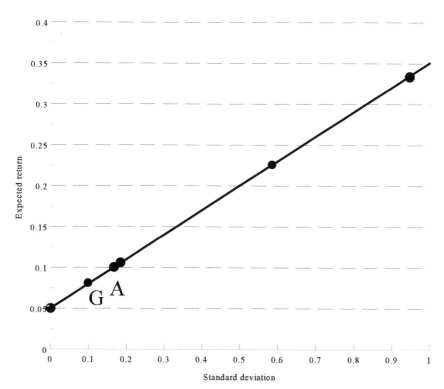

Figure 3
Risk and expected return for the index, options, and SIL CDs

CD, 0.0965, and has an expected return of 0.4187 (0.05) + 0.5813 (0.10) = 0.0791. Thus, the generic SIL CD provides an expected return that is 0.0791-0.0676 = 0.0115, or 1.15 percent per annum *less than* a fairly-valued portfolio with identical risk. Alternatively, a portfolio constructed using the riskfree asset and the underlying index with weights of -0.0235 and 1.0235, respectively, has the same risk as the average-value SIL CD, 0.1699, and has an expected return of 0.1012. Thus, the average-value SIL CD provides an expected return that is 0.1012-0.0927 = 0.0085, or 0.85 percent per annum less than a fairly-valued portfolio with identical risk. These results are consistent with the results in the previous section indicating that both of the SIL CDs are over-priced, but more so for the generic SIL CD, under current

Table 1
Measures of value and ex ante performance for SIL CDs for various values of the riskfree rate (r), index standard deviation (σ) and dividend yield (δ).

r	σ	δ	V/P ratio		Expected return difference (%)[a]		Yield difference (%)[b]	
			Generic	Avg. Value	Generic	Avg. Value	Generic	Avg. Value
0.05	0.15	0.00	1.039	1.036	0.75	0.81	1.02	0.96
		0.03	0.934	0.946	-1.38	-1.12	-1.64	-1.34
		0.04	0.906	0.921	-1.98	-1.66	-2.27	-1.93
		0.05	0.883	0.899	-2.52	-2.14	-2.81	-2.44
		0.06	0.862	0.879	-2.99	-2.59	-3.26	-2.88
0.05	0.20	0.00	1.070	1.073	1.33	1.38	1.89	1.96
		0.03	0.968	0.986	-0.65	-0.28	-0.80	-0.36
		0.04	0.941	0.961	-1.22	-0.80	-1.46	-0.97
		0.05	0.917	0.939	-1.75	-1.26	-2.03	-1.51
		0.06	0.895	0.918	-2.24	-1.72	-2.53	-1.99
0.10	0.15	0.00	1.008	0.964	0.15	-0.75	0.26	-1.17
		0.03	0.879	0.864	-0.26	-3.00	-3.63	-4.04
		0.04	0.843	0.835	-3.53	-3.72	-4.62	-4.82
		0.05	0.809	0.807	-4.37	-4.41	-5.48	-5.52
		0.06	0.779	0.782	-5.15	-5.07	-6.22	-6.15
0.10	0.20	0.00	1.023	0.982	0.44	-0.35	0.76	-0.57
		0.03	0.900	0.889	-2.15	-2.41	-3.05	-3.36
		0.04	0.865	0.861	-2.97	-3.07	-4.01	-4.11
		0.05	0.834	0.835	-3.75	-3.70	-4.85	-4.80
		0.06	0.804	0.811	-4.49	-4.31	-5.59	-5.42

[a]Difference between the instantaneous expected returns on the SIL CD and on a fairly-priced portfolio with identical risk, assuming the expected return on the index is 10 percent. Figures are in percent per annum.
[b]Difference between the yield on the bond component of the SIL CD and the riskfree rate, assuming the option component is fairly priced.

market conditions.

It is also interesting to note that, while the option component of the generic SIL CD represents only about 16.6 percent of its price, the risk borne by the investor is 58.1 percent of the risk of a 100% investment in the index. The corresponding figures for the average-value SIL CD are 18.0 percent and 102.3 percent, respectively. Thus, on the basis of instantaneous risk and return, the average-value SIL CD is nearly identical to a 100 percent investment in the index.[4]

An alternative measure of the ex ante performance of a SIL CD is given by the yield on the bond component in comparison to the riskfree rate, given that the call option is fairly priced (see equations (13) and (22)). Again using the base values of the parameters, the yield on the bond component of the generic SIL CD is 3.63 percent per annum. Thus, the bond component underperforms the riskfree asset by 5.00-3.63 = 1.37 percent per annum. The corresponding yield on the bond component of the average-value SIL CD is 3.97 percent, representing an underperformance of 1.03 percent per annum relative to the riskfree asset. Again, the average-value SIL CD appears to be more favorably priced relative to the generic SIL CD under current market conditions.

Table 1 provides a summary of the value and ex ante performance measures for both SIL CDs for commonly observed values of the parameters. Shown in column 4 and 5 are the V/P ratios for the generic and average-value SIL CDs, respectively, while columns 6 and 7 show their expected return performances relative to identical-risk, fairly priced portfolios, and columns 8 and 9 show the difference between the yield on the bond component of the SIL CD and the riskfree rate. Consistent with earlier results, the results in Table 1 indicate that (a) values and performances of both SIL CDs are sensitive to the values of the parameters, and thus to changes in market conditions (b) neither SIL CD dominates the other under all market conditions, and (c) both SIL CDs are generally overpriced, often to an extent that substantially affects their performances.[5]

4. BANK MOTIVATIONS FOR ISSUING SIL CDS

Changing economic conditions, changing regulations and increasing competition have required banks to make fundamental changes in their operations, including changes in the products they offer to investors and the manner in which they manage risk. For instance, in the last 20 years, banks have lost billions of dollars of potential deposits to money market mutual funds, and more recently, with short-term interest rates at their lowest levels in 20 years, many investors have opted to invest in stocks, largely through mutual funds, rather

---

[4]The relatively high risk of the average-value SIL CD as determined here is consistent with comments in the financial press indicating that early-on the Citibank CDs are very risky (see Granito (1993)).

[5]The investor also should be concerned about the tax treatment of SIL CDs (see Feldman (1993)).

than accepting the low current rates on CDs. These pressures have squeezed banks' profit margins tremendously. Banks have responded with innovations such as money market deposit accounts and, very recently, stock mutual funds (offered through their trust departments). In addition, in response to the substantial increase in interest rate volatility in the 1970's and 1980's, some banks have issued innovative securities such as yield curve notes or 'inverse floaters,' which pay interest at a rate that varies inversely with short-term interest rates. Having inverse floaters as liabilities serves to immunize the bank's exposure to interest rate risk (see Ogden (1987)).

The SIL CD may represent another important innovation for banks that may actually help them to both compete profitably for investors' funds as well as to manage market risk. Here we identify three possible motivations for a bank to issue SIL CDs:

Attracting Return-Oriented Investors: Even if we assume that SIL CDs are fairly priced (i.e., are not priced to yield an explicit profit for the bank), their issuance may attract many investors who, given low current interest rates, are willing to take limited market risk for the expectation of higher returns. As such, by offering SIL CDS the bank may lure investors out of mutual funds and back into CDs. And since, traditionally, the bank's greatest source of profits stems from borrowing via CDs and using these funds to engage in commercial lending, SIL CDs may be an efficient means of continuing this traditional structure under current conditions.

Pricing SIL CDs for Profit: If the pricing analysis discussed above reveals that SIL CDs are sold at a price that exceeds their fair value, it is possible that they can serve as a direct source of profit for a bank. Market imperfections such as transaction costs, combined with economies of scale that are greater for a bank than for the typical individual investor, may provide the reasons why a bank can offer the SIL CD at a premium over its fair value (i.e., the individual investor may face greater transaction costs in trying to purchase a portfolio that replicates the SIL CD). On the other hand, the opportunity for investors to replicate the SIL CD on their own, or for a brokerage firm to offer a similar package, ultimately limits the potential profitability of SIL CDs per se.

Managing Its Market Risk?: Having SIL CDs as liabilities may play a role in reducing a bank's market risk in a manner similar to the role that inverse floaters play in reducing the bank's interest rate risk. To see this, assume that, prior to the issuance of SIL CDs, a bank's stock has a positive 'beta'. Its beta is positive because the values of the assets it holds, including for instance business loans, are sensitive to changes in the market, while its traditional fixed-rate CDs are riskless. This leaves the bank's equity to 'absorb' the market risk of the assets. However, once the SIL CDs are in place as liabilities, they absorb market risk since they include a call option on the stock market, and thus the beta of the bank's equity will be reduced. This last motivation is analyzed in detail in the next section.

5. MANAGING A BANK'S MARKET RISK WITH SIL CDS

A bank's management, acting in the interest of the bank's shareholders, may be motivated to issue SIL CDs in order to change the market risk or 'beta' of the bank's equity. In this section, we analyze the likely effect of SIL CDs on the market risk of a bank's equity, and then discuss management's motivations for issuing SIL CDs as a risk management strategy.

5.1 Bank equity risk with SIL CDs

In order to analyze the effect of SIL CDs on the risk of a bank's equity, we assume a simple structure for the bank's assets and a simple capital structure. Regarding the assets, we assume that asset returns, R_{At} can be modeled effectively with the simple market model

$$R_{At} = \alpha_A + \beta_A R_{Mt} + \epsilon_{At}, \tag{23}$$

where R_{Mt} is the return on the market index, α_A is the intercept and β_A is the 'beta' of the assets. With this structure the variance of asset returns, σ_A^2, can be decomposed as

$$\sigma_A^2 = \beta_A^2 \sigma_{M2} + \sigma_{\varepsilon A}^2, \tag{24}$$

where σ_M^2 is the variance of market returns and $\sigma_{\varepsilon A}^2$ is the residual variance.

With the assets fixed, we now consider the characteristics of the bank's liabilities and equity. We assume that the bank has three types of securities outstanding, specifically, insured 'ordinary' deposits, insured SIL CDs, and common equity, in proportions W_d, W_{SIL} and W_e, respectively, where $W_d + W_{SIL} + W_e = 1$. Of course the risk of this "portfolio" must fully reflect the risk of the assets, and this must hold with respect to the total risk of the assets (σ_A^2) as well as the systematic and residual risk components of the assets ($\beta_A^2 \sigma_A^2$ and $\sigma_{\varepsilon A}^2$, respectively). We assume that ordinary deposits will bear neither systematic nor residual risk. The SIL CDs will bear systematic risk, since their returns are defined in terms of the return on the market, but will bear no residual risk. Finally, the equity, representing a residual claim on the assets, will bear all of the residual risk and also may bear systematic risk, depending on the amount of such risk remaining after the SIL CDs are in place, as we will shortly show.

Formally, we can decompose the risk of the assets as follows:

$$\sigma_A^2 = \left[W_{SIL}\beta_{SIL} + W_e\beta_e \right]^2 \sigma_M^2 + W_e^2 \sigma_\varepsilon e^2, \tag{25}$$

where β_{SIL} and β_e are the betas of the SIL CDs and the equity, respectively, and $\sigma_{\varepsilon e}^2$ is the residual variance of the equity. Using equations (24) and (25), we can separate the systematic and residual components of risk:

$$\beta_A^2 \sigma_{M2} = [W_{SIL}\beta_{SIL} + W_e\beta_e]^2 \sigma_{M2}, \tag{26}$$

and

$$\sigma_{\varepsilon A}^2 = W_e^2 \sigma_{\varepsilon e}^2. \tag{27}$$

Since our primary concern is the effect of the issuance of SIL CDs on the market risk of the equity, we focus on equation (26). Solving (26) for β_e yields

$$\beta_e = \frac{\beta_A - W_{SIL}\beta_{SIL}}{W_e}. \tag{28}$$

Assuming $\beta_{SIL} > 0$, equation (28) indicates that adding SIL CDs to the bank's capital structure will reduce the systematic risk of the equity, and when $W_{SIL}\,\beta_{SIL} > \beta_A$, the beta of the bank's equity will actually be negative. In order to explore the implications of equation (28), we must obtain estimates of the parameters β_A and W_e.

5.2 Empirical estimates of bank systematic risk and capital structure.

To obtain empirical estimates of banks' systematic risk and capital structure, we identified 11 bank holding companies whose stock traded on either the NYSE or the AMEX during the 6-year period 1987-1992. We regressed monthly returns on each of these stocks on the monthly returns on the value-weighted index provided by the University of Chicago's Center for Research in Security Prices (CRSP) data tape using equation (23), in order to obtain estimates of β_e. Next, we estimated each bank's capital structure by examining their balance sheets as of December 31, 1992, as reported in Moody's Bank and Finance Manual. Specifically, we calculated the proportion of the bank's capitalization represented by (a) deposits, (b) other liabilities, and (c) shareholders' equity. Although these figures represent book values, we assume that they provide reasonable estimates of the corresponding market values.

The results of the empirical analyses of the 11 banks are displayed in Table 2. Shown in column 2 and 3 are the banks' equity betas and annualized residual risk. All of the betas

Table 2
Betas, residual risk and book-value capitalization for 11 bank holding companies. Beta is obtained by regression using returns for 1987-1992, capitalization is based on balance sheet data for December 31, 1992.

Bank	Equity beta	Annualized residual risk (%)	Deposits (%)	Other liabilities (%)	Equity (%)
Bankers Trust	1.392	22.1	34.6	60.1	5.3
Bank of Boston	1.294	39.7	78.2	14.9	6.9
Bank of New York	1.354	30.4	72.0	19.4	8.6
Chase Manhattan	1.445	29.6	70.1	23.1	6.8
Chemical Bank	1.209	35.6	67.4	25.5	7.1
Citicorp	1.136	33.2	67.5	27.3	5.2
Continental	1.512	35.1	63.0	29.5	7.5
First Bank System	1.378	25.6	78.8	12.4	8.8
First Virginia	1.108	16.8	87.9	3.2	8.9
Mellon Bank	1.075	23.7	79.6	12.3	8.1
Sun Trust	1.039	20.8	80.0	12.5	7.5
Average	1.267	28.4	70.8	21.8	7.3

are greater than 1.0, and the average beta is 1.267. The average residual risk is 28.4 percent. Shown in columns 4,5 and 6 are the proportion of capitalization represented by deposits, other liabilities and equity, respectively. The average values of these proportions are 70.8%, 21.8% and 7.3%, respectively. We use these estimates to assess the impact of SIL CDs on equity risk.

5.3 An assessment of the effect of SIL CDs on bank equity risk.

In order to use the mathematical analysis and empirical results above to assess the affect of SIL CDs on a bank's equity risk, we must make two additional assumptions. The first assumption is that the bank's "other liabilities" are essentially equivalent to ordinary insured deposits in terms of risk (i.e., they are riskless). The second assumption is that the banks included in the sample were not affected by the presence of SIL CDs during the estimation period.[6] With these assumptions, we can use a simplified version of equation (28), in which $W_{SIL} = 0$, to relate a bank's equity beta to its asset beta. Solving for β_A, we obtain

---

[6]Obviously, some of these banks had issued SIL CDs during the sample period. We assume that they represented an insignificant proportion of total deposits during the period. To the extent that these banks had SIL CDs in this period, estimated equity betas represent *net* equity systematic risk.

$$\beta_A = W_e \beta_e. \tag{29}$$

Using equation (29) and the estimates in Table 2, we characterize the assets of a representative bank using $\beta_A = 0.0925(= 0.073(1.267))$, and $\sigma_{\epsilon A} = 2.073\%$ (=0.073(28.4)). In addition, the annualized standard deviation of the market index (i.e., the CRSP value-weighted index) over the estimation period was $\sigma_m = 16.6$ percent. Thus, our estimate of the total risk of the representative bank is $\sigma_A = [\ 0.092^2(16.6)^2 + 2.073^2\ ]^{.5} = 3.600$ percent per annum.

The final estimate required for the analysis is for β_{SIL}, the beta of the SIL CD. We will use estimates based on the analyses in the previous section. As the reader recalls, using the base values of the parameters, (which includes $\sigma_M = 0.166$) we found that the risk of the generic (average-value) SIL CD was equivalent to a portfolio consisting of the riskfree asset and the market index with weights of 0.4187(-0.0235) and 0.5813(1.0235), respectively. Thus, for the generic (average-value) SIL CD, $\beta_{SIL} = 0.5813$ ($\beta_{SIL} = 1.0235$).

We are now in a position to estimate both the beta and the total risk of the equity of the representative bank as a function of the proportion of the bank's capitalization represented by SIL CDs, W_{SIL}. Using equation (28), the estimated equation for equity beta associated with the generic SIL CD is

$$\beta_e = \frac{0.0925 - W_{SIL}(0.5813)}{0.073} = 1.267 - 7.963 W_{SIL}, \tag{30}$$

and the corresponding estimated equation associated with the average-value SIL CD is

$$\beta_e = \frac{0.0925 - W_{SIL}(1.0235)}{0.073} = 1.267 - 14.021 W_{SIL}. \tag{31}$$

Note that the coefficient of W_{SIL} is nearly twice as large (in magnitude) in equation (31) than in equation (30). This result is consistent with earlier results indicating that average-value SIL CDs are much more risky than generic SIL CDs. For both SIL CDs, the estimated equation for total equity risk is

$$\sigma_e^2 = \beta_e^2(16.6)^2 + (2.073/0.073)^2, \tag{32}$$

where, of course, β_e is given by equation (30) for the generic SIL CD and by equation (31) for the average-value SIL CD.

The estimated effects of SIL CDs on the beta and total risk of the representative bank

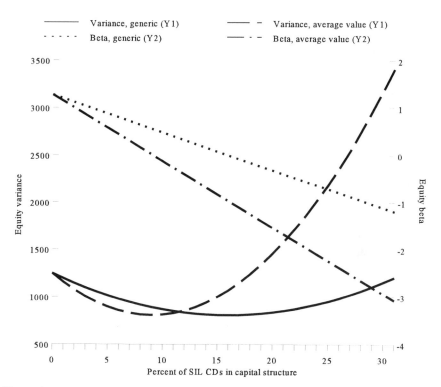

Figure 4
Equity variance and beta by percent SIL CDs in capital structure

are displayed in Figure 4. The effects are shown for both generic and average-value SIL CDs, as a function of W_{SIL}. Using the generic SIL CD, the bank's equity beta is zero, and total equity risk is minimized, when $W_{SIL} \equiv W_{SIL}^* = 0.159$, or 15.9 percent of the bank's assets. Using the average-value SIL CD, the corresponding figure is $W_{SIL}^* = 0.090$, or 9.0 percent of the bank's assets. If $W_{SIL} < W_{SIL}^*$ ($W_{SIL} > W_{SIL}^*$), the bank's equity has a positive (negative) beta. Note that due to the greater risk of the average-value SIL CDs, a smaller proportion of them is needed to have the same effect on equity risk.

5.4 A risk management motive for issuing SIL CDs.

As we noted in the previous sections, a bank's management may have a risk management motive for issuing SIL CDs. As illustrated in figure 4, even a small proportion of SIL CDs has a substantial effect on the bank's equity risk. The question is, what proportion of SIL CDs would be optimal—that is would maximize the value of the bank's equity?

We focus initially on the effect of changes in the bank's equity risk on the value of FDIC insurance. Assuming that the FDIC insurance premium, that is, the price of the insurance, is fixed, management has an incentive to increase the riskiness of the bank's equity in order to maximize the value of the insurance. As figure 4 illustrates, the issuance of SIL CDs initially reduces the risk of the bank's equity. Thus, initially any benefits provided by SIL CDs (as discussed in the previous section) are offset by a decrease in the value of the bank's FDIC insurance.[7] However, after the bank has issued SIL CDs totalling the critical (risk-minimizing) proportion W_{SIL}^*, issuing additional SIL CDs will increase equity risk and thus the value of the bank's FDIC insurance. Thus, assuming that SIL CDs provide fixed incremental benefits once the proportion is greater than W_{SIL}^*, there appears to be no optimal level of SIL CDs from this limited perspective. However, if the incremental cost of issuing SIL CDs (including the loss of FDIC insurance value) exceeds the incremental benefit when $W_{SIL} < W_{SIL}^*$ then we can argue that SIL CDs will benefit the bank's equity holders only if their proportion is substantially greater than W_{SIL}^*.

6. SUMMARY

This paper provides a rigorous analysis of the pricing of two types of stock index-linked CDs, and discusses motivations for banks to issue them. The pricing analysis indicates that SIL CDs are generally overpriced, and therefore provide a lower expected return than could be generated by replicating portfolios with identical risk in a perfect market. Nevertheless, investors may desire SIL CDs if transaction costs associated with creating the replicating portfolio negate its higher expected return. Banks may be motivated to offer SIL CDs because (1) they attract return-oriented investors who would otherwise place their funds in stocks, (2) the bank can offer these securities for a profit, or (3) having these securities as liabilities affects the risk and thus the value of the bank's equity.

---

[7]Quantifying this effect is beyond the scope of this paper, but the effect should be substantial, given the substantial effect of SIL CDs on bank equity risk.

REFERENCES

Black, F., and M. Scholes, 1973, The Pricing of Options and Corporate Liabilities, *Journal of Political Economy* 81, (May-June), 637-659.

Cantor, E. And B. Schachter, 1996, Indexed Certificates of Deposit, *Derivatives, Regulation and Banking*, Barry Schachter, Ed., Amsterdam: North-Holland, 159-192

Chance, D. and J. Broughton, 1988, Market Index Depository Liabilities: Analysis, Interpretation, and Performance. *Journal of Financial Services Research* 1, 335-352.

Chen, A. H. and J. W. Kensinger, 1990, An Analysis of Market-Index Certificates of Deposit, *Journal of Financial Services Research* 4, 93-110.

Chen, K. C. and R. S. Sears, 1990, Pricing the SPIN, *Financial Management* 19, (Summer), 36-47.

Feldman, A., 1993, CDs for CPAs, *Forbes*, July 19, 92-95.

Granito, 1993, New Derivative Products are Surprisingly Complex, *Wall Street Journal*, 72, april 8, C1-C2.

Ogden, J. P., 1987, An Analysis of Yield Curve Notes, *Journal of Finance* 42, 99-110.

Ogden, J. P. and T. Moon, 1993, An Analysis of Reset Notes and Rating Sensitive Notes, *Journal of Financial Engineering* 2, (June), 175-194.

Turnbull, S. M. and L. M. Wakeman, A Quick Algorithm for Pricing Average Options, *Journal of Financial and Quantitative Analysis* 26, 377-390.

Derivatives, Regulation and Banking
Edited by B. Schachter
1997 Elsevier Science B.V.

Chapter 9
OVER-THE-COUNTER DERIVATIVES AND SYSTEMIC RISK
TO THE GLOBAL FINANCIAL SYSTEM

Michael R. Darby[†]

University of California, Los Angeles, Los Angeles, California, USA

1. INTRODUCTION

The rapid rise of over-the-counter (OTC) derivatives to a central role in wholesale banking and finance with notional principal amounts rivaling stock market capitalization poses central policy issues for banking and financial regulation. In particular, policymakers are concerned with whether OTC derivatives have increased systemic risk of general failure of the global financial system. This paper attempts to bridge the gap between the academic literature and regulatory concerns by defining "systemic risk" rigorously and examining whether or not such risk has been increased or decreased by the advent of the OTC derivative market.

Since beginning work on what at the time seemed a somewhat esoteric theme, derivatives have become as timely as each morning's newspapers. This may point out one of the most salient features of the integrated global financial market — the speed of change and evolution. We must always remember that evolution in the financial markets — like in infectious viruses — is often responsive to attempted cures. As a result, we are constantly at risk with regulatory initiatives of engendering new financial products and procedures to get around the latest rules that may pose more risk to the system than the prior practices which were the reason for the new regulations.

While new regulations may always engender unintended consequences in the

[†]Warren C. Cordner Professor of Money and Financial Markets in the Anderson Graduate School of Management at UCLA and Research Associate of the National Bureau of Economic Research. The author acknowledges very useful comments from Andreas Grunbichler, Mark Levonian, Francis Longstaff, Susan M. Phillips, and Lynne G. Zucker and research assistance from Paul J. Alapat, Christine Beckman, and Lynda J. Kim. An earlier version of this paper was presented as the keynote speech at the Conference on International Financial Markets in the North-East Asia: Assessment and Prospects, organized by the Seoul National University and Korea Development Institute, Hilton Hotel, Seoul, Korea, May 26-27, 1994.

international financial markets, this is particularly likely when regulations are aimed at dealing with a loosely defined concept such as systemic risk. If regulators are not sure what target they are shooting at, it should not be surprising if they hit something else.

In Section 2, I first describe swaps and other derivatives, their magnitude and uses in the global financial market. Next I turn to the concept of systemic risk and the reasons that many officials believe that market forces cannot be relied upon to achieve appropriate self-regulation in the over-the-counter swaps and derivatives market. Section 4 contains an analysis of market arrangements in response to risk elements in the current lightly regulated regime. Section 5 is a review and evaluation of the "Basle II" proposals for capital requirements on derivatives. Finally, I draw some conclusions on the implications of these financial instruments for the operation of the global financial market.

2. SWAPS AND DERIVATIVES

Since the breakdown of the Bretton Woods system and the capital controls used to permit a modicum of monetary policy discretion while maintaining pegged exchange rates, the financial markets have become increasingly globally integrated.[2] In part this global integration is a return to earlier norms, but to a greater extent it reflects the revolution in communication which has occurred contemporaneously.

A parallel development which has perhaps proceeded furthest in the United States is the securitization of traditional bank liabilities. As banks' traditional intermediary functions have grown less and less profitable, major financial institutions have increasingly turned to trading and underwriting activities in order to remain competitive with alternative uses of their shareholders' capital. Furthermore, governments' efforts to regulate — and implicitly to tax — bank assets have played a significant role in banks' increasing concentration on off-balance-sheet products. In addition, needs to strengthen balance sheets and capital pressures, from both the market and regulators, have been particularly relevant in the general movement to off-balance-sheet activities and fee-producing initiatives. Over-the-counter (or OTC) derivative products today are a major if not the largest source of earnings for approximately 150 of the world's largest commercial banks and securities firms which are active dealers in these markets.[3]

---

[2] See Darby (1986, 1988) for fuller arguments on these points.

[3] These dealers are represented by a trade association known currently as the International Swaps and Derivatives Association and formerly as the International Swap Dealers Association (ISDA in either case). See ISDA (1993) for a current discussion of the membership. At the end of 1991, the 25 top dealers in interest rate and currency swaps comprised 19 banks, 4 securities firms, and 2 insurance

Derivatives are defined most generally to refer to a variety of bilateral contracts whose value derives from an underlying asset, reference rate, or index. Basically derivatives embody forward contracts, options, or some combination of these building blocks.[4] Exchange-traded futures and options as well as derivative securities are not the focus of current regulatory concerns although they play an important role in allowing dealers to lay off net risk and discover prices of the forward and options components of OTC derivatives.

OTC derivatives are generally privately-negotiated forwards (such as forward commodity or foreign-exchange contracts, forward rate agreements [FRAs] or currency, interest-rate, commodity, or equity swaps) or privately-negotiated options (such as commodity, currency, equity, FRA, swap, and bond options, and caps, floors, and collars). From the point of view of the end users, OTC derivatives provide customized tools to manage risk, reduce transactions costs, lower financing costs, and enhance portfolio yields.[5] OTC derivatives are available for longer maturities than are generally available for exchange-traded derivatives.[6] These end users — corporations, governments, institutional investors, and other financial institutions — could accomplish much the same results by using exchange-traded futures and options and derivative securities, but only at the higher cost of establishing a sophisticated in-house unit capable of continually managing the equivalent portfolios without the benefit of only having to layoff the net exposure of a dealer portfolio.[7]

Thus the market is organized so that a relatively small number of banks and other financial institutions serve as counterparties to a large number of OTC derivative transactions and then actively manage the risks of the resulting net portfolio position. End users are able

---

companies; 14 were U.S. based and 11 from other countries (Global Derivatives Study Group [G-30] 1993a, p. 42).

[4]The most comprehensive and comprehensible source on the OTC derivatives market is the Group of Thirty study, especially Global Derivatives Study Group [G-30] (1993a). I can only attempt to briefly summarize that material here.

[5]Although widely accepted by practitioners who appear to know their business, the idea that swaps or other derivatives can reduce financing costs or enhance portfolio returns is controversial in the academic literature. Significant contributions to the discussion include James Bicksler and Andrew H. Chen 1986, Marcelle Arak, Arturo Estrella, Laurie Goodman, and Andrew Silver 1988, Larry D. Wall 1989, Robert H. Litzenberger 1992, and Arie L. Melnik and Steven E. Plaut 1992.

[6] The availability of long maturities seems to be a particularly attractive feature to the end users. As we shall see, dealers are able to serve as counterparties in the place of a clearinghouse because they run trading books with closely matched exposures to underlying risk.

[7]Writing for the Federal Reserve Bank of Kansas City, Charles S. Morris (1989a and 1989b) and Morris and Thomas J. Merfeld (1988) lay out risk-management strategies for financial institutions using exchange-traded futures and options or combinations of those instruments with interest-rate swaps.

Table 1
Notional Amount of Derivatives Outstanding by Nature of the Underlying Risk 1989-1992

Underlying	1989	1990	1991	1992	Percent Growth[a]
Interest Rates	4,311	6,087	8,404	10,923	153
Exchange Rates	2,779	3,927	5,415	6,475	133
Equity/Commodity[b]	108	158	209	245	127
Total	7,198	10,172	14,028	17,643	145

Amounts in billions of U.S. dollar equivalents. Source: U.S. General Accounting Office (1994), 35.
[a]Percentage increase from 1989 to 1992.
[b]Data on individual-firm-equity-price and physical-commodity-price derivatives are especially incomplete.

to shift important elements of risk to those wishing to either hedge an offsetting risk or more willing to hold a speculative position.

These are powerful advantages which have contributed to the rapid growth of the OTC derivatives market from about US$1 trillion in 1987 to perhaps US$5 to US$10 trillion of underlying contract or notional principal amount now outstanding to end users.[8] The exact amount is hard to pin down because of substantial potential double-counting of intra-dealer transactions, but the market is clearly huge. Table 1 presents some gross estimates of the growth of the derivatives markets over 1989-1992 broken down by nature of the underlying risk. Although inclusive of intra-dealer contracts, these data are consistent but incomplete as measures of total global amounts.[9] The largest and fastest growing amount of contracts are concerned with interest rate risk. With notional amounts doubling every two years and currently of the same order of magnitude, it is not surprising that derivatives are receiving serious interest. However, the dealers' actual exposure to default is only a very small fraction of the principal amount, probably well less than US$1 trillion even in the event of a major market break. Even with all due caveats taken, this is indeed a large and rapidly

---

[8] Estimates vary widely depending on date and amount of netting out of double counting used. Global Derivatives Study Group [G-30] (1993a) uses ISDA data which exclude double-counting of intra-dealer transactions to estimate that swaps notional principal was US$4.5 trillion at the end of 1991. *Global Finance* reported in August 1993 that the notional principal amount exceeded US$10 trillion (Evans, Bere, and Massar 1994, p. 41). Eli M. Remolona (1992-93) reports intermediate estimates for the Federal Reserve Bank on New York. U.S. Board of Governors of the Federal Reserve System (1993b) reports a great detail of data on the derivatives activities of U.S. bank holding companies and their affiliates.

[9]These data include foreign exchange forward contracts which are generally excluded from industry estimates.

growing market.[10]

In Table 2, the totals in Table 1 are broken down by the type of derivative product. Forwards are the largest category because of inclusion of the traditional banking business of forward foreign exchange contracts in the GAO data. Excluding these contracts, the standard industry figures would place swaps in first place.

As alluded to earlier, there have also been recent horror stories as a number of end users appear to have moved from hedging risk to speculation on a scale that may have been literally inconceivable to their Boards of Directors. Surely, the best summary of the recent reports of speculative losses of such firms as Procter and Gamble was the *Financial Times* headline "Procter and guess what" (1994).[11] Perhaps that corporation's suit against Bankers Trust will help ensure that dealers obtain their clients' Boards' of Directors authorization for use of derivatives in a form that makes the directors aware of the crucial importance of internal controls to prevent officers from taking uncontemplated speculative positions.[12] Needless to say objections to these transactions occur only when they result in losses, and in some cases when the losses are offset by gains on the assets whose value they were intended to hedge.[13]

Despite the fact that OTC derivatives provide another channel for fraud and mismanagement, they have become an essential element of the global wholesale banking industry. Banks must be able to provide these risk management and financing services to major corporate, governmental, and institutional clients or else see their business increasingly flow elsewhere. Similarly a country which establishes burdensome regulations on its banks will either see the banks move their derivatives business offshore or, failing that,

---

[10] For example, gross credit risk for 14 major U.S. financial institutions with $6.5 trillion on notional amount outstanding was only $114 billion or 1.8 percent of the notional amount (U.S. General Accounting Office 1994, p. 53.)

[11] The Procter and Gamble loss is currently estimated at US$157 million. The January 1994 Metallgesellschaft AG bailout amounted to US$1.95 billion for losses from speculating both on and off exchange in the oil market (see Taylor and Bacon 1994).

[12] The House of Lords in 1991 found that the London Borough of Hammersmith and Fulham lacked the authority to undertake the swap contracts it had transacted at great loss during the 1980s. This finding resulted in: (a) most of the default losses since the inception of swap activity and (b) more fastidious concern as to whether dealers' customers were authorized to undertake the transactions which they were making.

[13] In the GAO's survey — which some observers considered a politically motivated search for horror stories to justify regulatory initiatives — only 1 percent (2 respondents) reported ever filing a complaint or litigating over a derivatives transaction. In one case, a complaint to a fund's management resulted in a resolution satisfactory to the respondent and the other case resulted in litigation. (U.S. General Accounting Office 1994, p. 135.)

Table 2
Notional Amount of Derivatives Outstanding by Type of Derivative Product 1989-1992

DerivativeProduct	1989	1990	1991	1992	Pct.Growth[a]
Forwards[b]	3,034	4,437	6,061	7,515	148
Futures	1,259	1,540	2,254	3,154	151
Options	953	1,305	1,841	2,263	137
Swaps	1,952	2,890	3,872	4,711	141
Total	7,198	10,172	14,028	17,643	145

Amounts in billions of U.S. dollar equivalents.Source: U.S. General Accounting Office (1994), 36.
[a]Percentage increase from 1989 to 1992.
[b]Forwards include foreign exchange, FRAs, equity and commodity forwards.

become mere correspondents of the global banks capable of offering wholesale clients a full range of demanded services.

In conclusion, OTC derivatives are now a mainstream element of the global banking business. The issue for national policymakers is what that implies for their economies and the appropriate regulatory environment.

3. SYSTEMIC RISK FROM DERIVATIVES

Despite the alarm with which those of us of a certain age respond to any sudden change, particularly one which favors younger colleagues, OTC derivatives have largely survived skeptical scrutiny. Looking first at the end user, derivatives provide a means to manage risk and reduce the risk-adjusted cost of capital, thus facilitating investment, economic growth, and rising living standards. It is true that they provide a new arena for fraud and mismanagement, but those activities surely will continue whether or not derivatives exist.

Considering the banks — and other financial institutions — which act as dealers and the regulatory agencies which supervise them, it turns out that the risks associated with derivatives are familiar ones and subject by and large to familiar solutions: market risk, credit risk, operational risk, and legal risk. The latter three types of risk have some interesting twists in this particular setting, but are basically amenable to management by existing best practices.[14] For example, before entering into a transaction dealers should and generally do assess both expected and worst case exposure and post that exposure against the

---

[14] There are many private and official analyses of the internal risk management and supervisory issues which come to similar conclusions. Most follow closely the analysis in Global Derivatives Study Group [G-30] (1993a, pp. 43-52).

client's overall institutional credit limit.[15] Furthermore, since end users of derivatives generally have access to the commercial paper market, they are the kind of credits which are increasingly absent from bank loan portfolios; thus the overall credit quality of the banks' exposure is generally strengthened by its derivatives operations.

Market risk for OTC derivatives is somewhat more difficult to measure than for most other bank balance sheet items, but there are important exceptions such as callable bonds and mortgage loans for which the borrower has the option to prepay.[16] The Board of Governors of the Federal Reserve System has recently informed the U.S. Congress (1993a, p. 91) that it "believes that the greater awareness and understanding of risk and the enhanced methods of managing risks probably have reduced the likelihood of systemic problems, and will continue to do so over time as industry and supervisory practices advance." They go on to note that the devotion of "substantial resources to the development of more sophisticated risk management tools and ... increasing use of netting to reduce their credit exposures ... have had favorable spill-over effects on institutions' abilities to manage their total portfolios, not just their derivative activities." (p. 92)

Indeed in private conversations, U.S. regulators see the greatest challenge due to the growing use of derivatives to be upgrading their staff of examiners so that there are sufficient numbers competent to assess the validity of the banks' more sophisticated and safer approach to market and other risks. Federal Reserve Governor Susan M. Phillips (1994, p.2) sees the current round of rulemaking on OTC derivatives "as offering opportunities to provide bankers with incentives to adopt more widely and to refine the new risk management practices that have begun to be implemented by the leading derivatives dealers."

3.1 Thinking about Systemic Risk

The main charge remaining against OTC derivatives is that they increase systemic risk. This is the essence of the so-called "Promisel report" prepared by a Working Group of the Central Banks of the Group of Ten countries. Systemic risk is defined in the Promisel report as "the risk that a disruption (at a firm, in a market segment, to a settlement system etc.) causes widespread difficulties at other firms, in other market segments or in the financial system as a whole."[17] Basically the fear is that derivatives will somehow increase

---

[15] James J. Calla and Sidney S. Pomper (1993, pp. 17-19) report on how this is done at one U.S. superregional bank.

[16] On the latter point, see Sean Becketti 1989.

[17] Bank for International Settlements ["Promisel Report"] (1992, p. 61).

the possibility of a general collapse of a significant part of if not the entire financial system: specifically, that firms' true financial conditions are less transparent, that risk may be substantially miscalculated for complicated instruments, that activity is concentrated in too few dealers, that market liquidity may be insufficient for management of very complex positions, and that increased volume may increase the level of settlement risk.[18]

Before returning to these specifics, I would first like to approach systemic risk from another, more personal point of view. In the summer before the October 1987 market crash, then-Federal Reserve Vice Chairman Manuel Johnson and I for the Treasury were made co-chairmen of a crisis contingency planning group which brought in representatives from the Securities and Exchange Commission, the Commodities Futures Trading Commission and other agencies as well. This provided valuable infrastructure when the crash occurred and more senior hands took over crisis management. At Treasury, I was principally responsible for oversight of the derivative markets during the crisis and had the opportunity to follow closely what was going on at our sister agencies as well. I must say that living through that experience, actually seeing the threat of major financial institutions being denied access to credit lines needed to cover cash flows required by hedged positions, and overcoming those threats only by Federal Reserve and Treasury officials giving assurances that the institutions were sound and in any case would not be allowed to fail gives me a personal sympathy for the concept of systemic risk that seems to be lacking among many academics. I believe that those who lived through that experience may be prone to require greater proof of safety than others might deem reasonable.

These concerns form the core of the following excerpt from the interim report of Treasury Under Secretary Gould, Federal Reserve Chairman Greenspan, S.E.C. Chairman Ruder, and C.F.T.C. Chairman Gramm:

> The size and speed of the decline initiated by fundamental revaluation of equity values was exacerbated on October 19 by a number of factors:
>
> > many participants pulled back from the markets because of fear and shock — and because of uncertainties and concerns over (i) the accuracy and timeliness of information, (ii) counter-party solvency, (iii) credit availability, and (iv) de facto, ad hoc market closures or other market disruptions.
>
> the financial system came under great stress in the credit, clearing, and settlement area.[19]

---

[18] See Global Derivatives Study Group [G-30] 1993b, pp. 127-129.

[19] U.S. Working Group on Financial Markets 1988, pp. 1-2.

Thus I see October 1987 as the crucible in which present regulatory concerns about systemic risk were formed. I would go further and say that the perceived failure in that episode of "portfolio insurance" to work as promised because of gapping prices, and the perception that the failed attempt to pursue dynamic hedging strategies made the situation worse, as argued by the Brady Commission,[20] leaves a residual of official distrust for derivative instruments in general and dynamic hedging strategies in particular. While other reports and subsequent academic literature indicate that portfolio insurance played a lesser role than sketched by the Brady Commission, the influence of the Brady report on official concerns remains profound.

Recently, William J. McDonough, the President of the Federal Reserve Bank of New York, worried about "systemic risk of liquidity failure in the OTC derivatives market." He admitted that "our admonitions have a nagging quality because we have not specified a concrete approach to controlling and managing this risk."[21]

The impasse between some regulators' concerns and the analyses of academics and practitioners over this ill-defined concept of systemic risk thus is hardly surprising. I am reminded of the hypothesis that car seat belts increase injuries and deaths because they give drivers a sense of security that leads them to take greater risks. This is pretty much the core of the systemic risk indictment: Instead of being diffuse where risk gets absorbed by much nonfinancial capital, derivatives permit nonfinancial corporations to take on riskier fundamental positions, the risk of which is transferred to and concentrated in the financial sector. Furthermore, the quantitative types in the financial markets lack the experience and judgement to weigh appropriately the danger of pricing gaps while the senior managers they report to do not really understand the risks they are taking.

4. MARKET SOLUTIONS AND SYSTEMIC RISK

Substantial regulatory proposals may be enacted on the basis of concerns such as just described. It is important to see what the market solutions are to the extent that these

---

[20] See, for example, the indictment of portfolio insurers and their "mechanical, price-insensitive selling" in the fourth and fifth paragraphs of the Brady Commission's Executive Summary. U.S. Presidential Task Force on Market Mechanisms 1988, p. v. The Promisel report returns to portfolio insurance "as an example of the destabilizing potential of the market linkages associated with dynamic hedging strategies." (Bank for International Settlements 1992, p. 26. Gerard Gennotte and Hayne Leland (1990) provide an academic analysis of how dynamic hedging strategies could have caused a large price drop in 1987.

[21] McDonough 1994, p. 6.

concerns can be made specific and testable. Let us now examine the specific components that underlie the systemic risk idea.

The Group of Thirty's Systemic Issues Subcommittee, following the Promisel Report, decomposed the systemic concerns into nine categories: the size and complexity of the exposures, concentration among a relatively small number of financial institutions, reduced transparency of financial activities, illiquidity in the hedging markets, settlement risk, credit risk, the importance of unregulated market participants, market linkages, and legal risks.[22] McDonough (1994, pp. 4-6) combines the more important of these into four thematic clusters:

- Instrument risks (complexity)
- Risks to institutions (size, credit risk, transparency)
- Risks to markets (illiquidity, market linkages)
- Evolution of risks (concentration)

The fourth of these is, in part, distinct from the Group of Thirty/Promisel list. The distinct idea is that risk borne by the derivative dealers is not only more concentrated but also in the aggregate larger. The increased aggregate risk is supposed to occur because the ability to shift risk at a low cost induces risk-taking in the nonfinancial sector. In essence this is the seat-belt argument, with no explanation why introduction of a risk reduction technology should not results in aggregate risks intermediate between those initially existing and those which would exist if there were no behavioral adjustment to the new technology. There are other taxonomies, but little substantively new beyond these.

Market participants have incentives to deal with these risks; so we need to examine what self-regulatory practices or institutions the market has developed to handle any or all of these concerns. This section first reviews them in terms of the Group of Thirty/Promisel taxonomy and then returns to the missing element added by the McDonough approach.[23]

Size and complexity. The size issue is real in the sense that these are clearly large enough positions that, if they were mismanaged, they could cause the failure of one of the large dealer institutions. However, the same could be said about a number of other lines of business, such as prepayable mortgages. It should be noted that actual exposure is normally

---

[22] Global Derivatives Study Group 1993b, pp. 128-129. Although theirs is the best analysis of systemic risk of which I am aware, I believe that their reading of the Promisel Report may overstress the importance of systemic risk as seen in that document.

[23] My review of the Group of Thirty/Promisel issues relies heavily on Global Derivatives Study Group 1993b and International Swaps and Derivatives Association, Inc. 1993.

only 2 or 3 percent of the notional principal amount — say, US$200 or US$300 billion on US$10 trillion. Losses on the rather rare defaults have averaged just over 3 percent of notional principal at risk for the defaulted transactions, and defaults are most likely where the counterparty is an unusually big loser.

Complexity is not nearly so significant an issue as it is made out to be. While tailored OTC derivatives cannot be directly hedged, they can always be broken down into their constituent components of forwards and options which can and should be managed at the portfolio level by hedging only the net position in each. Applying this sort of reasoning to such traditional bank products as mortgages is one of the very positive ways in which derivative risk management techniques have reduced the overall riskiness of banks.

Concentration. Because of the need for the highest credit standing and expensive talent and capital investment to be effective, the major dealers even in the United States can be counted on the fingers of two hands. Often, their derivatives business is conducted through AAA-rated subsidiaries continuously monitored by in-house representatives of the Moody's and Standard and Poors credit-rating firms. Moreover, these wholesale financial markets are truly global and no single firm has more than ten percent of the dealer activity.

On the other hand considerable risk has been shifted to these firms from other financial and nonfinancial corporations, and this concentration of risk could have the potential to leading to disruption of funding of the dealers' hedging activities in the hours of a major price break as lenders hold back to investigate rumors about individual dealers' creditworthiness.

Transparency. Perhaps in part as a result of this danger, the major dealers have worked closely with the Financial Accounting Standards Board to develop FASB Interpretation 39 effective this year to report current credit exposures from derivative transactions on dealer balance sheets. Clearly, ever increasing sophistication of risk management has made mark-to-market reporting and stress simulations standard tools for internal management and control as well. I would also note that an unhedged major underwriting of common stock was a major factor in the rumors which threatened financial flows in the October 1987 crisis; one wonders whether such a risk could have been undertaken today given current risk-management standards.

On the other hand, end users are not yet required to report in their financial statements on the hedges or speculative positions taken through derivative instruments. Such reporting is clearly desirable from the point of view of systemic risk, but also would help ensure that the Boards of Directors are aware of the risks that they are hedging or taking on.[24]

Illiquidity. As discussed above, portfolios are managed in term of individual risk components, so liquidity need not be present for individual products so long as there is risk liquidity. However, experience during October 1987 and the September 1992 EMS crisis has taught dealers that even these increasingly deep risk component markets can gap substantially.

As a result of their concern about potential price gapping as well as for other normal business reasons, dealers run relatively balanced portfolios and thus have little net exposure to hedge. What remains are mostly hedged by exchange-traded options so that only minor mismatches remain to be hedged through dynamic trading strategies. These strategies are subject to loss due to gapping, but stress simulations are used to ensure that the potential losses are manageable. Thus awareness of the potential danger has led to strategies that do not rely on the absence of discrete price movements.

Settlement risk. Settlement risks exist but are relatively small compared to other areas of these institutions' business, primarily because only net payments are routinely transferred. To provide perspective: aggregate daily cash flows associated with OTC derivatives appear to amount to less than 5 percent of those for traditional foreign exchange transactions.

Credit risk. As discussed previously, existing practices for management of credit risk are directly applicable to OTC derivatives credit exposures. Further, overall systemic risk has been reduced in this area by the growth of OTC derivatives, since "bank dealers have increased the average quality and diversity of [credit] risk to which they are exposed."[25]

Table 3 provides the best available evidence on the credit standing of dealers' counterparties in OTC derivative contracts. Nearly all are investment grade and 78 percent are rated A or higher. These are precisely the borrowers which banks have lost to the commercial paper and other direct lending markets. While the effect on the overall creditworthiness of bank exposures is salutary, this should not be overemphasized: Among

---

[24] Michael Schrage (1994) makes this point: "The greatest risk derivatives bring to the marketplace is not their complexity of volatility; it's the shadowy way in which they can be used by companies that would rather not tell the marketplace the truth about their investment intentions. The antiseptic for that infection is not more regulation; it's better and fuller disclosure."

[25] Global Derivatives Study Group [G-30], 1993b, p. 135. Academic economists have done some interesting work recently on the role of credit risk in the pricing of OTC derivatives; see Francis A. Longstaff and Eduardo S. Schwartz (1994) and the references cited there.

Table 3
Credit Ratings of 200 Companies with More than $1 Billion in Swaps Outstanding as of Year-End 1991

Credit Rating	Firms	Notional Amounts	Percent
AAA of Aaa	21	535	9.7
AA or Aa	34	1,747	31.7
A	78	2,023	36.7
Total A or better	**133**	**4,305**	**78.2**
BBB or Baa	38	1,066	19.4
Total Investment Grade	**171**	**5,371**	**97.5**
Speculative	15	30	0.6
Unrated	14	106	1.9
Total Noninvestment Grade	**29**	**136**	**2.5**
Total All Grades	**200**	**5,507**	**100.0**

Amounts in billions of U.S. dollar equivalents. Source: U.S. General Accounting Office (1994), 59.

the seven largest U.S. bank dealers only Bankers Trust had larger credit exposure from derivatives than loans, and for five of the others the loan exposure was three or more times as large as the derivatives exposure.[26]

Market participants have endorsed the desirability of the legal and regulatory reforms that would be required to establish an international netting scheme as recommended by a high-level Working Group of the Central Banks of the Group of Ten countries in the so-called "Lamfalussy report." If these changes were made, such an entity would somewhat further reduce credit risk.

Unregulated entities. Central bankers and securities regulators sometimes express concern about the unregulated status of several major OTC derivatives dealers such as insurance company affiliates. Given the high credit standards required to compete as a dealer, this concern does not appear to have much substance beyond a universal desire for more data.

Market linkages. While the OTC derivatives markets seem to be very much an element of the integrated global financial market, there is no apparent net contribution to systemic risk from this fact. A recent joint study by the U.S. Federal Reserve System, Federal Deposit Insurance Corporation, and Comptroller of the Currency concluded that "it is unlikely that the underlying markets would have performed as well as they did in [the] September [1992 EMS crisis] without the existence of related derivatives markets that enabled currency

---

[26] U.S. General Accounting Office (1994), pp. 53-55.

positions to be managed, albeit with some difficulty in some instruments."[27]

Legal risks. While market participants appear to be cognizant of and responsive to legal risk, the U.K. local authorities case illustrates that residual systemic risk from an unforeseen legal ruling remains. Dealers have concerns about the enforceability in bankruptcy in some jurisdictions of netting agreements, particularly for cross-product exposures.

The international regulatory groups, such as the Bank for International Settlements, the Basle Committee on Banking Supervision, and the Group of 10, are involved in a major effort to address legal risks. These efforts are likely to result ultimately in new legislation.

This review of the Group of Thirty/Promisel laundry list of risk factors suggests that while there is some systemic risk associated with the OTC derivatives markets, they do not appear to be unusual or disproportionate to that element in other bank activities such as commercial or mortgage lending. Nonetheless, there are areas which could be improved and national and international regulatory bodies are working to do so.

We are left then with McDonough's fourth point (the evolution of risks) to consider: Has aggregate risk been increased because it is now possible to manage risk so much better through derivatives?

The first question is whether or not nonfinancial risk taking has increased. Of course, reducing the cost of an activity — including taking risks — will increase the amount of it, but such an increase does not imply an increase in aggregate or systemic risk as an unintended by-product of growth in these markets since the cost reduction results from a risk reduction technology.

To that latter issue, I conclude that on balance there has been a decrease in systemic risk. The reason that this is true is because systemic risk at root is about failure of firms and fears of resulting failure of other firms, especially financial firms. The growth of the derivatives markets have reduced that risk through widespread cancelling of risk as well as shifting of risk to those most able to manage and bear it.

If we look at each derivatives transaction, we see a principle of conservation of risk apparently at work — risk can be transferred but not eliminated. But, as discussed above, dealers generally run closely balanced books, with the fundamental risk components closely balanced. Residual risk is generally laid off with other dealers or through exchange-traded options or futures. This entire process involves a great deal of cancellation of offsetting hedges placed by the end users, and that cancellation eliminates risk in the system as a whole.

---

[27] U.S. Board of Governors of the Federal Reserve System, Federal Deposit Insurance Corporation, and Comptroller of the Currency 1993, p. 18.

This result should not be surprising. After all, most of the real economic transactions which give rise to the end users' demand for hedging involve symmetric risks of loss and gains to the parties to the transaction. In principle, those risks could be directly cancelled through appropriately constructed contingent contracts. Since the costs of negotiating such contracts are generally quite large relative to the underlying value, it makes sense for the parties instead to collect their risks and hedge them with risk specialists who can do so in a cost effective manner.

It is in just this manner that the derivatives markets promotes production and trade, and the associated risk-taking, by the end users. This is a clear channel by which financial institutions contribute to growth and development.

Note finally that growth in the OTC derivatives markets reduces a number of features that those involved in crisis management in October 1987 found troublesome: Because they are largely options-based contingent contracts, they involve thought-out positions of what should happen in case of large market price changes and thus reduce the potential for panic-motivated sales. Since the dealers' books are managed so as to be as close as practicable to balanced, there is relatively little need for potentially destabilizing dynamic hedging strategies. Most of these transactions are settled at fixed dates; so large cash flows are not required among the potential confusion of rumors associated with a financial crisis.

Thus, concerns about systemic threats of OTC derivatives are not sustained by this analysis of the market structure. Indeed, it appears that these instruments have contributed to reduction in the overall level of economic risk.

5. THE BASLE II PROPOSALS

In April 1993 the Basle Committee on Banking Supervision released through its constituent Group of Ten central banks three supervisory documents addressing market risk and bank capital for banks active in the Global capital market. These proposals are seen to supplement the original Basle Capital Accord which was primarily concerned with credit risk, including credit risk on OTC derivatives.

One of these three documents, a consultative proposal entitled "The Supervisory Treatment of Market Risks," has been the subject of considerable debate. In fact, a number of observers see this "Basle II proposal" as so fatally flawed in its measurement of risk as to set up incentives for unbalanced portfolios which could result in higher probability of failure of individual institutions and significant increase in systemic risk. Obviously, that result is not the intention of the G-10 central-bank governors and since that time the Basle II proposals have been subject to considerable revision, though much debate about their flaws still is ongoing.

Indeed, now that these proposals are being enacted in the G-10 countries and elsewhere, they may provide an opportunity for nonadopting jurisdictions to develop as an offshore venue for the OTC derivatives business just as recent regulatory increases in transactions costs in Japan have promoted growth in exchange-traded Japanese derivatives in Singapore. To demonstrate this potential market shift, I first review Basle II and then show why it would create a demand for doing business in jurisdictions which treat risk more consistently with the underlying economics.

First, Basle II establishes the principle that a bank or other financial institution's trading book is to be treated separately from the rest of the bank's business and have minimum capital requirements based on a separate set of rules. This would not necessarily increase overall capital requirements for banks with significant trading activities, since moving certain bonds to the trading book could lower the capital requirements against those bonds so as to more of less than offset increased requirements against other activities.

Next, Basle II follows economic theory and market practice in separating exposure to interest rates, exchange rates, and equity prices, and in treating specific risk and general market risk differentially.[28] Capital requirements for market risk are then based on a standard of 99 percent confidence intervals for historic two-week moves for the various market factors.

Despite these firm foundations, Basle II implements risk measurement in an adding up with disallowances manner which seems to have been designed by accountants rather than economists or market practitioners. Practitioners are alarmed that depending on interpretation of some of the rules, capital requirements on what appears a well-balanced book could in fact be doubled.

One exception to the general dismay over Basle II is the analysis of Mark Levonian at the Federal Reserve Bank of San Francisco, who has recently done a remarkable job of defending the seemingly indefensible. Levonian (1994) interprets the Basle II capital standards as a linear approximation to the results of a more economically appropriate but administratively costly measure of risk based on the variance-covariance matrix of a bank's exposures. Specifically, Levonian shows that the Basle II standards can be more generally interpreted as proportionate to a weighted average of a bank's long and short positions with the weights varying according to whether applied to foreign-exchange, debt, or equity

---

[28]See Robert Gumerlock (1993) for a careful analysis of the strengths and weaknesses of the proposal. The ISDA comment letter (International Swaps and Derivatives Association, Inc. 1993) is also an important piece of analysis.

positions. Levonian showed that the weights used for foreign-exchange risk would have resulted in an acceptable approximation to actual risk in the foreign-exchange markets for the few banks in the San Francisco district which had any such exposure. Levonian did not show that the other weighting schemes were sensible even within that district nor that the approximation schemes would continue to work if capital requirements were laid against positions in this way.

Formal comments have generally taken a different view on administrative costliness than has Basle II. Commentators have generally pointed out that realistically very few banks run the kind of trading book to which Basle II applies. Other banks should be exempted from regulation for those few through de minimis rules, and such rules have been enacted in the market risk capital rule in the US.

For the relatively few trading banks in the global financial market, the Basle II capital approach would at best require them to calculate a redundant measure of the risks they face, and more likely impose taxes on some, possibly fully hedged, transactions which would otherwise contribute to their profitability and at the same time provide effective subsidies to taking on market risks which would otherwise not be undertaken. Why not simply require them to do what is already in their self interest to do? That is, why not require trading banks to measure risk appropriately and then apply capital standards based on the actual risks undertaken as a result of their activities?

Once this question is asked, all the administrative practicality arguments for the building-blocks with disallowances approach ("standard model") disappear. Clearly, the compliance costs are lower for the regulated firms because they don't have to create a set of economically meaningless reports nor take on risks which would not be taken except in order to reduce their capital requirements. From the point of view of the regulators, the argument is made that the arithmetically simpler process of adding and subtracting is necessary because budgetary requirements limit severely the number they can hire and retain of examiners qualified to understand the more complicated, correct computation of risks. But, if the examiners for these institutions cannot understand the business well enough to audit whether the banks' internal risk management systems and controls are well designed and effectively implemented, there is little hope that they would do any good against a sophisticated effort to circumvent Basle II. Since regulators ultimately must rely on self-enforcement, compliance is far more likely if the rules are seen as reasonable and as not putting particular institutions at an unfair competitive disadvantage relative to other institutions.[29] Indeed, in

---

[29]Commenting on a draft of this paper, Mark Levonian has made two important points (a) the internal systems adopted by dealers might differ if they knew their capital requirements would be based

the US the enactment of Basle II did not include reference to the standard model approach of the original proposals.

6. CONCLUSIONS

OTC derivatives are an important innovation which have contributed substantially to risk management wherever they have been available and used. As a result at the same time that the market has grown rapidly, risks faced by end users have declined. These risks have not simply been shifted to the dealers, however, as many of the risks can be cancelled in the market. Furthermore, the growing size of the market has led to the development of new risk management techniques and skills in dealer financial institutions which have had the effect of reducing their overall riskiness by managing risks which were previously not actively faced and managed.

This general reduction of risk in the system has on balance contributed to the overall reduction of systemic risk. There are several areas where further improvements are underway to ensure that balance is maintained and enhanced:

- Increased transparency of the derivatives positions in financial statements, particularly in those of end users, would reduce unfounded rumors during a crisis.
- A proposed international netting arrangement could make some further contribution to reducing credit and settlement risks.

Turning finally to the Basle II market risk capital rules, we see that these regulatory changes could ultimately increase systemic risk or drive the derivatives offshore from adopting jurisdictions. The problem is not with the intentions or even analytical approach of that document, but rather with short-cuts taken where none are required.

---

on the indicated net risks and (b) "nobody knows as well as the insiders how to game the bank's internal systems." I think that the Lucas critique [point (a)] is wrong in this case because one cannot really bias the calculations in general unless one also knows the desired bias to be maintained in the book. Since dealers do not show any desired bias, it is hard to cook the books. I agree that insiders may try to game the internal risk control system, but in that case their supervisors have a clear reason to try to catch them before they cause disaster. Their supervisors would have little reason to do the same in the face of avoidance of capital controls.

REFERENCES

Arak, Marcelle, Arturo Estrella, Laurie Goodman, and Andrew Silver, 1988, Interest Rate Swaps: An Alternative Explanation, *Financial Management*, Summer, 17: 12-18.

Bank for International Settlements, 1990, *Report of the Committee on Interbank Netting Schemes of the Central Banks of the Group of Ten Countries*, [Lamfalussy Report], Basle: Bank for International Settlements, November.

Bank for International Settlements, 1992, *Recent Developments in International Interbank Relations*, Report prepared by a Working Group established by the Central Banks of the Group of Ten countries, [Promisel Report], Basle: Bank for International Settlements, October.

Basle Committee on Banking Supervision, 1993, The Supervisory Treatment of Market Risks, Basle, April.

Becketti, Sean, 1989, The Prepayment Risk of Mortgage-backed Securities, Federal Reserve Bank of Kansas City *Economic Review*, February, 74: 43-57.

Bicksler, James, and Andrew H. Chen, 1986, An Economic Analysis of Interest Rate Swaps, *The Journal of Finance*, July, 41: 645-655.

Calla, James J., and Sidney S. Pomper, 1993, Interest Rate Swaps: A Derivative Product for Portfolio Management, *Journal of Commercial Lending*, June, 75: 12-22.

Darby, Michael R., 1986, The Internationalization of American Banking and Finance: Structure, Risk, and World Interest Rates, *Journal of International Money and Finance*, December, 5: 403-428. [Reprinted in *Internationalization of Banking and Finance -- Analysis and Prospects, Proceedings of the Second International Symposium on Financial Development*, Seoul, Korea: Korea Federation of Banks, 1986.]

Darby, Michael R., 1988, Real Exchange Rates and Freedom of International Trade and Capital Flows, *Cato Journal*, Fall, 8: 473-475.

Evans, Richard, Carol Bere, and Betsy Massar, 1994, Derivatives Superstars: Anonymous No Longer, *Global Finance*, February, 8(2): 39-74.

Gennotte, Gerard, and Hayne Leland, 1990, Market Liquidity, Hedging, and Crashes, *American Economic Review*, December, 80: 999-1021.

Global Derivatives Study Group [G-30], 1993a, *Derivatives: Practices and Principles*, Washington, DC: The Group of Thirty, July.

Global Derivatives Study Group [G-30], 1993b, *Derivatives: Practices and Principles. Appendix I: Working Papers*, Washington, DC: The Group of Thirty, July.

Gumerlock, Robert, 1993, Double Trouble, *Risk*, September, 6(9).

International Swaps and Derivatives Association, Inc. [ISDA], Consultative Proposal by the Basle Committee: Capital Adequacy for Market Risk, comment letter to the Basle Committee on Banking Supervision, December 28, 1993.

Levonian, Mark E., Bank Capital Standards for Foreign Exchange and Other Market Risks, *Federal Reserve Bank of San Francisco Economic Review*, 1994, Number 1, pp. 3-18.

Litzenberger, Robert H., 1992, Swaps: Plain and Fanciful, *The Journal of Finance*, July, 47: 831-850.

Longstaff, Francis A., and Eduardo S. Schwartz, 1994, A Simple Approach to Valuing Risky Fixed and Floating Rate Debt and Determining Swap Spreads, UCLA Finance Working Paper no. 22-93, revised April.

Melnik, Arie L., and Steven E. Plaut, 1992, Currency Swaps, Hedging, and the Exchange of Collateral, *Journal of International Money and Finance*, October, 11: 446-461.

McDonough, William J., 1994, remarks presented at the Conference on Financial Markets, sponsored by the Federal Reserve Bank of Atlanta, Coconut Grove, Florida, February.

Morris, Charles S., 1989, Managing Interest Rate Risk with Interest Rate Futures, Federal Reserve Bank of Kansas City *Economic Review*, March, 74: 3-20.

Morris, Charles S., 1989, Managing Stock Market Risk with Stock Index Futures, Federal Reserve Bank of Kansas City *Economic Review*, June, 74: 3-16.

Morris, Charles S., and Thomas J. Merfeld, 1988, New Methods for Savings and Loans to Hedge Interest Rate Risk, Federal Reserve Bank of Kansas City *Economic Review*, March, 73: 3-15.

Phillips, Susan M., 1994, Derivatives and Risk Management: Challenges and Opportunities, remarks presented at the Conference on Financial Markets, sponsored by the Federal Reserve Bank of Atlanta, Coconut Grove, Florida, February 25.

Procter and Guess What, 1994, editorial, *Financial Times*, April 21, 21.

Remolona, Eli M., 1993, The Recent Growth of Financial Derivative Markets, *Federal Reserve Bank of New York Quarterly Review*, Winter, 17: 28-43.

Schrage, Michael, 1994, Innovation: As Derivatives Debacles Add Up, It's Time to Ask: Hedge or Risk, *Los Angeles Times*, May 5, D1 & D3.

Taylor, Jeffrey, and Kenneth H. Bacon, 1994, How the Nymex Cooled MG's Oil Crisis, *Wall Street Journal*, April 5, C1 & C6.

U.S. Board of Governors of the Federal Reserve System, 1993a, Responses to Questions on Financial Derivatives Posed by Congressman James A. Leach, Committee on Banking, Finance, and Urban Affairs, U.S. House of Representatives, Washington: Board of Governors of the Federal Reserve System, October 6.

U.S. Board of Governors of the Federal Reserve System, 1993b, Responses to Questions on

Financial Derivatives Posed by Congressman Henry B. Gonzalez, Chairman, Committee on Banking, Finance, and Urban Affairs, U.S. House of Representatives, Washington: Board of Governors of the Federal Reserve System, October 26.

U.S. Board of Governors of the Federal Reserve System, 1993, Federal Deposit Insurance Corporation, and Comptroller of the Currency, *Derivative Product Activities of Commercial Banks*, Joint study conducted in response to questions posed by Senator Riegle on derivative products, Washington: Board of Governors of the Federal Reserve System, January 27.

U.S. General Accounting Office, 1994, *Financial Derivatives: Actions Needed to Protect the Financial System*, Report GAO/GGD-94-133, Washington: General Accounting Office, May.

U.S. Presidential Task Force on Market Mechanisms, 1988, *Report*, [Brady Commission Report], U.S. Government Printing Office: Washington, January.

U.S. Working Group on Financial Markets, 1988, Interim Report of the Working Group on Financial Markets, submitted to The President of the United States, U.S. Government Printing Office: Washington, May.

Wall, Larry D., 1989, Interest Rate Swaps in an Agency Theoretic Model with Uncertain Interest Rates, *Journal of Banking and Finance*, May, 13: 261-270.

Derivatives, Regulation and Banking
Edited by B. Schachter
© 1997 Elsevier Science B.V. All rights reserved.

Chapter 10
Derivatives Regulation

John Board, Charles Goodhart, Michael Power, Dirk Schoenmaker[†]
London School of Economics, London, England, UK

1. INTRODUCTION

The study of the effects of derivatives can be divided into two major categories: the analysis of exchange-traded derivatives and the implications that over-the-counter (OTC) derivatives may have for the wider banking sector. One of our purposes is to examine the implications of both of these for derivative regulation, as well as the wider effects of derivatives on financial stability. This chapter will also draw lessons from the collapse of Barings.

Three general points can be made about derivatives and regulation. First, economics suggests that regulation is justified only when manifest harm, or the potential for harm, can be demonstrated. This harm is usually expressed in terms of externalities imposed on other participants or in terms of market failure. Second, there has been a very large amount of academic research into the effects of derivatives markets. The overwhelming evidence (including that for the UK) is that derivatives markets are not destabilising, either in theory or in practice. In particular, the evidence is not consistent with the view that derivatives cause undue volatility in the underlying spot market. Finally, in terms of OTC derivatives, the major problems arise from problems of capital adequacy and internal control. We regard these as being general issues relating to banking, rather than being specifically related to banks' derivatives activities.

Positions in derivatives can change from minute to minute, so annual or even quarterly reporting is unlikely to be useful for monitoring positions. One of the main managerial challenges is to track derivatives positions for control and capital adequacy purposes. However, in practice, this can only be done internally by banks. Consequently there is a need for supervisors to move from rule-based regulation (e.g. detailed capital

---

[†] Financial Markets Group. An earlier version of this paper was submitted as written evidence to the Treasury and Civil Service Committee of the House of Commons in the UK as part of the Committee's inquiry into derivatives.

adequacy rules) to self-regulation (e.g. reliance on internal risk control systems). This raises the question of how the official regulators may best test and monitor internal risk control systems. Another challenge is to obtain useful information: for OTC markets on counterparties (credit risk) and total net positions (market risk); for exchanges on total positions (preferably consolidated at headquarters and known by home supervisors).

Our main conclusion is to emphasize the pre-eminence of the need continuously to improve and monitor the performance of internal risk control systems. The power of the internal auditor to check internal control procedures should be enhanced – the challenge is to do this without reducing the incentive for firms to engage actively in such self-examination. However, even in the aftermath of Barings, we do not believe that external or internal auditors should be brought into the regulatory process. We do see a need for reinforcing the role of the Bank of England's derivatives team for checking on internal risk control systems.

The derivatives activities of banks should be brought fully into the regulatory framework for banks, insofar as it has not already been done. In this context, international proposals (BIS, EU) to incorporate market risks in the capital adequacy framework are significant. We also welcome the trend towards use of banks' internal risk measurement models (which are more flexible and advanced) for capital purposes.

We reject calls for narrow banking. Prohibition of derivatives trading by banks may, in our view, destabilize the banking system rather than stabilize it. The focus should be on how to control banks' involvement in derivatives business rather than on forbidding it. We endorse initiatives to collect more data on the size and structure of OTC markets. Such information could greatly assist supervisors to analyze the systemic consequences of the collapse of one participant.

Margins are a useful device to reduce counterparty risk for exchange-traded derivatives. The clearing house is the appropriate party to assess the size of such margins, and no regulatory action is needed. Because derivatives are useful, if only for hedging purposes, attempts to limit their use is likely to fail. Furthermore, regulation which is not introduced on an international level will just drive business elsewhere and ultimately off-shore.

2. ISSUES AND REGULATORY RESPONSES

2.1 The Role of Derivatives

The main economic function of derivatives is to allow individual parties to transform risks arising from changing interest rates, foreign exchange rates, equity prices and commodity prices. Derivatives do not create new risks, but redistribute existing risks among participants. Derivatives increase economic efficiency in that they enable participants to unbundle risk components and trade them in a manner which they could not do, or not nearly as effectively, previously. It is now widely accepted that derivatives are hedging vehicles which do not cause volatility but have developed in response to volatility (BIS, 1994b). However, it should also be acknowledged that, although risks can be reduced, they can also be amplified by trading speculatively in futures, options and other derivative instruments.

2.2 Differences between Exchange-traded and OTC Derivatives

Over-the-counter (OTC) derivatives are simply derivatives which are created as the result of bilateral negotiation between the parties to the trade, rather than through trade on a formal market. The benefit of OTC derivatives is that all terms of the contract (including, for example, the delivery date and contract volume) can be negotiated, whereas most terms of exchange-traded derivatives are pre-specified. The disadvantages of OTC products arise from the absence of a formal market place which leads to reduced liquidity and the absence of market oriented counterparty risk assessments. Data on the scale of OTC activity is scarce, but an ISDA survey suggests that in 1993, the notional value of OTC swaps activity was about 15% greater than that of all exchange traded derivatives.

The leading participants in the OTC market are banks, both commercial and investment. Risk reduction measures have arisen in the OTC market as part of prudent commercial activity (Group of Thirty, 1993). Such measures to reduce risk by financial institutions include: credit risk enhancement (e.g. third party guarantees, partial collateral requirements and early termination agreements) and daily marking-to-market (discussed below). In addition, derivative traders regularly use stress tests to simulate the impact of a large swing in certain foreign exchange or interest rates on their portfolio. Regulators may offer guidelines to encourage good practice. An alternative to formal regulation has recently emerged in the form of codes of 'best practice' as published by many trade associations and also, most importantly, by the Derivatives Policy Group of six major US investment houses. It seems likely that this will emerge as a *de facto* standard with which all firms wishing to enter the market will have to comply.

In the case of exchange-traded derivatives, the clearing house is the central counterparty of all derivative deals. The solvency of the clearing house is crucial for the stability of the exchange. To protect itself against potential failures of traders, the clearing house typically requires traders to deposit an initial margin. Positions are marked-to-market daily or sometimes even intradaily and variation margin calls are made when prices change. Most clearing houses have a loss sharing agreement among members and/or a reserve fund in case a member fails and its margins are not sufficient to cover its positions. For example, in the case of Barings the margins deposited at the Singapore and Osaka exchanges were sufficient to close Barings' outstanding contracts without a loss to the other members. Margin requirements are thus a very useful protective device against failure.

It has been suggested to bring 'standard' OTC derivatives to centralized exchanges as a method of reducing counterparty risk (Folkerts-Landau and Steinherr, 1994). Bringing 'standard' OTC products to exchanges is useful and some-OTC-products have come to exchanges once standardized. A recent example is the introduction of so-called flex options. But we doubt whether this approach is feasible for the majority of OTC-products for the following reasons. First, specialized products cannot be traded on an exchange. Second, the demand for new specialized or customized products will continue. Finally, some participants may *prefer* the less transparent OTC market and would move business elsewhere if this was changed. Therefore, without prohibition of OTC-trading, exchanges and OTC-markets will continue to co-exist.

2.3 The Importance of Internal Control

There is a long term trend in all areas of regulation towards internal control and self-regulation (indeed, self-regulation is the explicit basis of UK securities regulation under the Financial Services Act 1986) so that internal and external audits have become important regulatory instruments. There are also economic pressures for the substitution of internal control for external supervision and oversight, possibly reflecting a fundamental trade-off between formal independence and expertise (i.e. that only insiders really know what is going on, particularly in areas such as derivatives operations). Control techniques are well known: authorization controls; segregation of access to assets and recording. But these controls can always be circumvented. For example, there was no segregation of trade and settlement in the case of Barings Futures Singapore, even though no evidence of collusion in Singapore and/or between Singapore and London emerged from the inquiry by the Board of Banking Supervision (1995).

Although there may be a role for strengthening the culture of internal control, this requires internal auditors to be sufficiently strong to carry authority. At Barings, for example, internal auditors reported, in considerable detail, the lack of controls in the Singapore unit to the Board in London in August 1994. However, if, as at Barings, their recommendations carry no weight, so that no effective follow-up action is taken, internal audits are not useful.

It is tempting, if only because it is relatively cheap, to devise further roles for internal and external auditors post-Barings. Our view is that this would be a mistake. The main difficulty is that attempts to use internal audit functions for regulatory purposes would lead, in our view, to a deliberate reduction in the information contained in such reports. This would reduce their value both to the firm (which might use alternative channels to obtain the necessary information) and to the regulator. Ultimately, the internal audit would be exposed to some of the criticisms levelled at the operation of quality assurance initiatives, such as British Standard 5750 on quality systems. It would lead to an auditing of the procedural form rather than the substance of performance for the banking sector. Another example of these effects is found in the Cadbury code on the financial aspects of corporate governance for large UK companies, under which a voluntary code of best practice requires company directors to report on the effectiveness of internal controls. This remains controversial and, in practice, minimal information is provided in a statement that the directors have 'reviewed' internal controls with no statement on their effectiveness. This shows the sensitivity which exists in making any kind of strong 'certifying' statement in this area.

Finally, it should be emphasized that those bank supervisors which do active on-site examinations (e.g. the Federal Reserve and the Office of the Comptroller of the Currency in the USA) pay regular visits as well as surprise visits to banks. The UK style of relying on external auditors involves only regular visits (which are expected and prepared for by banks; fraud can more easily be hidden from pre-announced annual checks) and thus eliminates the surprise element. One alternative is that the Bank recruits its own investigators to pay surprise visits to banks to check controls. While the cost of stronger inspection is sizeable, the benefit is difficult to assess – how likely are examiners to detect fraud? The Bank has recently established a small specialist team for derivatives. This team should not only check on valuation models for capital adequacy purposes, but also on internal risk control models.

While it is easy to check whether the internal control procedures are adequate in principle, it is extremely difficult to assess whether procedures are applied. Moreover, the current structure of bonus payments makes the conscious adoption of a risky strategy the rational course for any trader, subject only to concern about his own future employment. Thus the internal control systems of a bank need to be tougher and more comprehensive, because they have to contend against an incentive structure which that same bank has put in place. Seen in this light Leeson was not just a unique 'rogue trader'. The bonus system tempts traders everywhere to emulate Leeson, but just to be luckier.

Another problem is how to control activities in foreign centres. The examples of Barings in Singapore and Standard Chartered in India show how difficult it is to control activities in foreign centres. As suggested above, only insiders know what is going on[1] and the challenge is to put an appropriate incentive structure in place. Since shareholders have lost money, they (or rather their delegates, the non-executive directors) can be expected to demand adequate control systems and monitoring mechanisms.

2.4 Cooperation between Regulators

There are conflicting demands for geographical and functional coordination of supervision, as national and institutional boundaries between previously distinct financial sectors continue to diminish. In particular, trading in derivatives has cut down cross-border and cross-sectoral barriers. We first discuss the consequences of global integration of financial institutions and next the impact of functional integration between banks and securities houses (and insurance companies as well) for cooperation among regulators. While the US, Japan and Canada still have legislation in place to separate commercial and investment banking[2], the European Union has universal banks which combine banking and securities business within the same legal entity.

2.4.1 International level

The main bodies for international regulatory cooperation are the Basle Committee on Banking Supervision of the Bank for International Settlements (BIS) and the International Organization of Securities Commissioners (IOSCO). Over the last two decades cooperation between bank regulators has been more successful than that between securities regulators, because systemic risk (with cross-border effects as first illustrated by the failure of Herstatt Bank in 1974) is more serious in banking and international banking regulators are a more cohesive (and less competitive) group than securities regulators (see, for example, Steil, 1994). The Basle Committee and the IOSCO Technical Committee started to coordinate efforts, but failed to reach agreement on the major issue of capital adequacy requirements for market risks (see section 3.2). However, cooperation between the Basle Committee and IOSCO has recently improved as witnessed by the joint guidelines issued for world-wide supervisors on the information necessary to evaluate derivatives risks incurred by banks and

---

[1]In the BCCI case, an aggrieved formal employee, Mr. Rahman, acted as a whistle-blower. As a former chief officer, he had inside knowledge about some of the irregularities in BCCI. He talked first to the New York District Attorney and the New York Federal Reserve Bank, and later to the Bank of England (Bingham, 1992, 130-1).

[2]There are proposals in the US Congress to abolish the Glass-Steagall Act, but it is not clear, at the time of the writing, whether they will pass the legislative hurdle. Japan has gradually allowed banks to enter into securities activities and *vice versa*.

securities firms (Joint Framework Document, 1995).

In May 1995, regulators of futures and option exchanges from sixteen countries signed the so-called Windsor Declaration. The Declaration was subsequently adopted by the IOSCO at its annual meeting in July 1995. This Declaration aims at cooperation between market authorities and, importantly, regulatory cooperation in emergency cases. This initiative to strengthen supervision of exchanges and improve information flows across international markets is much needed. But it remains to be seen how effective regulatory cooperation between exchanges, which are fiercely competing for market share, will be in practice.

2.4.2 National level

While it is generally recognized that cooperation among international regulators may be difficult to establish (e.g. due to cultural and linguistic differences), it is sometimes assumed that cooperation between national regulators is less burdensome. This is again highlighted in the Board of Banking Supervision Report (1995) on the collapse of Barings. The authors go at considerable length to explain the difficulties the Bank experienced in getting information from the Singapore authorities. While this may be true, there were serious fault lines in the cooperation between the Securities and Futures Authority (SFA) and the Bank of England as well. As functional regulators, the SFA was responsible for Barings Securities London and the Bank of England for Barings Bank. In addition, the Bank of England acted as lead regulator for the entity. The role of a lead regulator is to monitor the soundness and solvency of the financial institution on a consolidated basis and to coordinate regulatory actions, if needed.

To illustrate the difficulties in national cooperation between regulators, we discuss two problems in the cooperation between the Bank and the SFA in their supervision of Barings.[3] First, it appears that Barings in London reported its funding of Baring Futures Singapore (BFS) - to meet its substantial margin requirements on SIMEX - differently to the Bank and the SFA. The advances to BFS were neither included in the large exposures reports to the Bank, because they were believed to represent modest advances for a large number of clients, nor were they included in the returns to the SFA as advances to clients but were reported as amounts due from affiliated companies (Board of Banking Supervision Report, 1995, p.240-1). In other words, Barings reported the funding of margin requirements to the

---

[3]Another problem is that the SFA only supervised the UK operations of Barings Securities, but not the activities of overseas affiliates, such as Barings Futures in Singapore and Barings Securities in Japan.

Bank as funding for clients' positions and to the SFA as funding for proprietary positions of BFS. A reconciliation of the prudential returns between the Bank and the SFA would probably have revealed these differences, which rose from £150m on 1 January 1995 to £300m on 24 February 1995. Second, it appears that during the Barings crisis the Bank of England, as lead regulator of Barings, did not call upon the Securities and Investments Board (SIB) or the SFA, as functional regulator of Barings Securities. While the expertise on futures markets was available at the SIB and the SFA, it was not used by the Bank to assess the position of Barings Securities on the Singapore and Osaka futures exchanges. In this context, Dale (1995) has argued that the separation of banking and securities regulation between different agencies makes sense only if the risk exposures of these two businesses can also be segregated.

3. OTC/BANKING ISSUES

There are two particular issues which affect OTC derivatives. These are the possibility of systemic risk (i.e. the chance that problems at one bank will produce a widespread failure) and transparency (i.e. the fact that the risks of each trade must be evaluated by each party to the trade, in contrast to reliance on exchange clearance and the clearing house). It should be noted that although the former is economically very significant, it is really an issue in banking, rather than derivatives, regulation. This focus on bank regulation raises the question as to whether all derivatives players, and not just banks, should be brought into the regulatory framework. Apart from the systemic consequences, it is not clear that regulation of derivatives activity should bear harder on banks than on other institutions. In addition, the distinction between banks and non-banks is becoming less clear. For example, it has been argued that the large US mutual funds now have many of the characteristics of banks.

3.1 Problem – Systemic Risk

An important issue for banking supervision is whether derivatives contribute to systemic risk. Systemic issues arise when an incident at one financial institution (usually a bank) spreads to other financial institutions and/or financial markets.[4] The banking sector may be more susceptible to systemic problems than other financial intermediaries because

---

[4]There have been suggestions that the role of Barings as clearer for other agents in financial markets, which did not have adequate procedures for shifting that function in the case of a failure, almost led to some systemic externalities.

they are interconnected (for example, through the payment system and the interbank market; see Goodhart and Schoenmaker, 1995). Moreover, there are linkages between the large-money-centre-banks that are trading OTC-derivatives. Almost half of all interest rate swaps and a quarter of all currency swaps are negotiated between banks rather than with end-users (IMF, 1995). Furthermore, a loss of confidence in certain banks or the banking sector as a whole may give rise to runs on banks not directly implicated in the original problem. This suggests that, although banking regulation and supervision should be designed to minimize the chance of any bank failing, rescues should be limited to cases of potential systemic break-down.

Another type of systemic crisis starts with a market wide plunge in certain asset prices, such as the stock market crash in October 1987. Without central bank intervention (providing liquidity to the system), such a systemic crisis may easily cause multiple direct failures and further indirect failures by institutions which are exposed to the originally failing institutions. The question is whether derivatives contribute to the likelihood of a systemic collapse of financial markets. Certain trading strategies such as dynamic hedging may (see below) contribute to volatility in these markets.

Apart from proposals to improve, and enforce, internal controls (see above), there have been several proposals for regulation which are discussed below.

3.2 Regulatory Response I – Capital Adequacy

Capital Adequacy rules are instructions issued by regulators to ensure that financial institutions have sufficient capital to cover their investment activities (which may differ in riskiness from bank to bank). The difficulty is to devise rules which incorporate the main risk categories and which do not permit manipulation designed to avoid capital requirements without reducing risk.

The major current international guidelines are the 'Basle Capital Adequacy Accord' and the 'EC Own Funds and Solvency Ratio Directives', adopted in 1988 and 1989 respectively. These are both designed to deal with credit risk which is the most important risk relating to bank loans. However, the main risks in a bank's trading activities (which includes derivatives and other short-term operations), are market risks such as foreign exchange, interest rate and equity price risk. The capital requirements for these types of risk are contained in the '1993 Basle Proposals' (not adopted) and the 'EC Capital Adequacy Directive' (adopted in 1993). These are critically assessed in IMF (1994).

The main advantage of the Basle approach is that, as it applies to all international banks, it creates a level playing field. Although there are some notable deficiencies (e.g. Japanese banks are permitted to include unrealized gains on equities in their capital base), a multilateral approach is required in today's global financial markets. A unilateral attempt by a single country to impose tough capital standards would simply drive business to less restrictive jurisdictions.

One of the main problems with these systems is the simplifications which must be made to design a useable method for calculating total risk, which is suitable for all market participants including smaller banks. The 1993 Basle Proposals used a simple building block approach to the calculation of value at risk, and hence, of capital requirements. However, large banks which have sophisticated models to measure 'value at risk' argued that this would result in a 'lowest common denominator' approach to risk measurement and demanded to be allowed to use their own internal systems for risk measurement. In its new proposals, which supersede the earlier 1993 Proposals, the Basle Committee (BIS, 1995b) has accepted this and suggests that banks use their own value at risk models subject to certain common standards.

The Committee proposes the following parameters: a holding period of two weeks (ten business days), a short-term and long-term observation period over which to calculate historical volatilities and correlations (use the higher value at risk numbers obtained by using the two sample periods), a confidence level of 99%, limits on aggregation (aggregation within risk categories but not between risk categories such as interest rates, foreign exchange rates, equity and commodity prices). Even then, firms with the same portfolio of derivatives can have different outcomes when they are using different derivatives pricing models (experiments with existing models have produced variations of over 45%). To be conservative, the capital charge is obtained by multiplying the value at risk measure by a factor of three or more, but there is no theoretical basis for this factor. Finally, measures based on historical volatilities and correlations tend to overlook major market disturbances which have a low probability of occurrence but a large impact if they occur. Examples of such disturbances are the October '87 stock market crash and, more recently, the Mexican crisis. Stress tests should therefore supplement the value at risk methodology.

Under this regime, the challenge for banking supervisors is to test and monitor such models. This suggests that, rather than prescribing a certain format for risk measurement models or risk control systems, supervisors should encourage innovation by allowing such models and systems to develop and improve, while examining them against a benchmark of best practice.

Although capital rules are a valuable vehicle to internalize the riskiness of banks' activities, other forms of risk (e.g. liquidity or funding risk) are also important, but not yet addressed under these proposals. Any firm, industrial or financial, has to plan its cash inflows and outflows, and arrange for expected (and unexpected) cash shortfalls or liquidity gaps. The same is true for derivatives business. A derivatives trader should have sufficient liquid funds or borrowing capacity available to meet potential margin calls on its derivatives positions. The recent example of Metallgesellschaft highlights the importance of having adequate funding facilities in place (Edwards, 1994). Metallgesellschaft was using futures (and swaps) as a hedge against a large volume of fixed-price, forward supply contracts for oil. Because of falling energy prices, Metallgesellschaft had to fund sizeable cash outflows due to margin calls on its futures contracts. Even if Metallgesellschaft had equal and offsetting unrealized gains on its forward supply contracts, it would still have had to borrow to meet these cash outflows because of the illiquid nature of its forward contracts.

Finally, the European Large Exposures Directive, LED, extends the concept of the large exposure limit, which already applied to UK banks, to the wider investment community. Under the LED, no institution may advance more than 25% of its capital to a single counterparty without making additional capital provisions. This limit was notionally in force for Barings, but an 'informal concession' had been granted by the Bank of England. The discretion to do this was removed under the LED, although it included transitional provisions. However, there is no evidence that the Bank of England relied on these in permitting Barings to continue exceeding the large exposure limits.

3.3 Regulatory Response II – Narrow Banking and Ring-Fencing

There have been several calls for narrow banking in the wake of the Barings crisis (*Financial Times*, 27 Feb 1995; *The Economist*, 4 March 1995). In its purest form, narrow banking means that deposit-taking banks are only allowed to invest in highly liquid, safe assets such as government securities (Litan, 1987). Government guaranteed deposit insurance is then exclusively available for these narrow banks, although there will be (almost) no need for such deposit insurance as these narrow banks are relatively safe. Lending (as well as other risky activities) has then to be channelled through financial institutions which fund themselves with uninsured liabilities such as commercial paper.

A more moderate form of narrow banking is that relatively risky activities have to be conducted through a separate subsidiary. The risky part is then 'ring-fenced' and the insured part of the bank is not allowed to channel funds to the uninsured subsidiaries unless prior approval from the bank supervisor is obtained. This structure ensures that the deposit-taking part of the bank will not be contaminated by the risky parts of the bank. Apart from the question whether such narrow banking proposals are feasible (essentially whether banking supervision and the public safety-net could really be confined to these narrow banks)[5], it is not clear whether such narrow banking schemes are desirable.

A market based version of this approach is the recent trend (noted in Dale, 1995) for major US securities firms to establish derivative product companies, *DPCs*, arguably to escape the SEC's regulatory oversight (including capital adequacy rules).[6] This arrangement allows banks' derivatives trading to be assessed by credit rating agencies, which act as surrogate but market based regulators of the *DPCs*, and which will base their rating (*AAA* for most banks which have made this change) on assessments of capital adequacy, maximum counterparty risk, transfer of market risk etc. Whether this should be viewed as an interesting development or a potential regulatory problem is unclear. It should be noted that the motivation for the creation of *DPCs* is the separation of high quality derivatives trading from risky and low quality banking activities – not the reverse.

Dis-intermediation has resulted in a decline in the charter value of banks over the last two decades, but banks have found new ways to make profits in securities (e.g. by underwriting) and derivatives activities. This means that derivatives activities have moved closer to the core of banks' activities and means that there may be severe operational difficulties in attempting to separate derivatives from banking activities. For example, should only proprietary trading be ring-fenced or should OTC derivative trading with clients (i.e. acting as counterparty to a client who wants a particular derivative) also be separated? A similar type of market risk is involved in each case and the level of risk is dependent on the degree of hedging, not the motivation for the position. Furthermore, preventing a bank from entering the derivatives market altogether will prevent it from hedging its own potentially risky mis-matches. The result could be worse, as the banking system might be less stable without the opportunity to hedge. Allowing banks to use derivatives for hedging, but not for speculating purposes raises the thorny issue of dividing derivatives activities into hedging and speculating. We would argue that such a distinction cannot be effectively assessed by outsiders. Finally, forbidding deposit-taking banks from engaging in derivatives trading on their own account (i.e. by banning proprietary trading) would make banks less profitable and might even encourage them to take on more risk in their traditional business. This might, therefore, make the banking system less stable in the long run.

---

[5]Is it really possible for the authorities to confine the public safety-net to the insured narrow banks? What happens, for example, if one or more of the uninsured fiinancial institutions gets into trouble? Are these uninsured banks able to cause a systemic crisis and may thecentral bank as lender of last resort then wish to intervene to prevent a systemic break-down of the financial system?

[6]It is not clear under existing UK regulations whether DPCs would still be regarded as banks and therefore remain subject to bnaking supervision.

The calls for ring-fencing or narrow banking in the wake of the Barings collapse is comparable with the response to the US banking crisis in 1930s. The Glass-Steagall Act was introduced to separate commercial (loan business) and investment (securities business) banking. Stock holdings by banks were thought to be one of the main causes of the multiple bank failures during the Great Depression and were subsequently forbidden[7]. Recent research (e.g. Benston, 1990), indicates that this view was premature and without much foundation. But reversing the Glass-Steagall legislation has so far proved to be very difficult. We believe that the focus should be on how to control banks' involvement in derivatives business rather than on ring-fencing or forbidding it.

3.4 Problem – Counter-Party Risk and Transparency

It is important that parties can assess counterparty risk. Over-the-counter (OTC) traded derivatives are not transparent, in that the information required to assess correctly a bank's derivatives exposure is mostly lacking. We separate the transparency issue into two parts: at the *participant* level, the focus is on the information required by potential counterparties to a trade, while, at the *supervisory* level, the focus is on the information required by regulators to assess the overall structure of markets. Increased transparency is also very useful in times of a crisis as it enables the authorities, as well as individual agents, to evaluate the impact of the crisis on the different market players. Without information to differentiate between affected and non-affected financial institutions, rumours can adversely affect healthy institutions.

3.5 Regulatory Response – Mandatory Information Provision

3.5.1 Participant Level

At this level the participants to any OTC derivatives deal need the information to assess each other's risk. It can be argued that derivatives and other off-balance instruments have reduced the transparency and information content of balance sheets; however, while this may be true, it is unlikely to affect the decisions of OTC participants, who can demand detailed information of each other.

Nevertheless, some general information will be required, if only to facilitate comparison between institutions. This suggests that a minimum degree of standardization of accounting for derivatives may be required. The Fisher Report (BIS, 1994a) argues that differences in the information about risk and risk management available to managers and to

---

[7]Another reason for separating banking and securities activities was to avoid conflicts of interest between debt and equity holders.

outsiders may lead to a mis-allocation of capital among firms. To improve transparency, the Fisher Report proposes that information generated by internal risk management systems should be adapted for public disclosure purposes. Such information would complement, but not substitute for, disclosures based on traditional accounting. The Report recommends that all financial institutions (regulated and unregulated) should move into the direction of publicly disclosing periodic quantitative information on the market risks in the relevant portfolio, the actual performance in managing these risks over the reporting period, and counterparty credit risks arising from its trading activities.

The Report suggests, as an example of market risk reporting the presentation of 'value at risk' (for a given confidence interval and period) at the reporting date, and as an example of the actual performance of managing market risk reporting the presentation of the average daily value at risk, or a diagram of daily changes in portfolio value over the reporting period. The example of credit risk reporting includes: current credit exposure, broken down by credit quality class. A more profound change would be the adoption of 'scenario reporting' in which banks report the value of their derivatives positions under a variety of different scenarios (rather than emphasising a single figure as required under present accounting rules). While the definition of these scenarios could, in principle, be left to individual firms, one alternative would be to standardize scenarios by adopting the methods used by derivatives clearing houses (e.g. SPAN) or the recently published RiskMetrics (originated by J.P. Morgan).

Another response is to require all OTC trades are marked to market on a regular and frequent basis (daily or weekly). At a minimum, this would involve regular, formal, valuation of open positions and the possible exchange of cash when this value changes. Since many OTC positions are already marked to market, a requirement to do so might not be excessively onerous, though one reason often given for the popularity of OTC trades is that it leaves marking-to-market to the discretionary decisions of the parties involved.[8]

Although there is scope for improvement in disclosure, there are limits to what can be achieved. Even with mark-to-market accounting and frequent reporting (e.g. each quarter), information can still be outdated. As credit rating agencies are gathering information on a continuous basis, credit ratings of institutions may be a useful tool in the assessment of counterparty risk.

---

[8]Conceptually, an OTC product negotiated between a bank and its client can be seen as a pure derivative and a credit line. As mentioned in section 2.2, banks actively manage the credit risk inherent in OTC derivatives. If banks would like to reduce their credit exposure to certain clients, they could, for example, ask for a letter of credit or collateral (see also Group of Thirty, 1993).

3.5.2 Supervisory Level

The Brockmeijer Report (BIS, 1995a) identifies a need for better statistical data to assess the implications of derivative markets for the policy responsibilities of various public authorities. An internationally coordinated approach (by central banks) to collecting these data would aim to shed light primarily on the size and structure of the global OTC derivatives markets. The existing data on derivatives markets, whether gathered by central banks or by market associations, have a number of important shortcomings (e.g. differences among various reporting systems in terms of range of instruments and institutions covered; existing data focus on notional amounts and are uninformative as to size and risk incurred; existing data provide only limited information on the structure of participation).

The Report recommends two complementary approaches for the collection of data needed for compilation of global market size characteristics: (1) occasional surveys of a large number of participants to obtain broad scans of derivatives market activity; (2) a system of regular market reporting confined to the main intermediaries in the derivatives markets. Both the survey and regular market reporting would collect data on the notional and market values of outstanding contracts, dis-aggregated by broad underlying market risk classes (i.e. exchange rates, interest rates, equity prices and commodity prices) and by instrument type, counterparty type, maturity and currency. To shed light on linkages between OTC and exchange-traded markets, it also recommends collecting data on the exchange-traded activities of the reporting institutions. It is not clear how large the resulting reporting burdens will be.

Initiatives to gather industry-wide information such as the Brockmeijer Report (BIS, 1995a) are informative and helpful, especially to reduce systemic risk. Only with regular information on the major players and on the derivatives markets (both OTC and exchanges), can supervisors and individual agents alike better assess the situation during times of stress. It will be easier to neutralize rumour driven panics. Moreover, supervisors will be in a better position to analyze the impact of the collapse of one participant on other participants and on the stability of the wider financial system. As noted above, banks are the major players in the OTC derivatives markets and a substantial part of the OTC trading is between banks. Information on the linkages between these OTC traders is therefore crucial to assess the systemic consequences of the failure of a bank that is active in the OTC market.

4. EXCHANGE-TRADED DERIVATIVES

4.1 Do Derivatives Increase Risk?

Derivatives are often criticized on the argument that they increase risks, particularly of the underlying market. We consider some different aspects of this question below.

4.1.1 Volatility

A large amount of evidence (e.g. Board, Goodhart and Sutcliffe, 1991, 1992) suggests that exchange-traded derivatives do not induce additional volatility in the spot market. This means that the measured volatility of the underlying market does not increase either with the opening of derivatives markets or with growth in the volume of trade on those markets.

It is important to recognize that volatility is not in itself undesirable. Volatility is caused by trade and the arrival of new information leads to trade in an efficient market. What is undesirable is excessive volatility which is unrelated to informed trade. There is considerable evidence that transactions costs (i.e. bid/ask spreads and commissions) are much lower in derivatives markets than in the underlying equity market. One implication of this is that traders with information might prefer to trade in derivatives markets. This suggests that 'price discovery' is facilitated by the existence of derivatives, and academic evidence consistently suggests that futures markets *lead* the corresponding underlying market by about 5 minutes. This suggests that derivatives enhance market efficiency.

It is also interesting that both the Bank of England and the London Stock Exchange reports on the crash of 1987 highlight the *low* level of derivatives and arbitrage activity as reasons why recovery from the crash was slow. There is no evidence from either the US or UK that derivatives caused, or contributed substantially to, the crash.

4.1.2 Speculation

It is often asserted that excessive volatility is caused by the speculative nature of derivatives markets. This behaviour will, it is alleged, induce large price swings in both derivatives and spot markets. However, if the spot market is 'correctly' priced, it would be sensible (and profitable) for spot market participants to take riskless positions against speculators (e.g. if futures prices are driven too high by speculators, selling futures backed by equity, will be very profitable). This would eliminate any excess volatility. It is of interest that there are reports that some large investors were taking positions against Leeson (i.e. selling him the futures contracts which he was buying).

A second issue arises when it is alleged that negative market sentiment is expressed through, levered, derivatives positions. While this is possible, negative sentiment could be expressed equally well by selling the underlying asset using borrowed funds (or broker's credit). Therefore, it is unclear why derivatives should encourage such speculative behaviour.

4.1.3 Liquidity

Another question is whether derivatives activity reduces spot liquidity. The suggestion is that, as derivatives markets typically have much lower transactions costs than the spot market, it is possible that derivatives markets will begin to dominate the spot. This might lead to a drift of capital away from the spot market, leading to a loss of liquidity and a fall in efficiency. This is an open question, but no sign of this effect has been reported in the UK or Japan/US (where in these latter countries nominal equity derivatives activity is several times that of the underlying equity levels). Equally, equity market inefficiency would be exploitable by traders, and their (arbitrage) actions would tend to eliminate any price disparity between markets.

4.1.4 Knowledge

A contentious issue is whether there is a need for suitability criteria for users of derivatives. In the aftermath of the Gibson Greetings and Procter & Gamble cases, there have been calls for such criteria. Mis-representation appeared to be an important element in these cases. It can e argued that access to civil law provides an adequate remedy against these cases of mis-representation. Moreover, a suitability criterion is already part of the core conduct of business rules published by the SIB and SROs (rule 16, SIB, 1991). This principle of 'know your customer' is applicable to derivatives as well, so there is no automatic requirement for new regulation here. Clearly, however, derivatives are more complex than other investment vehicles and reinforcement, particularly for private business, of these rules may be beneficial.

4.2 Inter Market Linkages

The existence of derivatives markets may also have implications for the operation of the market in the underlying asset. One example of this is the current concern with the transparency (i.e. the fact that publication of the details of almost 50% of the value of Stock Exchange transactions is delayed for 90 minutes). There are arguments that this structure imposes costs on the system as a whole (e.g. Board and Sutcliffe, 1995). It is also claimed that derivatives growth is hindered by lack of spot market transparency. This is unproved, but it cannot be desirable for the current spot price to be unobserved when trading derivatives. At a minimum, this creates asymmetries of information which may lead to volatility or a withdrawal from the market (this latter effect is alleged by LIFFE). Whether this is the case or not, LIFFE's equity options (in contrast to most of their other products) are measurably less successful than those in other competing markets.

A second issue is whether programme (i.e. automated) trading strategies can cause problems in the cash market. These strategies need not involve the explicit use of derivatives. The major problem is that an institution which, say, wants to sell a large volume of stock may be doing so because it has negative information about the stock or because it has decided to rebalance its portfolio (i.e. a programme trade). The former will lead, correctly, to a large price fall; the problem arises if the latter were mistakenly to be interpreted as being information related. 'Sunshine trading' (under which firms pre-announce their intention to buy or sell as part of a programme trade) has been suggested as a method of avoiding this problem. In the US, this practice was ruled to be in conflict with pre-arranged markets rules. In the UK, the system of 'one day protection' can be argued to achieve the same effect. There is also evidence that information about the parties involved in block trades filters into the market informally.

4.3 Margins and the Clearing House

There are two separate roles for margins and the distinction between them is important. First, margins act as an initial deposit to minimize the risk of default to the clearing house (which acts as the counterparty to all deals on the exchange). To protect itself against potential failures of traders, the clearing house typically requires traders to deposit an initial margin and further variation margin calls are made as prices change. The size of these margin payments seems most appropriately assessed by the clearing house itself (presumably in consultation with its members), and is likely to be based on the average daily price movement and the probability of default. In these terms, there is no particular evidence that margins are generally too low (note that, for example, Barings' positions were closed within 36 hours with minimal price impact and no calls for additional funds by clearing houses in either Singapore or Osaka). This use of margins for the avoidance of default risk is the principal purpose of margins on derivatives markets.

Second, margins can be used to control the leverage of individual positions (e.g. a multiplier). This is often used as the basis of arguments that control over margins would stabilize the market. However, there is no evidence from the US (e.g. Hsieh and Miller, 1990) that margins act as an effective control over volatility. It should also be emphasized that raising margins reduces liquidity and reduces the attractiveness of markets. This may drive business overseas or onto OTC markets.

It is important to realize that any system which advances credit is susceptible to Barings type problems. For example, on the London Stock Exchange, even rolling $T+5$ settlement gives 5 days to run up levered speculative positions. Note also that brokers often allow clients significant private credit which may be of longer duration than the exchange's settlement period (c.f. in a different context, the Stock Exchange's current concern with short selling of new equity issues).

There are occasional proposals to reinforce the requirement of marking-to-market of OTC derivatives by the establishment of a clearing house. This proposal deserves some consideration, but because of the concentrated nature of much OTC business and the difficulty of credit screening for the remaining customers, this idea is unlikely to be practicable. Were it a viable and efficient possibility, banks might be expected to create such a mechanism themselves, without regulatory intervention.

5. THE BARINGS CRISIS

5.1 How Did It Happen?

The most startling and worrying aspect of the Barings failure is the realization that Leeson's trading strategies were very simple and that the reasons why they were not recognized sooner was the absence of the most rudimentary controls within the bank. The failure was not caused by a failure to understand complex trading strategies nor by sophisticated fraud by Leeson or others. In addition, it is important to recognize that derivatives positions of this size are not unusual (a number of UK banks have greater exposure than this), but that the problems arose because of the size of the open positions relative to the bank's capital.

It is known that, although Leeson was authorized only to take large fully hedged positions (so as to exploit small pricing differences between Nikkei index futures traded on the Singapore and Osaka futures exchanges), he actually took large unhedged positions. Is seems that, since arriving in Singapore in 1992, Leeson consistently took unauthorized positions (both unhedged futures and written options). In January 1995, he held a total of 1,080 unhedged futures contracts, by 26 February 1995, this had risen to 61,039. The positions were based on simple exchange-traded derivative instruments; there is no question, therefore, that the lack of transparency attributed to OTC derivatives could have been involved.

The Board of Banking Supervision (BBS) Report (1995) revealed an 'absolute' failure of Baring's internal control systems. The most cited shortcoming was in Barings' failure to separate front and back office management in Singapore. This allowed Leeson to fabricate trades and to falsify records so as to conceal the nature of his activities. These activities allowed Leeson not only to report false positions to London, but also to mislead SIMEX as to which trades were on behalf of Barings' clients and which were 'house' positions. The BBS report estimates that Leeson may have underpaid margin payments to SIMEX in the amount of £250m during the 1995.

Barings seemed to lack even the most rudimentary controls, such as a reconciliation of margin payments to client business. If house positions had been hedged, then contracts/positions running into deficit should be offset by contracts showing a surplus. While the negative positions have to be covered via margin calls in exchange-traded contracts, surpluses should arise at the other contracts and the net margin payment at any time should be close to zero. Indeed, SIMEX allows reduced margin payments for positions fully hedged in Osaka. A simple check whether Barings Futures Singapore had unrealized surpluses on the other contracts would have indicated that these supposedly offsetting contracts were not in place and hence that positions were unhedged. Instead, senior management in London authorized the transfer of liquid funds from London to Singapore to meet the required margin calls so that, by the time of failure, the banks entire capital had been transferred to the far east.

Both futures markets involved were aware of the large positions adopted by Barings. Indeed Osaka periodically publishes details naming institutions and their holdings. There is evidence of concern by SIMEX over the size of Barings' positions (SIMEX wrote to and met Barings representatives and noted both that Barings had large long positions, at a time when Leeson was reporting short positions, and questioning the role of account 88888, which Leeson used for all of his unauthorized activities and of whose existence Barings in London was unaware). However, neither exchange could have observed directly the size of the bank's net unhedged position. To do this would have required data from the other markets in which the bank could have been trading (to hedge or to lever further the position on its own market) and not just from one market. Consequently it is difficult for any one market to observe and to warn (either the firm or the supervisor) about the effect of large positions between markets or on the interactions of such positions. The issue of the extent to which competing exchanges will voluntarily exchange information is an open one.

One question which deserves some consideration is whether an international official body should be established, when several derivative markets are trading the same contract, to receive and collate data from both. An argument against this is that a trader wishing to disguise fraudulent trades could move part of his dealing to the OTC market. Nevertheless this does raise one of the key questions which is whether the information available on a systematic basis to regulators, internal or external, is sufficient, and, if not, how it can be enhanced.

5.2 Should Barings have been Saved?

Bailing out by the central bank is justified only if there is a demonstrable systemic consequence to failure. The initial assessment in the weekend of 25/26 February 1995, that there was limited, systemic risk arising from the Barings collapse, proved to be correct. This assessment will, in part have been made on the grounds that Barings was actually a rather small institution. Following the collapse of Barings, all other banks in the world should have reassessed whether their own bank's internal risk control system would have prevented that happening to them. Had Barings been bailed out, that signal would have been muted. Thus, the decision not to rescue Barings is likely to have reinforced market discipline.

The attempt by the Bank of England to organize a lifeboat for Barings was, however, justified, as long as it was to be financed by the banking sector itself. But the use of taxpayers' money (either indirectly via the Bank's accounts or directly by the HM Treasury) is not justified under such circumstances. It would have sent the wrong signal to the market.

In a 'traditional' bank failure, the major task is to assess the real value of bad loans. Although this value will be lower than the nominal loan value, the potential loss is cannot exceed the face value of the bad loan. However, with large open positions in derivatives and a market aware that large positions will have to be unwound, the potential losses are potentially unlimited. Particularly as normal statistical relationships tend to break down during crisis situations, the potential downward risk is difficult to calculate both in terms of the loss and the time required to complete the unwinding. It is reported that the lifeboat failed because the participating banks wanted to cap the overall size of the support action, which was impossible given Barings' outstanding derivative contracts.

Although there were only limited systemic risks arising from the failure, some related aspects of bank behaviour were revealed. Barings had been acting as clearing agent for certain other financial intermediaries in some markets. When it failed alternative mechanisms for switching the clearing arrangements were not in place in some cases, leaving those intermediaries who had used Barings in this capacity in an exposed position. The participants in the markets involved, and those markets, need to review their own procedures on this. But, while the official regulators have an interest, the initiative on this should come from the private sector participants.

5.3 Lessons from Barings

The main lesson of the Barings case is that there is no alternative to the establishment of effective and stringent internal risk control systems. In Barings, there was no separation of trade and settlement, which allowed Leeson's activities to be concealed. In addition, there was no formal, and independent, risk management division which monitored Leeson's activities. The failure makes clear that stringent internal investigations are the principal mechanisms by which the management can inform themselves of the efficiency of their control procedures. These reports should be regularly commissioned and their recommendations must be acted upon.

The second lesson is that with investment in several competing markets, let alone OTC trading, it is difficult for the regulators (be they the markets, clearing houses or supervisors) to obtain information on net positions, and thus to establish whether regulations are being followed. Even the bank itself, if its internal control and reporting systems are inadequate, may face these problems; for example, Barings believed (and assured SIMEX) that they were 31,000 contracts short, at a time when they were actually 30,000 contracts long. This raises the importance of international co-operation and coordination between of regulators. The Windsor declaration is a recent example of this, as noted in section 2.4.

Finally, one feature of the derivatives market is the speed and extent to which speculative positions can be created, or unwound. When traders can take huge unauthorized positions (even to the event of destroying their own bank) within a few days, the invasiveness of central bank supervision required to prevent such activity would be neither feasible nor acceptable. The implication of this is that the principal regulatory burden falls on the bank itself – if the bank itself does not know what is going on, the regulators cannot be expected to do so. Ultimately, any regulated bank must be assumed to be run professionally, and regulation be designed to encourage such professionalism. It is hard to imagine any system of regulation or supervision being able to prevent determined fraud or sudden and catastrophic failure of competence.

6. RECOMMENDATIONS AND CONCLUSIONS

There is no evidence (in theory or practice) that derivatives destabilize the financial system. Derivatives trading is beneficial in that it allows agents to unbundle risk components and trade them in a cost-efficient way.

As derivatives traders can change their positions intraday, it is difficult for outsiders to keep abreast of traders' positions. Our main recommendation therefore is to improve and monitor internal risk control systems. Traders should set internal limits and ensure adequate mechanisms to control these limits on a regular (at least daily) basis. The role of the internal auditor to monitor internal control procedures should be strengthened. In the aftermath of Barings, we expect both shareholders and management of banks to step up the monitoring of internal risk control systems.

We do not believe that external or internal auditors should be brought into the regulatory process. Requirements for internal auditors to report their findings to banking supervisors, for example, may lead to an auditing of form rather than substance. But we see a need for reinforcing the role of the Bank of England's derivatives team for checking on internal risk control systems.

The banking system is subject to systemic risk. Derivatives, as well as other banking activities, may cause a systemic failure. We recommend therefore that derivatives activities of banks should be brought fully into the regulatory framework for banks, insofar as it has not already been done. Regulators have been working on an international basis (BIS, EU) to formulate minimum capital adequacy rules for market risks. We welcome the trend towards relying on banks' internal risk measurement models for capital purposes, as such models are more flexible and advanced. Risk reduction measures (e.g. third party guarantees, partly collateral requirements) have arisen in the OTC market as part of prudent commercial activity. Regulators may offer guidelines to encourage good practice.

We reject calls for narrow banking. Prohibition of derivatives trading by banks may, in our view, destabilize the banking system rather than stabilize it. The focus should be on how to control banks' involvement in derivatives business rather than on forbidding it. We endorse initiatives to collect more data on the size and structure of OTC markets and exchanges. Such information, if effectively shared between market regulators and bank supervisors, could greatly assist regulators and supervisors to analyze the systemic consequences of the collapse of one participant.

Clearing houses rely on margins to reduce counterparty risk of derivatives traded on exchanges. The clearing house is the appropriate party to assess the size of these margin positions. There is no particular evidence that margins are generally too low. Although we see some merit in initiatives to bring 'standard' OTC products to exchanges, we do not believe that intervention by regulators to 'force' OTC traders to shift (part of) their business to exchanges would be warranted or successful.

Because derivatives are useful, if only for hedging purposes, attempts to limit their use is likely to fail. Finance theory reveals how portfolios with characteristics equivalent to derivatives (including their leverage) can be constructed from traditional securities, attempts to ban or to restrict explicit derivatives (or their markets) will simply lead to increased use of less heavily regulated markets. Furthermore, regulation which is not introduced on an international level (e.g. Basle) will just drive business elsewhere and ultimately off-shore.

REFERENCES

Bank for International Settlements, 1994a, *A Discussion Paper on Public Disclosure of Market and Credit Risks by Financial Intermediaries* (Fisher Report), Prepared by the Euro-Currency Standing Committee of the G-10 Central Banks, Basle, September.

Bank for International Settlements, 1994b, *Macroeconomic and Monetary Policy Issues Raised by the Growth of Derivatives Markets* (Hannoun Report), Prepared by the Euro-Currency Standing Committee of the G-10 Central Banks, Basle, November.

Bank for International Settlements, 1995a, *Issues of Measurement Related to Market Size and Macroprudential Risks in Derivatives Markets* (Brockmeijer Report), Prepared by the Euro-Currency Standing Committee of the G-10 Central Banks, Basle, February.

Bank for International Settlements, 1995b, Proposal to Issue a Supplement to the Basle Capital Accord to Cover Market Risks, Basle Committee on Banking Supervision, Basle, April.

Board of Banking Supervision, 1995, Report of the Board of Banking Supervision Inquiry into the Circumstances of the Collapse of Barings, HMSO, London.

Benston, George, 1990, *The Separation of Commercial and Investment Banking*, MacMillan, London.

Bingham, Lord Justice, 1992, *Inquiry into the Supervision of The Bank of Credit and Commerce International*, House of Commons, London, October.

Board, John, Charles Goodhart and Charles Sutcliffe, 1991, *Equity and Derivatives Markets: Linkages and Regulatory Implications*, London School of Economics.

Board, John, Charles Goodhart and Charles Sutcliffe, 1992, *Inter Market Volatility Linkages,* London School of Economics.

Board, John and Charles Sutcliffe, 1995, *The Effects of Trade Transparency on the London Stock Exchange*, LSE Financial Markets Group, Special Paper No 67, January.

Dale, Richard, 1995, Derivatives: The New Regulatory Challenge, *Butterworths Journal of International Banking and Financial Law*, January, p.1-7.

Economist, The, 1995, The Bank That Disappeared, 4 March, p.11-12.

Edwards, Franklin, 1994, *Derivatives Can Be Hazardous to Your Health: The Case of Metallgesellschaft*, LSE Financial Markets Group, Special Paper No 64, December.

Financial Times, 1995, Body Blow to Barings, 27 February.

Folkerts-Landau, David and Alfred Steinherr, 1994, The Wild Beast of Derivatives: To Be Chained Up, Fenced In or Tamed?, in: Richard O'Brien (ed., *Finance and the International Economy: The AMEX Bank Review Awards*, Vol 8, Oxford University

Press, Oxford.

Goodhart, Charles and Dirk Schoenmaker, 1995, Should the Functions of Monetary Policy and Banking Supervision be Separated?, *Oxford Economic Papers*, forthcoming.

Group of Thirty, 1993, *Derivatives: Practices and Principles*, Prepared by the Global Derivatives Study Group, Washington DC, July.

Hsieh, David and Merton Miller, 1990, Margin Regulation and Stock Market Volatility, *Journal of Finance*, 45, p.3-29.

International Monetary Fund, 1994, *International Capital Markets: Developments, Prospects, and Policy Issues*, World Economic and Financial Surveys, Washington DC, September.

International Monetary Fund, 1995, *International Capital Markets: Developments, Prospects, and Policy Issues*, World Economic and Financial Surveys, Washington DC, August.

Joint Framework Document, 1995, Framework for Supervisory Information about Derivatives Activities, Basle Committee on Banking Supervision and the Technical Committee of the International Organization of Securities Commissioners.

Litan, Robert, 1987, *What Should Banks Do?*, Brookings Institution, Washington DC.

Securities and Investments Board, 1991, *The Core Conduct of Business Rules*, Rulebook Amendments and Additions Release 94, January.

Steil, Benn, 1994, *International Financial Market Regulation*, John Wiley and Sons, New York.

Derivatives, Regulation and Banking
Edited by B. Schachter
© 1997 Elsevier Science B.V. All rights reserved.

Chapter 11
Financial Innovation, Money Banking and Financial Fragility in the UK

Andy Mullineux[†]
University of Birmingham, Edgbaston, Birmingham, UK

1. INTRODUCTION

This chapter assesses the impact of financial innovation and liberalization in the personal banking sector in the UK. Financial innovation has reduced transaction costs and increased the liquidity of some financial assets leading to wealth portfolio adjustment and a consequent blurring of the definition of money. Financial liberalization has increased competition in banking, further stimulating reductions in transaction costs and increasing the supply of bank loans and credit. The dramatic reduction in credit rationing since the early 1980s led to over-indulgence in the late 1980s and a debt overhang in the early 1990s. The question thus arises: has financial innovation and liberalization increased financial fragility in the UK?

2. FINANCIAL INNOVATION, MONEY AND BANKING IN THE UK

The key innovative themes in the personal banking sector in the UK in the 1970s and 1980s were: rapid innovation in the provision of Money Transmission Services (MTS) [1] (the spread of Automated Teller Machines (ATMs), Electronic Funds Transfer (EFT), credit, debit and charge cards, and interest bearing cheque accounts); increased liquidity of traditional savings accounts, such as bank time deposit accounts or building society

---

[†]Director of Money, Banking & Finance Programmes Department of Economics. Tel: 021 414 6642; Fax: 021 414 6625

[1]In Bank of England (1992), it is noted that the upward trend in narrow money velocity in the UK dates back to (at least) the mid 1950s and that this may reflect financial innovation in the form of the introduction and more widespread use of alternative means of payment; including cheque books and credit cards.

'passbook' savings accounts; and a blurring of distinctions between financial intermediaries which had traditionally specialized in particular spheres of business as demarcations were rescinded and they encroached upon each other's traditional business. The Appendix provides a summary of some of the key innovations in the UK.

The increased availability of interest bearing cheque accounts (IBCAs) since the mid 1980s would be expected to induce the public to economize on cash and traditional non-interest bearing current account (NIBCA) holdings because of the 'opportunity cost' of holding them. The components of transactions money aggregates can thus no longer be regarded as perfect substitutes. It may be that cash and NIBCAs have never been perfect substitutes, however, since their rates of return have in fact differed. This is because UK banks have not sought to charge fully for MTS provision and this means that they implicitly pay (non-taxable) interest. One reason for the adoption of such a policy is to gain custom in order to facilitate the cross-selling of other products.[2] Another, and closely related, reason is to gain information from monitoring current accounts. This is useful for marketing traditional and new products and gives banks information on credit worthiness which may not be available in the market.

The blurring of distinctions between banks and non-bank financial intermediary (NBFIs), and particularly building societies in the UK, has meant that some of the liabilities of NBFIs have become widely accepted as means of payment and their traditional savings instruments, such as building society share accounts, have become more liquid. In effect, some NBFIs have become banks or have entered the banking market. Consequently, their means of payment liabilities should be included in narrow money aggregates and these, along with their liquid liabilities, should be included in broad money aggregates; but then, perhaps, so should the liquid liabilities of the remaining NBFIs. These are, however, traditionally ignored.

The concept of liquidity used here accords with that of the Bank of England (1982), which regards liquidity as a matter of degree. Liquid assets are defined as assets which can be realized (converted into means of payment) at short notice with little or no actual or potential financial penalty (as a result of forfeited interest or capital value loss). The question of degree arises out of interpretation of the words "little"and "short" and a degree of uncertainty over liquidity is introduced by the word "potential", implying that liquidity can vary with expectations of asset prices (the sale price at short notice will depend upon the

---

[2]Initially loans and overdrafts but, latterly, a much broader range of products, including participation in unit trusts and insurance products, as banks diversified their activities in the 1970s and 1980s.

'depth' of the market) and anticipated holding-periods.

One guide to the liquidity of capital value uncertain financial assets is the maturity (at time of issue) of financial assets which have well established and active ('deep') secondary markets.[3] At some stage, however, an arbitrary cut-off point has to be imposed to divide assets into those liquid enough to be included as components of a monetary aggregate and those deemed insufficiently liquid. Economic theory seems unable to help here, and the appropriate dividing line in the liquidity spectrum may change over time as a result of financial innovation, especially if it reduces transactions costs and thereby increases the liquidity of assets previously regarded as too illiquid to include (Hicks, 1935). The introduction of new financial instruments (product innovation) also has the effect of filling out the liquidity spectrum.

Product innovations, such as IBCAs, may not only encourage economic agents to economize on non-interest bearing financial assets, but, because of changes in relative prices ('own rates of interest'), induce a portfolio reallocation away from more risky assets into safer (normally capital value certain and, therefore, more liquid) assets, particularly IBCAs. Accordingly, some savings balances may be transferred into IBCAs. If this occurs, it will not be possible to make an unequivocal distinction between means of payment balances and savings balances in the wealth portfolio, even if the speculative holding of liquid assets is ignored. A sophisticated analysis would therefore require means of payment and liquid balances to be separated from savings balances when modeling the allocation of wealth across a portfolio of financial and non-financial (including housing) assets. Although portfolio selection theory is well developed (see e.g. Markowitz, 1991) given certain objectives (e.g. maximizing accumulation), the objectives underlying wealth accumulation and savings, and their implications are not well understood.[4]

In the second half of the 1980s the increased availability of IBCAs has been complimented by that of tiered-interest-instant-access- accounts. Such accounts pay progressively higher interest as balances accumulate to exceed certain thresholds. Some of these now combine features of cheque and savings accounts and reduce transactions costs, in terms of time spent managing accounts, and facilitate economization of transactions balance holdings.

This is consistent with Hicks (1935) who argued that, as transaction costs decline and wealth increases, it becomes economical for individuals to hold a more varied portfolios of assets because fixed brokerage fees (investment costs) can be spread across viable blocks of

---

[3]'Term to maturity' may be more appropriate and would encompass a wider set of assets.

[4]See Chrystal (1992) for an introductory survey of the issues.

investments in particular assets. The asset (particularly house) price inflation in the 1970s and 1980s contributed significantly to the growth in personal sector wealth and was itself aided and abetted by financial liberalization and innovation. The reduction in transaction (investment) costs is likely to result in a larger proportion of the more liquid (than hitherto), but nevertheless more risky (less capital value certain), financial assets being held (in place of cash and NIBCA balances) for precautionary purposes.

The traditional view of banks has been called into question by developments in wholesale banking which have led many banks to adopt 'asset driven liability management' techniques.[5] Banks no longer passively take deposits and then seek profitable lending opportunities. Instead, they aggressively pursue profitable lending opportunities and then raise extra funds on the domestic and international ('Eurocurrency') interbank markets, as required. They also lend surplus funds via these markets. As a result, banks have increasingly come to be regarded as managers of portfolios of assets and liabilities, and the risks they entail (Harrington, 1987). To manage these risks they make use of portfolio management techniques such as pooling and diversification (Markowitz, 1991). Consequently, the origin of modern bank behaviour is not so much the goldsmiths' discovery of the 'law of large numbers' as the bill brokers discovery that open positions for certain maturities may be worth the risk (Niehans, 1978, Chapter 9). Hence, the key uncertainty may relate to interest rates or yields, rather than the uncertainty about the maturity of deposits. The latter is traditionally modeled mechanistically using multipliers based on fractional reserve holdings, but has more recently been analyzed in a more sophisticated manner.[6]

Financial intermediaries, including banks, can thus be regarded as insurers holding portfolios of (generally less liquid) assets to back portfolios of (generally more liquid) liabilities (Lewis and Davis, 1987; Artis and Lewis, 1991). The banks then become a special case because they guarantee the nominal value of some of their liabilities (current account deposits) and promise to redeem them on demand. Other financial intermediaries, such as money market mutual funds (MMMFs) and unit trusts, have liabilities which, like their assets, vary with market prices and they are not therefore exposed to 'runs'. In contrast, the confidence in banks' commitments may occasionally be called into question (Goodhart, 1987, 1989, chapter VIII). Therefore, unlike banks, NBFIs don't need the monetary authorities to underwrite (usually via the central bank acting as crisis 'lender of last resort') their system; and a concomitant moral hazard problem, which in turn creates a need or

---

[5]See Harrington (1987) for a comprehensive survey.

[6]By Niehans (1978, chapter 9), for example. See Lewis (1991) for a recent survey of the theory of the banking firm.

prudential regulation and supervision to prevent abuse of the insurers, and ultimately taxpayers, (Mullineux, 1993) is not created.

Banks can, therefore, be regarded as portfolio managers and providers of brokering and accounting services, as well as creators of bank credit and liquidity and providers of money transmission services (MTS). Hence many functions are performed by both banks and NBFIs and, in the absence of regulatory and/or cartelistic constraints, banks might be expected to diversify into activities traditionally associated with NBFIs and *vice versa.*

In addition, Hicks (1935) and others[7] have anticipated that, as transaction (investment) costs are reduced, the importance of money as a means of payment will decline and could, if transactions costs go to zero, disappear. If this were to happen, only a unit of account would be required and banker/brokers would supply portfolio management services. The 'electronification' of the payments system has raised the prospect of a 'cashless society', but it seems unlikely that transaction costs will tend to zero in the near future because uncertainty and information deficiencies seem likely to persist.

Financial innovation in the 1970s and 1980s has, however, undoubtedly reduced portfolio related transaction costs sufficiently to allow people to economize considerably on cash and NIBCAs. The increasing use of prepayment cards, such as telephone cards, is also like to reduce the usage of cash (notes and coins). The recent introduction of rechargeable 'electronic purse' cards, whose memory chip, can be 'charged-up' with bank money at ATMs, and rechargeable prepayment cards, whose value can be increased by phoning a central computer, will take this process further. The situation where all financial assets bear interest was dubbed a credit economy by Hicks (1935). In such an economy, credit, rather than (transactions) monetary aggregates, are clearly appropriate. Such developments will make it even more difficult for the central bank to control the 'money' supply and might well reduce their ability to influence short term interest rates.

Another feasible implication of the reduction in transactions costs is that, as Hicks (1935) warned (see Ford, 1991), rising wealth could lead personal sector investors to hold riskier portfolios; thereby exposing the economy to greater financial fragility. In such a situation, regulatory tightening would be natural response by the authorities. We may, indeed, be part of the way through a regulatory cycle (Gowland, 1991); having experienced a period of liberalization in the 1970s and 1980s in which regulatory reform resulted in fewer restrictions on banking activities. However, tightening, by one country in isolation would tend to put domestic banks at a competitive disadvantage in the increasingly 'globalized' banking market. Regulatory tightening would, therefore, require coordinated action by the

---

[7]Black, 1970; Fama, 1980; and Greenfield and Yeager, 1983.

authorities responsible for the major international banks. As well as allowing commercial banks to diversify, particularly into securities related business, this liberalization led to significant entry into the traditional banking sector in the UK and to a substantial increase in competition in retail and wholesale banking markets. Defensive (and aggressive) product innovation aimed at retaining ('capturing') market share has resulted in a 'filling-in' of the spectrum of liquid financial instruments, as noted previously.

To the extent that product innovation is induced by a desire to circumvent monetary and prudential regulations, attempts to restrict the growth of a chosen monetary aggregate are likely to encourage the use of substitute liquid assets. The monetary aggregates 'targeted' or used as indicators, by the monetary authorities have traditionally been based on narrow or broad sets of bank liabilities and attempts to control their growth have restricted intermediation by banks and hence encouraged disintermediation. In regard to the latter, funds have been raised directly from the wholesale money or the securities markets and, via the use of alternative liquid financial instruments, often supplied by NBFIs. Hence, the 'targeting' of monetary aggregates has been distortionary.

The UK government's policy appears to have been to inject competition into the personal banking sector by creating a 'level playing field' between banks and building societies.[8] This was reflected in tax changes in the 1984 budget and the 1986 Building Societies Act; which cleared the way for building societies to diversify (within prescribed limits) into providing non-home loans and to offer a full range of money transmission and other, to the household sector.

The removal of reserve requirements imposed for monetary control purposes in August 1981 is also consistent with the attempt to treat banks and building societies even-handedly. Banks and building societies are, however, subject to prudential liquid reserve, as well as and capital adequacy, requirements. These regulatory 'taxes' have also become increasingly conformable following the 1986 Building Societies Act and the 1987 Banking Act and both sets of credit institutions must conform to various EC Directives.[9]

If restricting the ability of banks to create credit encourages the use of substitute liquid financial instruments, circumventive innovation, and disintermediation; then the only way to control liquidity is to impose controls on all financial institutions which contribute to liquidity, whether they have liabilities that serve as means of payment or not, and to

---

[8]Podolski 1986, Chapter 6 traces public pressure for a more competitive and responsive financial sector back to the Radcliffe Report (1959). The recommendations of that report were reinforced by subsequent official enquiries (see Podolski, 1986 p 137; and Mullineux, 1987a, Chapter 2).

[9]See Mullineux, 1992, Chapter 1.

restrict entry into the financial markets to firms willing to abide by the controls. This appears to be at variance with the current policy of encouraging competition in the financial sector in order to increase efficiency and anyway, if (transactions) money's function is primarily to facilitate exchange, why interfere with its supply? Why not let it respond elastically to demand for it? Financial liberalization makes it necessary to abandon attempts to control the supply of transactions money and liquidity directly and to concentrate on manipulating the price of liquid assets (own rates of interest and yields) instead. This is the approach now pursued by the Bank of England.

If, however, a European Central Bank (ECB) were to decide to adopt broad money targeting, whilst using short term interest rates as the instruments for hitting the target, then it is a moot point whether liquid reserve requirements are useful for this purpose (Fry, 1992). In one camp sits the Bank of England, which abandoned monetary control reserve requirements in 1981, in the other sits the Bundesbank, which argues that reserve requirements provide an extra degree of freedom in monetary control.[10]

In line with earlier observations, it should be stressed that, to minimize distortionary effects, it seems necessary for the ECB to ensure that any reserve requirements imposed for monetary control purposes apply to the broadest possible range of 'credit' institutions. However, the risk will remain that reserve requirements, to the extent that they exceed prudential requirements, will impose a differential tax on credit-creating financial intermediaries and thereby encourage disintermediation.

Rybczynski (1986) has argued that as economies mature their financial sectors evolve from being (more) bank oriented towards being (more) capital market oriented. The USA and the UK are commonly cited as the countries furthest along this road. If the role of banks and other financial intermediaries is founded on information deficiencies (Diamond, 1984) and uncertainty over credit ratings (Goodhart, 1989, Chapter II) then this trend, which encompasses securitization, may be due to the increased ability of the markets to gain access (via enhanced reporting requirements, improved accounting standards and credit rating agencies), to information; and to signal more information through changes in yields. The imposition of stricter monetary and prudential reserve and capital adequacy requirements on banks (than on securities firms) may, however, accelerate this process by encouraging disintermediation.

The higher 'taxation' of traditional banking, relative to other financial services, may

---

[10]Though the Bundesbank was forced to reduce the reserve requirement 'tax' on banks in 1993 in order to reduce the competitive advantage of Luxembourg, which impose no such requirements, as a banking center.

have encouraged banks to diversify. In continental Europe, particularly Germany and Switzerland, universal banking, which combines commercial (including merchant) banking and securities business (brokering, trust management, underwriting), has long been practiced. In other European countries, such as France and the UK, there was more segregation in the banking sector, either due to regulations (France) or due to traditional demarcations (UK). Securities business was also separated; again by statute in Paris and by tradition in London. Re-regulation in France in the mid 1960s led to the abandonment of banking segregation and in the late 1980s banks were permitted to deal in the securities business. In the UK, the major clearing banks diversified: into instalment credit and leasing ('Finance House') business, in the 1960s; into merchant banking, in the 1970s; and into securities business, following the 'Big Bang' reform of the London Stock Exchange in October 1986. The universal banking model has therefore become prevalent in Europe in the 1980s.[11] Furthermore, the traditional demarcation between banking and insurance business also began to breakdown in the late 1980s with the emergence of 'Allfinanz' or 'bancassurance'.[12] This involves the development, usually through cross shareholdings or acquisition, of financial conglomerates involved in both banking and insurance business. The symbiosis in personal finance arises from the ability of banks to cross-sell insurance products and the access to potential customers that insurance companies gain by entering banking.

3. FINANCIAL INNOVATION AND FINANCIAL FRAGILITY

Financial innovation is as old as banking.[13] Our current level of understanding of the process generating it is not, however, sufficiently advanced to permit us to predict future innovation. Prominent amongst the theoretical explanations of financial innovation is the attempt by financial institutions to circumvent controls imposed upon their profitable activities by the monetary authorities. It is not obvious, however, that the distinction which is made between regulation induced and market induced innovation (Sinkey, 1992), is as sharp as it at first appears to be; for even circumventive innovation is not costless, and will not be pursued unless it is justified by market conditions.

In the personal banking sector, innovation has predominantly involved the marketing

---

[11]There remains, however, considerable variation in the extent to which major European banks hold equity investments in non-financial firms.

[12]See Mullineux (1992) for further discussion.

[13]Podolski (1986, Part II) Gowland (1991) and Thornton and Stone (1992) provide recent surveys of the literature.

of new financial services or products, and the marketing theory view of the product adoption process (see e.g. Rogers, 1962) may well be appropriate in explaining the diffusion of innovations. The marketing approach views the individual as passing through a five stage 'adoption' process: awareness, interest, evaluation, trial, and adoption. Not all individuals become aware at the same time, some adopt quickly, others are more cautious and yet others reject the product. The overall picture is often assumed to be representable by an ogive (elongated 'S')-shaped learning curve.[14]

Even if much of the innovation is circumventive, the 'learning curve' may still be relevant because, once new techniques have been introduced, they are unlikely to be unlearnt and may be transferable to other markets. It seems to be the case that much of the innovation takes place in the highly competitive corporate banking markets and is then adapted and transferred to the personal banking sector, in which habits are slower to change. Additionally, where there are significant economies of scale, such as in electronic banking (Revell, 1983), rapid innovation may be inhibited by the need to conclude cost sharing and network sharing agreements (Mullineux, 1985; 1987a, Chapter 3).

Tobin (1963) considered whether banks are different (from NBFIs) because they are regulated or regulated because they are different. The answer is probably a bit of both. The prevailing fractional reserve system of banking, combined with a promise to repay the nominal value of deposits on demand, renders the banking system fragile in times when depositor confidence is undermined. This in turn creates the need for prudential regulation. It is also notable that banking and financial systems differ markedly between countries and that, at least in part, this may be due to differential prudential regulatory regimes.[15] Additionally, it has been noted that, because they have liabilities which serve as means of payment, banks have traditionally borne the brunt of monetary control regulations; despite the fact that NBFIs also create liquidity and provide means of payments and substitutes for bank created liquid assets. As a result, some NBFIs, such as building societies in the UK, can be regarded as having become banks.

There is some official concern that the rapid financial innovation of the 1980s has increased fragility in major financial markets (BIS 1986, 1991, 1992). The authorities have responded by raising capital adequacy requirements on banks; a policy which induced further financial innovation. The process started following the onset of the Mexican Debt Crisis in

---

[14]As assumed in Ford, Peng and Mullineux, 1992.

[15]See Mullineux (1987b) for further discussion.

1982 and was coordinated internationally by the Basle Committee,[16] which concluded the Basle Agreement on risk-related capital adequacy requirements in 1988. The ensuing Latin American debt crisis was the first of a series of instances in the 1980s where major international banks miscalculated risks and adopted 'herd-like' behaviour (Davis, 1992). Their subsequent substantial exposures to the highly leveraged debt and property markets[17] are further examples, and there is a suspicion that much of the product innovation has involved underpriced risks,[18] perhaps in an endeavour to gain rapid and widespread acceptance of new products.

The initial response of the authorities to the Latin American debt crisis was to raise capital-to-asset ratios. This increased the cost of bank intermediation, to the extent that banks were able to pass on the costs, and reduced its profitability, to the extent that they were not. In addition, the cost of raising capital rose for banks as the quality of their loans deteriorated (credit risks increased). Consequently, the credit ratings of major corporate clients improved relative to those of their banks and their clients found it cheaper to raise funds directly from the wholesale money and securities markets. The banks then had an incentive to move into the securities business to retain the custom of their major corporate clients, earn fees and evade the 'capital tax' by developing 'off-balance' sheet business. In addition, to complement their increasingly active liability management, they began to securitize the loan markets by issuing asset (loan) backed securities to facilitate asset management. The 1988 Basle

---

[16]Its formal title is the Committee on Banking Regulation and Supervisory Practices. It was known for a time as the Cooke Committee, taking its name from it is long serving chairman, and meets at the Bank for International Settlements in Basle. It consists of representatives of bank supervisory authorities in the G.10 countries and aims to allocate supervisory responsibilities between countries (the Basle Concordat) and promote efficient (and consistent) regulatory practices. To date its activities in the latter sphere are reflected in the 1988 Basle Agreement. The original Basle Concordat was concluded in 1975. It was revised in 1983 following the 'Banco Ambrosiano Affair' (see Dale, 1986 and Mullineux, 1987c Chapter 4) and in 1992, following the 1991 'BCCI (Bank of Credit and Commerce International) Affair', see Dale (1992).

[17]Associated with a wave of mergers and acquisitions activity in the late 1980s the USA and the UK, there was rapid growth in the highly leveraged debt (including 'junk bonds' in the USA) of the corporate sector to banks. Also, asset-price inflation was both driven by and encouraged property sector lending growth in the USA and Japan and in the UK, despite warnings from the Bank of England. The 'bubble' burst first in the mid 1980s in the USA and later, at the beginning of the 1990s, in Japan and the UK. The result was that banks were heavily exposed to the property sector and, in each country, a large quantity of office space remained unlet.

[18]See BIS (1986).

agreement provided for the phasing-in[19] of minimum (credit) risk-related balance sheet capital adequacy requirements and also, for the first time, capital adequacy requirements (also credit risk-related) on banks' off-balance sheet credit risks were introduced.

In 1988, the Basle Committee began considering extending the range of risks for which capital backing is required to encompass market- related risks such as exchange and interest rate risks. It issued proposals for revised capital adequacy requirements in April 1995. This process is reminiscent of the kind of dialectic discussed by Kane (1981, 1984) in connection with the regulatory system in the US. The impression is gained that the regulators are continually trying to plug holes in the regulatory dyke whilst the financial institutions are continually finding new ones. This would perhaps not be too serious were it not that the institutions themselves seem to be incapable of gauging the risks involved and of operating adequate internal auditing, compliance, and control systems and so repeatedly get their fingers burnt (Davis, 1992). This was amply illustrated in 1995 by the Barings Bank and Daiwa Bank debacles.

The Basle agreement also attempted to harmonize capital adequacy requirements in order to create a more level international playing field. This became necessary following the rapid growth of 'offshore banking', which went hand in hand with the internationalization of banking in the 1970s (Pecchioli, 1983). Dale (1986) has argued that the proliferation of offshore banking centers reflected regulatory arbitrage, because international banks were taking advantage of more permissive regulatory regimes. The influx of US banks into London in the 1960s marked the start of this process, which then gathered momentum and became an international phenomenon. The subsequent global deregulation in banking can be regarded as competition in laxity (Dale, 1986) and the Basle Concordats and the Basle agreement can be seen as an attempt to establish minimum prudential standards to safeguard institutions and markets in the new, intensely competitive, environment.

As noted in the previous section, for policy motives which have never been clearly spelt out, the UK monetary authorities have encouraged greater competition in all parts of the UK banking sector and the dismantling of the traditional City 'clubs' (Goodhart, 1985; Llewellyn, 1985, 1986) since the early 1970s. The City has, therefore, been in the vanguard of change. The 1986 'Big Bang' reform of the London Stock Exchange, for example, was followed, by a series of 'little bangs' in Europe and by a major overhaul of the financial system in Canada.

---

[19]Interim target ratios were successfully hit in 1990. The final (8%) target risk-related capital-asset ratios are supposed to be reached at the end of 1992. At that stage at least half the 8% capital ratio should consist of 'Tier 1' (equity-like) capital. The remainder can consist of 'Tier 2' (subordinated debt-like) capital.

In the UK and elsewhere, substantial re-regulation has accompanied the liberalization.[20] The net effect of the regulatory reform, or re-regulation, in the UK, has been: to give greater statutory backing to the traditional practitioner-led self-regulatory practices; and to replace monetary and prudential regulations which restrict risk-taking with regulations that require adequate liquid and capital reserves be held to cover the risks in the portfolios of financial intermediaries.

Financial liberalization does, however, seem to have encouraged asset-price inflation, particularly on the stock and property markets (Davis, 1992). This culminated in: the 1987 'price correction' on most countries stock exchanges; the 1990, and subsequent, slump in Tokyo stock exchange prices; and in the collapse of property markets, at the end of the 1980s in the USA, and in the early 1990s in Japan, Norway, Sweden and the UK. It may also have increased financial fragility and could yet result in pressure for further, more restrictive, re-regulation coordinated at the international level.

In the UK personal sector, the asset-price inflation in the late 1980s, particularly in the housing market, both raised wealth and as a consequence, the demand for more risky financial instruments (Hicks, 1935). This in turn drove share prices up, and was itself driven by the greater availability of mortgage finance. The latter came from banks, released from the restraint of the 'corset' (see Appendix, Dec 1973) and lending guidance by the Bank of England, and new, wholesale funded, specialist mortgage lenders. These wholesale lenders entered a market traditionally dominated by building societies operating an interest rate cartel, which was itself abandoned in 1983, and took advantage of the lower costs of wholesale, relative to retail, funding at the time.

The internationalization of banking, 'securitization', the 'Big Bang', new financial legislation in the UK, removal of interest rate controls in the US, and the spread of liability management can all be regarded as 'clusters' of innovations; to which we might add the spread of variable interest rate lending since the 1970s. The latter has had the effect of passing interest risks from banks to their customers at the cost of increasing the banks' exposure to credit risks, as the 1980s Latin American debt crisis and the rise in UK house repossessions in the early 1990s, due to an inability to maintain mortgage payments attest. Clearly not all of these 'clusters' are the result of induced, circumventive, innovation. There is substantial evidence of innovation in response to regulatory liberalization as a result of banking markets becoming more contestable (Baumol, 1982).

In other cases, the 'clusters' reflect responses to changing market conditions. These

---

[20]In the UK there were the Banking Acts in 1979 and 1987; a Building Society Act in 1986; and a Financial Services Act in 1986.

include the development of markets in financial derivatives (such as futures, options and swaps), in response to the greater interest and exchange rate variability (risks) since the early 1970s. There have also been different responses in different countries. In the US, fixed interest rate home loans were common and the savings and loan associations, the main mortgage lenders, were undermined by rising interest rates because they borrowed short to lend long at fixed rates. They were subsequently encouraged to introduce variable rate loans to transfer the interest rate risks to borrowers. In contrast, in the UK, where variable rate home loans had long been the norm, the increased interest rate variability, along with high interest rates in the late 1980s and early 1990s, created a demand for fixed rate mortgages. With greater access to the Euronote and Eurobond markets, the mortgage lenders (including building societies post-1986) could meet this demand, without exposing themselves to interest rate risks, by raising matching term finance.

This review of some of the 'clusters' of financial innovations indicates that much, but by no means all, of the innovation was induced by regulation which became onerous due to changes in market conditions and other market changes. The role of technology in the 1970s and 1980s appears to have been to facilitate an acceleration of innovation because the financial sector had failed to exploit advances in telecommunication and information technology fully. There was plenty of opportunity to exploit the technology given the labour and paper intensive nature of financial, and especially banking, services. In the absence of widespread use of patents, the technological innovation also facilitated rapid diffusion, by making copying easier. It could also be employed to design more sophisticated and complex products, such as financial derivatives, as well as other new instruments whose purpose was to exploit regulatory loopholes. Even if interest and exchange rates become less volatile in the future and international regulatory harmonization is enhanced, so that the incentive for regulatory arbitrage and competitive deregulation is reduced, the innovations are unlikely to be abandoned. The pace of financial innovation may, however, decelerate, once the opportunities offered by the new technology have been fully exploited.

Another market related factor forcing the pace of financial innovation in the 1970s and 1980s was increased competition. In oligopolistic banking markets, such as the UK's, where an interest rate cartel was in operation until 1971, non-price competition, particularly through advertising, was evident. The UK wholesale and corporate banking markets became much more competitive following the influx of US banks in the 1960s, and UK government policy in the 1980s seems to have successfully induced a significant increase in competition in personal sector retail banking.[21] There have also been new entrants[22] into various sectors of the banking market. Many banking markets do seem to have become more contestable (Baumol, 1982) and it seems likely that the new technology being employed in banking since the late 1980s has made them more so (e.g. 'telephone banking' and 'direct sales' of financial products, especially insurance and home and other loans, over the telephone). It is notable that the UK market for financing small and medium sized enterprises remains dominated by the major clearing banks and seems to be an exception.

In the personal banking sector, the pace of change accelerated following the removal of monetary policy-induced credit rationing in the early 1980s. This followed a revision of monetary control techniques which led to greater reliance on controlling interest rates and hence the price of credit, rather than its availability. The result seems to have been 'overshooting' in the sense that the private sector as whole (household and business) took on more debt in aggregate than it could manage because, given the post-war history of credit rationing, there was little experience in optimizing debt levels. The banks seemed to become less cautious, perhaps due to increased competition (Davis, 1992), and reduced their reliance on voluntary credit rationing (Stiglitz and Weiss, 1981) as a means of reducing their exposure to risk in the face of information deficiencies.

The resulting 'debt overhang' made borrowers more cautious about taking on new debt and banks more cautious about lending in the early 1990s recession.

4. CONCLUDING REMARKS

The key financial innovations effecting the personal sector in the UK relate to changes in payments technology and availability of credit. These impact on the means of payment function of money by reducing transaction costs and the need to hold cash and non-interest bearing deposits, which pay implicit interest by non-full recovery of the costs of providing money transmission services (MTS). Examples include: the widespread availability of credit cards; an increase in the number of people with one (or more) current accounts;[23] networked ATMs; the introduction of debit cards and Eftpos; the widespread availability of interest

---

[21]Via the amalgamation and privatization of the Trustee Savings Banks and the aforementioned Building Societies Act 1986.

[22]Including foreign banks and the aforementioned, wholesale funded specialist mortgage lenders.

[23]This increase was encouraged by a change in the UK law on the payment of wages and salaries. This has allowed firms to encourage employees to accept monthly payments via the Bank Automated Clearing Services (BACS), rather than weekly wage packets containing cash.

bearing cheque accounts and the increasing availability, of instant-access-tiered-interest-accounts; and the provision of MTS and 'instant access' savings accounts by building societies.

There have also been significant changes in wholesale banking, leading to more active asset and liability management by banks and major corporations (the 'treasury function') and a rapid development of the financial derivatives markets. It seems clear that it is necessary to disaggregate to take account of these changes; so that the money and liquidity holdings managed by the treasury departments of major corporations can be analyzed separately from the requirements of the personal sector and small and medium-sized enterprises, which may be differently motivated. A summary of some of the financial innovation that has occurred in retail banking in the UK in the last two decades is provided in the Appendix. The innovations appear to provide a bewildering array of changes. However, most of them can be classified into two groups, with some straddling both. One group of innovations has led to an increase in the range of (potential) liquid assets; whilst the other group has reduced transactions costs and altered the liquidity, and perhaps other, characteristics of already-existing financial claims.

This innovation has occurred at a time when competition in UK domestic banking has been increasing, particularly since the early 1980s when quantitative and quantitative controls over bank lending were abandoned in a shift to interest rate based monetary control. Superimposed on this has been a government policy of stimulating competition in the retail financial sector, the most important example being the liberalization of building societies. These institutions traditionally took savings deposits and advanced home loans but were permitted to offer cheque accounts and other MTS and to advance personal loans, for car purchase etc, in the second half of the 1980s.

The increased freedom to lend and borrow and the growing competition combined to stimulate financial innovation and a credit boom. This in turn fueled retail price and asset price, particularly house price, inflation. The rise in wealth associated with the house price bubble itself stimulated the demand and supply of credit. Once the house price bubble burst the debt overhang and 'negative equity'[24] helped contribute to a relatively sharp recession and subdued recovery.

The 'drag' caused by these debt problems was particularly great in the UK because by far the most common means of house purchase was via 'endowment' mortgages with variable interest rates. An endowment mortgage provides for the repayment of the principal

---

[24]Which affected a significant proportion of households and occurs when the house price falls below the value of the outstanding home loan.

of a home loan in a lump sum at the end of the contract period, following the payment over the life of the loan of monthly premia to an insurance company, which invests the funds. The lender receives only the interest due on a monthly basis and the value of the debt remains constant. However, the interest due changes in response to, often policy induced, changes in market interest rates over the period of the loan. During the housing boom in the mid to late 1980s, many households took on endowment loans of between 90% and 100% of the value of their property. Following the collapse of the bubble, when houses in many areas of the UK fell by between 20% and 30%, these households were left not only with negative equity, but also the problem of servicing a debt which might have been taken on when the bank base rate was 7.5% (in 1987). To squeeze inflation out of the system, the government engineered a rise in interest rates. They had risen to 15% by 1989 and were held at this level for about 12 months before they being gradually reduced, following sterling's entry into the ERM in September 1990. During this period, and indeed throughout the first half of the 1990s, real interest rates were consistently positive and above 2%. Under such condition debt servicing and reduction causes a significant drain on real income and wealth and it is not surprising that many households remained heavily indebted and suffered from 'negative equity' in the UK.

What lessons can be drawn from this salutary tale? The UK was in many respects uniquely exposed to the risk of an asset price inflation in the housing market. It is notable that the lenders are now much less willing to grant home loans of a value exceeding 90% of the value of the house being purchased and take more account of ability to service the loan than they did in the frenzy of the mid to late 1980s boom. The supply and uptake of fixed rate mortgages has also increased. Further, repayment mortgages have become much more popular, the regulatory authorities having expressed concern that many households were wrongly advised to take out endowment policies by lenders eager to earn front-loaded commission from the insurers. That having been said, variable rate home loans remain prevalent and housing remains the main wealth asset of the majority of households. The UK thus remains particularly sensitive to the impact of variations in interest rates and thus monetary policy is a particularly potent weapon. Perhaps not surprisingly, the removal of the post war rationing of the supply of credit to the personal sector perhaps not surprisingly seems to have led to celebratory overindulgence by many lenders and borrowers. The 'debt hangover', including the bad debt problems experienced by banks and building societies, has hopefully instilled a more sober attitude amongst both sets of parties. Competition continues to intensify, however, and lending margins over cost of funds are being severely squeezed. This is particularly true of the home loan market, where demand remained depressed in 1995, but also in the wider personal, large corporate and even the small and medium sized enterprise sectors. The experience of the UK, as well as that of the US and Japan, indicates that financial fragility, in the sense of potential for asset price inflations and subsequent financial slumps, and perhaps crises, appears to have been increased by financial liberalization.

The hope is that the regulatory and supervisory system, bolstered by judicious preemptive use of interest rate policy, can contain the threat in future. If it can, then the major further cause for concern is financial shocks emanating from abroad. These too have become more likely following the progressive liberalization of international capital flows since the early 1980s. This chapter has concentrated primarily on personal sector banking in the UK. We have noted, however, that another area in which there has been significant innovation over the past decade or so is financial derivatives. Following the extremely rapid growth in their usage, there is some doubt that the managers and supervisors of the financial institutions involved in dealing in these products are fully cognizant of the associated risks and have established adequate internal and external controls to contain them; especially as the latter require full international cooperation and coordination amongst bank and securities regulators. The February 1995 'Barings' and the September 1995 'Daiwa' crises, which were not caused by financial derivatives *per se*, but followed a series of other instances in Europe and the US where misperception of the risks involved in financial derivatives was evident, have hopefully provided a timely warning and galvanized supervisors and financial firms to re-examine external and internal controls. Further, at the July 1995 meetings of the International Organization of Securities Commissions (IOSCO), it was agreed that in future there should be closer liaison in this sphere with the Basle Committee of Bank Supervisors, which coordinates supervision in international banking.

APPENDIX

UK Financial Innovation in the Retail Banking Sector in the 1970s and 1980s

Date	Innovation	Impact
1966	Introduction of Barclaycard - 1st nationally (UK) available on credit card.	Combined convenient payment method with (free for a month or so) overdraft facilities
1967	Introduction of primitive automated teller machines (ATMS) (Barclays).	Facilitated economization on cash holding.
Mid Sept 1971	Competition and Credit Control (CCC) - Reform of methods of monetary control and end of clearing bank's interest rate 'cartel' - becomes operative.	Increased Competition in banking sectors and reduced reliance on Bank of England 'guidance' to control the bank credit creation.
Dec 1973	Supplementary Special Deposit Scheme ('Corset') introduced. (Suspended Feb 1975, re-imposed Nov 1976, suspended Aug 1977, reimposed June 1978).	Marked a return to direct credit controls by 'taxing' deposit taking beyond prescribed limits and encouraged disintermediation (especially via 'bill-leak'[1]).
July and October 1979	Removal of exchange controls.	Undermined 'Corset' and allowed rapid growth of foreign exchange balance holdings and trading.
June 1980	'Corset' abolished.	Led to reintermediation via reversal of 'bill-leak'.[1]
August 1981	Monetary Control: Provisions - Change of method of monetary control.	Removal of Reserve/Asset Ratio requirements and other controls on bank lending offensive in the home loans market.
July 1982	Term controls on consumer (instalment/'Hire Purchase') credit removed.	Further relaxation of credit rationing.
October 1983	Building Society interest rate cartel abandoned.	Greater competition amongst building societies in savings and home loan markets.
1984	Midland Bank introduces 'free' (if in credit) 'banking'.	Rise in 'implicit interest'[2] paid on cheque accounts.
1985	Nationwide Building Society introduces Flex-Account.	Introduction of first mass-marketed[3] interest bearing cheque account with no charges (if in credit). Other major building societies soon followed.

UK Financial Innovation in the Retail Banking Sector in the 1970s and 1980s

Date	Innovation	Impact
1985	APACS (Association of Payments Clearing Systems) established.	Opened membership of the clearing systems to a wider range of banks and to building societies.
October 1985	Mansion House Speech announced the end of 'overfunding'[4]	Reduced disintermediation and allowed Bank of England to rundown the 'bill-mountain'[5].
October 1986	Trustee Savings Banks privatized in accordance with the 1985 TSB Act.	Increased competition in banking.
October 1986	'Big Bang' reform of stock exchange.	Encouraged wider share holding and saving via unit and investment trusts.
January 1987	Provisions of the 1986 Building Societies Act become operational.	Allowed building societies to diversify into non-home loans to the household sector *inter-alia* and intensified competition in the retail banking sector.
June 1987	Barclays launch the Connect (debit) card.	First nationally issued debit card, designed to replace the cheque.
October 1987	Black Monday (19th) Stock exchange price collapse.	Outflow of savings from unit trusts to banks and building societies and decline of household investment in (non-privatization) shares.
January 1988	Building Societies' wholesale funding limit raised.	Allowed expansion of building society lending and greater competitive equality with banks and specialized mortgage lenders.
1988	Switch network established.	Introduced nationwide EFTPOS[6] network accepting debit cards issued by various banks under Switch logo.
1988	The four major banks became members of <u>both</u> the Visa and the Mastercard credit and debit card networks.[7]	Increased competition in the credit and debit sectors.
January 1989	Lloyds Bank introduced interest-bearing 'free' (if in credit)cheque account.	Soon followed by other major clearing banks;adding to 'implicit interest' payments on cheque accounts and inducing a steady decline in non-interest bearing deposits.
July 1989	Following stock exchange flotation, Abbey National 'con verts', from a building society to a bank.	Further increase in competition in the retail banking sector.

UK Financial Innovation in the Retail Banking Sector in the 1970s and 1980s

Date	Innovation	Impact

1. 'Bill-leak' refers to funding via the issue of commercial bills rather than bank borrowing.

2. 'Implicit interest' is paid when banks do not fully recover the costs of providing payment related services through cheque accounts.

3. The Co-operative Bank was already offering a free if in credit interest bearing cheque account with overdraft facilities.

4. 'Overfunding' results from selling more medium to long term bonds than necessary to 'fund' the government borrowing requirements.

5. The 'bill-mountain' was created by the Bank of England releaving liquidity shortages by purchasing commercial bills.

6. EFTPOS is electronic funds transfer at point of scale.

7. Previously they had been members either of the Visa or of the Mastercard (ACCESS) networks.

REFERENCES

Artis, M.J. and Lewis, M.K., 1991, *Money in Britain: Monetary Policy, Innovation and Europe*, London: Philip Allan.

Bank of England, 1982, The Measurement of Liquidity, *Bank of England Quarterly Bulletin*, 22(2) 145-49.

Bank of England, 1992, The Demand for MO Revisited, *Bank of England Quarterly Bulletin*, 32(3), 305-13.

Baumol, W.J., 1982, Contestable Markets, *American Economic Review*, 72(1), 1-15.

BIS, 1986, *Recent Innovations in International Banking*, Basle: Bank for International Settlements.

BIS, 1991, *61st Annual Report*, June 1991, Basle: Bank for International Settlements.

BIS, 1992, *62nd Annual Report*, June 1992, Basle: Bank for International Settlements.

Black, F., 1970, Banking and Interest in a World Without Money, *Journal of Bank Research, Autumn*, 9-20.

Chrystal, A. 1992, The Fall and Rise of Saving, *National Westminster Bank Quarterly Review*, February, 24-41.

Dale, R.S., 1986, *The Regulation of International Banking*, London: Woodhead-Faulkner.

Dale, R.S., 1992, *International Banking Deregulation*, Oxford: Basil Blackwell.

Davis, E.P., 1992),*Debt, Financial Fragility and System Risk*, Oxford: Oxford University Press.

Diamond, D., 1984, Financial Intermediation and Delegated Monitoring, *Review of Economic Studies* 51, 393-414.

Fama, G.F., 1980, Banking in the Theory of Finance, *Journal of Monetary Economics* 12, 7-28.

Ford, J.L., 1991, Uncertainty, Liquidity Preference and Portfolio Choice: Aspects of the Hicksian Approach, *Review of Political Economy* 3(3), 320-348.

Ford, J.L., Peng, W.S. and Mullineux, A.W., Financial Innovation and Divisia Monetary Aggregates, *Oxford Bulletin of Economics and Statistics* 54(1), 87-102.

Fry, M.J., 1992, Monetary Policy Implementation During Europe's Transition to a Single Currency, *Chapter 3 in Mullineux (1992)*, 44-64

Goodhart, C.A.E., 1985, *The Evolution of Central Banks: A Natural Development*, London: Sticero (L.S.E.).

Goodhart, C.A.E., 1987, Why Do Banks Need a Central Bank?, *Oxford Economic Papers* 39 (March), 750-89.

Goodhart, C.A.E., 1989, *Money, Information and Uncertainty, (2nd Edition)*, London:

Macmillan

Gowland, D.H., 1991, Financial Innovation in Theory and Practices, Chapter 3 in Green, C.J. and Llewellyn, D.T. (Eds), *Surveys in Monetary Economics: Volume 2, Financial Markets and Institutions*, 79-115, Oxford: Basil Blackwell.

Greenfield, R.L. and Yeager, L.B., 1983, A Laissez-Faire Aroach to Monetary Stability, *Journal of Money, Credit and Banking*, Augast, 302-15.

Harrington, R., 1987, *Asset and Liability Management by Banks*, Paris: OECD.

Hicks, J.R., 1935, A Suggestion for Simplifying the Theory of Money, *Economica*, February, 1-19.

Kane, E.J., 1981, Accelerating Inflation, Techological Innovation and Decreasing Effectiveness of Bank Regulation, *Journal of Finance* 36 (May), 355-67.

Kane, E.J., 1984, Technological and Regulatory Forces in the Developing Fusion of Financial - Services Competition, *Journal of Finance* 39 (June), 759-72.

Lewis, M.K.,, 1991, Theory and Practice of the Banking Firm, Chapter 4 in Green, C.J. and Llewellyn, D.T. (Eds.), *Surveys in Monetary Economics, Volume 2, Financial Institutions and Markets*, 116-65, Oxford: Basil Blackwell.

Lewis, M.K. and Davis, L.T., 1987, *Domestic and International Banking*, Oxford: Philip Allan.

Llewellyn, D.T., 1985, *The Evolution of the British Banking System, London: Institute of Banking.*

Llewellyn, D.T., 1986, *The Regulation and Supervision of Financial Institutions, London: Institute of Banks.*

Markowitz, H.M., 1991, *Portfolio Selection: Efficient Diversification of Investments (2nd Edition)*, Oxford: Basil Blackwell.

Mullineux, A.W., 1985, Sharing out the Costs of Eftpos, *The Banker* 135, 38-42.

Mullineux, A.W., 1987a, *UK Banking after Deregulation*, London: Croom Helm.

Mullineux, A.W., 1987b, *International Banking and Financial Systems: A Comparison*, London: Graham and Trotman.

Mullineux, A.W., 1987c, *International Money and Banking: The Creation of a New Order*, Brighton, UK: Wheatsheaf.

Mullineux, A.W., 1992, *European Banking*, Oxford: Basil Blackwell.

Mullineux, A.W., 1993, Bank Regulation, Uncertainty and Business Cycles in *Risk and Uncertainty in Economics: Essays in Honour of James L. Ford*, Cheltenham: Edward Elgar.

Niehans, J., 1978, *The Theory of Money, Maryland,* Baltimore and London: John Hopkins.

Pecchioli, R.M., 1983, *The Internationalisation of Banking*, Paris: OECD.

Podolski, T.M., 1986, *Financial Innovation and the Money Suly*, Oxford: Blackwell.

Radcliffe Report, 1959, *Report on the Working of the Monetary System*, Command Paper

827, London: HMSO.

Revell, J.R.S., 1983, *Banking and Electronic Funds Transfers*, in Trends in Banking Structure and Regulation Series, Paris: OECD.

Rogers, E.M., 1982, *Diffusion in Innovation*, New York: The Free Press.

Rybczynski, T.M., 1986, The UK Financial System in Transition, *National Westminster Bank Quarterly Review*, November, 26-42.

Sinkey, J.F., 1992, Innovation as a Diffusion Process: Bank Technological Innovation, the Payments System, and Information Processing in *The Financial Serivces Industry (4th Edition)*, New York: MacMillan, 113-43.

Stiglitz, J.E. and Weiss, A., 1981, Credit Rationing in Markets with Imperfect Information, *American Economic Review* 71, 393-410.

Thornton, D.C. and Stone, C.C.,, 1992, Financial Innovation: Causes and Consequences, Chapter 5 in Dowd, K. and Lewis, M.K. (Eds.), *Current Issues in Financial and Monetary Economics* 81-109, Houndmills (UK): Macmillan.

Tobin, J., 1963, Commercial Banks as Creators of Money in Carson, D. (Ed), *Banking and Monetary Studies 408-79, Economics, Vol 1, Macroeconomics* reprinted in Tobin, J., Amsterdam: Norlt Holland.

Derivatives, Regulation and Banking
Edited by B. Schachter
© 1997 Elsevier Science B.V. All rights reserved.

Chapter 12
VALUE-AT-RISK ANALYSIS AND THE PROPOSED BASLE ACCORD AMENDMENT

Patricia Jackson and David J. Maude
Bank of England, London, England, UK
William Perraudin[†]
Birkbeck College and CEPR, London, England, UK

1. INTRODUCTION

1.1 Trading Risk and the Basle Accord

In the last decade, banks have greatly increased their holdings of trading assets such as bonds, equities, interest rate and equity derivatives, foreign exchange and commodity positions. Their motive in this has been to make trading profits and the desire to hedge exposures elsewhere in their banking portfolios. The swap market has been especially important in enabling banks to raise funds in a wider range of markets while avoiding mismatched portfolios.

The increase in the relative importance of trading risk rather than traditional credit risk has obliged bank regulators to reconsider the system of capital requirements agreed in the 1988 Basle Capital Accord. The common framework for treating risk laid down by the 1988 Accord was designed primarily for limiting credit risk and had clear drawbacks in its treatment of trading risk. For example, short positions and holdings of government securities were not covered.[1] Also, the counter-party risk of off-balance sheet positions was included but not their position risk.

The capital charge imposed by the 1988 Accord was a minimum of 8% of private sector assets regardless of maturity and made no allowance for the volatility of different

---

[†]The views expressed here are those of the authors and not necessarily those of the Bank of England. We thank Lina El-Jahel and Adrian Chalcraft for research assistance, Xavier Freixas and Bank of England staff for useful comments, and J. P. Morgan, Tokai Bank Europe and various financial institutions for generously supplying us with data. Any errors remain our responsibility.

[1]Although the latter were included in the UK.

security prices. Thus, low-risk short maturity private sector bonds were effectively penalized much more than longer-dated corporate debt. In certain markets, this placed banks at a competitive disadvantage compared to securities firms for whom capital requirements, at least in the UK and US, allow for such risk in a more sophisticated way.

These problems led the Basle Supervisors' Committee and also the European Commission to study alternative ways of treating trading book positions. The Commission's Capital Adequacy Directive (CAD) introduced at the beginning of this year and Basle's proposed standardised method, which is very similar, are a major advance on what preceded them. Under these approaches, which were heavily influenced by the systems of capital requirements operated by UK and US securities regulators, capital must exceed a weighted sum of the bank's holdings in different asset categories, where the weights reflect the assets' price volatilities, after allowing for hedging.

1.2 Additive Capital Requirements

An important limitation of the risk adjustments in the CAD and Basle standardised approach is the *additive* nature of the capital required for broad asset categories. The capital requirement for a long position in UK equities, for example, takes into account hedging in the same market but not, say, any offset from holding a short position in US equities even though the value of the positions is probably strongly negatively correlated. Ignoring such correlations is innocuous only if short and long positions are all perfectly positively correlated, a very unlikely possibility.

In effect, additive capital requirement systems make no allowance for diversification across different broad categories of securities.[2] The effect is to favour specialised market-makers at the expense of globally diversified banks. Thus, banks that run global portfolios have pressed the Basle Committee to consider approaches to capital requirements that do recognise the benefits of diversification.

Clearly, achieving this in a regime where the supervisors set the percentage capital requirements and hedging allowances for different types of position would have been extremely complex. But, the firms had themselves been developing methods of measuring the risk of given losses on a their total portfolio and these internal whole book or Value at Risk (VaR) models have provided a way of making the problem tractable, leading to a proposed alternative to the Basle standard approach.

---

[2]The UK securities regulators address this problem for equity positions by using a simplified Sharpe portfolio model but this approach was not adopted by either CAD or Basle.

1.3 Decentralised Risk Assessment

In this alternative approach, rather than laying down the percentage capital requirements for different types of position, it is proposed that standards would be established for the in-house models which would then form the basis for the calculation of capital requirement. This would have the additional key advantage of aligning the capital calculation with the risk measurement approach of the particular firm.

The January 1996 Basle paper 'Overview of the Amendment of the Capital Accord to Incorporate Market Risks' proposes that G-10 supervisory authorities should implement the standard and the alternative models by end-1997. Using internal models to generate capital requirements is a radical change in approach but supervisors have for some time been moving steadily in this direction. In the CAD and the Basle standardised method there is a recognition that only by employing the firms' internal models can some positions be correctly processed for inclusion in the capital calculation.

This is particularly the case for options but sensitivity models to convert large books of swaps into equivalent bond exposures and to assess the risk on foreign exchange books were also allowed. In effect, reliance on in-house models provides the only way of closely aligning the assessment of the capital requirement needed for a particular portfolio with the actual risk of loss on that portfolio and therefore reducing the distortionary effects of the requirements.

It does, however, raise a number of issues for supervisors concerning the safeguards which should be put in place to ensure that the capital requirements generated are adequate. Basle has addressed this in several ways. One is to lay down standards for the construction of the models. For example, they must calculate the distribution of losses over a 10-day holding period using at least 12 months of data and must yield capital requirements sufficient to cover losses on 99% of occasions.

Adopting general standards is necessary both to increase consistency between firms and ensure capital requirements really are adequate to the task. In theory, however, they might drive a wedge between the regulatory model and the one which the firm uses for its own purposes. Typically the firms' VaR models use a 95% confidence interval and a 24-hour holding period. Basle will not, however, prescribe the type (parametric v. non-parametric) of model to be used.

1.4 Back-Testing

As a post hoc check on the accuracy of the models, under the proposed alternative Basle approach, the supervisors will carry out back-testing — the comparison of actual trading results with model generated risk measures. This may pose problems in that trading results are often affected by changes in portfolios in the period following the calculation of the VaR. Basle has urged banks to develop the capability to perform back-tests using the losses which would have been made if the book had been held constant over a 24 hour period. Also, Kupiec (1995) argues that back-testing requires a large number of observations in order to make a judgement about the accuracy of the model.

But back-testing and some kind of penalty is essential to provide incentives for firms to increase the accuracy of the models. Basle is proposing that firms not meeting the back-testing criterion for accuracy should have an additional capital charge. A further safeguard is the use of an over-riding multiplier. This will provide a cushion sufficient to cover, for example, extended periods of market turbulence and failings in the models. Thus, Basle is proposing that the capital requirement should be equivalent to the higher of (1) the current VaR estimate and (2) three times the average VaR estimate over the previous 60 days.

The incorporation of a multiplier has the advantage that, while making the system more conservative, it will not distort the treatment of trading books with different risk profiles. However, if the multiplier is too high, it could discourage firms from developing in-house models and lead them to choose the standard approach which the Basle proposals permit as an alternative.

1.5 Value-at-Risk Analysis

What then is the nature of the 'whole-book' or VaR models that will be used in capital requirement calculations by banks that take the Basle Committee's alternative approach? The typical VaR models developed by the firms for their internal risk-management purposes attempt to measure the loss on a portfolio over a specified period (often the next 24 hours) that will only be exceeded on a given fraction of occasions (typically 1% or 5%). Two broad types of VaR analysis are employed.

First, under parametric VaR analysis, the distribution of asset returns is estimated from historical data under the assumption that it is a member of a given parametric class. The commonest procedure is to suppose that returns are stationary, joint normal and independent over time. Using estimates of the means and covariances of returns, one may calculate the daily loss that will be exceeded with a given probability. Second, the simulation approach to VaR analysis consists of finding from a long run of historical data the loss that is exceeded on a given percentage of the days in the sample. As a non-parametric procedure, the latter imposes no distributional assumptions.[3]

In this paper, we examine various aspects of VaR analysis and its use as an instrument of banking regulation from an empirical point of view. Using data on the interest and foreign exchange (FX) rate exposure of a bank with significant trading activity, we compare the empirical performance of parametric and simulation-based VaR analysis.

Even though the proposed Basle Accord Amendment does not specify which approach banks should use, the penalties envisaged for banks whose models fail to forecast loss probabilities accurately makes this an important question. We also look at the impact of window length (ie the length of returns data used) and weighting factors for the returns. The alternative Basle system requires the use of at least one year of data and we assess whether this appears sensible.

Lastly, we investigate the precise formula for required capital proposed in the Basle alternative approach. The current proposal is that capital exceed the maximum of the previous day's VaR and of three times the average VaR of the previous 60 days. It is interesting to ask with our 'real life' books, how the scaling factor and the fact that one must take the maximum of two quantities affect the outcome.

2. EMPIRICAL ANALYSIS OF VaRs

2.1 Trading Books

In this section, we compare the performance of simulation-based VaR methods with parametric VaR analysis that assumes joint normality of asset return distributions. The Basle proposals do not specify which of these two approaches banks should follow. However, the intended system of back-testing and penalties for banks whose models fail to predict loss probabilities, make it important for banks to study the relative performance of the different methods.

In evaluating different VaR techniques, we employ data on the trading book of a large bank with significant trading exposure. From these data,[4] provided to us on condition of anonymity, one may deduce the amounts held by the bank in a number of asset categories. The asset breakdown consists of 14 maturity 'buckets' (i.e., intervals along the

---

[3]The terminology used to distinguish these two forms of VaR analysis varies across authors in a somewhat confusing manner. For example, Laycock and Paxson (1995) refer to what we call parametric and simulation-based VaRs as simulation and back-testing approaches respectively. The former is also often referred to as the variance-covariance approach.

[4]The data consisted of sensitivities of the different assets in the book to market moves.

Table 1
Portfolio Amounts (Sterling Millions)

	FFR	GBP	USD	YEN	DM
Portfolio 1					
FX	-10.89		-46.02	4.31	40.95
3-12 mo	24.04	56.82	-191.56	-590.78	462.35
2-5 yr	-11.45	-336.42	83.13	1247.51	-139.10
6-10 yr	-3.52	-14.62	69.96	-65.45	-144.32
11+ yr	0.00	0.00	-3.19	5.52	-41.66
Portfolio 2					
FX	-5.95		5.72	-22.23	10.20
3-12 mo	64.96	40.01	-135.10	-529.87	629.90
2-5 year	-130.29	-268.84	-33.18	1194.70	-178.89
6-10 yr	19.39	11.17	0.93	-58.66	-107.47
11+year	0.00	0.00	-2.71	5.20	-8.76
Portfolio 3					
FX	-9.86		33.50	-5.59	22.48
3-12 mo	-237.72	105.39	4.56	-1314.62	11.69
2-5 year	43.46	-245.85	11.11	346.49	89.64
6-10 yr	39.53	22.44	0.26	-58.31	-69.96
11+year	0.00	-26.70	-2.72	4.75	-8.81
Stylised Portfolio					
FX	-10.89		-46.02	4.31	40.95
3-12 mo	24.04	56.82	-191.56	-590.78	462.35
2-5 year	-11.45	-336.42	83.13	1247.51	-139.10
6-10 yr	-3.52	-14.62	69.96	-65.45	-144.32
11+year	0.00	0.00	-3.19	5.52	-41.66
Equities	50.00	50.00	50.00	50.00	50.00

yield curve) for five different government bond markets (UK, US, Japan, Germany and France). The time buckets comprised four bands for maturities less than one year, annual bands for one to ten year maturities, and a single band for maturities greater than ten-years.

Table 1 shows the break-down of the four different books that we employed in our statistical analysis. The first three portfolios were those held by the bank on three consecutive months. Two interesting features of the data are: (i) the degree to which the bank's fixed income exposure fluctuates over relatively short periods of time; and (ii) the fact that the FX position of the bank is to a significant degree hedged so that net exposures are small. Other data we have suggests that in both of these aspects, the months we chose were fairly typical of the bank's general behaviour.

The main advantage of using actual books for the predominant bank trading risks (interest rate and FX) is that it ensures that the pattern of risk exposures along the yield curve and between markets is realistic. The amount of exposure taken at different points on the yield curve and between markets clearly reflects the degree of risk and likely return. Two of the factors taken into account are the relative illiquidity in particular time bands and markets and the ease with which positions can be hedged.

Randomly generated portfolios would therefore not be representative and it would be difficult to build stylised books which were representative without basing them on actual books. The fourth book used, which was stylised by adding positions in equity indices in each market to one of the actual books (encompassing interest rate and FX risk), has this drawback. The results may well be sensitive to the books used but that makes it all the more important that the books are realistic.

2.2 Return Data

We thought it important to examine whether VaR analysis performed differently when applied to portfolios containing equities rather than just fixed income and FX positions. We therefore supplemented the three portfolios supplied to us by the anonymous bank with a fourth stylised portfolio comprising the fixed income and FX exposures of the bank's portfolio 1, plus holdings of £50 million in the market indices for five equity markets, i.e., the French CAC-40, the British FT-All Share, the German DAX, the US S&P Composite and the Japanese Nikkei-225. The inclusion of equities meant that in total we were dealing with 79 different sources of risk. Corresponding to the different asset categories, we constructed a dataset of FX rates, zero coupon bond holding returns, and equity index returns. All returns were included in log form.

Throughout the analysis we took sterling to be the base currency and employed data from July 1987 to April 1995. Table 2 shows the annualized sample standard deviations of the daily returns on our 79 different rates of return. The volatilities shown in this table imply that fixed income books are much less volatile than books including significant equity exposure unless the portfolio includes very long-dated securities. Since holdings that include large amounts of long-dated bonds will still have relatively low average durations, even portfolios with substantial net exposures at the long end of the yield curve would have lower volatilities than portfolios that   include equities.

Although the returns data covered the period July 1987 to April 1995, estimates of the VaRs were made only for the period June 1989 to April 1995. The data covering the earlier period was used in whole or in part (depending on the length of the data window) to construct the first VaR estimate. This meant that it was not possible to compute a VaR estimate for the 1987 equity market crash although the crash did appear in the past data when VaR estimates were calculated using a 24 month window. (This explains the high estimates that were found for the stylised portfolio at the start of the estimation period.) The

Table 2
Standard Deviations of Daily Returns

	FFR	GBP	USD	YEN	DM
FX	9.22		15.68	14.59	9.68
<3 months	1.32	0.70	0.45	0.32	0.37
3-6 months	1.59	1.26	0.77	0.50	0.66
6-9 months	1.92	1.93	1.21	0.77	0.98
9-12 months	2.17	2.57	1.70	1.02	1.29
1-2 years	3.84	4.85	3.05	1.90	2.51
2-3 years	5.28	6.45	4.53	2.85	3.32
3-4 years	6.70	8.07	6.03	3.90	4.28
4-5 years	8.14	9.59	7.52	5.01	5.11
5-6 years	9.71	11.02	8.97	6.36	5.93
6-7 years	11.66	12.48	10.42	8.20	7.26
7-8 years	13.66	14.30	11.88	9.82	9.04
8-9 years	14.81	16.01	13.26	11.18	10.71
9-10 years	15.17	17.58	14.52	12.31	12.45
10+ years	16.72	19.94	16.98	14.73	15.33
Equities	28.44	20.78	24.10	32.74	29.22

Standard deviations are annualized (multiplied by $\sqrt{250}$) and stated in percent

equity market crash of October 1987 is included only when a 24 month window for past data was used and hence does not figure amongst the spike periods discussed below.

2.3 Parametric VaR Analysis

The first issue we wish to address in our empirical analysis is the sensitivity of parametric VaR analysis to the precise way in which the volatilities are estimated. As mentioned above, Basle does not specify what approach is to be taken except that at least 12 months of data should be employed. However, the penalties incurred if forecast loss probabilities are inaccurate should serve as a strong incentive for banks to seek out accurate techniques that yield unbiased estimates.

The approach to volatility estimation typically used in VaR applications is to take a weighted average of the squared deviation from an estimate of the mean return using a window of lagged data. Thus, if r_t is the holding return at t, a typical estimator for $\sigma^2 = \text{Var}(r_t)$ would be:

$$\hat{\sigma}_t^2 = \frac{1}{T-1}\sum_{i=0}^{T-1} \lambda_i (r_{t-T+1} - \bar{r}_t)^2, \tag{1}$$

where $\lambda_i \in [0, 1]$, $\sum_{i=0}^{T-1} \lambda_i \frac{1}{T} = 1$, and $\bar{r} \equiv \sum_{j=0}^{T-1} r_{t-T+j} \frac{1}{T}$.

Three choices must be made in implementing the parametric VaR described above,

Table 3
Parametric VaRs and Window Length

	3 mths	6 mths	12 mths	24 mths
Mean Absolute Forecast Error				
Portfolio 1	50.81	50.42*	50.52	50.62
Portfolio 2	21.22	21.06	21.02	20.80*
Portfolio 3	2.15	2.11	2.10	2.08*
Stylised	32.00	31.65*	31.85	33.22
Tail Probabilities				
Portfolio 1	1.72	1.39	1.32*	1.32*
Portfolio 2	2.11	1.91	1.58	1.52*
Portfolio 3	1.52	1.06*	1.52	1.39
Stylised	1.65	1.38*	1.45	1.32

Calculations employ equal weights $(\lambda_i = 1, \forall i)$, and daily returns.
* Indicates lowest for the portfolio.

namely (i) what is an appropriate length for the lagged data 'window,' T; (ii) what weighting scheme should be adopted, $(\lambda_0, \lambda_1, ...\lambda_{T-1})$; and (iii) should the mean be estimated using the sample mean, $\sum_{j=0}^{T-1} r_{t-T+j} \frac{1}{T}$, or set to zero as some empirical researchers have advocated.[5]

2.4 Forecasting Performance and Window Length

Table 3 shows two ways of assessing the sensitivity of the VaR results to the choice of T. In the upper block of the Table, we show the mean absolute forecast error where we define the forecast error at period t as:

$$(r_t - \bar{r}_t)^2 - \hat{\sigma}_t^2. \tag{2}$$

Averaging the absolute forecast errors over the entire sample period, yields a measure of the accuracy of the volatility estimates.

As one may see from Table 3, the mean absolute forecast errors for the first three portfolios (with returns dominated by low volatility fixed-income risk) are quite insensitive to the length of the data window. On the face of it, this is surprising since plots of the forecasts based on long or short windows look quite different — see Figure 1. However, the results reflect the very low explanatory power of the volatility forecasts. Hence, even if the volatility forecasts vary substantially with different window lengths, the variation in the forecast is uninformative about the actual outcome.

---

[5]See, for example, J.P. Morgan (1995), 66.

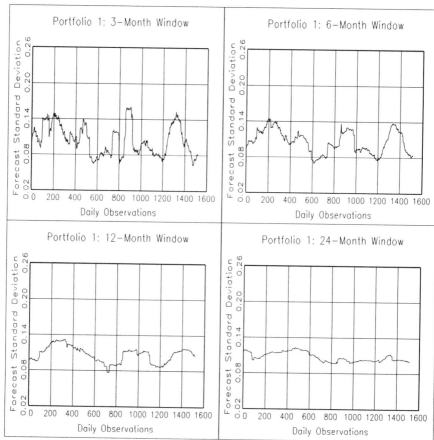

Figure 1
Plots of forecast volatilities

This may seem surprising to those who have worked with GARCH volatility models since a common presumption is that volatilities are highly forecastable. However, it is important to distinguish between the contributions made to volatility by 'moderate' and 'large' price changes. Moderate squared price changes are easy to forecast but large ones, which is what matters for our VaR loss probability estimates, are very hard to predict. One implication is that it is not appropriate to evaluate VaR models based on their ability to forecast total volatility. Hendricks (1995), for example, compares VaR techniques in this way.

Table 4
Parametric VaRs and Exponential Weights

	Equal Weights	$\lambda = 0.97$	$\lambda = 0.94$
Mean Absolute Errors			
Portfolio 1	50.62	50.00*	50.08
Portfolio 2	20.80*	20.88	20.90
Portfolio 3	2.08*	2.10	2.12
Stylised	32.22	31.61*	31.77
Tail Probabilities			
Portfolio 1	1.32*	1.32*	1.72
Portfolio 2	1.52*	1.72	1.91
Portfolio 3	1.39*	1.45	1.78
Stylised	1.32*	1.51	1.71

Calculations employ zero means, daily returns, and a 24-month window.
* Indicates lowest for the portfolio.

Assuming normally distributed returns, one may deduce from the time series of estimated volatilities a corresponding series for what we shall call 1% cut-off points meaning those points such that the loss in the next period should on average exceed the cut-off point 1% of the time. More precisely, the cut-off points may be obtained by inverting the equation:

$$Prob\left[\sum_{n=1}^{N} r_{nt} a_n < -\gamma \mid \sigma^2, \mu \right] = 0.01, \tag{3}$$

for γ_t on a period by period basis. (In equation (3), a_n is the holding of the nth asset. Throughout our analysis, we shall normalise initial wealth to unity so that $\sum_{n=1}^{N} a_n = 1$.) Carrying out the inversion yields:

$$\gamma_t \equiv -\mu - \Phi^{-1}(0.01)\sigma, \tag{4}$$

where $\Phi(\cdot)$ is the cumulative distribution function for a standard normal random variable.

The lower panel in Table 3 shows the proportion of actual portfolio returns that fall below the 1% cut-off points. In general, the figures substantially exceed 1%, demonstrating the inaccuracy of the tail probability measures implied by parametric VaRs based on normal distributions. This finding is not surprising given the widely documented leptokurtosis of interest rates and stock returns. Two less obvious points that emerge from the Table however are: (i) the tail probability bias is sensitive to the window size; but (ii) the effect of window size varies from book to book, so the preferred window length depends upon which book is being analysed.

As noted above, the alternative approach in the proposed Basle Accord Amendment requires that VaR's be carried out using at least 12 months of data. The results in Table 3 certainly suggest that use of very small amounts of data is not advisable. But, for the parametric approach, it is less clear whether 12 months of data is preferable to using either 6 or 24 months. The mean absolute errors are slightly lower for two of our four portfolios using 6 months of data but for the other two portfolios, the maximum of 24 months of data appears better. Four 3 out of out four portfolios the biases in the tail probabilities are smaller when one uses 24 months rather than 12 months or less.

2.5 Weighting Schemes

As mentioned before, a common procedure is to calculate variance estimates for VaR-type analyses using *weighted* squared deviations from an estimate of the mean. Rapidly declining weights mean that variance estimates are largely determined by the last few observations although information contained in more lagged observations is not totally ignored. The motivation for this approach is the widely recognised fact that financial market returns are conditionally heteroskedastic.

A range of more or less complicated techniques have been developed to model this

Table 5
Parametric and Simulation VaRs: Tail Probabilities

	Return and method	3 mths Data	6 mths Data	12 mths Data	24 mths Data
Portfolio 1	1-day, parametric	1.72	1.39	1.32	1.32
	10-day, parametric†	1.78	1.06	1.32	1.06
	1-day, simulation	1.71	0.79	1.38	0.92
	10-day, simulation‡	3.69	1.97	2.30	1.78
Portfolio 2	1-day, parametric	2.11	1.91	1.58	1.52
	10-day, parametric†	0.79	0.73	0.99	0.92
	1-day, simulation	1.78	0.99	1.18	1.18
	10-day, simulation‡	2.63	1.32	1.45	1.65
Portfolio 3	1-day, parametric	1.52	1.06	1.52	1.39
	10-day, parametric†	0.40	0.40	0.20	0.07
	1-day, simulation	1.71	0.53	1.12	0.92
	10-day, simulation‡	2.24	0.99	1.12	0.92
Stylised	1-day, parametric	1.65	1.38	1.45	1.32
	10-day, parametric†	2.11	2.24	1.91	1.85
	1-day, simulation	1.58	0.66	1.18	1.12
	10-day, simulation‡	2.96	1.32	2.24	1.38

†Calculated by multiplying the 1-day VaR estimate by $\sqrt{10}$ and comparing with the subsequent realised 10-day log returns.
‡Calculated by estimating the VaR from the portfolio losses over 10-day periods and comparing these with the subsequent realised 10-day log returns.

feature of financial returns. In particular, Generalised Autoregressive and Conditionally Heteroskedastic (GARCH) models are specifically designed for such purposes. Most implementations of VaR analysis have taken the simpler approach of estimating variances using the weighted average of squared deviations from the mean described above with weights that decline exponentially as the lag length increases. The weights are thus of the form:

$$\lambda_i \equiv T\frac{1-\lambda}{1-\lambda^{T-1}}\lambda^i, \quad i=0,1,2,\ldots,T-1, \tag{5}$$

for a constant $\lambda_i \in [0, 1]$. Standard results on geometric series imply that $\sum_0^{T-1} \lambda_i = T$.

Table 4 shows mean absolute volatility forecast errors under different weighting scheme assumptions. The calculations are carried out using daily returns with 24-month windows of lagged data and means fixed at zero. Once again, the volatility forecasts for the fixed income and FX books are quite insensitive to the precise approach followed. Equal weighted volatility forecasts seem slightly preferable for two of the three fixed income porfolios while rapidly declining weights perform better for portfolio 1 and the stylised

Table 6
Parametric VaRs: Mean Absolute Forecast Error, Sample Mean Included

		Sample Mean	Zero Mean
Portfolio 1	1-day return	50.68	50.62*
	10-day return†	440.39	434.16*
Portfolio 2	1-day return	20.83	20.80*
	10-day return†	16.99	16.74*
Portfolio 3	1-day return	2.08*	2.08*
	10-day return†	16.99	16.74*
Stylised	1-day return	33.27	33.22*
	10-day return†	300.68	296.47*

Equal weights, daily returns, 24-month window.
* Indicates lowest for the portfolio.
†Calculated by mutiplying 1-day returns by $\sqrt{10}$.

portfolio. The lower panel of Table 4 shows the tail probabilities for different weighting schemes. It is apparent that weighting schemes with rapidly declining weights increase the upward bias in the tail probabilities.

To summarise, there appears to be a trade-off in that weighting schemes may improve slightly the degree to which the VaR calculations track time-varying volatilities (i.e., the mean absolute forecast errors may be reduced to some small degree). However, in the portfolios we analysed, the bias in the tail probabilities is exacerbated by weighting schemes.

The Basle alternative approach makes no particular recommendations about weighting schemes; but it does require that even with a weighting scheme in place, the effective observation period must be at least one year (i.e. the weighted average age of the different observations cannot be less than 6 months). This is important because a weighting scheme with rapidly declining weights effectively throws out most of the information in all except very recent data points. Given the penalties for banks whose VaR models yield loss probabilities that are biased down, the fact that equal weights in our estimates yield smaller

Table 7
'Spike' Losses --- Stylised Portfolio

Date		Fr	UK	US	JP	Ger	Total
16/10/89	FX	0.01		-0.07	-0.00	-0.06	-0.12
	Bonds	-0.04	-1.08	-0.09	-0.43	-0.53	-2.16
	Equities	-0.72	-0.46	0.30	-0.21	-1.52	-2.61
	Total	-0.75	-1.54	0.15	-0.64	-2.11	-4.89
21/02/90	FX	-0.00		-0.07	0.01	0.01	-0.05
	Bonds	-0.03	-0.30	0.01	0.02	-0.75	-1.04
	Equities	-0.10	-0.09	-0.01	-0.36	-0.10	-0.66
	Total	-0.13	-0.39	-0.06	-0.33	-0.84	-0.76
23/08/90	FX	-0.02		-0.12	0.02	0.08	-0.05
	Bonds	0.04	-0.32	-0.14	-0.70	0.38	-0.74
	Equities	-0.23	-0.18	-0.34	-0.67	-0.39	-1.82
	Total	-0.21	-0.51	-0.61	-1.35	0.06	-2.61
18/03/91	FX	0.01		0.24	-0.02	-0.02	0.20
	Bonds	0.02	0.12	-0.11	-1.53	0.16	-1.34
	Equities	-0.10	-0.02	-0.04	0.13	-0.13	-0.16
	Total	-0.07	0.10	0.08	-1.43	0.01	-1.30
19/08/91	FX	-0.02		0.20	-0.01	0.12	0.28
	Bonds	0.03	-0.08	-0.02	-0.63	0.60	-0.10
	Equities	-0.84	-0.35	-0.20	-0.68	-1.10	-3.23
	Total	-0.83	-0.43	-0.09	-1.32	-0.38	-3.05
03/04/9	FX	0.01		-0.08	0.00	-0.03	-0.10
	Bonds	-0.01	-0.05	0.18	-2.09	-0.05	-2.02
	Equities	0.00	-0.10	0.03	0.16	-0.01	0.09
	Total	0.00	-0.15	0.13	-1.92	-0.09	-2.03

biases suggests that rapidly declining weights should probably be avoided.

2.6 Parametric Versus Non-Parametric VaRs

Let us now compare the performance of parametric and non-parametric-based VaR models. Since non-parametric-based VaRs do not yield a time series of volatility forecast errors, we restrict our comparison to the tail probabilities that the two kinds of model produce. Table 5 shows the results for data window lengths ranging from 3 to 24 months. For the parametric approach, 10-day return tail probabilities were calculated by scaling up the 1-day VaR estimates by $\sqrt{10}$ and then taking the fraction of observations for which the 10-day loss outturns exceed the implied cut-off level. The 1-day tail probabilities are calculated as in previous sections. For the non-parametric approach, 10-day return tail probabilities were calculated using 10-day portfolio losses to compute the VaR and then taking the fraction of observations for which the 10-day loss outturns exceed the implied

Table 7 (continued)
'Spike' Losses --- Stylised Portfolio

Date		Fr.	UK	US	Jap.	Ger.	Total
17/09/92	FX	0.08	--	0.17	-0.02	-0.37	-0.14
	Bond	-0.10	-2.90	0.02	0.24	0.09	-2.65
	Equities	-0.04	0.48	0.00	0.11	-0.04	0.50
	Total	-0.06	-2.42	0.19	0.33	-0.32	-2.29
16/02/93	FX	-0.01	--	-0.21	0.01	0.04	-0.18
	Bond	-0.00	0.04	0.02	-0.34	-0.21	-0.50
	Equities	-0.13	-0.11	-0.27	-0.13	-0.00	-0.64
	Total	-0.14	-0.07	-0.46	-0.46	-0.18	-1.31
18/06/93	FX	-0.00	--	0.13	0.01	0.01	0.15
	Bond	-0.05	-0.06	-0.06	-0.61	-0.17	-0.94
	Equities	0.06	0.01	-0.12	-0.07	-0.04	-0.15
	Total	0.01	-0.05	-0.05	-0.66	-0.20	-0.95
01/03/94	FX	-0.00	--	0.00	0.00	0.01	0.01
	Bond	0.02	0.28	-0.28	-0.17	-0.71	-0.87
	Equities	-0.28	-0.15	-0.06	0.12	-0.13	-0.50
	Total	-0.27	0.13	-0.34	-0.05	-0.83	-1.36
28/04/94	FX	0.01	--	-0.01	-0.01	-0.01	-0.02
	Bond	0.01	0.07	-0.40	-0.26	-0.43	-1.02
	Equities	0.02	-0.05	-0.07	-0.00	-0.01	-0.11
	Total	0.03	0.02	-0.48	-0.27	-0.45	-1.15
17/10/94	FX	-0.00	--	-0.10	0.00	-0.01	-0.11
	Bond	0.00	-0.16	-0.06	-0.34	-0.34	-0.91
	Equities	-0.15	0.04	-0.00	-0.01	-0.08	-0.20
	Total	-0.15	-0.12	-0.16	-0.35	-0.43	-1.21

cut-off level. For the 1-day tail probabilities, the VaR was computed using 1-day portfolio losses and the result compared with the 1-day outturns. For both the parametric and the non-parametric approaches, the 10-day return outturns were computed on a rolling basis by summing the log daily returns — see below.

The results in the Table suggest that, as one might expect, calculating the 24-hour and 10-day VaR cut-off points from short data windows is inadvisable in that the small sample biases are very substantial. For longer data windows, the non-parametric approach for the 1-day returns consistently out performs the parametric VaR model in that the tail probabilities are matched more accurately. For the parametric approach, the tail probabilities computed using the different lag lengths consistently exceed the 1% level, reflecting the well-known non-normality of financial returns.

Looking at the 10-day returns, for some portfolios, the non-parametric approach appears to perform worse than the parametric VaR estimates. However, for the stylised book returns, the parametric calculations of tail probabilities suggest there are substantial biases. Thus, the tail probability figures for 10-day returns probably serve to underline the statistical problems involved in attempting to deduce 10-day volatilities directly from estimates of 1-day volatilities.

The Basle alternative approach makes no recommendations about the use of parametric versus non-parametric approaches. The biases in the loss probability estimates implied by the former approach might well suggest non-parametric approaches are preferable, however.

2.7 The Inclusion of Estimated Means

The last exercise we perform to assess the sensitivity of VaR analyses to different assumptions is to calculate mean absolute forecast errors for parametric VaRs (i) with means estimated from lagged returns, and (ii) with the means set to zero. Fixing the means at zero might seem an unconventional statistical procedure but the estimation error associated with badly determined mean estimates may significantly reduce the efficiency of the estimated volatilities. (Figlewski (1994) makes a similar point in the context of return variance estimation.) If the true mean returns are, as seems likely, very close to zero, fixing them at this level could enhance the forecasts.

The results in Table 6 show that, for our books and dataset of rates of return, this conjecture is indeed correct. The mean absolute forecast errors with means set to zero are consistently lower than in cases in which the means are freely estimated. However, the reduction in mean absolute forecast errors is very small for the 1-day returns which are easiest to interpret. For the 10-day returns, the reduction in mean absolute forecast errors is more sizeable.

2.8 Calculation of Value at Risk Over 10-day Periods

As discussed above, we looked at the effect of trying to estimate the VaR over a 10-day period. We did not have a sufficiently long run of data to estimate the VaR using returns calculated over non-overlapping 10-day periods (this would reduce the number of observations by a factor of 10). Hence, for the parametric approach we had to choose between using the VaR estimated for a 24-hour period grossed up by $\sqrt{10}$, or using overlapping returns based on rolling 10-day periods. Since the use of overlapping data induces artificial autocorrelation in the series (which makes them appear smoother than they actually are), for the parametric approach we did not attempt to calculate the VaR using 10-day rolling returns.

Table 8
Stylised Portfolio — Descriptive Statistics

Component	Covariance Matrix			Standard	Skewness	Kurtosis
	FX	I/R	Equities	Deviation		
Period: 10/07/87 to 18/04/95						
FX	0.45			0.67	0.09	4.87
I/R	-0.01	18.07		4.25	-0.03	6.37
Equities	0.39	-2.11	20.90	4.57	-1.65	27.85
Whole Portfolio				6.00	-1.03	12.52
Period: 22/06/89 to 17/04/95*						
FX	0.46			0.68	0.05	4.83
I/R	-0.15	17.45		4.18	-0.10	5.95
Equities	0.20	-2.68	16.52	4.06	-0.33	10.01
Whole Portfolio				5.40	-0.65	9.14

* Period corresponds to that on Figures 1 and 2.
Covariance matrix elements are $\times 10^6$.
Standard deviations are $\times 10^3$.

For the non-parametric approach we calculated the VaR using portfolio losses calculated over rolling 10-day periods. As illustrated in Table 5, the 10-day VaR estimates using both the parametric and the non-parametric approaches were substantially biased. Moreover, the direction of the bias appears to be portfolio dependent.

2.9 'Spike' Loss Periods

An important question is whether the ability of parametric VaR analysis to 'track' the time series behaviour of volatility enables it to out-perform simulation-based VaRs in predictions of large, 'spike' losses in portfolio values. It is possible that even if parametric VaRs do not yield lower mean absolute forecast errors as we saw above, they are better at picking out large market movements. This issue is particularly important if VaR analysis is to be used for regulatory purposes since the primary concern of regulators regarding trading-book risks is that banks will be wiped out by sudden large losses that occur before action could be taken to reduce the riskiness of the bank's portfolio.

To examine this issue, we split our sample period into six-month intervals and identified for each of our portfolios, the day within each period on which the largest loss occurred. By way of illustration, Table 7 provides detailed break-downs of the constituent parts of each of these large value declines for the stylised portfolio containing equity as well as interest rate and FX risk. The most striking fact that emerges from Table 7 is the importance of equity declines in generating large losses in the overall portfolio on a number of the spike dates. (The equity declines were a dominant factor on three dates and were a major contributory factor on a further four dates.)

Recall that the equity exposure we have added to the fixed income and FX book was just £50 million for each of five national equity markets. Compared with net fixed income exposure, these figures are small (although for many banks, equity exposures may well be a very small proportion of their total exposures). Table 2 showed that equity returns are distinctly more volatile than any except the very long-dated bond returns. The results on spike loss dates suggest that the contribution of equity returns to the fourth moment of the distribution of returns on the overall portfolio is even higher. In Table 8 we present descriptive statistics for the returns of the stylised portfolio and its component asset categories (FX, interest rate exposures and equities). All three components of the portfolio exhibit excess kurtosis (greater than the level of three characteristic of normally distributed random variables). For the equity component, the degree of kurtosis is particularly marked; and even when the 1987 stock market crash is excluded, as shown in the lower panel of the Table, the kurtosis remains much higher than that of the other portfolio components.[6]

The fact that the spike losses were, on a large number of occasions, the result of equity rather than bond market developments is confirmed by ex post reports of the market movements in the *Financial Times* summarised in the Appendix. These suggest that even when the basic shock to the economy was news affecting expectations of future interest rate policy, the equities provided a more highly geared exposure to such developments.

2.10 Model Performance in 'Spike' Loss Periods

Table 9 shows the capital requirement[7] implied by the VaR estimates less the actual loss sustained. We term this quantity the capital surplus (+) or capital short-fall (-). As one may see, the differences between the performance of parametric and simulation-based VaR models according to this measure is not great. For each of the portfolios, the parametric model generates a larger number of capital short-falls but the differences are relatively small. The implication is that the spike losses are the result of sudden, unforecastable, market movements that the parametric VaRs, despite their ability to 'track' volatility over time, are unable to detect in advance. If anything, the simulation approach that does not

---

[6]The more 'spiky' and volatile nature of equities has been recognised, for instance, in the CAD building-block approach. A single position in a ten-year government bond would carry a capital requirement of 2.4%, whereas a single position in an equity index would carry a charge of 8%; for a single equity the charge would be 12%.

[7]The capital "requirement" is the VaR for the whole book produced using a 99% confidence level. It does not build-in any other aspects of the Basle proposals such as the treatment of correlations between asset classes or the three-times multiplier.

Table 9
Model Performance on 'Spike' Loss Dates

Model	Portfolio		Portfolio 2	
	Simulation	Parametric.	Simulation	Parametric.
Period 1	-2.39	-2.20	-0.72	-0.68
Period 2	-0.82	-0.93	-0.62	-0.62
Period 3	-1.09	-1.30	-0.70	-0.79
Period 4	0.04	-0.12	-0.42	-0.57
Period 5	0.41	0.16	0.22	0.04
Period 6	-1.58	-1.95	-1.53	-1.75
Period 7	-2.64	-3.05	-2.03	-2.16
Period 8	0.06	-0.35	-0.45	-0.50
Period 9	0.58	0.22	-0.12	-0.14
Period 10	0.15	-0.11	0.09	-0.00
Period 11	-0.10	-0.14	-0.06	-0.05
Period 12	-0.24	-0.11	0.26	0.18
Model	Portfolio 3		Stylised Portfolio	
	Simulation	Parametric.	Simulation	Parametric.
Period 1	-0.05	-0.06	-3.56	-3.66
Period 2	-0.08	-0.09	-0.54	-0.48
Period 3	-0.01	-0.04	-1.18	-1.30
Period 4	-0.20	-0.22	0.24	0.19
Period 5	0.05	0.03	-1.51	-1.56
Period 6	-0.26	-0.28	-0.62	-0.74
Period 7	-0.07	-0.16	-1.05	-1.06
Period 8	0.01	-0.07	0.41	-0.12
Period 9	0.16	0.08	0.78	0.27
Period 10	-0.01	-0.02	-0.05	-0.17
Period 11	-0.02	-0.02	0.16	0.03
Period 12	-0.11	-0.12	-0.05	-0.14

Note: Table shows the capital shortfall (-) or surplus (+) for the largest loss in each 6-month period
Equal weights, daily returns, 24-month window.
Parametric approach uses zero mean.

exploit the conditional structure of volatility, does a better job of establishing appropriate capital requirements.

2.11 Basle Alternative Approach Capital Calculations

One issue is how much of a capital cushion the proposed Basle alternative approach would deliver for actual books. We looked at this for our portfolios by comparing the capital requirement which would be generated by one part of the proposed two-stage test — 3 times the 60-day average of the VaRs calculated to cover a 10-day holding period using the parameters laid down by Basle. The bank must hold capital equivalent to the higher of this amount and the VaR for the current book. But because of the magnitude of the multiplier, it is, in most circumstances, likely to be the first of these tests which 'bites'. Only when the bank's current book was abnormally risky would this not be the case.

We compared the 10-day returns which would have been secured on our four portfolios over the period July 1989 to April 1995 with the capital requirement based on 3 times the 60-day average of the daily VaRs. We used the parametric approach with a 24-month window of past returns data, equal weights, and a zero mean. We also calculated the capital requirement which would result from setting the multiplier at 2 and 2.5.

For all the portfolios there were no loss outliers (losses which exceeded the capital requirement) for a multiplier of 2.5 or 3. Two of the portfolios had a single (marginal) loss outlier for a multiplier of 2. But these are of course results on only a small number of portfolios and ones which do not include options.

A further issue is whether back-testing will be able to sift among the models. The proposed alternative Basle approach envisages that banks will suffer increases in their capital requirements if their VaR models under-predict the number of losses exceeding the 1% cut-off point for a 250-day period. The capital requirement for banks whose models generate more than four exceptions may be increased by regulators.

We ran back-tests for all four of our portfolios, comparing the VaR figures calculated for 24-hour holding periods (again using the parametric approach) with the 24-hour returns which would have been secured on each book. For each portfolio, the number of loss outliers, or 'exceptions', for each discrete period of 250 days are set out in Table 10.

For three of the six periods, the model would be in the 'yellow zone'. The highest number of exceptions was 7, for portfolio 2 in the first and second periods. (This reflects the high tail probability for the model when run on this portfolio (1.52%), shown in Table 5.) According to the Basle guidelines, this would normally lead to an increase in the scaling factor of 0.65 unless the supervisor was persuaded that it would not be appropriate to increase the charge because of special factors. The fact that the model moves from the green to the yellow zone from period to period reflects the difficulty of using 250 observations to sift between accurate and moderately inaccurate models. A grossly

Table 10
Back-testing Results

Portfolio	1	2	3	Stylised
Period 1	6	7	5	5
Period 2	4	7	5	4
Period 3	3	2	2	3
Period 4	4	5	5	4
Period 5	1	1	1	3
Period 6	2	1	2	1

Table shows the number of exceptions in each 250-day period. (Green zone = 0-4; Yellow zone = 5-9; Red zone = 10+)

inaccurate model would, however, be picked up.

3. CONCLUSION

In writing this paper, we have sought to provide practical analysis of help to those contemplating the use of VaR models either for risk measurement within a bank or for regulatory control of bank risk taking. We have related our results at various points to the recommendations and provisions of the alternative approach of the Basle Accord Amendment. A strength of our study is our use of data on the actual trading books of a bank active in a wide range of markets. We expect that prescriptions about whether one approach dominates another are sensitive to the kind of portfolios held. Thus, studies that analyse VaR modelling on the basis of, for example, a single equity index or FX rate seem to us to be ill-advised and it is important to look at realistic portfolios.

The main conclusions that emerge from the empirical section of our study are as follows:

1.   In parametric VaR modelling, volatility forecasts look quite different for different window lengths but the accuracy of the volatility forecasts varies little. On the other hand, different window lengths affect tail probabilities quite significantly. But the window length that gives most accurate tail probabilities varies across different portfolios, although very short window lengths (i.e., 3 month) consistently perform poorly.

2.   For some portfolios, declining weights in parametric VaR models appear to improve the accuracy of volatility forecasts. But this is at the expense of greater bias in the implied tail probability measures: for all four portfolios, declining weights increased the biases.

3.   The ability of parametric VaR analysis to track the time series behaviour of volatility does not, in fact, yield significantly superior forecasts compared with non-parametric, simulation-based techniques.

4.   Simulation-based VaR techniques yield more accurate measures of tail probabilities than parametric VaR models. This arises from the severe non-normality of financial returns. The common argument that mismeasurement by parametric VaRs of the *level* of tail probabilities does not matter since they correctly rank different portfolios seems unconvincing since different asset returns will be more or less fat-tailed leading to varying biases.

5.   It appears preferable in parametric VaR modelling to set mean returns to zero rather than to include estimated sample means. The reason is that estimated means are so ill-determined that their inclusion injects substantial noise impairing the volatility forecasts.

6.   If one concentrates on spike loss periods, in our sample, simulation VaRs slightly out-perform parametric VaRs in that there are fewer occasions on which the required capital fails to cover the loss.

7.   The results indicate that without very long runs of data (which would enable discrete 10-day periods to be used to calculate past returns) it is not possible accurately to estimate Value at Risk over 10-day holding periods. Either using rolling 10-day periods for calculation of the returns or grossing up the daily figures would lead to considerable biases in the parametric approach. The same is true for the use of rolling 10-day periods in the calculation of losses in the non-parametric approach.

8.   The system of additional capital charges suggested under the Basle Accord Amendment for banks whose VaR model under-predicts losses exceeding the estimated 1% cut-off point will help to sift between the models. The parametric approach using 24 months of data would have triggered an extra capital charge in some periods.

APPENDIX

Explanations for Stylised Portfolio 'Spike' Losses

1.   Monday 16/10/89 – A sharp fall in Wall Street the previous Friday led to price falls on all the major equity markets. The less liquid European markets tended to magnify the movements of the big stock markets. The security of government stock commanded a premium; UK gilt prices rose particularly strongly.

2.   Wednesday 21/2/90 – Equity prices in Europe and in the US showed only modest falls following a substantial fall in Japanese equity prices. German government bond prices strengthened following a late rally in the Japanese bond market.

3.   Thursday 23/8/90 – Gulf war tension led to an increase in oil prices to $32 per barrel and fears of an energy crisis. Equity prices fell in all the major markets. Sterling strengthened supporting UK gilt prices. Japanese government bond prices fell sharply due to fears of higher inflation from increasing oil prices.

4.   Monday 18/3/91 – The possibility of a strong recovery from recession in America led to a stronger dollar but inflation fears caused US bond prices to fall. Sterling weakened on the expectation of a UK base rate cut and the possibility of the Bundesbank raising rates. The Bank of France cut its intervention rate.

5.   Monday 19/8/91 – Concerns about a political crisis in the Soviet Union led to falls in equity prices around the world, and to an increase in oil prices. Sterling fell against a strong dollar but rose against the deutschemark. Japanese bond prices fell, linked to the Soviet political concerns.

6.   Friday 3/4/92 – Sterling was under pressure due to election worries. Japanese government bond prices fell.

7.   Thursday 17/9/92 – UK short-term interest rates fell sharply on the day following sterling's exit from the ERM and the yield curve flattened. UK equity prices rose on hopes of lower interest rates.

8.   Tuesday 16/2/93 – Pessimism over the forthcoming State of the Union address in the US led to sharp falls in the dollar and in US equity prices. European equity prices fell in response. The Japanese equity market closed down due to profit taking. The German Bund was seen as a safe haven and prices rose. Sterling was strong against the deutschemark.

9.   Friday 18/6/93 – The dollar moved sharply up against the Deutschemark, yen and sterling on concerns over deteriorating economic conditions in Germany and political upheaval in Japan. UK equities were helped by positive economic data. Political

uncertainties pushed the Nikkei and the yen lower.

10. Tuesday 1/3/94 – Fears of rising inflation and tightening economic policy led to falls in US bond and equity prices. European government bonds fell in response to the falls in the US, and a smaller than expected easing of the repo rate in Germany. Signs of an upturn in the Japanese economy led to a rise in equity prices in Japan.

11. Thursday 28/4/94 – A negative reaction to mixed economic data in America led to a fall in US equity prices and to a weaker dollar. US government bond prices fell and this led to falls in the prices of some European government bonds.

12. Monday 17/10/94 – Chancellor Kohl's victory in the German elections strengthened the Deutschemark, pushing the dollar downwards. German bonds strengthened, followed by UK gilts. UK equities also gained slightly.

REFERENCES

Alexander, C., 1995, After the Event: A Review of the Volatility and Correlation Forecasts in the Third Edition of RiskMetrics, *Risk Magazine*.

Basle Committee on Banking Supervision, 1994, *Risk Management Guidelines for Derivatives*, Basle.

Basle Committee on Banking Supervision, 1995a, *Planned Supplement to the Capital Accord to Incorporate Market Risks*, Basle.

Basle Committee on Banking Supervision, 1995b, *An Internal Model-Based Approach to Market Risk Capital Requirements*, Basle.

Basle Committee on Banking Supervision, 1996, *Overview of the Amendment to the Capital Accord to Incorporate Market Risk*, Basle.

Dewatripont, M., and J. Tirole, 1994, *The Prudential Regulation of Banks*, MIT Press.

Dimson, E., and P. Marsh, 1995, Capital Requirements for Securities Firms, *Journal of Finance*, Vol. 50, No. 3, July, 821-851.

Figlewski, S., 1994, Forecasting Volatility Using Historical Data, New York University working paper, S-94-13.

Harlow, W.V., 1991, Asset Allocation in a Downside-Risk Framework, *Financial Analysts Journal*, Vol. 47, No. 5, September-October, 28-40.

Hendricks, D., 1995, Evaluation of Value-at-Risk Models Using Historical Data, Federal Reserve Bank of New York mimeo, July.

Jackson, P., 1995, Risk Measurement and Capital Requirements for Banks, *Bank of England Quarterly Bulletin*, May, 177-184.

Kendall, Sir M., and A. Stuart, 1977, *The Advanced Theory of Statistics, Volume 1, Distribution Theory*, Fourth edition, Charles Griffin: London.

Kupiec, P.H., 1995, Techniques for Verifying the Accuracy of Risk Measurement Models, Board of Governors of the Federal Reserve System mimeo.

Laycock, M.S., and D.A. Paxson, 1995, Capital Adequacy Risks: Return Normality and Confidence Intervals, Bank of England mimeo, presented at the 1995 Annual Meeting of the European Financial Management Association.

Lewis, A.L., 1990, Semivariance and the Performance of Portfolios with Options, *Financial Analysts Journal*, Vol. 46, No. 4, July-August, 67-76.

Markowitz, H.M., 1959, *Portfolio Selection: Efficient Diversification of Investments*, Basil Blackwell: Oxford.

Merton, R.C., and Z. Bodie, 1993, Deposit Insurance: A Functional Approach, Carnegie-Rochester Conference Series on Public Policy, Vol. 38, 1-34.

Morgan, J.P., 1995, *RiskMetrics Technical Document*, Third edition, J. P. Morgan: New York.

West, K., and D. Cho, 1994, The Predictive Ability of Several Models of Exchange Rate Volatility, NBER Technical Working Paper No. 152.

Derivatives, Regulation and Banking
Edited by B. Schachter
1997 Elsevier Science B.V.

Chapter 13
RECENT DEVELOPMENTS IN BANK CAPITAL REGULATION
OF MARKET RISKS

Paul H. Kupiec and James M. O'Brien[t]

Board of Governors of the Federal Reserve System, Washington, DC, USA

1. INTRODUCTION

Prior to 1992, uniform minimum capital standards were applied to all bank regardless of any differences in the levels of their investment risks. The task of limiting banks' portfolio risks and ensuring capital adequacy was left to regulatory monitoring and supervision, and to some degree, to market pressures. In the 1988 Basle Accord, U.S. banking regulatory agencies along with the regulatory agencies of other G-10 countries, Luxembourg, and Switzerland, under the rubric of the Basle Supervisory Committee (BSC), proposed minimum capital standards for banks' credit risk exposures.[1]

In linking bank capital standards to credit risk exposures, the 1988 Basle Accord represents a first step both in substituting rules for supervisory judgment and in promoting international harmonization of bank capital requirements. The latter objective is intended to avoid a multiplicity of capital rules for internationally active banks and limit opportunities for regulatory arbitrage.[2] Current BSC proposals that extend risk-based capital requirements to market risks are a second step in this process. In a related endeavor, bank supervisors in EC countries are scheduled to implement (by January 1996) market risk capital standards for the trading exposures of EC banks under the Capital Adequacy Directive (CAD).

The BSC proposals consist of two alternative approaches for setting market risk

---

[t]Division of Research and Statistics. The conclusions herein are those of the authors and do not represent the views of the Federal Reserve Board or any of the Federal Reserve Banks.

[1]US representatives on the BSC include officials form the Federal Reserve Board, the Federal Reserve Bank of New York, the Comptroller of the Currency, and the Federal Deposit Insurance Corporation.

[2]See King (1990), Carosio (1990), or Schaefer (1990), for a more extensive discussion of the issues.

capital standards for bank trading accounts. A third approach, distinct from the BSC efforts, is also being developed for possible future consideration.[3]

One of the two BSC approaches, the so-called standardized approach (Basle (1993), revised May 1995), consists of a set of rules that assign risk charges to specific instruments and crudely account for selected portfolio effects on banks' risk exposures. The standardized approach uses a "building block" framework, a framework it shares with the 1988 Basle Accord credit risk capital standards as well as national capital requirements that apply to securities dealers in some countries. Under the CAD, EC bank supervisors will be implementing a market risk capital approach similar to the standardized BSC measure. In both cases, the required market risk capital will supplement the regulatory capital required under the current capital standards for credit risk.

A second approach proposed by the BSC is fundamentally different. Under the internal models approach, capital charges would be based on market risk estimates from banks' internal risk measurement models (FRB July 1995a). The bank would use its proprietary risk measurement models to estimate its trading risk exposure which would become the basis for the regulatory capital charge for market risk. Regulators also would impose a number of standardizing restrictions on banks' models in an attempt to create rough comparability across banks that will use the internal models approach.

A third proposal is known as the pre-commitment approach. This approach is a concept release of the Federal Reserve Board (July 1995b). It is undergoing continued development and may be considered more formally at a future date. Under this approach, each bank pre-commits to a maximum loss exposure over a designated horizon. This maximum loss commitment becomes the bank's market risk capital charge. If the bank incurs trading losses in excess of its capital commitment it is subject to penalties which may include fines, a capital surcharge in future periods, or other regulatory discipline.

The slow progress and competing market risk proposals produced by the BSC have generated criticism of the process underlying the international negotiations and lead some to question the feasibility or desirability of international harmonization (e.g., Dimson and Marsh (1995), Hartmann (1995), Schaefer (1990)). While there may be merit in some of these criticisms, the tepid pace of development owes in part to an evolution of views among

---

[3]Market risk capital standards are being developed for the trading account independently of the non-trading component of the bank. The trading account is distinguished by the requirement that its positions be carried at their current market values. This paper focuses on the trading account proposals. U.S. supervisors have under development somewhat similar approaches for market risk (mostly interest rate risk) in the banking book. At present, however, the banking book proposals would use risk measurement systems only as an examiner tool and not for setting formal market risk capital requirements. See Federal Reserve Board, July 1995c.

bank regulators and the banking industry about how best to measure market risk for regulatory capital purposes. From an initial presumption that market risk measurement would be based on an approach similar to the BSC standardized measure, the view that risk exposures are better measured using banks' proprietary systems has gained favor. The issue of precisely how a bank's risk measurement system should be used to best advantage in the regulatory capital process is still in debate, a debate that is reflected in the internal models and pre-commitment alternative capital proposals.

In what follows, the details of these alternative approaches for setting market risk capital requirements will be reviewed.[4] Following this review, the different alternatives will be analyzed with an emphasis on bringing out the weaknesses that have provided the impetuous for the development of the alternative approaches. In this respect, the discussion will mirror the evolution in thought that has transpired in the negotiations surrounding the development of a set of market risk capital standards. A summary and reference to some important omitted issues concludes the paper.

2. ALTERNATIVE APPROACHES

2.1 The BSC Standardized Measure

The BSC regulatory standardized measure, and its EC counterpart embodied in the CAD, use a building-block approach for setting market risk capital requirements. Capital charges are determined separately for each of four major market risk categories (interest rate, foreign exchange, equity, and commodities) and are then aggregated. Different procedures are used for each category to determine the category's respective capital charge.

Interest rate and exchange rate risks dominate the market risks for most bank trading departments. Under the building-block approach, debt securities incur a specific and a market risk capital charge. The specific risk charge is intended to cover changes in the market value of securities owing to changes in credit quality. It is a weighted aggregate of gross debt security positions where the weights vary between zero and 8 percent according to quality measures of the security (issuer, maturity, rating). These specific risk capital charges for interest rate products would substitute for the credit risk capital requirement these positions currently require under the 1988 Basle Capital Accord.

The market risk charge covers changes in the value of the debt positions that owe to changes in the general level of (risk free) interest rates. For this charge, positions are

---

[4]As of November 1995, the details of the approaches have not been finalized. The final international agreement may contain some differences in the details of the approaches described herein.

aggregated and netted within each of 13 time bands. Net positions in each time band are then multiplied by a risk weight and aggregated across time bands. The prescribed weights are intended to roughly reflect durations for an assumed shift in the yield curve 100 basis points at the short end and 60 basis points at the long end.[5]

The netting of positions within a time band and aggregation of weighted positions across time bands assumes perfect correlation among (risk-free) debt instrument price changes. Under this rule, opposite sign positions in different securities within and across maturity bands hedge dollar for dollar, while positions of the same sign are not assigned any diversification benefit. The standardized measure does make an adjustment to account for imperfect hedges due to imperfectly correlated interest rate (price) changes. The adjustment takes the form of additional capital charges that are imposed to cover basis risk within a maturity band ("vertical disallowances") and imperfect correlations across maturity bands ("horizontal disallowances").[6] The size of the added capital requirements are related to the smaller of (variously aggregated) shorts and (variously aggregated) longs within and across the different maturity categories.[7] There is no attempt to recognize diversification benefits for positions of the same sign in different securities or maturities. Interest rate risk capital charges are separately determined for positions in each currency unit (e.g., dollar, yen, etc.) and are then aggregated across currency units using spot exchange rates to determine the total capital requirement for interest rate risk. There is no netting of positions or recognition of diversification across currency units. In addition, the present value of each foreign currency-based interest rate book is also included as an FX exposure in the FX risk capital requirement calculation. Unlike securities, the FX capital requirement covers positions both in the bank book and the trading book. Foreign exchange exposures generated by outright FX positions and foreign-currency denominated interest rate and equity products are assessed an 8 percent capital charge on the larger of the sum of net short cash and forward positions or

---

[5]Alternatively, the bank itself may calculate the durations on its debt securities and multiply these by a prescribed set of changes in interest rates.

[6]There may be some redundancy in the disallowances for basis risk and the imposition of a specific risk capital charge, since some basis risk may come from changes in credit quality on instruments with default risk.

[7]Within time bands, a percent of the smaller of the offsetting (short or long) positions is disallowed (short and long positions in the same instrument are reported only as a single position). For disallowances of hedging between time bands, the 13 maturity bands are divided into three zones. There is a larger disallowance for offsetting (short or long) positions between adjacent zones than within a zone, and a still larger disallowance for offsetting positions between zones 1 and 3 than between adjacent zones.

the sum of net long cash and forward positions in each currency (forward positions can be measured in a present value form). This is a "compromise" between no off-setting and complete off-setting of long and short FX exposures in that it is equal to ½ the sum of the gross and the net exposures across currencies (Levonian (1994)). Only in this crude sense do the FX capital charges give recognition for the diversification effects generated from imperfectly correlated changes in foreign exchange rates.[8]

Equity positions are subject to both a specific risk and a market risk capital charge. Equity capital charges are determined on a national market basis and are then aggregated across markets at current exchange rates with no offsets permitted for hedging or diversification among markets.[9] The present value of each foreign-currency denominated equity book is also included in the FX capital requirement calculation. For market risk, the difference between the sum of long and short positions at current market value is assessed an 8 percent capital charge. For specific risk, the absolute sum of all the bank's long and short (non-index) equity positions are subject to an 8 percent capital charge. However, if the portfolio is judged to be liquid and well diversified by the examiner, the specific risk capital charge is 4 percent. If the equity investment is in a well-diversified index instrument, the specific capital charge is 2 percent of the net long or short position (to cover risks associated with contract execution).

Though there is some variation in the method of assessment, commodity capital charges are essentially 15 percent of the net position in each commodity (excepting gold, see above). Some additional capital charges are also assessed for basis risk, interest rate risk, and forward gap risk.

The general approach for assessing capital requirements for derivatives positions is the same for interest rate, FX, and equity contracts. Firm commitment contracts (futures, forwards, swaps) are expressed as long and short positions in the underlying instruments. The positions are then treated in the same way as outright positions in the respective instruments in determining capital requirements.[10]

---

[8]Under the CAD, a bank may be allowed to use an alternative backtesting method for FX capital requirements based on estimates of FX losses that would have occurred with its current positions over the past five years.

[9]Subject to certain limitations, the CAD permits reductions in the market risk capital charge for offsetting cross-country equity positions.

[10]For example, a purchased futures contract to receive $1 million in 5 year Treasury notes in 1 month is treated as a long position in a 5 year (plus 1 month) note valued at its current market value, which is slotted in the 4-5 year maturity band, and a short position in $1 million 1-month T-bills. slotted in the 1-3 month band.

Options positions also may be included in the measure for securities risks by weighting the value of the underlying instruments by the options' deltas. When this method is used, referred to as the delta plus method, there is an additional capital charge to cover volatility risk and, in certain cases, a charge to cover delta measurement errors (gama effects). However, where there is substantial trading activity in options, the bank is expected to measure the options risk paired with any associated hedging positions using a suitable options model under a carve out method. Under this method, the option and its associated hedging positions' risk is determined over for a specified range of underlying security values and a range of return volatilities. The resulting capital charge is added to those for other components of the portfolio.

2.2 The Internal Models Approach

Banks who would qualify for the internal models approach must satisfy various qualitative risk management standards. These standards include the requirement that the bank's risk exposure estimates be fully integrated into its daily trading risk management process and that the model be subject to review and evaluation at various levels within the bank. The bank's risk management model also must be validated by the supervisory authority. Additionally, the bank must keep a record of its daily risk exposure estimates and its trading book's daily profits and losses so that supervisors have data upon which to judge model accuracy. If supervisors judge the model or risk controls to be inadequate, they may disallow the use of the model or require capital above the minimum specified in the proposal.

Various quantitative restrictions are also being proposed for the model's use in determining required capital. Although no specific modeling technique is prescribed, a bank's model must: (1) measure all material risks in the trading book; (2) provide a risk estimate of the worst 1 percent of potential losses over a subsequent period of 10 business days (referred to as Value at Risk or VaR); (3) account for the non-linear pricing characteristics of options instruments, including their sensitivity to implied volatility;[11] (4) include at least six factors (e.g. maturity categories) in measuring interest rate risk for debt instruments in currencies where there are significant exposures; and (5) measure aggregate risk exposure as the sum of the individual risk exposure estimates for each major product group-equity, foreign exchange, and fixed income positions. In addition, options exposures must be measured by directly considering the variance of two-week price movements whereas linear instruments can be modeled by scaling one-day exposure estimates by the

---

[11]At present, the internal models used by banks in daily operations do not account fully for the option nonlinearities associated with 10-day price movements. As a consequence, this requirement may be phased in over a period of time.

square root of time. The quantitative standards also require that the historical sample used for parameter estimation be at least a year in length and updated at least once a quarter.

The bank's capital charge at date t is based on the larger of the bank's current 10-day-ahead risk estimate or the average of its risk estimates over the prior 60 business days subject to a multiplication factor. Let VaR_{t-1} represent a bank's risk exposure estimate for date $t-1$, and CMR_t represent the banks market risk capital requirement for date t. The bank's regulatory market risk capital requirement is,

$$CMR_t = Max[\frac{SM_t}{60}\sum_{i=1}^{60} VaR_{t-1}, VaR_{t-1}] + SR_{t-1},$$ (1)

where SM_t is a supervisory determined multiplication factor and SR_{t-1} is an additional capital charge for the specific risk of trading book positions. The proposed minimum value for the multiplication factor, SM_t is 3. The multiplier can be increased if the supervisor is not satisfied with the accuracy of a bank's risk exposure estimates. For verifying risk estimates, a "back-testing" methodology is proposed which would be based on the frequency of realized daily losses exceeding the models' predicted daily losses at the 1 percent critical values. The specific risk capital charge applies to traded debt and equity positions. It is intended to account for idiosyncratic risks, as risk measurement models generally measure risks generated by market-wide factors. The specific risk charge is equal to one-half of the specific risk capital charge as calculated under the standardized approach.

2.3 The Pre-Commitment Approach

Under the pre-commitment approach, a bank would specify a maximum loss over a designated horizon which becomes its market risk capital requirement. Subsequently, if cumulative trading losses breech the capital commitment, the bank is subjected to closer supervisory examination and penalties are imposed. At this stage of development, no formal penalty structure has been specified although there has been some analysis of fines and capital surcharges (Kupiec and O'Brien 1995b) and less formal penalties, such as restricting trading activity, are also possible. Penalties give the bank an incentive to align its capital pre-commitment with its internal evaluation of trading risks and its self-assessment of its risk management capabilities. Public disclosure of the pre-commitment is also recommended to enhance these incentives and strengthen the credibility of the regulatory policy.

The pre-commitment approach, besides taking a more inclusive approach to bank trading risks, reflects several practical considerations. Treating losses in excess of the capital commitment as a breech of the bank's maximum loss pre-commitment substantially simplifies ex post verification by making a violation an observable result. Because penalties are applied ex post and only in the event of losses, the approach does not protect against a "go-for-broke" strategy. Thus bank regulators need to identify banks for whom the penalties would not act as a deterrent to taking excessive trading risk. In this respect, the pre-commitment approach is designed to minimize supervisory micro-management of trading risks and excessive resource expenditure for banks that are judged to be in a sound condition and have acceptable risk management abilities. There would still be normal regulatory monitoring of trading activities and review of trading risk management in periodic bank examinations.

Another practical concern requires that in the event of an unusual systemic situation as judged by the authorities, ex post penalties for capital violations may be waived. In order to maintain the proper incentives, forbearance can only be a policy option under exceptional circumstances. Public disclosure of bank pre-commitments and subsequent trading performance would help deter unwarranted forbearance as public pressures to impose sanctions on those that violate their pre-commitments may offset regulatory incentives to waive the penalties and forebear violations.[12]

As the pre-commitment approach is still in its formative stages, no specific incentive mechanism has been formally proposed. Some operational alternatives have been suggested however. For example, if both the pre-commitment and the internal models approaches were adopted as alternative schemes for determining market risk capital requirements, some who have commented have suggested that a potential penalty for a pre-commitment violation might be to require the bank to use the internal models approach with a "penalty" multiplication factor for some subsequent time period. The negative publicity impact of a pre-commitment violation along with the increased backtesting costs and the regulatory restrictions on the bank's risk management models imposed by the internal models approach would serve as the incentives to encourage accurate capital pre-commitments. Although such a scheme might provide a basic operational penalty rule that could be augmented as circumstances warrant, the incentives it creates are difficult to quantify and theoretically illustrate. An example of a monetary penalty scheme is provided to more concretely illustrate the conceptual underpinnings of the pre-commitment approach and quantify the capital coverage that is possible under such a scheme.[13]

Assume that the bank's overall financial position is such that the bank could pay any penalty that it might incur for a capital violation. The penalty is assumed to be a direct dollar charge proportional to the excess of the loss over the pre-committed capital. Let KT denote the

---

[12] See for example Kane (1995).

[13] For an analysis of other forms of penalties see Kupiec and O'Brien (July 1995b).

capital committed to cover trading losses. The *ex post* charge for a capital commitment breach is

$$\Psi(\Delta V) = -\psi Min\{\Delta V + K_T, 0\},$$

(2)

where ΔV represents the change in the value of the trading portfolio realized at the end of the period. Thus, the bank incurs a penalty if

$$\Delta V < -K_T.$$

(3)

In determining the appropriate incentives, the cost of regulatory capital to the bank plays an important role in determining the appropriate regulatory choice of a penalty rate, ψ. Among other things, this cost will depend on the bank's leverage and will vary with the leverage ratio. For purposes of this illustration, the bank's cost of regulatory capital is assumed strictly proportional at the rate R to the level of capital. Let $f(\Delta V)$ be the probability density for ΔV, $F(\Delta V)$ the associated distribution function, and r the required discount rate on a payoff described by $\Psi(\Delta V)$. The full cost of the capital commitment, inclusive the potential penalty, is

$$RK_T - \frac{\psi}{1+r}\int_{-\infty}^{-K_T}(\Delta V + K_T)d\Delta V.$$

(4)

The first term of expression (4) is the current cost of committing K_T of capital to trading risk. The second term is the current value of the monetary penalty for a pre-commitment violation.

Assuming the bank minimizes (4), the capital commitment KT that satisfies an interior optimum first-order condition is,

$$R = \frac{\psi}{1+r}F(-K_T^*).$$

(5)

Expression (5) suggests how the regulator might set an appropriate penalty rate. Solving (5) for ψ leads to a penalty rate

$$\psi^* = \frac{R(1+r)}{F^*},$$

(6)

where F* represents the regulator's objective in terms of the probability of trading losses exceeding committed capital. Replacing ψ in expression (5) with the optimal penalty rate in expression (6) shows that a cost-minimizing bank will choose a capital commitment K_T^* such that

$$F(K_T^*) = F^*.$$

(7)

Expression (6) indicates that the penalty rate, +, is inversely related to the regulator's acceptable probability of losses exceeding capital. Lowering the desired prob ability of observing a breach of capital lowers the likelihood of a penalty and thereby lowers the expected penalty cost. To counter this effect, a higher penalty rate is needed. Expression (6) also indicates that the appropriate penalty rate depends on the cost to the bank of meeting the regulatory capital commitment, R (with r being of second-order importance). In general, it is difficult to know this cost as it will depend on the value of leverage to the bank. A single penalty rate that reflects the highest cost of regulatory capital will be a conservative approach in that it will lead to over-commitment by most banks. Thus, some flexibility in the penalty rate based on the likely cost of regulatory capital would be desirable.[14]

3. ANALYSIS OF THE ALTERNATIVE PROPOSALS

3.1 Regulatory Capital Objectives

It is generally believed that government's role in banking is necessitated by externalities associated with bank failures.[15] Alternative approaches can be used to reduce the severity of these externalities. A direct approach is to limit entry into banking and apply strict supervisory regulation of banks to ensure financial integrity and reduce the incidence of bank failure. Formally or informally, this requires capital standards related to bank insolvency risk. Alternatively, if the externalities are primarily generated by bank limitations in meeting depositor obligations, the externalities might be mitigated by government deposit guarantees or insurance. With deposit insurance or guarantees, moral hazard problems also necessitate risk-based capital standards to limit the potential insurance fund liability when the insurance premiums are not fully risk based (as is always the case). Thus, under either approach to reducing the risks associated with bank insolvency, risk-based capital standards are necessary.

Given their purpose, risk-based capital standards can be judged to be effective if they appropriately control the level of insolvency risk. In general, this requires relating capital standards to the bank's total risk since piecemeal measures of bank risk will not aggregate to the bank's total insolvency risk. Nonetheless, bank capital standards have been designed on a piecemeal basis. For example, current approaches divide risk according to credit (default) risks and price risks, and price risk is subdivided according to accounting

---

[14]Where R is zero, the bank would want commit equity even if $F(-K_T) < F^*$.

[15]For a review of the role of capital regulation in banking institutions, see Berger, Herring and Szego (1995).

treatment–whether the position is marked to market or valued at historical costs. Because they ignore the effects of diversification and hedging across different components of bank risk, these approaches reduce the overall effectiveness of the capital standards and make it difficult to evaluate the level of insolvency risk coverage achieved. An alternative but more limited criteria is based on a measure of the efficacy of each piecemeal standard in achieving a stipulated level of risk coverage for the portfolio component to which the standard is being applied.

In addition to the prudential efficacy objective, regulatory capital goals include efficiency objectives as well. Risk-based capital rules that fix the portfolio composition of a bank might provide the appropriate level of insolvency risk but might also make the bank unprofitable. In principal, risk-based capital requirements should leave the portfolio allocation unchanged from what it would be if shareholders had to fully bear the bank's investments' risk. Thus, given the appropriate level of insolvency coverage, the effects of the risk-based capital standards on the bank's portfolio should be neutral. Otherwise, the capital rules will distort portfolio choices and will reduce the risk-transfer efficiency of the banking system. However, because the neutrality criterion requires the consideration of the effects of individual positions on the risk of the entire portfolio, the objective cannot be satisfied when risk-based capital standards are imposed on a piecemeal basis. Under a piecemeal approach, a more limited objective is that the risk-based capital standard imply risk weights consistent with the individual positions' contributions to the risk component to which the standard is being applied. In addition to portfolio allocation consequences, efficiency must also include recognition of compliance costs, including reporting, legal, and administrative costs.

Still another objective for capital regulation is international harmonization. This goal calls for the same capital standards being applied to banks domiciled in different countries and, in principal, equal capital requirements for equal insolvency risk. Harmonization of capital regulation is believed important because of the internationalization of banking and, particularly, the move to establish a common market in financial services in EC countries. Compliance costs could be substantial if internationally active banks had to satisfy a different set of risk-based standards in every country in which they operated. If banks are subject only to the standards of the country in which they are officially domiciled, regulatory arbitrage would lead banks to locate in the country with minimum standards while maintaining operations in other EC countries with more stringent standards.

3.2 Evaluating the Alternative Approaches
3.2.1 BSC Standardized Measure
Since all three approaches to capital regulation of market trading risk are piecemeal

approaches, none can be easily quantified as to their coverage of banks' insolvency risk. As measured by the risk coverage for the trading book, the BSC standardized measure appears the weakest on both efficacy and efficiency criteria.

The standardized approach is not explicit about the intended level of overall trading risk coverage nor about the holding period over which risk is being measured. For protection against insolvency risk, the holding period should depend on the regulatory monitoring interval plus a defeasance period to enable a bank to adjust its risk exposure to satisfy possible regulatory concerns when trading account positions are reviewed. Two or three different holding periods can be detected among the various building blocks in the standardized measure.[16] How these different holding periods were arrived at and whether they are intended to reflect different defeasance periods within the trading portfolio is unclear. It seems unlikely that appropriate defeasance periods will be related simply to broad instrument category types.

The effectiveness of the standardized measure in providing an appropriate level of (trading) risk coverage is also hampered by its violation of basic principles of portfolio risk measurement. The building block method itself, because it adds measured risks across various instrument categories, is inconsistent with a measure of the total risk in the trading book. The addition of risks ignores hedging and diversification benefits among the different building blocks as it assumes return correlations of +1 for same sign positions and -1 for opposite sign positions. In reality, correlations in returns across different instrument categories are highly diverse and frequently far from unity.

Further, capital charges applied to instrument category risk exposures at best only loosely correspond to proper risk measurements. A uniform capital charge of 8 percent is applied against FX, gold, and (market risk) equity positions without regard to differences in statistically calibrated return volatilities. Where diversification and hedging are recognized, the recognition is crude and not based on explicit statistical calculations.[17] Moreover, methods for recognizing hedging and/or diversification differ among different instrument

---

[16] As described in Basle (1993), risk coverage for interest rate instruments is roughly based on a measure of monthly interest rate volatility while for FX risk, a 10-day holding period is suggested. Dimson and Marsh (1995) suggest that for the equity component weekly return uncertainty is the norm

[17] The most elaborate methodology regarding imperfect hedging are the disallowances applied to interest rate positions. The disallowance methodology-the *smaller* of the short or long weighted positions-does not correctly capture correlation effects. Under standard measures of portfolio risk the disallowances would depend on the product of weighted positions: the disallowance for positions in debt instruments I and j would be $2W_iW_j(\rho_{ij} - 1)$ where W_iW_j is the risk-weighted position and ρ_{ij} is the return correlation.

categories (e.g., methods differ among interest rate, equity, and FX categories).

Options risk measurement is also deficient. A bank with significant activity in options is required to carve out the options positions along with directly related hedging positions and measure the options risks separately from the rest of the portfolio. In general, options risk will not be separable from the rest of the portfolio. With options, the sensitivity of the portfolio value to changes in the underling securities values can be highly nonlinear and even non-monotonic. Maximum exposures need not occur at maximum changes in the underlying securities values.[18]

The deficiencies of the standardized measure suggest that it is not designed to provide any uniform measure of risk coverage across different instrument categories or trading portfolios. As the actual risk coverage will be portfolio specific, there is no single overall coverage level that is consistent with the standardized measure.

The many measurement deficiencies of the standardized approach also suggest that it will be a very inefficient system of capital regulation. The mismeasurement of positions' relative risks may distort portfolio choices if these choices are influenced by the capital requirements they engender. Further, by not granting appropriate capital relief for various hedging techniques or other risk reduction methods, the capital standards reduce the value of employing or developing such methods. An additional inefficiency comes from compliance costs. The standardized measure is different from risk measures used for internal purposes by banks with large trading operations. As such, it has the potential to generate significant reporting burdens by requiring banks to set up and maintain a complex and detailed set of records that would not be used for internal purposes but simply to enable regulators to verify compliance.[19]

Risk mismeasurement problems with the standardized risk measure have been noted by the banks in their comment letters. Some studies have argued that modern portfolio theory should be used to provide a guiding principal for a proper regulatory standard measure (e.g., Dimson and Marsh (1995), or Kim and Santomero (1988).) While the application of the principals of portfolio theory would greatly improve the BSC standardized measure, those advocating a portfolio approach have advanced these arguments in the context of a single class of instruments (equities) and have thereby side-stepped the many practical measurement

---

[18]A simple example of non-monotonicity is a butterfly spread. In a butterfly spread, the greater risk exposure occurs when the underlying instrument price changes little or not at all.

[19]For a detailed and complete elaboration of the requirements for implementation of a standardized measure, see the Bank of England (1995) document for implementation of the CAD in the United Kingdom.

difficulties created when a portfolio contains many disparate classes of instruments. In a classical equity portfolio setting, variances, covariances, and position information are sufficient statistics to construct an estimate of the risk exposure. When currencies, commodities, and interest rate products are added, risk exposure estimation is no longer as simple as it is for the case of a common stock portfolio. Risk measurement practices for multi-product portfolios are not standardized either in the academic literature or in practice at financial institutions.[20]

Further complications are introduced once non-normality of security returns are recognized (especially heavy tails and time variation in return variances) along with the substantial nonlinearities involved in options-related risks. Moreover, even among the largest and most sophisticated dealer banks who have developed techniques to estimate the risk exposure generated by the institution's global portfolio, such risk measurement practices continue to evolve.

The lack of a generally accepted standard portfolio risk measure is a major weakness of any regulatory standard measure. Any single measure, regardless of sophistication, is likely to differ significantly from the risk measure that is best for many individual bank trading portfolios and from the measures actually employed by management. These considerations suggest that it would be imprudent to codify a single regulatory standard measure for market risk. Aside from design issues, the demonstrated reluctance of supervisors to base regulations on intricate analytical and statistical formulas and the political compromises that accompany regulatory enactments at the international level (see Dimson and Marsh (1995)) further dim the prospects for a theoretically satisfactory regulatory standard risk measure.

3.2.2 *Internal Models Approach*

By relying on bank trading risk estimates used for internal purposes, the internal models approach resolves many of the problems associated with the BSC standardized approach. As currently proposed, the internal models proposal specifies a level of trading risk coverage for a particular holding period-i.e., a minimum capital charge of three times the average of the estimated two-week VaR over the last 60 days.

---

[20]For example, there is a large academic literature that investigates how many factors are required to model stock returns. As large covariance matrices require simplifying statistical structures to facilitate their estimation (e.g. the single factor market model of Sharpe(1963)), this debate and similar debates in the term structure literature illustrate that there is no commonly accepted procedure for estimating the variance-covariance matrix for large numbers of instruments covering stocks, bonds, foreign exchange and commodities in terms of a relatively small number of common factors.

Bank internal models are likely to provide a considerably more accurate measure of the bank's market trading risks and avoid the "one size fits all" criticism applicable to any regulatory standard measure. Self interest leads banks to develop internal risk measurement models specialized to efficiently measure the risks that the bank itself faces. By shifting much of the burden of market risk measurement from the supervisory agencies to the banks, regulatory capital charges can be more closely aligned with the banks' own risk exposure estimates used for operational purposes. Thus, the capital standards can more accurately reflect the regulator's desired risk coverage than with the standardized model.

The internal models' approach also is more efficient. In principal, this approach leaves to the bank the determination of individual positions relative risks and thus the capital standards should not distort portfolio choices. In practice, the quantitative standards will compromise the efficiency of the approach. Compared to the standardized measure, reporting burdens may be reduced. Aside from the limits of quantitative restrictions imposed on model estimates by the regulators, the internal models approach allows regulatory risk measures to evolve as risk measurement techniques improve and are incorporated into the risk measurement models.

Given its superiority over the BSC standardized approach, the internal models approach would appear to be a better candidate model for an international risk-based capital standard. How much international harmonization would be achieved in terms of equivalency of risk coverage for a given exposure will depend on the uniformity with which it is implemented by bank examiners across national boundaries. In any case, current proposals are for the internal models approach to be offered alongside the standardized approach. It is envisioned that the standardized measure would be adopted by EC banks and the internal models approach by U.S. banks. While this may be a temporary development, it does not further international harmonization objectives as it creates different standards in different countries. Attempting to equalize "on-average" capital charges between the two approaches by ad hoc regulator-imposed parameter adjustments to give the appearance of harmonization does not resolve their basic differences.

Although the internal models approach represents an important advance over the standardized risk measure, it still has important shortcomings that will impair its effectiveness and efficiency. The advantages of the internal models approach will be realized only if: (1) the bank's internal risk measurement model is capable of providing an accurate measure of the bank's risk exposure over a holding period of concern to regulators; and (2), that the regulatory authority can verify that each bank's model is indeed providing such an accurate measure of the bank's risk exposure. In practice, there are reasons to suspect that neither of these conditions are completely satisfied.

Operational risk measurement models are principally used to evaluate one-day trading risk exposures to aid in daily risk management operations. Even putting aside limitations in estimating one-day risk exposures, the models are not designed to measure the longer-horizon exposure that is the intended basis of a regulatory capital requirement. Time aggregation introduces complications into the statistical measurement of a portfolio's risk exposure (see Kupiec and O'Brien (1995a)). While the inaccuracies in distributional assumptions created by time-aggregation may not be insurmountable impediments to successfully implementing an internal models approach, the endogeneity of risk exposure over longer horizons creates a more fundamental problem.

Long-horizon risk exposure depends not simply on a bank's initial risk exposure, but also on its management risk strategy and the risk control system that the bank has in place. Risks are managed daily. The longer the horizon, the less important will be the initial risk exposure and the more important will be management's risk objectives and the bank's risk management system. The internal models proposal sets the capital requirement at some multiple of the model risk-estimate for an initial portfolio composition. This risk measure places undue emphasis on the initial portfolio at the expense of ignoring the importance of the bank's risk management objectives and the efficacy of its risk control systems.

Notwithstanding difficulties associated with accurate assessment of long-horizon risk exposures, even at the one-day horizon the accuracy of reported internal model risk exposure estimates is difficult to verify (Kupiec (1995)). The conceptual problem is that it is difficult to determine whether a loss that exceeds a risk model's exposure estimate is a true rare event or if the failure owes to an understatement of portfolio risk exposure. Statistical methods of discriminating among these alternatives require many years of data to reliably judge the accuracy of a risk measurement model. The verification issues suggest that it may be difficult to reliably certify a bank model's accuracy and thereby establish risk capital comparability across banks using the internal model's approach.

Because reliable performance-based verification tests require significant amounts of data, the verification process is necessarily time consuming. If a model is determined to be inaccurate, the model will be altered and the institution will begin accumulating a new performance data sample. Given the statistical properties of performance-based tests, a substantial amount of time must transpire before the accuracy of the new model can be confidently accepted. Time considerations have implications for the multiplication factor applied to the model risk estimate in the internal model proposal. If the magnitude of the factor is linked to statistical verification, in the event a bank's model is deemed inaccurate, the data requirements of verification tests suggest that the bank's scaling factor should remain elevated for a significant time period.

Partly to address these risk measurement shortcomings and to provide model comparability across banks, the internal models proposal includes various quantitative restrictions on model risk estimates-restrictions on sample estimation period, factor return covariances, measurement of options risks. The quantitative restrictions, even if necessary to address measurement and verification shortcomings, tend to make the reported risk estimates different from those the bank would prefer to use for internal purposes. The quantitative restrictions will likely reduce the accuracy of the bank's risk measures. Both the model restrictions and the qualitative standards associated with model verification will increase the cost of compliance.

3.2.3 The Pre-Commitment Approach

As with the internal models approach, the pre-commitment approach seeks a level of trading risk coverage consistent with that desired by bank regulators over a specified holding period. However, the risk coverage level under pre-commitment is not an explicit regulation as in the internal models' proposal. Rather it is determined endogenously by the pre-commitment incentive structure. By increasing the severity of the penalties, the pre-commitment approach makes it optimal for banks to commit ever larger amounts of capital for a given level of trading risk or to reduce the amount of trading risk exposure taken by the bank. While there is not a specific one-to-one observable relationship between a particular incentive schedule and the coverage a bank endogenously chooses, theoretical considerations (illustrated above) suggest that there is an approximate correspondence between the penalty structure and the coverage provided by the approach.

The pre-commitment approach also differs from the internal models approach in that it does not attempt to measure the risk associated with a fixed portfolio. Instead, it relates capital coverage to risk exposure defined by the distribution of potential profits or losses on trading activity over the designated holding period. By basing the capital requirement explicitly on a maximum loss pledge, the bank's risk taking strategy and risk management ability, as well as standard determinants of portfolio risk as reflected in its internal model risk estimates, become directly involved in setting its capital commitment. The penalties associated with a breach of the capital commitment provide the incentives to commit honestly and to manage risk to stay within the commitment.

The pre-commitment approach is less intrusive into the bank's risk management function than is the internal models approach. If a bank is well-managed and never violates its pre-commitment, there is no demonstrated need for supervisory intrusion into the risk management process beyond normal regulatory monitoring and periodic examinations. Should a bank violate its pre-commitment, it has demonstrated a risk management shortcoming that may merit supervisory attention. The approach significantly reduces the reporting burden generated under the standardized approach and (perhaps to a lesser degree) under the internal models approach. Further, under the pre-commitment approach, the need for statistical risk exposure estimate verification schemes are eliminated because a violation of the pre-commitment can be observed in changes in the mark-to-market values of the bank's trading book.

Two limitations of the pre-commitment approach are its failure to cover go-for- broke behavior without supervisory monitoring and its failure to distinguish between a bank's intentions and its results when imposing a penalty. The first of these concerns limits the applicability of the pre-commitment approach to banks for whom go-for- broke is not a realistic possibility. The second imposes a cost on banks (in expected value terms) even when their capital commitment is appropriate and their trading risk is well managed. There are capital incentive mechanisms in the banking literature that ostensibly would avoid the particular limitations of the pre-commitment approach, but these mechanisms may have even less desirable features.

To remove the go-for-broke incentive, John, John, and Senbet (1991) advance an incentive scheme that imposes a tax on high returns earned by a bank. In this scheme, there is no penalty when there are losses. Despite the attractiveness of removing the go-for-broke complication, this proposal is not practical. It is doubtful that regulators (much less an international organization) legally would be allowed to judgementally impose a 100 percent tax on a bank's trading profits or that the U.S. Congress would (or should) enact a tax specifically aimed at expropriating high bank profits.

More narrowly, there is no objective method to determine the threshold level of acceptable profit associated with prudent risk choices. This threshold cannot be determined via a pre-commitment approach since banks would simply indicate a profit so high as to never violate it under any risk choice. The upper tail of the prudently managed portfolio must be specified by the regulator or some outside party. Such a determination raises criticisms identical too those that surround the BSC standard risk measure.[21]

Chan, Greenbaum, and Thakor (1992) (CGT) take a different approach. CGT design a risk-based insurance and capital scheme where each institution chooses from a downward sloping schedule of insurance premiums and capital. Applied to trading risk, banks might pay an additional insurance premium inversely related to the amount of capital earmarked for the trading book. There would be no *ex post* penalty or evaluation of trading returns relative to

---

[21]Regulator judgments of abnormally high trading profits for a specific bank, however, can be useful as a signal to more closely monitor the bank's actions.

committed capital.[22] If the capital and premium schedule is appropriately constructed, banks with higher trading risk choose higher premiums and lower capital commitments and lower risk banks choose lower premiums and higher capital. Bank risk choice is revealed *ex ante* and thus the scheme does not require penalties for poor performance.

This scheme, however, is not as attractive at it might first seem.[23] Under the common view that underlies risk-based capital standards, firms with high asset or portfolio risk should hold a higher capital (and possibly pay higher default or insurance premiums).[24] In contrast, under CGT, the greater the risk of the portfolio the lower the capital committed. It is doubtful this result will appeal to those concerned with preventing bank failures even if the deposit insurance fund is being adequately compensated. It is also possible that the potential for unmonitored risk-taking is so great as to dictate a very steep inverse schedule of premiums and capital that makes a high level of capital and low risk the norm for the industry.

The CGT mechanism is a pure incentive scheme, without monitoring or information on returns. Campbell, Chan, and Marino (1992) (CCM) make an effective argument that monitoring, though costly, can still be cost effective as a partial substitute for higher capital requirements. CCM also consider the need for regulator incentives to assure the effectiveness and appropriate level of monitoring. While lacking formal analysis, the pre-commitment approach would use public disclosure to provide credibility to the policy, as well as to enhance bank capital commitment incentives

4. CONCLUDING COMMENTS

Regulatory and industry views on the appropriate method for setting bank capital standards for market risks have evolved away from the use of regulatory standard model approaches and toward the use of banks' internal risk estimates. This evolution represents a promising development as internal-model based approaches have clear advantages both in terms of the

---

[22]CGT assume that realized returns are not observable. This assumption is not entirely consistent with their assumption that capital is observable. For an ongoing bank, income for period t-1 is a part of capital at the start of period t.

[23]To be fair, CGT use their model principally to argue that fairly-priced deposit insurance is possible only if shareholders earn profits on deposit issuance, significantly extending the arguments in Buser, Chen, and Kane (1981). Given a deposit-related value, they do then suggest their incentive scheme as a potential risk-based insurance pricing mechanism.

[24]While the recently enacted FDIC risk-based insurance schedule makes the insurance premium inversely related to the bank's capital ratio, the insurance premium is related to the risk based capital ratio.

effectiveness and efficiency of risk-based capital standards. Although the growing recognition of the potential usefulness of internal models is a promising development, an internal models approach may not represent the optimal method as it focuses only on the risk measurement of a static portfolio and thereby ignores fundamentally important determinants of a bank's trading risk-its risk-taking strategy and its risk management ability. Although the pre-commitment approach has yet to gain international support and is still in its conceptual stage, it attempts to improve upon the shortcomings of the internal models approach by basing capital requirements on a more inclusive and inherently more efficient measure of trading risk.

A clear weakness in existing and proposed risk-based capital standards is their piecemeal approach to the bank's total risk. This weakness is likely to become even more noticeable as products and techniques for allocating risks, such as credit derivatives and structured notes, continue to develop. While a whole-bank approach to capital standards appears to be a desirable goal, it does not appear achievable at this juncture. Aside from the important limitations generated by differences in accounting treatments across components of the bank, few banks (and no regulators) currently could provide an acceptable measure of all-in bank risk.

This review has been selective. Among important issues not covered is the issue of what to include in a measure of bank capital. Standard finance conventions would define capital as the bank's equity value less the net implicit value of any deposit insurance guarantees which would approximately correspond to the market value of the bank's assets less the risk-free discounted value of the bank's liabilities. Current market risk proposals are also considering including limited amounts and forms of bank debt in the measure of bank capital.

REFERENCES

Bank of England 1995, Implementation in the United Kingdom of the Capital Adequacy Directive, April.

Basle Committee on Banking Supervision, 1995, The Supervisory Treatment of Market Risks, April, Bank for International Settlements, Basle Switzerland.

Berger Allen, Richard Herring and Giorgio Szego, 1995, The Role of Capital in Financial Institutions, *Journal of Banking and Finance*, 19, June, 393-430.

Buser, S. A., A.H. Chen, and E.J. Kane, 1981, Federal deposit insurance, regulatory policy, and optimal bank capital, *Journal of Finance*, September, 51-60.

Campbell, Tim, Yuk-Shee Chan, and Anthony Marino, 1992, An Incentive- Based Theory of Bank Regulation, *Journal of Financial Intermediation* 2, 255-276.

Chan, Yuk-Shee, Stuart I Greenbaum, and Anjon Thakor, 1992, Is Fairly- Priced Deposit Insurance Possible? *The Journal of Finance* 47, March, 227-245.

Carosio, Giovanni 1990, Problems of Harmonization of the Regulation of Financial Intermediation in the European Community, *European Economic Review*, 34, 578-586.

Dimson, Elroy, and Paul Marsh 1995, Capital Requirements for Securities Firms, *Journal of Finance* 50, No. 3, 1219-1233.

Federal Reserve Board, 1995a, Risk-Based Capital Standards: Market Risks, July.

Federal Reserve Board, 1995b, Request for Comment on the Pre-Commitment Approach for Market Risks, docket No. R-0886, July.

Federal Reserve Board, 1995c, Final Rule on Interest Rate Market Risk Pursuant to Section 305 FIDICIA, docket No. R-0884, July.

Hartman, Phillip, 1995, Capital Adequacy and Foreign Exchange Risk Regulation, mimeo, June, DELTA (ENS), Paris, France.

John, K., T. John, and L. Senbet, 1991, Risk-shifting incentives of depository institutions: A new perspective on federal deposit insurance reform, *Journal of Banking and Finance* 15, 895-915.

Kane, Edward, 1995, Three paradigms for the role of capitalization requirements in insured financial institutions, *Journal of Banking and Finance*, June, 431-459.

Kim, Daesih and Anthony Santomero, 1988, Risk in Banking and Capital Regulation, *The Journal of Finance*, December, 1219-1233.

King, Mervyn, 1990, International Harmonization of the Regulation of Capital Markets: An Introduction, *European Economic Review* 34, 569-577.

Kupiec, Paul and James O'Brien, 1995a, The Use of Bank Measurement Models for

Regulatory Capital Purposes, FEDS Working Paper No. 95-11, Federal Reserve Board, March.

Kupiec, Paul and James O'Brien 1995b, A Pre-Commitment Approach to Capital Requirements for Market Risk, FEDS Working Paper No. 95-34, Federal Reserve Board, July.

Kupiec, Paul 1995, Techniques for Verifying the Accuracy of Risk Measurement Models, *Journal of Derivatives* 3 (Winter), 73-84.

Levonian, Mark, 1994, Bank Capital Standards for Foreign Exchange and Other Market Risks, *Economic Review* 1, 3-18, Federal Reserve Bank of San Francisco.

Schaefer, Stephen 1990, The Regulation of Banks and Securities Firms, *European Economic Review* 34, 587-597.

Sharpe, William 1963, A Simplified Model for Portfolio Analysis, *Management Science* 9, 277-293.

Derivatives, Regulation and Banking
Edited by B. Schachter
© 1997 Elsevier Science B.V. All rights reserved.

Chapter 14
NETTING AGREEMENTS AND POTENTIAL CREDIT EXPOSURE

Darryll Hendricks[†]
Federal Reserve Bank of New York, New York, NY, USA

1. INTRODUCTION

The dramatic growth of over-the-counter (OTC) derivatives markets in recent years has necessarily created substantial credit exposures for institutions, particularly dealers, that are active in these markets. Indeed, recent data suggests that the outstanding notional amounts of interest-rate and cross-currency swap instruments alone come to nearly US$4 trillion. A crude and conservatively low estimate of the actual credit exposures of these contracts would be based on 1% of the notional amount, or $40 billion. Clearly, the appropriate management of these credit exposures is a topic of major concern for OTC market participants, in spite of the very low rates of contract default observed to date.

Bilateral close-out netting agreements are an important tool for managing the credit exposures faced by active participants in OTC derivatives markets. These agreements are intended to provide legal certainty that, in the event of a counterparty's default, legal obligations arising from transactions covered by the netting agreement are based solely on the net value of such transactions. In other words, with an enforceable netting agreement in place a defaulting firm could not simultaneously claim payment for positively-valued derivative contracts while withholding payment on negatively-valued contracts. Thus, an institution's credit exposure to another firm will be equal not to its gross exposure (the sum of all positive-value contracts), but to its net exposure (the sum of all contract values or zero, whichever is greater).

[†]The views expressed here are those of the author and not necessarily those of the Federal Reserve Bank of New York or the Federal Reserve System. I would like to thank Arturo Estrella, Beverly Hirtle, John Simpson, Philip Strahan, and participants at the Queen's University conference on Managing and Regulating Off-Balance Sheet Risks for helpful comments and discussions. I am grateful to Greg Duffee for providing me with access to the CRSP bond file data. All errors are the sole responsibility of the author.

Clearly, the reduction of current credit exposure from a gross to a net value can be substantial, particularly if an institution has many positive- and negative-value contracts with a counterparty. Current credit exposures, however, are only one facet of the credit-risk management problem faced by active participants in derivatives markets. Because of the speed with which the market values of derivative instruments can change, especially when measured as a percentage of their current market values, current credit exposures are typically highly volatile. It is therefore prudent for institutions to develop estimates of the extent to which credit exposures can increase over measured time intervals. This component of credit exposure is typically referred to as potential or contingent credit exposure.

It is clear that, while potential credit exposure could be measured in a variety of ways, it is crucially related to the volatility of current credit exposures. In fact, a common way of measuring potential exposure is to express it as a multiple (typically two or three times) of the standard deviation of current exposure over a specified time interval. A somewhat more robust approach to measuring potential credit exposure is to base it on a specified percentile of the probability distribution of the change in current credit exposure. Conservative measures of potential exposure (e.g., 95th percentile) can frequently rival or even exceed the current credit exposure in magnitude.

The main focus of the current paper is an investigation of whether netting agreements reduce potential exposure. I attempt to specify the conditions under which netting agreements will reduce potential exposure and to identify the major factors influencing the extent of this reduction. These issues turn out to be surprisingly complex, given the obvious reduction in current credit exposures that netting agreements typically provide.

The plan of the paper is as follows. Section 2 introduces a conceptual framework for thinking about potential credit exposure. Section 3 analyzes the factors that influence the potential credit exposure of a portfolio of contracts with a single counterparty but not covered by a netting agreement. Section 4 analyzes the case where a netting agreement is in force. Section 5 extends the analysis to a portfolio encompassing multiple counterparties. Section 6 concludes.

2. POTENTIAL CREDIT EXPOSURE — BASIC CONCEPTS

Potential credit exposure is a significant concern for institutions with active OTC derivatives portfolios. Since OTC contracts do not typically entail such credit-risk-reducing measures as daily variation margin, the high levels of volatility (as a percentage of contract value) imply the possibility of substantial increases in credit exposure over time. This potential credit exposure can be assessed by calculating the probability distribution of the change in credit exposure over the relevant time interval. If the time interval is short, one day for example, then potential exposure is small. The drawback to such a short time interval, of course, is that the calculation of current credit exposure and the allocation of capital to cover current and potential exposures must also be performed on a daily basis. For these reasons, a longer horizon on the order of three or six months may be more appropriate.

A separate issue is the question of what feature of the probability distribution of the change in credit exposure to focus on in assessing the degree of potential exposure. A natural candidate is the 95th percentile of the probability distribution. The use of this measure would imply only a 5% chance that the actual credit exposure would increase by more than this amount over the relevant time period. Obviously, the 90th percentile would be a more liberal measure, while the 99th percentile would be more stringent. In general, percentile-based measures have a great deal to recommend them; risks can be gauged with consistency, for example. On the other hand, it is difficult to develop intuition about percentiles.

An alternative measure that is often used is the mean of the probability distribution plus either two or three standard deviations of the distribution. If the probability distribution of the change in exposure is normal, then a two-standard-deviation measure is equivalent to a 97.7th percentile measure, and a three-standard-deviation measure is equivalent to a 99.9th percentile measure. If the distribution is not normal, then it is not possible to establish exact equivalencies, although Chebyshev's inequality guarantees that a two- (three-)standard-deviation measure cannot be equivalent to anything less than a 75th (89th) percentile measure.[1]

In the discussions below, I often focus on the standard deviation of the probability distribution of the change in credit exposure rather than the 95th percentile of the distribution. This is because it is usually much easier to think about the behavior of the standard deviation than the behavior of the 95th percentile. Moreover, the behavior of the standard deviation is also a reasonably good guide to the behavior of the 95th percentile. This is borne out by the simulation results I present later on, where I show both the standard deviation and the 95th percentile. In other words, even though the standard deviation is almost never the whole story, it is almost always a large part of the story.

The arguments below will therefore frequently refer to both the mean and the standard deviation of the change in credit exposure, either of a single contract or of a set of contracts. It is important to understand that these measures are not the same as the mean and the standard deviation of the change in value of the contract or the set of contracts. The value

---

[1] Chebyshev's inequality requires finite first and second moments of the probability distribution.

of a contract can be either positive or negative.[2] Credit exposure can only be positive; if a contract has negative value, the credit exposure on that contract is zero.[3] Mathematically, the relation between contract value and credit exposure can be expressed as follows.

$$x_t = \max(0, v_t).$$ (1)

In this equation, v_t represents the value of a contract at time t, and x_t represents the credit exposure associated with this contract at time t. It naturally follows that the expression for the change in the credit exposure between time s and time t is that shown in equation 2.

$$\Delta x = x_t - x_s = \max(0, v_t) - \max(0, v_s) = \max(0, v_s + \Delta v) - \max(0, v_s).$$ (2)

It should be clear from this expression that the change in credit exposure, Δx, will not necessarily be equal to the change in the value of the contract, Δv. Furthermore, then, it cannot be expected that the mean and standard deviation of the change in credit exposure will equal the mean and standard deviation of the change in contract value.

In general, the mean change in exposure is positive. One way of seeing this is to focus on the possible scenarios. Assuming that the distribution of changes in contract value is symmetric about zero, the definition of credit exposure implies that negative changes to a positively-valued contract will not always be fully reflected in the change in credit exposure since exposure cannot fall below zero. Similarly, the only changes in the value of an initially negatively-valued contract that are reflected in a change in exposure are positive ones. Thus, a symmetric (and mean zero) distribution of contract value changes is translated into an asymmetric distribution of credit exposure changes that has a positive mean.

It is also clear that the level of credit exposure itself, given in equation 1, has a positive mean. In fact, it can be shown that the mean credit exposure is proportionately related to the standard deviation of the contract value.[4] Intuitively, this makes sense since large negative contract values lead to zero exposure while large positive values lead to large positive exposures. Thus, if the probability of observing both large positive and large negative contract values rises, the mean value will not rise, but the mean exposure will.

A similar result can also be obtained for the mean change in credit exposure over a given time interval. Namely, the expected change in credit exposure over this interval will tend to rise proportionately with the standard deviation of the change in contract value.

---

[2]The arguments that follow in this section apply equally well to a set of contracts taken as a whole.

[3]Bankruptcy of the counterparty in this case would not typically result in a windfall gain. That is, the bankruptcy of the counterparty would not imply a release from the obligation to pay off on the contract.

[4]An excellent summary of results on truncated distributions can be found in the appendix to Maddala (1983).

Moreover, the standard deviation of the change in exposure also turns out to depend greatly on the standard deviation of the change in contract value. This too conforms with intuition. The more widely contract values fluctuate over a given time interval, the more widely we would expect credit exposures to fluctuate over the time interval as well.

This implies that the standard deviation of the change in contract value is a very important determinant of the distribution of the change in credit exposure and therefore of potential credit exposure. This is true since both the mean change in credit exposure and the standard deviation of the change in credit exposure will tend to be linearly related to the standard deviation of the change in contract value. Thus, a measure of potential exposure based on the mean change in exposure plus two standard deviations of the change in exposure will be very sensitive to the standard deviation of the change in contract value.

3. POTENTIAL CREDIT EXPOSURE — NO NETTING

This section analyzes potential credit exposure for a portfolio of contracts with a single counterparty, but not covered by a netting agreement. It is common to refer to the credit exposure on such a portfolio as the gross exposure of the portfolio. In the absence of a netting agreement, the portfolio credit exposure is found by summing the credit exposures of the individual contracts. This contrasts with a net exposure calculation, where the individual contract values are aggregated first, and the portfolio credit exposure is based on this net portfolio value. These two methods of calculating credit exposure are summarizedbelow.

No Netting Agreement — Gross Exposure

$$X_t = \sum_{i=1}^{N} \max(0, v_{it})$$

Netting Agreement — Net Exposure

$$X_t = \max(0, \sum_{i=1}^{N} v_{it})$$

In the equations above, the summations are taken over the N contracts with the single counterparty. X_t represents the credit exposure of the entire portfolio with the counterparty. It is immediately clear from the equations that the net exposure cannot be larger than the gross exposure. This does not imply, however, that the potential exposure measured using gross exposures will always be larger than the potential exposure measured using net exposures. In fact, appendix A contains a simple example where the reverse is true.

3.1 Influences on Gross Potential Exposure — Statistical Argument

Since the gross exposure of a portfolio of contracts is simply the sum of the exposures of the individual contracts, it follows that the change in the gross exposure of a portfolio is equal to the sum of the changes in the exposures of the individual contracts. Thus, the expected change in the exposure of the portfolio will simply equal the sum of the expected changes in exposure of each individual contract. This means that the expected change in the gross exposure of a portfolio of contracts will tend to rise linearly with the volume of contracts.[5] A similar line of reasoning can be used to show that this is also true of the expected level of gross credit exposure.

As discussed in section II, the volatility of the change in credit exposure is a very important determinant of potential exposure. In fact, as simulation results below bear out, the standard deviation of the change in gross credit exposure tends to be much more important than the mean change in gross credit exposure. This implies that an understanding of potential exposure requires an analysis of the factors that determine the standard deviation of the change in gross exposure. Unfortunately, the properties of the standard deviation of the change in gross exposure are not as simple to derive as those of the expected change in gross exposure.

It is possible, however, to make some simplifying assumptions that render the problem more tractable. While these assumptions do remove some elements of realism from the analysis, they make it possible to develop intuition about the major determinants of potential exposure. The first assumption made is that all contracts have distributions of both current values and changes in value that are symmetric about zero. This assumption seems particularly reasonable for a portfolio of interest-rate swaps. Second, I assume that the variance of the change in value over a given time interval is the same for all of the contracts in the portfolio. This assumption greatly simplifies the analysis while likely sacrificing little in terms of understanding.

Changes in the credit exposures of individual contracts over a given time interval will tend to be concentrated among those contracts that have positive value at the beginning of the interval. I will refer to such contracts as ITM (in-the-money) contracts, and to negatively-valued contracts as OTM (out-of-the-money) contracts. For the sake of exposition, I focus on the extreme case where no contract changes sign over the interval.[6] That is, the natural tendency for changes in exposure to be concentrated in the ITM subset of contracts is taken to the limit. Under these conditions, the change in the gross exposure of the portfolio simply equals the sum of the changes in the values of the ITM contracts.

The standard deviation of the change in gross exposure under these conditions, $\sigma_{\Delta G}$

---

[5] I use the term "volume of contracts" rather than "number of contracts" since contracts are not all alike in terms of notional principal, among other features.

[6] I stress that this assumption is made for exposition only. It is not necessary for the results below and is not imposed on the simulations.

can therefore be written in terms of the standard deviation of the change in the value of each contract, σ, and the correlations of changes across different contracts, ρ_{ij}. Of course, if $i=j$, then this correlation equals one. Assuming that there are k ITM contracts, the following expression results.

$$\sigma_{\Delta G} = \sigma \sqrt{k + \sum_{\substack{i=1}}^{k} \sum_{\substack{j=1 \\ i \neq j}}^{k} \rho_{ij}} \;. \tag{3}$$

The double summation sums over all of the $(k^2 - k)$ correlations between the changes in the value of different ITM contracts. It is clear from equation 3 that the standard deviation of the change in the gross exposure of the portfolio will tend to rise proportionately with the standard deviation of the change in individual contract values. Furthermore, it is also positively related to the sum of the correlations between different contracts. Note that it is the sum of these correlations that matters; any combination of correlations that results in the same sum yields the same result in equation 3.

Now let $\bar{\rho}_{ITM}$ equal the average correlation across all of the ITM contracts, excluding the correlations between each contract and itself. Thus,

$$\bar{\rho}_{ITM} = \frac{\displaystyle\sum_{\substack{i=1}}^{k} \sum_{\substack{j=1 \\ i \neq j}}^{k} \rho_{ij}}{k^2 - k} \tag{4}$$

This quantity can be thought of as a measure of the extent to which changes in the values of the ITM contracts move together. If $\bar{\rho}_{ITM}$ is zero, then there is no tendency for the changes in the values of the ITM contracts to move together. The maximum value of $\bar{\rho}_{ITM}$ is one, in which case, the changes in the values of all ITM contracts are perfectly correlated with each other. The minimum value of $\bar{\rho}_{ITM}$ is achieved when the changes in the ITM contract values are such that they always offset each other so that the sum of the changes is always zero. This occurs when $\bar{\rho}_{ITM}$ equals -1/(k-1). Note that this is typically far closer to zero than it is to -1 if k is large.

The definition of $\bar{\rho}_{ITM}$ allows equation 3 to be rewritten in the following simpler form.

$$\sigma_{\Delta G} = \sigma \sqrt{k + (k^2 - k)\bar{\rho}_{ITM}} \tag{5}$$

This equation implies that the standard deviation of the change in gross exposure of the portfolio depends on three variables: (1) the standard deviation of the change in contract value, (2) the number of ITM contracts in the portfolio, and (3) the average correlation of changes across different ITM contracts. The first two of these variables are relatively

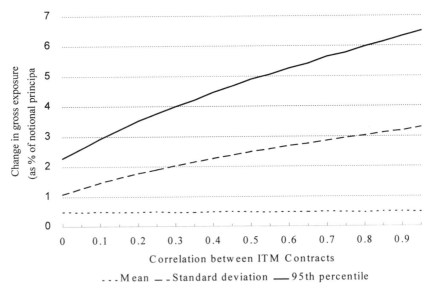

Figure 1
Figures for gross exposures in the chart are based on 50,000 simulations of portfolios of 25 swaps with a single counterparty. The initial values of the swaps are drawn from independent standard normal distributions. The changes in swap values are drawn from normal distributions with variance = 0.1, and correlations as given on the x-axis based on the signs of the initial values. Swaps whose initial values have the same sign have a correlation equal to the value shown on the x-axis. Swaps whose initial values are of opposite sign have a correlation equal to the negative of the value shown on the x-axis.

straightforward. The third, however, depends on the nature of the contracts held in the portfolio. Before analyzing this issue further, however, I now turn to simulation evidence on the effect of each of these variables on gross potential exposure.

3.2 Influences on Gross Potential Exposure — Simulation Evidence

This sub-section reports the results of simulation experiments designed to examine the distributions of changes in gross exposure under a variety of conditions. Simulations are needed because the probability distributions of the changes in exposure are, in general, too difficult to derive analytically.[7] Each simulation iteration begins by drawing contract values

---

[7]This is primarily the result of relaxing the assumption that ITM contracts cannot become OTM and vice-versa.

randomly from independent standard normal distributions. Thus, on average, the portfolio of contracts will consist of equal numbers of both ITM and OTM contracts. This and other features of the simulation are designed to mimic the characteristics of an inter-dealer portfolio as opposed to a portfolio with an end-user, which would be expected to be more one-sided on average. The reason for focusing on inter-dealer-like portfolios is that the scope for netting is generally greater for such portfolios.

Given a set of initial contract values, the gross exposure of the portfolio is then calculated by summing the values of the ITM contracts. Next, random changes are added to the initial contract values. These changes are also drawn from normal distributions with mean zero. However, the variance of the distribution of the changes is less than one. Even more important, however, the simulations induce correlations between these changes depending on the contracts' initial values. If the initial values of a pair of contracts have the same sign, then the correlation between the pair is set to a positive value. If the initial values have the opposite sign, then the correlation of the pair is set to a negative value. The absolute value that correlations are set to is the same for all pairs of contracts and all iterations of a given simulation. In this way, the simulation explicitly controls the value of $\bar{\rho}_{ITM}$.

Figures 1, 2, and 3 depict the mean, standard deviation, and the 95th percentile of the change in gross exposure as three parameters are adjusted. Figure 1 adjusts the magnitude of the induced correlation ($\bar{\rho}_{ITM}$) between zero (ITM contracts uncorrelated) and 0.95 (ITM contracts nearly perfectly correlated). Figure 2 adjusts the number of contracts in the simulated portfolio. Figure 3 adjusts the variance of the change in individual contract value. Because the volatilities of the changes in the values of the simulated contracts are set arbitrarily, the vertical scale is also arbitrary in the sense that it does not reflect actual instrument volatilities. The numbers are comparable, however, across the three figures. Note also that since the numbers are not calculated as percentages of the initial exposure, they can be interpreted as percentages of (arbitrary) notional principal amounts.

As is seen clearly in Figure 1, an increase in the correlation of ITM contracts ($\bar{\rho}_{ITM}$) produces a corresponding increase in the standard deviation and 95th percentile of the distribution of the change in gross exposure. In other words, if the ITM contracts are highly correlated, potential exposure measured on a gross basis is high. This result is exactly what the statistical argument developed above predicted. Moreover, equation 5 also would have predicted that the standard deviation of the change in gross exposure would rise roughly with the square root of $\bar{\rho}_{ITM}$. This too appears to be the case in the simulation experiment. Needless to say, this reinforces that it would be very useful to know what the correlation of the ITM contracts is in a typical swap portfolio.

Figure 2 shows that, when $\bar{\rho}_{ITM}$ is set to 0.5, potential exposure (as a % of notional

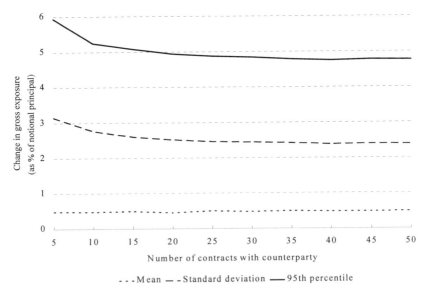

Figure 2
Figures for gross exposures in the chart are based on 50,000 simulations of portfolios of swaps with a single counterparty. The initial values of the swaps are drawn from independent standard normal distributions. The changes in swap values are drawn from normal distributions with variance = 0.1, and correlations equal to either 0.5 or -0.5. Swaps whose initial values have the same sign have a correlation equal to 0.5. Swaps whose initial values are of opposite sign have a correlation equal to -0.5. The x-axis shows the number of swaps with the counterparty.

principal) tends to fall as the number of contracts in the portfolio (and thus the notional principal) increases. As the analysis above suggested, the mean change in gross exposure as a percentage of notional principal remains constant as the size of the portfolio increases. The standard deviation of the change in gross exposure does, however, tend to fall somewhat with the number of contracts in the portfolio. This is because the effect of changes in k in equation 5 is not necessarily proportional. If $\bar{\rho}_{ITM}$ were equal to one, then the standard

deviation of the change in gross exposure would rise proportionately with k, and would thus remain constant as a percentage of total notional principal. If $\bar{\rho}_{ITM}$ were equal to zero, then the standard deviation of the change in gross exposure would tend to rise proportionately with the square root of k, and would thus decline with the square root of the total notional principal. The results in Figure 2 fall somewhere between these two extremes.

Figure 3 shows how the distributional characteristics of the change in gross exposure vary with the variance of the changes in contract value. Since many financial contract values have a variance of future value that grows linearly with time, Figure 3 can also be interpreted as showing the effect of a lengthening time horizon on potential exposure.[8] As expected from equation 5, the standard deviation of the change in gross exposure grows less than proportionately with the increase in variance (time horizon).

3.3 What is the Average Correlation of ITM Contracts?

As predicted by statistical argument and confirmed by simulation experiment, the correlation between the changes in contract values of those contracts that are currently ITM ($\bar{\rho}_{ITM}$) is crucial to the magnitude of gross potential exposure. Thus far, little has been said about the likely values of this quantity except that it must lie between -1/(k-1) and 1. In fact, the value of $\bar{\rho}_{ITM}$ will depend on the nature of the contracts held in the portfolio. This sub-section focuses on the case where the portfolio of contracts consists of U.S. dollar interest-rate swaps. While this a somewhat special case, it is an extremely important case, and it illustrates the complexity of this issue.

When attention is restricted to only the ITM subset of a typical interest-rate swap portfolio, it is quite likely that the correlation between changes in contract value is positive. To see this, consider a swap portfolio with an equal mixture of pay-fixed and pay-floating swaps. Swaps of like type (that is, two pay-fixed swaps or two pay-floating swaps) tend to be highly positively correlated with each other, while swaps of opposite type (that is, a pay-fixed paired with a pay-floating or vice-versa) tend to be highly negatively correlated. Thus, two swaps randomly chosen from this portfolio (with replacement) will tend to be have an average correlation of zero, since it's equally probable that the correlation between the two swaps will be highly positive or highly negative.

On the other hand, if we restrict our selection of swaps to the subset that it is currently ITM, then it is less likely that this correlation will average out to zero. This is because the subset of the portfolio that is ITM may be biased toward one or the other type of swap. For example, if interest rates have been moving steadily downward for some time, then it is probable that the ITM swaps will be predominantly of the pay-floating type. On the other hand, if interest rates have been moving upward for a long time, then it is more likely that the ITM swaps will be predominantly pay-fixed. In either of these cases, the correlation of the changes in value of two ITM swaps chosen at random will be positive, leading to greater

---

[8]Importantly, however, these simulations do not include payments. Thus, there is only a diffusion effect evident here, no amortization effect.

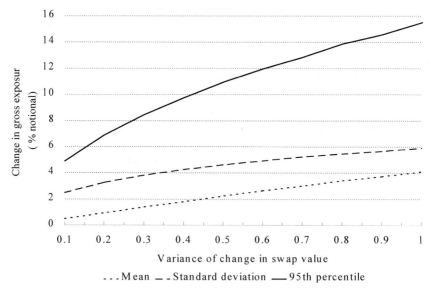

Figure 3
Figures for gross exposures in the chart are based on 50,000 simulations of portfolios of 25 swaps with a single counterparty. The initial values of the swaps are drawn from independent standard normal distributions. The changes in swap values are drawn from normal distributions with the variance shown on the x-axis, and correlations equal to either 0.5 or -0.5. Swaps whose initial values have the same sign have a correlation equal to 0.5. Swaps whose initial values are of opposite sign have a correlation equal to -0.5.

potential exposure.

In general, this argument implies the possibility that the average correlation of ITM swaps ($\bar{\rho}_{ITM}$) will be positive. Moreover, if interest rates have been moving steadily in one direction, then we would expect $\bar{\rho}_{ITM}$ to be closer to one, while if rates have been moving more or less aimlessly, we would expect $\bar{\rho}_{ITM}$ to be closer to zero. To provide further insight into the possible values of $\bar{\rho}_{ITM}$ for an interest-rate swap portfolio, I also examine historical and simulated term structures and their effects on a simulated swap portfolio.

Consider a swap portfolio that adds new matched pairs of one-year, two-year, three-year, four-year, and five-year swaps each month. In steady-state, this portfolio will consist of sixty pairs of swaps that were originally five-year swaps, forty-eight pairs that were originally four-year swaps, thirty-six pairs that were originally three-year swaps, twenty-four pairs that were originally two-years swaps, and twelve pairs that were originally one-year

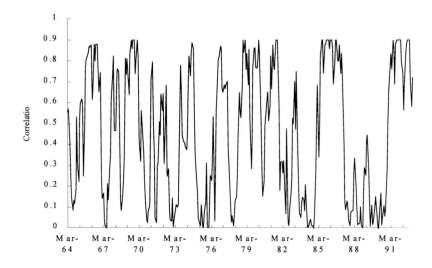

Figure 4
The figure is based on a simulation of a perfectly matched interest-rate swap portfolio. Each month during the simulation, new matched pairs of one-year, two-year, three-year, four-year, and five-year swaps are initiated. The portfolio therefore consists of 360 swaps, of which 180 always have positive value. The fixed rates for the swaps are chosen so that the swap values are zero at initiation. Yield curve movements are based on historical discount bond yields in the United States from February 1959 to December 1992 (see footnote 9 in the text for sources). The correlation of the in-the-money (ITM) swaps on a given date is calculated by averaging the correlations of the positive-value swaps. These correlations were calculated via a separate, initial simulation that calculated the correlations of the change in values of swaps of different maturities over this time period.

swaps. The distribution of swaps by remaining maturity will be staggered; at any given time there will be five pairs with one month remaining, for example, while only one pair with fifty-four months remaining. The greater concentration of swaps with shorter remaining maturities is consistent with the composition of typical inter-dealer portfolios.

This hypothetical swap portfolio is tracked as the underlying term structure of interest rates evolves through time. Two term-structure evolutions are considered: (1) the actual observed term structure in the U.S. from February 1959 to December 1992[9], and (2) a

---

[9]Yields for months 1-6 are from the Six-Month Treasury Bill Yield file and yields for months 12, 24, 36, 48, and 60 are from the Fama-Bliss Discount Bond file, both from the Center for Research in

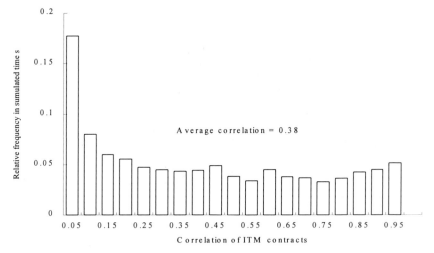

Figure 5
The figure is based on a 500-year simulation of a perfectly matched interest-rate swap portfolio. Each month during the simulation, new matched pairs of one-year, two-year, three-year, four-year, and five-year swaps are initiated. The portfolio therefore consists of 360 swaps, of which 180 always have positive value. The fixed rates for the swaps are chosen so that the swap values are zero at initiation. Yield curve movements are based on the Longstaff-Schwartz (1992) two-factor term-structure model. The correlation of the in-the-money (ITM) swaps on a given date is calculated by averaging the correlations of the positive-value swaps. These correlations were calculated via a separate, initial simulation that calculated the correlations of the change in values of swaps of different maturities. The figure shows the frequency distribution of the simulated time series of ITM contract correlations.

simulated term structure evolution generated by the two-factor term-structure model developed by Longstaff and Schwartz (1992). In both cases, new swaps are added to the portfolio every month with fixed rates set so that the values of the new swaps are zero. As the term structure evolves, some of these swaps move ITM, while others move OTM. Every month, the correlations between all ITM swaps are calculated. If there are k ITM swaps, then there will be $(k^2 - k)/2$ correlations to calculate.

Calculation of the correlation between any two swaps in the portfolio is straightforward. The process begins with calculation of the correlation between pay-fixed

Security Prices (CRSP) Bond File. Linear interpolation is used to determine other zero-coupon yields. These data can be used to construct the pure discount-bond term structure needed to correctly price and value interest-rate swaps.

(pay-floating) swaps of different maturities. That is, the term structure data is first used to develop a database that contains, as an example, the correlation between a pay-fixed swap with three years remaining and one with two years remaining.[10] Correlations between like-type instruments are always substantially positive, while correlations between opposite-type instruments are always highly negative. The absolute value of the correlation between any pair tends to rise as their maturities converge. This database of correlations is used as a look-up table for the correlations of the ITM instruments.

If the ITM subset currently consists of predominantly pay-fixed swaps, then most of the look-ups for that point in time will lead to positive correlations. If the ITM subset has a number of both pay-fixed and pay-floating instruments, then there will be many look-ups that lead to negative correlations. The $(k^2 - k)/2$ correlations thus calculated can then be averaged to provide a summary measure of the extent of correlation between ITM swaps at that point in time. This procedure is repeated every month to produce a time series of this summary correlation measure ($\bar{\rho}_{ITM}$).

The time series so generated using historical data is depicted in Figure 4. It covers the years 1964-1992, since a five-year initialization period is needed to determine the fixed rates for all of the swaps. As can be seen, the correlation of the ITM contracts in this hypothetical portfolio is almost always positive, although it varies dramatically between zero and a maximum value. This maximum value is equal to the average correlation across all pay-fixed (pay-floating) contracts. Attaining this maximum implies that all of the ITM contracts are of only one type. A clear implication of Figure 4 is that $\bar{\rho}_{ITM}$ can change extremely rapidly. Yet if $\bar{\rho}_{ITM}$ can change very rapidly, the earlier results of this section (equation 5 and Figure 1) imply that gross potential exposure can also change very rapidly, since it depends crucially on the correlation of the subset of ITM contracts.

On average, the time series shown in Figure 4 equals 0.45. This is relatively close to the value produced when a simulated term structure is used instead of historical data. Figure 5 depicts the frequency distribution of the observed summary correlation of ITM contracts based on a 500-year simulation of monthly observations using the Longstaff-Schwartz model. The average correlation using this model is 0.38.[11] From Figure 1, these results imply an

---

[10]It is possible to implement this because the correlation between two swap instruments is not very sensitive to the fixed rates of the swaps.

[11]Results from a hypothetical portfolio where the distribution of swaps by remaining maturity is flat (i.e., only a new five-year swap is initiated each month) are similar. The average value of $\bar{\rho}_{ITM}$ for this portfolio is 0.49 using historical data and 0.45 using the Longstaff-Schwartz model.

average level of potential exposure roughly double that for a portfolio where ITM contracts are uncorrelated. Bear in mind, however, that actual portfolios will consist of instruments with different base currencies and will also possibly include different instrument types. Thus, these values likely overstate the actual correlation of the ITM contracts that would be observed for a typical portfolio of OTC derivative products.

4. POTENTIAL CREDIT EXPOSURE — WITH NETTING

This section focuses on the potential credit exposure of a portfolio of contracts with a single counterparty that are covered by a valid close-out netting agreement. I refer to the potential exposure of this portfolio as the net potential exposure since the credit exposure is based on the net value of all contracts, including both ITM contracts and OTM contracts.

4.1 Influences on Net Potential Exposure — Statistical Argument

The analysis of net potential exposure is in fact somewhat simpler than the analysis of gross potential exposure. This is because it is possible to apply the analysis of the credit exposure on a single contract directly to the entire portfolio of contracts, by virtue of the ability to net contract values before assessing the credit exposure. That is, equation 2 above can be applied directly to the case of a netted portfolio of contracts, where x_t now represents the net exposure of the portfolio at time t and v_t represents the net value of the portfolio at time t. Furthermore, the analysis of section 2 can also be applied directly to the case of a netted portfolio of contracts.

The analysis of section 2 implies that both the expected change in credit exposure and the standard deviation of the change in credit exposure of a single contract are linearly related to the standard deviation of the change in the value of that contract. Since this analysis applies equally to a netted portfolio of contracts, it follows that the standard deviation of the change in the value of the netted portfolio is the crucial determinant of net potential exposure.

As in section 3, I assume that all of the contracts in the portfolio have distributions of both levels and changes that are symmetric about zero and that the variances of the changes in contract values are identical across contracts. These assumptions imply that the standard deviation of the change in the value of the netted portfolio of contracts is given by the following expression, where σ is the standard deviation of the change in the value of an individual contract, and n is the number of contracts in the portfolio.

$$\sigma_{\Delta N} = \sigma \sqrt{n + (n^2 - n)\overline{\rho}_{ALL}}. \tag{6}$$

The quantity ρ_{ALL} is defined analogously to $\bar{\rho}_{ITM}$, except that ρ_{ALL} is the average correlation over all n contracts in the portfolio, not simply the k ITM contracts.

$$\bar{\rho}_{ALL} = \frac{\displaystyle\sum_{i=1}^{n}\sum_{j=1,j\neq i}^{n} \rho_{ij}}{n^2 - n}. \tag{7}$$

Note that $\sigma_{\Delta N}$ is <u>not</u> itself the standard deviation of the change in net credit exposure; it is rather the standard deviation of the change in the net value of the portfolio. Of course, these two quantities are very closely linked, and $\sigma_{\Delta N}$ is much easier to work with.

As with the analysis of gross credit exposure, there are three variables with significant influences on the size of net potential exposure. These are (1) the standard deviation of the change in contract value, σ, (2) the number of contracts with the counterparty, n, and (3) the average correlation between changes in contract value, ρ_{ALL}. From equation 6, the effect of σ will be similar to its effect on gross exposures. Namely, net potential exposure will tend to rise linearly with the standard deviation of the change in the value of an individual contract.

The effect of the number of contracts in the portfolio, n, will depend on the value of ρ_{ALL}. If ρ_{ALL} is close to zero, then the standard deviation of the change in the net portfolio value will increase at the same rate as the square root of the number of contracts. Since the standard deviation of the change in net portfolio value is the major determinant of both the mean change in net exposure and the standard deviation of the change in net exposure, this implies that if ρ_{ALL} is close to zero, net potential exposure will tend to increase at the same rate as the square root of the number of contracts. This contrasts with gross exposure, where the expected change in gross exposure increases at the same rate as the number of contracts and the standard deviation of the change in gross exposure increases at a rate somewhere between the number of contracts itself and its square root.

These statistical arguments thus suggest that, if ρ_{ALL} is close to zero, then the expected change in net exposure will be smaller than the expected change in gross exposure. In addition, if $\bar{\rho}_{ITM}$ is significantly above zero, then the standard deviation of the change in net exposure will also be smaller than the standard deviation of the change in gross exposure. This gives rise to one clear conclusion with regard to netting agreements. If the average correlation of the change in contract value across all contracts (ρ_{ALL}) is close to zero and if the average correlation of the change in contract value across the ITM contracts ($\bar{\rho}_{ITM}$) is substantially positive, then a netting agreement will reduce the potential exposure of the portfolio.

It is also clear that equation 6 implies that the standard deviation of the change in the net portfolio value will increase with ρ_{ALL}. In the last several paragraphs, it has been implied

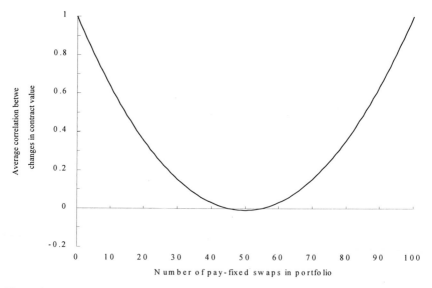

Figure 6
The figure is based on a hypothetical portfolio of 100 swaps, each with a standard deviation of the change in swap value equal to one. The figure shows how the average correlation between the changes in the values of the swaps ($\bar{\rho}_{ALL}$ from the text) changes as the number of pay-fixed swaps in the portfolio is varied. All pay-fixed swaps are assumed to be perfectly correlated with each other, as are all pay-floating swaps. Pay-fixed swaps are assumed to be perfectly negatively correlated with pay-floating swaps. The figure shows that the average correlation falls below zero only if the number of pay-fixed swaps in the portfolio is between 45 and 55.

that a likely value for ρ_{ALL} is near zero. The reason for this assumption is a focus on inter-dealer portfolios. If the portfolio is with an end-user, then all of the contracts in the portfolio are likely to be similar and ρ_{ALL} is likely to be substantially positive. On the other hand, an inter-dealer portfolio is likely to consist of a variety of contract types, so that the correlation across different contracts will average close to zero.

Some market participants might even be tempted to argue that, in an inter-dealer portfolio, $\bar{\rho}_{ALL}$ is likely to come close to achieving its minimum value of $-1/(n-1)$. This would occur, for example, if the portfolio consisted entirely of exactly matched pairs of contracts. While it is unlikely that many portfolios have exactly this composition, it is very likely that inter-dealer portfolios will tend to have equal numbers of opposite-type contracts. For example, if the portfolio is an interest-rate swap portfolio, then it is likely to have roughly equal numbers of pay-fixed and pay-floating contracts. If this caused $\bar{\rho}_{ALL}$ to achieve its minimum value then the standard deviation of the change in the net value of the portfolio would shrink to zero and there would be no potential exposure at all. While this extreme case is unlikely, it is clearly important to know where $\bar{\rho}_{ALL}$ is likely to fall within the range from $-1/(n-1)$ and 0.

Some insight into this question can be gained by imagining a hypothetical portfolio of 100 interest-rate swaps. In this hypothetical portfolio, there are only two types of swap, a pay-fixed variety and a pay-floating variety. All swaps of each type are identical in every respect, and swaps of opposite type are perfectly negatively correlated. Now consider how the average correlation of this portfolio ($\bar{\rho}_{ALL}$) changes as the number of pay-fixed swaps in the portfolio varies from 0 to 100. At both extremes, if all of the swaps in the portfolio are pay-floating or pay-fixed, then $\bar{\rho}_{ALL}$ will equal 1. If there are exactly 50 of each type, then $\bar{\rho}_{ALL}$ will achieve its minimum value (in this case, -0.0101). A graph of the average correlation of the portfolio as the number of pay-fixed swaps is varied is shown in Figure 6.

It is somewhat difficult to discern from Figure 6, but the average correlation crosses the zero-boundary when there are either 45 or 55 pay-fixed swaps in the hypothetical portfolio. The implication is that a portfolio needs to be quite closely matched in order to push the average correlation below zero. In fact, if we imagine a portfolio of 100 swaps where the percentage of pay-fixed swaps is the result of random draws of swaps, and where it is equally likely to draw a swap of either type, then the long-run average of the average correlation is zero.[12] This implies that the assumption of a value of zero for $\bar{\rho}_{ALL}$ is likely the correct assumption for a swap portfolio that maintains an equality between different types of swaps only on average.

The assumption of matching opposite types of contracts only on average would seem to be the appropriate one for most inter-dealer portfolios. If, however, active risk-management measures are taken to keep the portfolio more closely matched at all times, then the appropriate value of $\bar{\rho}_{ALL}$ for the portfolio will fall below zero and thus equation 6 would imply a further reduction in the net potential exposure of the portfolio. By active risk-management measures, I have in mind a system where the choice of a dealer for a new contract would be based on the relative degree of matching in the existing portfolios with other dealers. That is, if a new pay-fixed contract needed to be assigned to a dealer (perhaps because of the demand for a pay-floating contract with an end-user), the chosen dealer would be the one with the lowest current proportion of pay-fixed contracts.

---

[12]FMore precisely, if the number of pay-fixed swaps in the portfolio is binomially distributed with 100 trials and a 50% chance of success (pay-fixed) on each trial, then the expected value of $\bar{\rho}_{ALL}$ for this portfolio is zero.

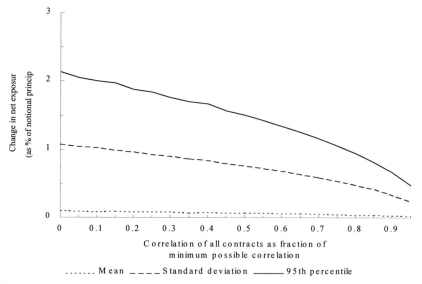

Figure 7
Figures for net exposures in the chart are based on 50,000 simulations of portfolios of 25 swaps with a single counterparty. The initial values of the swaps are drawn from independent standard normal distributions. The changes in swap values are drawn from normal distributions with variance = 0.1, and correlations between zero and a minimum possible value (in this case, -0.042) as given on the x-axis. The values on the x-axis are not themselves correlations, but instead are ratios of the actual correlation to the minimum possible correlation. Thus, the correlations between changes in swap values decline as one moves right across the x-axis.

A simple simulation example illustrates the potential benefits of such a risk-management scheme. On the one hand, imagine ten inter-dealer portfolios with a mixture of 100 swaps as described in the previous few paragraphs. Each period, there is a turnover of one swap in each portfolio. That is, one swap matures while a new one is added. The chance of the new swap being a pay-fixed swap is 50%. Thus, on average, each portfolio consists of an even mixture of pay-fixed and pay-floating swaps. Over a long period of time, the average value of the average correlation of each portfolio ($\bar{\rho}_{ALL}$) is zero, as was shown above. Contrast this with the situation where the ten new swaps each period are allocated based on existing proportions of swaps. That is, the new pay-fixed swaps are allocated first to those dealers with the lowest proportion of pay-fixed swaps. Under this scheme, each portfolio continues to consist of an even mixture of both types of swaps, on average. Importantly, however, the long-run average value of $\bar{\rho}_{ALL}$ under this scheme falls to -0.009.

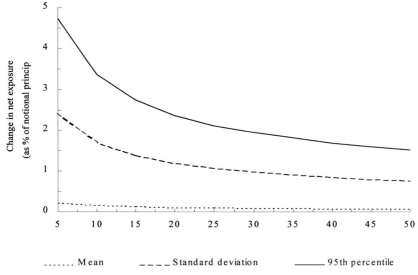

Figure 8
Figures for net exposures in the chart are based on 50,000 simulations of portfolios of swaps with a single counterparty. The initial values of the swaps are drawn from independent standard normal distributions. The changes in swap values are drawn from normal distributions with variance = 0.1, and zero correlation. The x-axis shows the number of swaps with the counterparty.

This number may appear to be trivially different from zero, but it is not. In fact, it is 89% of the way between zero and the minimum possible value of $\bar{\rho}_{ALL}$. Examination of either equation 6 or the simulation results below show that this would result in a significant further reduction in net potential exposure.

4.2 Simulations of Changes in Net Exposure

This sub-section reports the results of simulation experiments designed to examine the factors influencing the probability distribution of changes in net exposure. The design of the experiments is similar to those of section 3. Each simulation iteration begins by drawing contract values randomly from independent standard normal distributions. Given a set of initial contract values, the net exposure of the portfolio is then calculated by summing the values of all of the contracts and then comparing this sum with zero. If the sum is positive, the net exposure is equal to the sum; if negative, it is equal to zero. Next, random changes are added to the initial contract values. These changes are also drawn from normal distributions with mean zero. However, the variance of the distribution of the changes is less than one. The simulations also induce correlations between these changes. The induced correlation is the same across all contracts.

Figures 7, 8, and 9 are the net counterparts to Figures 1, 2, and 3. In this case, however, Figure 7 shows how the distribution of changes in net exposure is affected as the average correlation between all contracts ($\bar{\rho}_{ALL}$) varies between zero and its minimum possible value. The horizontal axis plots $\bar{\rho}_{ALL}$ as a fraction of the minimum possible correlation, so that $\bar{\rho}_{ALL}$ is becoming more negative (i.e., closer to its minimum value) reading right across the axis.[13]

Notice that, if the average correlation across contracts is zero (i.e., $\bar{\rho}_{ALL}$ achieves zero percent of its minimum possible value), the standard deviation of the change in net exposure is essentially identical to the standard deviation of the change in gross exposure when the average correlation of ITM contracts is also zero (see Figure 1). As the average correlation becomes more negative, however, the standard deviation and therefore the 95th percentile of the change in net exposure fall substantially. For example, Figure 7 suggests that a reduction in $\bar{\rho}_{ALL}$ from zero to 90% of its minimum possible value would result in a reduction of potential exposure on the order of 50%.[14]

Figures 8 and 9 demonstrate the sensitivity of net exposures to the number of contracts and to the variance of the change in the value of individual contracts. Note from Figure 8 that, when $\bar{\rho}_{ALL}$ equals zero, the expected change in net exposure falls with the number of contracts. This result could be easily predicted from equation 6, and is in contrast to the results from Figure 2, which demonstrate that the expected change in gross exposure does not change with the number of contracts. Even more importantly, the standard deviation of the change in net exposure falls off more rapidly as the size of the portfolio increases than does its gross counterpart (see Figure 2). This result, predictable from equations 5 and 6, implies that reductions in potential exposure due to netting, if any, will be more pronounced (in percentage terms) for larger portfolios.

The results of Figure 9, however, are similar to those of Figure 3, suggesting that the

---

[13]he reason for reporting the horizontal axis in this fashion is that the changes in the average correlation itself occur over a very small numerical range. It thus seemed more informative to indicate the extent to which this correlation came close to its minimum possible value.

[14]Not shown on Figure 7 is the possibility that $\bar{\rho}_{ALL}$ might be positive. For portfolios with end-users, is very likely to be positive, implying little or no reduction in potential exposure.

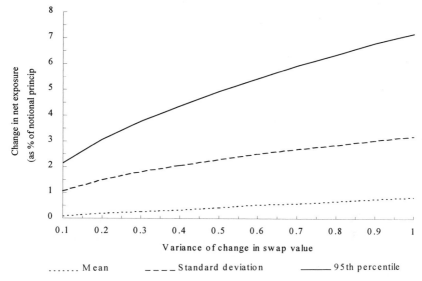

Figure 9
Figures for net exposures in the chart are based on 50,000 simulations of portfolios of 25 swaps with a single counterparty. The initial values of the swaps are drawn from independent standard normal distributions. The changes in swap values are drawn from normal distributions with the variance shown on the x-axis, and correlations equal to zero.

degree of reduction in potential exposure from netting agreements, if any, is not affected by either the time horizon over which potential exposure is measured or by the relative volatility of the instruments under consideration.[15]

5. EXTENSION TO MULTIPLE COUNTERPARTIES

The two previous sections have explored the factors that influence the potential exposure of a portfolio of contracts with a single counterparty, both with and without a valid netting agreement in place. The analysis in those sections suggests that there are conditions under which netting agreements can reduce potential exposure for individual counterparties.

---

[15]This does not mean that the nature of the instruments is irrelevant. As noted at the end of section III, the wider the range of instruments covered by the netting agreement, the less one would expect to observe extremely high values of $\overline{p}_{ITM}$.

In particular, if changes in the values of ITM contracts are typically more highly correlated than are the changes in the values of all contracts taken together, then netting agreements will tend to reduce potential exposure. Moreover, this effect will be visible for individual counterparties. Yet most active institutions deal with a large number of counterparties, and this remains true even if attention is restricted to dealer counterparties.

At first glance, it might seem that the addition of multiple counterparties does little to alter the conclusions of the analysis. Since bilateral netting agreements cover only one counterparty's contracts, there would seem to be no reason to examine the interaction between the portfolios of multiple counterparties. This is incorrect, however. The analysis of credit exposure to multiple counterparties is nearly exactly analogous to the analysis of gross credit exposures to a single counterparty. Because netting is not allowed across counterparties, the exposures to multiple counterparties must be aggregated on a gross rather than a net basis.

The aggregate (across multiple counterparties) potential exposure will be large if the standard deviation of the change in the aggregate credit exposure is large. Recall from section III, however, that the standard deviation of the change in gross exposure is strongly influenced by the correlation between the changes in the values of the ITM contracts. In the current context, this implies that the size of the change in aggregate potential exposure will be strongly influenced by the correlation between the changes in the values of the ITM counterparty portfolios. This correlation measures the degree to which positively-valued counterparty exposures tend to move together. If all counterparty exposures tend to move in unison, then obviously the change in aggregate potential exposure is greater than if there is diversity in their movements.

Netting agreements influence this correlation because they affect the nature of the quantities that are relevant. Without netting agreements, counterparty exposures are measured on a gross basis, but with netting agreements, they are measured on a net basis. If changes in net counterparty exposures are less highly correlated across counterparties than are gross counterparty exposures, then netting agreements provide a benefit in addition to those discussed in previous sections. Needless to say, the existence of this benefit depends on the scale of these two correlations.

On the one hand, it is quite likely that the correlation of the changes in gross counterparty exposures across counterparties is substantially positive. This will be the case if changes in the values of ITM contracts are even mildly correlated, as long as the gross exposure of each counterparty consists of a sum of many such ITM contracts. A simple illustration should make this point clear. Assume that the correlation of the change in the value of ITM contracts with each other is given by ρ. Now assume that there are two counterparties, each of whom has n ITM contracts in their portfolio and that no netting agreements are in place. The correlation of the change in the sum of the values of these n contracts between the two counterparties, P, is given by the following expression.

$$P = \frac{\rho n}{\rho n + (1 - \rho)}. \tag{8}$$

Thus, if there are 25 ITM contracts with each counterparty, and changes in the values of ITM contracts have a correlation equal to 0.05, the correlation between the counterparty sums will be 0.57. This calculation dramatically underscores the general point that the sums of even mildly correlated variables will turn to be quite highly correlated.

It is much more difficult to predict the correlation between changes in counterparty exposures if these exposures are measured on a net basis. While in general it seems unlikely that net exposures will be as highly correlated as the previous paragraphs suggest that gross exposures will be, it is difficult to know for sure. Net exposures will tend to be the product of greater or lesser imbalances between different types of instruments, some currently ITM and some currently OTM. It makes sense that those counterparties with positive net exposures will tend to have some similarities in portfolio composition so that there is likely to be positive correlation across counterparties even when exposures are measured on a net basis.

There is simply a great deal of variety, however, in the types of portfolios that would have a positive net exposure at any given moment. On the one hand, this variety makes it very difficult to generalize about the likely correlation across net counterparty exposures. On the other hand, it also suggests a lesser tendency toward high, positive correlations than I have argued is likely for gross counterparty exposures.

Unfortunately, the conclusions of this section are less clear-cut than those of previous sections. In summary, however, netting agreements can provide additional reductions in aggregate potential exposure if changes in gross counterparty exposures tend to be more highly correlated across counterparties than are changes in net counterparty exposures. While there are good reasons for suspecting that changes in gross counterparty exposures will be substantially positively correlated across counterparties, generalizations about changes in net counterparty exposures are difficult.

6. CONCLUSIONS

The appropriate management of credit exposure is an increasingly important task for institutions that are actively involved in OTC derivatives markets. While bilateral netting agreements clearly serve a valuable purpose in limiting the size of current credit exposures, the extent of their efficacy in limiting potential exposures is much less clear. This paper has attempted to cast some light on this issue, primarily by focusing on the ability of netting agreements to reduce the volatility of current credit exposures.

In the absence of a netting agreement, changes in the credit exposures to individual counterparties can be large. To a significant extent, this is the result of the fact that changes in gross credit exposure are primarily driven by a non-random subset of the contracts with the counterparty. The subset of in-the-money (ITM) contracts will tend to share similar sensitivities to changes in market factors, thereby rendering this subset more volatile than a diversified subset of contracts. For example, if the ITM subset of an interest-rate swap portfolio consists primarily of either pay-fixed or pay-floating contracts, then the volatility of this subset of contracts will be high and gross potential exposure will also be high.

In contrast, net exposures will be based on all of the contracts with the counterparty. Particularly if the counterparty is another dealer, this set of contracts will probably be more diverse in type than the ITM subset. If this is the case, then net exposures can be expected to be less volatile than gross exposures. This result is very sensitive, however, to the makeup of the ITM subset of contracts. Figure 4 demonstrates that, even for a portfolio of interest-rate swaps, the behavior of the ITM subset of contracts can change drastically over short periods of time.

This implies that observed changes in the ratio of the change in net exposure to the change in the gross exposure will fluctuate with changes in the makeup of the ITM subset of instruments. Thus, the ratio of net to gross will be low when ITM contracts are similar and therefore highly correlated. The ratio of net to gross will be high when the subset of ITM contracts is a diverse one, implying low correlations across ITM instruments. In general, the volatility of changes in gross exposures is itself quite a volatile quantity.

It seems obvious that additional reductions in potential exposure can be achieved if counterparty portfolios consist of closely-matched pairs of contracts. While this is true, it is also the case that the matching must be quite close to reduce net exposures below that of a random selection of different contract types. This, then, is likely not the primary reason why netting agreements can reduce potential credit exposure. The primary reason is the one summarized in the last few paragraphs.

It is worth considering, however, the role that risk management systems could play in keeping inter-dealer portfolios more closely matched. The results in section IV suggest that even a simple system could possibly reduce net potential exposures by up to 50%.

Finally, it is also important to consider the possibility that changes in net counterparty exposures may be less correlated across counterparties than are gross counterparty exposures.

If so, then netting agreements can reduce potential exposures by an even larger amount.

Under the right conditions, netting agreements can reduce potential credit exposures as well as current credit exposures. There will not always be a reduction, however, and evaluating the probable size of the reduction accurately requires significant knowledge of the portfolio's composition. Clearly, netting agreements are an important tool for managing some of the risks inherent in the contemporary financial system. The properties of these agreements turn out to be surprisingly complex, however, suggesting that their usage be accompanied by a sound analysis of their likely effects.

APPENDIX

This Appendix demonstrates the possibility that netting agreements can, in fact, increase potential credit exposure under certain conditions. The table below illustrates possible changes in portfolio credit exposure, both with and without counterparty netting agreements. The initial values for each of the four hypothetical swaps are given in the row entitled "Initial Swap Value". Swaps 1 and 2 are with counterparty A, while swaps 3 and 4 are with counterparty B. It is assumed that the values of each of the swaps can either rise by $5 or fall by $5. There are thus sixteen possible cases to consider. The shaded columns give the changes in net replacement costs for each of the sixteeen cases with and without netting agreements. Assuming that each of the sixteen cases is equally likely, it is clear that regardless of the measure of potential exposure used, it is higher if netting agreements are in place.

	Counter-party A		Counter-party B		Without Netting		With Netting	
	Swap				Portfolio Exposure	Change	Portfolio Exposure	Change
	1	2	3	4				
Initial value	10	-10	10	-10	20	NA	0	NA
Case 1	-5	-5	-5	-5	10	-10	0	0
Case 2	5	-5	-5	-5	20	0	0	0
Case 3	-5	5	-5	-5	10	-10	0	0
Case 4	5	5	-5	-5	20	0	10	10
Case 5	-5	-5	5	-5	20	0	0	0
Case 6	5	-5	5	-5	30	10	0	0
Case 7	-5	5	5	-5	20	0	0	0
Case 8	5	5	5	-5	30	10	10	10
Case 9	-5	-5	-5	5	10	-10	0	0
Case 10	5	-5	-5	5	20	0	0	0
Case 11	-5	5	-5	5	10	-10	0	0
Case 12	5	5	-5	5	20	0	0	10
Case 13	-5	-5	5	5	20	0	0	10
Case 14	5	-5	5	5	30	10	10	10
Case 15	-5	5	5	5	20	0	0	10
Case 16	5	5	5	5	30	10	20	20

REFERENCES

Duffee, Greg, 1993, Historical Simulations of Interest-Rate Swap Replacement Costs, unpublished memorandum, Federal Reserve Board of Governors, Washington, D.C.

Estrella, Arturo, 1992, Gross Notional Principal, Net Replacement Cost, and the Potential Credit Exposure of Plain Vanilla Swaps, unpublished paper, Federal Reserve Bank of New York, New York.

Estrella, Arturo and Darryll Hendricks, 1993, Netting and Potential Exposure: A Simple Statistical Illustration, unpublished paper, Federal Reserve Bank of New York, New York.

Hendricks, Darryll, 1992, Swap Credit Exposure Add-ons: Portfolio and Netting Effects, unpublished paper, Federal Reserve Bank of New York, New York.

Longstaff, Francis and Eduardo Schwartz, 1992, Interest Rate Volatility and the Term Structure: A Two-Factor General Equilibrium Model, *Journal of Finance* 47, 1259-82.

Maddala, G.S., 1983, *Limited-Dependent and Qualitative Variables in Econometrics*, Cambridge University Press, Cambridge, England.

Derivatives, Regulation and Banking
Edited by B. Schachter
© 1997 Elsevier Science B.V. All rights reserved.

365

Chapter 15
A PROPOSED FRAMEWORK FOR STUDYING THE DOMINO EFFECT

Leonard Schneck[†]

University of Kentucky, Lexington, KY, USA

1. INTRODUCTION

Many government officials, regulators, and others have described scenarios whereby the failure of an intermediary in the swap market causes other intermediaries to fail in a "domino"-like effect, with potentially significant adverse systemic consequences. While the prediction is indeed a dire one, no careful analysis of this problem has appeared to date.[1]

This chapter describes a model that, while a simplification of the realities[2] of the actual swaps market, nevertheless is rich enough to capture the important stylized elements of that market. The model incorprates varying hedging horizons for for counterparties, interdealer hedging by intermediaries (possibly with futures), diversification by intermediaries, both systematic and idiosyncratic risk, and innovations to counterparty hedging needs. In the first section of this paper, the formal model is developed. Therein the important parameters that describe the functioning of this model swap market are described, and include the swap tenor; the variance of the uncertain cash flow, the variance of both the systematic risk factor and the idiosyncratic risk; the sensitivity of the cash flows to the factor risk; the number of counterparties, the amount of capital of the intermediary, the effectiveness of the intermediary's hedge, and the number of marketmakers.

This model gives us a framework that will permit exploration of a multitude of issues surrounding the swaps market, such as the parameters that contribute to the risk of a swap

---

[†]Assistant Professor of Finance.

[1]As Peter Field, Editor-in-Chief of *Risk* magazine, reported, "...no-one at the [International Swap and Derivatives Association's July 1993 conference] could cite any serious academic research in progress on the subject.". Field (1993).

[2]As must be all models.

portfolio and the parameters that help to ameliorate this risk, the role of the interdealer market in serving to reduce systemic risk and the other risks introduced by interdealer trades, and the scenarios producing a possible domino effect and how controls, such as marking-to-market, concentration limits, and risk-based capital, help to lower the possibilities of such an effect.

The second section of the paper outlines an analysis of the probability of multiple inter-related bankruptcies, hence a domino effect. A complete analysis of this issue awaits follow-up work

2. ANALYTICAL FRAMEWORK

As it is commonly described, the domino effect is initiated by a default affecting a swap dealer. A default that affects OTC derivatives positions can occur either as a result of a failure to perform under the terms of an OTC derivatives contract or as a result of a failure to perform under other financial obligations, for example, omitting an interest payment on a debt obligation, which may trigger early termination of the defaulting party's swaps through cross-default clauses. If a default by one market participant imposes cash flow constraints on its counterparties of sufficient magnitude, then it is possible that one or more of the defaulting party's counterparties may be unable to meet some of their payment obligations, thus generating a chain of defaults. In order for this to occur, the amount owed by the defaulting party to the counterparty must represent a significant source of funds to the counterparty for meeting its other obligations and the counterparty must be unable to fund the shortfall with borrowing. Thus concerns over concentration are tied closely to the domino effect. In order to assess the likelihood and potential consequences of a domino effect, we should formulate an analytical framework that can evaluate the composition and quality of OTC derivatives portfolios' counterparties, the market values of the transactions in the portfolios, internal control mechanisms for limiting concentration risk, the effect of default on the ability of counterparties to continue making payments on other obligations, the speed with which the portfolio of the defaulting party can be unwound and the losses attendant thereto, and the impact of regulatory intervention. Such a task would be a formidable challenge. We choose to approach the problem within a simpler framework, which we believe still offers the possibility of important insights, leaving a more fully articulated model for future work. As will be seen below, even the simple framework adopted here contains several fairly complex elements.

In order to develop a model for better understanding the interdependencies among swaps dealers, we start by adapting the model of Campbell and Kracaw (1991).[3] In this model there exist several counterparties or end-users (the total number of whom is represented by n and indexed by i) who wish to hedge a series of uncertain future cash flows. We expand this model to include several intermediaries or marketmakers or dealers (the total number of which is represented by ℓ and indexed by k) who offer marketmaking services for fixed for floating swaps, customized as to their payment terms. We denote the expectation at time t of the uncertain future cash flow of a counterparty at time τ periods after t as

$$v_{it}^{k}(t+\tau).$$

It is usually asserted that a principal advantage of a swap over exchange listed instruments is the flexibility with which the transaction may be designed. We will therefore assume that all swap contracts are tailored to perfectly hedge the risk exposure of the counterparty. Therefore, the floating or future payment that a marketmaker promises at time t to deliver to the counterparty τ periods in the future under the swap, is structured to match the end-user's time t evaluation of the random future cash flow, or

$$v_{it}^{k}(t+\tau).$$

The corresponding promised fixed payment from the counterparty to the marketmaker is

$$f_{it}^{k}(t+\tau).$$

We will assume that all end-users wish to convert a floating cash outflow to a fixed one, so they all will receive floating and pay fixed under their swaps. Note also that it is possible that, as time passes, the end-user may revise his estimate of the random future cash flow, which will induce him to enter into additional swaps in the future, as we shall see below.

We assume that each swap has a zero value initially. Additionally, for simplicity, and with no loss of generality, we assume that transaction costs are zero (i.e., no bid-ask spread, front-end fees, etc.), so that the promised fixed payment is equal to the expected floating payment.

$$f_{it}^{k}(t+\tau) \;=\; v_{it}^{k}(t+\tau). \tag{1}$$

In this model all counterparties who decide to directly hedge via available instruments are beyond our scope. Rather we are interested only in those counterparties who enter into a swap from a marketmaker. Assume each counterparty deals exclusively with a single

---

[3]Campbell and Kracaw (1991).

marketmaker,[4] with marketmaker k constructing a portfolio of n^k swaps[5] such that

$$\sum_{k=1}^{\ell} n^k = n. \tag{2}$$

That is, each counterparty enters into one swap to hedge its exposure, so the total number of swaps equals the total number of counterparties. Note we are not modelling the choice among dealers by the end-user.[6]

The marketmaker is only interested in the net cash flow at $t+\tau$ from all swap transactions, taking into account any natural hedges on her book; or

$$c_t^k(t+\tau) = \sum_{i=1}^{n^k} \left[v_{it}^k(t+\tau) - f_{it}^k(t+\tau) \right]. \tag{3}$$

The term in brackets is the profit or loss in that period from the swap with one counterparty. There will be a profit if the floating rate is less than fixed rate. In order to model these cash flows, it is necessary to make some further simplifications.

Assume that each counterparty has a cash flow horizon of τ_{max}; that is, counterparties have expected cash flows from the current time t until time $t+\tau_{max}$. Each end user must re-evaluate all his future hedging needs each period as each future cash flow within his horizon experiences an innovation $\epsilon_{it}^k(t+\tau)$ in each time period τ within the τ_{max} window.[7] To keep things relatively simple, we assume that the new information each end user receives about any given future cash flow is independent of the new information received about all other future cash flows, and the information one end-user receives about his future cash flows is independent of the information received by other end-users (more specifically, the innovations are independently and identically normally distributed with zero mean and standard deviation σ_ϵ).

---

[4]This is strictly not true in practice, as large end-users may have more than a dozen dealer relationships. We use this simplifying assumption, while conceptualizing a counterparty who deals with multiple dealers as having his transactions with each dealer indexed by a different i subscript (i.e., as if each dealer relationship were a different end-user). We must later take this into consideration when we introduce idiosyncratic shocks to single counterparties.

[5]We will label all actual swap contracts executed with a single intermediary over all time horizons a swap where any cash flows with the same horizon have been netted.

[6]Modelling this decision would require substantially more analysis, inasmuch as the equilibrium distribution of end-user business would have to be determined.

[7]Since the future cash flow was perfectly hedged, this innovation represents a shock to the future business or financing needs of the counterparty.

We assume that each end user's cash flow can be affected by one market wide factor which affects all end-users' cash flows in the same way and one idiosyncratic factor, so that the uncertain cash flows evolve from period to period as

$$v_{it}^k(t+\tau) = v_{i,t-1}^k(t+\tau)\left[1 + \beta\delta_t + \zeta_{it}^k(t+\tau)\right],$$

$$\begin{bmatrix} \delta_t \\ \zeta_{i_1 t}^k(t+\tau) \\ \zeta_{i_2 t}^k(t+\tau) \end{bmatrix} \sim \text{IID MVN} \begin{bmatrix} \sigma_\delta^2 & 0 & 0 \\ 0 & \sigma_\zeta^2 & 0 \\ 0 & 0 & \sigma_\zeta^2 \end{bmatrix}, \quad \forall i_2 \neq i_1, \tag{4}$$

where δ_t is the factor shock, $\zeta_{it}^k(t+\tau)$ is the idiosyncratic shock, and β is the common, time-invariant sensitivity of the cash flows to the factor shock.[8] The net cash flow at time $t+\tau$ from all swaps between an intermediary and a counterparty is then

$$\begin{aligned} c_i^k(t+\tau) &= v_i^k(t+\tau) - f_i^k(t+\tau) \\ &= \sum_{\iota=1}^{\tau_{max}}\left[\epsilon_{i,t-1}^k(t+\tau)\prod_{\kappa=0}^{\iota-1}\left(1 + \beta\delta_{t-\kappa} + \zeta_{t-\kappa}\right) - \epsilon_{i,t-1}^k(t+\tau)\right]. \end{aligned} \tag{5}$$

At any time t within the cash flow horizon, the variable cash flow at $t+\tau$ consists of a portion which is known (innovations prior to or at t) and a portion which has not yet occurred (after t). Since the innovations have zero mean, the known past quantities are also the expectation of the variable cash flow, resulting in a time t expectation of the net cash flow from intermediary k to counterparty i at $t+\tau$ of[9]

$$\begin{aligned} c_{it}^k(t+\tau) &= v_{it}^k(t+\tau) - f_{it}^k(t+\tau) \\ &= \sum_{\iota=1}^{\tau_{max}-\tau}\left[\epsilon_{i,t-1}^k(t+\tau)\prod_{\kappa=0}^{\iota-1}\left(1 + \beta\delta_{t-\kappa} + \zeta_{t-\kappa}\right) - \epsilon_{i,t-1}^k(t+\tau)\right] \end{aligned} \tag{6}$$

and an uncertain future cash flow, given this known cash flow at time t, of

---

[8]For simplicity of notation, the idiosyncratic shock will from now on be represented as ζ_t, where the dependence on i, k, and $(t+\tau)$ is understood.

[9]Note that, while $\epsilon_{it}^k(t+\tau)$ is a known cash flow need at time t and is included in both the variable and fixed cash flows at time t, it nets to zero in this equation and is thus not explicitly included.

$$c_{i,t+\lambda}^k(t+\tau) = v_{it}^k(t+\tau)\prod_{\iota=1}^{\lambda}\left(1 + \beta\delta_{t+\iota} + \zeta_{t+\iota}\right) +$$

$$\sum_{\iota=1}^{\lambda-1}\epsilon_{i,t+\iota}^k(t+\tau)\prod_{\kappa=\iota+1}^{\lambda}\left(1 + \beta\delta_{t+\kappa} + \zeta_{t+\kappa}\right) - f_{it}^k(t+\tau) - \sum_{\iota=1}^{\lambda-1}\epsilon_{i,t+\iota}^k(t+\tau), \tag{7}$$

Because the cash flows from the swaps the dealer enters into are uncertain, the dealer will choosed to hedge its swap book to reduct this risk. The risk in the book related to future period $t+\tau$ is given by the conditional variance of these cash flows, or

$$\begin{aligned}
\text{Var}_t[c_{i,t+\lambda}^k(t+\tau)] &= \text{Var}_t\left[v_{i,t+\lambda}^k(t+\tau) - f_{i,t+\lambda}^k(t+\tau)\right]\\
&= \text{Var}_t\left[v_{i,t+\lambda}^k(t+\tau)\right] + \text{Var}_t\left[f_{i,t+\lambda}^k(t+\tau)\right] - 2\text{Cov}_t\left[v_{i,t+\lambda}^k(t+\tau)f_{i,t+\lambda}^k(t+\tau)\right]\\
&= \left\{\left[v_{it}^k(t+\tau)\right]^2\left[\left(1 + \beta^2\sigma_\delta^2 + \sigma_\zeta^2\right)^\lambda - 1\right] + \sigma_\epsilon^2\sum_{\iota=1}^{\lambda-1}\left(1 + \beta^2\sigma_\delta^2 + \sigma_\zeta^2\right)^\iota\right\}\\
&\quad + \left\{(\lambda-1)\sigma_\epsilon^2\right\} - \left\{2(\lambda-1)\sigma_\epsilon^2\right\}\\
&= \left[v_{it}^k(t+\tau)\right]^2\left[\left(1 + \beta^2\sigma_\delta^2 + \sigma_\zeta^2\right)^\lambda - 1\right] + \sigma_\epsilon^2\left[\sum_{\iota=1}^{\lambda-1}\left(1 + \beta^2\sigma_\delta^2 + \sigma_\zeta^2\right)^\iota - (\lambda-1)\right].
\end{aligned} \tag{8}$$

The conditional variance of the net $t+\tau$ cash flow for intermediary k then is

$$\begin{aligned}
\text{Var}_t[c^k(t+\tau)] &= \sum_{i_1=1}^{n^k}\left\{\text{Var}_t\left[c_{i_1,t+\tau}^k(t+\tau)\right] + \sum_{i_2\neq i_1}\text{Cov}_t\left[c_{i_1,t+\tau}^k(t+\tau),c_{i_2,t+\tau}^k(t+\tau)\right]\right\}\\
&= \left[\left(1 + \beta^2\sigma_\delta^2\right)^\tau - 1\right]\sum_{i_1=1}^{n^k}\sum_{i_2\neq i_1}^{n^k}\left[v_{i_1t}^k(t+\tau)v_{i_2t}^k(t+\tau)\right]\\
&\quad + \left[\left(1 + \beta^2\sigma_\delta^2 + \sigma_\zeta^2\right)^\tau - 1\right]\sum_{i=1}^{n^k}\left[v_{it}^k(t+\tau)\right]^2\\
&\quad + n^k\sigma_\epsilon^2\left[\sum_{\iota=1}^{\tau-1}\left(1 + \beta^2\sigma_\delta^2 + \sigma_\zeta^2\right)^\iota - (\tau-1)\right].
\end{aligned} \tag{9}$$

Let there exist a single potential hedging instrument (for example a futures contract market) for laying off factor risk. For simplicity, assuming zero transaction costs, marketmaker k will seek to identify the hedge ratio $b^k(t+\tau)$ that minimizes the variance of her exposure at date $t+1$ to the $t+\tau$ horizon. This is accomplished in the standard way, namely, by minimizing the variance of the error term $e_{t+1}^k(t+\tau)$ in the regression[10]

---

[10]Since hedging transaction costs are zero and innovations occur in each period, the marketmaker will need only a single period hedge for her entire portfolio and will rehedge the portfolio each time period. Furthermore, with zero transaction costs, the total portfolio hedge may be viewed as the net of the hedge for each horizon individually.

$$e_{t+1}^k(t + \tau) = c_{t+1}^k(t + \tau) - b_t^k(t + \tau)p_{t+1}, \tag{10}$$

where p_t is the price of the hedge instrument at time t and

$$p_{t+1} = p_t\left(1 + \Delta p_{t+1}\right),$$
$$\Delta p_t \sim \text{IID } N(0, \sigma_p^2),$$
$$\text{Corr}[\Delta p_t, \delta_t] = \rho, \tag{11}$$
$$\text{Corr}[\Delta p_t, \zeta_t] = \text{Corr}[\Delta p_t, \epsilon_{it}] = 0 \ \forall i \ \forall \tau.$$

The standard hedging result for this problem gives the following hedge ratio:

$$
\begin{aligned}
b_t^k(t+\tau) &= \frac{\text{Cov}_t\left[c_{t+1}^k(t+\tau), p_{t+1}\right]}{\text{Var}_t\left[p_{t+1}\right]} \\
&= \frac{\beta\rho\sigma_\delta}{\sigma_p p_t} \sum_{i=1}^{n^k} v_{it}^k(t+\tau).
\end{aligned}
\tag{12}
$$

In practice we would expect that it would be impossible to find a hedging vehicle that would eliminate all risk. For example, Eurodollar futures trade for specific expiration dates only, so that it would be unlikely to be able to match all swap cash flows with a portfolio of futures. As a result, even after using the hedging instrument, the marketmaker will face "basis" risk of the following form with respect to future period $t + \tau$:

$$
\begin{aligned}
\text{Var}_t[e_{t+1}^k(t+\tau)] &= \sum_{i_1=1}^{n^k} \sum_{i_2 \neq i_1} v_{i_1 t}^k(t+\tau) v_{i_2 t}^k(t+\tau)\left[\beta^2 \sigma_\delta^2(1 - \rho^2)\right] \\
&\quad + \sum_{i=1}^{n^k}\left[v_{i_1 t}^k(t+\tau)\right]^2\left[\beta^2 \sigma_\delta^2(1 - \rho^2) + \sigma_\zeta^2\right],
\end{aligned}
\tag{13}
$$

which cannot be hedged with the available instruments. This will be done for all $1 < \tau < \tau_{max}$.

Once marketmakers have hedged for each future period given the available hedging instrument, they can reduce their residual risk by trading amongst themselves.[11] As described in Campbell and Kracaw (1991), there exists a beneficial (i.e., Pareto superior) risk sharing arrangement between any two marketmakers so long as their error terms are not perfectly

---

[11]They will each own a portion of each other's portfolio in the sense that they share the economy-wide innovations. However, neither this risk-reduction methodology nor hedging as described above ameliorates a marketmaker's exposure to her own counterparty risk; for that, a clearing house arrangement would be necessary.

correlated.[12] Similar to the usual treatment of risky asset diversification, the pareto superior solution is a set of $\frac{1}{2}(\ell-1)$ two party inter-marketmaker swaps.[13] Each marketmaker will then, in essence, own a portion of each other marketmaker's portfolio. This "distributed" portfolio for marketmaker k will have residual risk

$$d_{t+1}^{k}(t+\tau) = \sum_{k_1=1}^{\ell} w_{k_1} e_{t+1}^{k_1}(t+\tau),$$ (14)

where the w's represent the weights of the marketmakers' portfolios in this "shared" portfolio. Note that it is this hedging by dealers that gives rise to the interdealer market. The conditional variance of this residual risk for marketmaker k will be

$$\text{Var}_t[d_{t+1}^{k}(t+\tau)] = \sum_{k_1=1}^{\ell} \sum_{k_2=1}^{\ell} w_{k_1} w_{k_2} \text{Cov}_t\left[e_{t+1}^{k_1}(t+\tau), e_{t+1}^{k_2}(t+\tau)\right].$$ (15)

The weights can be calculated as in standard portfolio diversification by

$$\min_{\{w_k\}} \text{Var}_t\left[d_{t+1}^{k}(t+\tau)\right], \quad \text{s.t.} \sum_{k=1}^{\ell} w_k = 1.$$ (16)

This can be easily solved in matrix form by constructing the Lagrangian

$$\mathcal{L} = \tfrac{1}{2}\mathbf{w}'\mathbf{V}\mathbf{w} + \lambda(1 - \mathbf{w}'\mathbf{1}),$$ (17)

where $\mathbf{w}$ is the ℓ vector of portfolio weights, $\mathbf{V}$ is the $\ell \times \ell$ variance-covariance matrix of $d_{t+1}^{k}(t+tau)$, λ is the Lagrange multiplier, and $\mathbf{1}$ is an ℓ vector of ones. The first order conditions are

$$\frac{\partial \mathcal{L}}{\partial \mathbf{w}} = \mathbf{v}\mathbf{w}_p - \lambda\mathbf{1} = \mathbf{0},$$

$$\frac{\partial \mathcal{L}}{\partial \lambda} = 1 - \mathbf{w}_p'\mathbf{1} = 0,$$ (18)

where $\mathbf{w}_p$ is the optimal weight vector and $\mathbf{0}$ is an ℓ vector of zeroes, yielding optimal portfolio weights of

---

[12]Again, with zero transaction costs and innovations in each period, marketmakers need only be concerned with the risk in a single period and can be modelled as trading amongst themselves anew in each period.

[13]The pareto superior solution will not be obtained, however, so long as each marketmaker's residual risk is unobservable. We will assume at this point, however, that all such risks are observable.

$$\mathbf{w}_p = \left(\mathbf{1'V}^{-1}\mathbf{1}\right)^{-1}\mathbf{V}^{-1}\mathbf{1}. \tag{19}$$

While conditional means and variances describe the pertinent decision-making factors when, say, a swap dealer attempts to hedge or lay off the risk in her swap book, it is the unconditional means and variances that determine overall probabilities of events, such as a domino effect, occurring. Thus, the unconditional means of all three portfolios are zero, while the unconditional variances are

$$\text{Var}[c^k] = n^k\sigma_\epsilon^2 \left\{ \sum_{t=1}^{\tau_{max}} \left[1 + \beta^2\sigma_\delta^2 + \sigma_\zeta^2\right] - \tau_{max} \right\}, \tag{20}$$

for the unhedged and undistributed portfolio,

$$\text{Var}[e^k] = n^k\sigma_\epsilon^2 \left\{ \sum_{t=1}^{\tau_{max}} \left[1 + \beta^2\sigma_\delta^2(1-\rho^2) + \sigma_\zeta^2\right] - \tau_{max} \right\}, \tag{21}$$

for the hedged but undistributed portfolio, and

$$\text{Var}[d^k] = n^k\sigma_\epsilon^2 \left\{ \sum_{t=1}^{\tau_{max}} \left[1 + \beta^2\sigma_\delta^2(1-\rho^2) + \frac{\sigma_\zeta^2}{\ell}\right]^k - \tau_{max} \right\}, \tag{22}$$

for the hedged and distributed portfolio, assuming, for now, that all marketmakers have the same scale of operations (that is, n^k is the same for all marketmakers).

3. ANALYSIS OF DOMINO EFFECT PROBABILITIES

Let the capital of marketmaker k at time t be represented by q_t^k. The probability of bankruptcy of an intermediary is simply the probability that the cash outflow at time t is greater than the capital at time t. Since we have set up the model such that, whether hedged, distributed or not, the marketmaker's capital exhibits a random walk, the probability of eventual bankruptcy of any marketmaker is 1. However, this is not true in finite time, nor does it address the problem of simultaneous bankruptcy of multiple marketmakers in a domino effect. This will be addressed below.

Except for independent and separately capitalized subsidiaries, the financial institution's capital will be a function of all the activities of the bank and is thus a random variable. We will define bankruptcy of a marketmaker to be when her capital drops to zero and assume that bankruptcy is an absorbing state.

Since the definition of bankruptcy used in this paper is when the intermediary's capital drops to zero, this is equivalent to

$$d^k(t) > q_t^k, \tag{23}$$

where the $d^k(t)$ term is as defined above, and would be replaced by $e(t)$ or $c(t)$ if the portfolio is undistributed or unhedged, respectively.

Result 1.

What is the probability of a bankruptcy occurring for an intermediary with capital q_t^k? It is simply

$$\mathrm{Prob}\!\left[d^k(t) > q_t^k\right] = 1 - \Phi\!\left\{\frac{q_t^k}{\sqrt{\mathrm{Var}\!\left[d^k(t)\right]}}\right\}, \tag{24}$$

where $\Phi(\bullet)$ is the standard normal cumulative distribution function and $\mathrm{Var}[d^k(t)]$ is given by (22).

Implications.

The probability of any single marketmaker default increases with the following:

- the swap horizon (τ_{max});
- the variances of the cash flow innovation;
- the factor shock and the idiosyncratic shock (σ_ϵ^2, σ_δ^2, and σ_ζ^2, respectively);
- the sensitivity of the cash flows to the factor shock (β); and
- the number of counterparties (n^k).

The probability is decreasing in the following:

- amount of capital (q_t^k);
- the effectiveness of the hedge (ρ); and
- the number of marketmakers(ℓ).

In order to investigate the probability of multiple bankruptcies, it is necessary to specify how marketmaker capital is distributed. An obvious distribution would have capital gamma distributed with shape parameters α and γ, since this distribution is non-negative and not overly restrictive.

Result 2.

The probability of a second marketmaker going bankrupt given that another has gone bankrupt is

$$\text{Prob}\left[d^{k_2}(t)>q_t^{k_2}\mid d^{k_1}(t)>q_t^{k_1}\right] = \frac{\text{Prob}\left[d^{k_2}(t)>q_t^{k_2}\ \&\ d^{k_1}(t)>q_t^{k_1}\right]}{\text{Prob}\left[d^{k_1}(t)>q_t^{k_1}\right]}, \tag{25}$$

where the denominator is (24).

Implications.

If the two marketmakers have the same capital, the same number of counterparties, and no idiosyncratic innovations then this probability is 1. Otherwise, it will be less than 1, and this dependence can be investigated by specifying specific values for the relevant parameters.

In this way we may be able to construct a tabular analysis of the conditions which will induce multiple defaults and compare the results with empirical observations on those parameters. Further we can use this framework to examine simulated events and by relaxing the assumptions examine the robustness of the framework. Specific analysis of this issues should be addressed in further work.

REFERENCES

Campbell, Tim S. and William A Kracaw, 1991, Intermediation and the Market for Interest Rate Swaps, *Journal of Financial Intermediation*, 362-384.

Field, Peter, 1993, Publisher's Letter, *Risk* 6 (August), 4.